LIVING WELL IN RETIREMENT

NOEL WHITTAKER

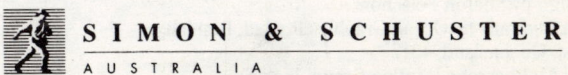

SIMON & SCHUSTER

AUSTRALIA

The laws relating to superannuation, taxation, social security benefits, and the investment and handling of money, are constantly changing and are often subject to departmental discretion. While every care has been taken to ensure the accuracy of the material contained herein at the time of publication, neither the author nor the publisher will bear responsibility or liability for any action taken by any person, persons or organisation on the purported basis of information contained herein.

Without limiting the generality of the foregoing, no person, persons or organisation should invest monies or take other action on reliance of the material contained herein, but instead should satisfy themelves independently (whether by expert advice or otherwise) of the appropriateness of any such action.

Other bestsellers by the same author:

MAKING MONEY MADE SIMPLE

MORE MONEY WITH NOEL WHITTAKER

GETTING IT TOGETHER

GOLDEN RULES OF WEALTH

LIVING WELL IN RETIREMENT

First published in Australia in 1994 by
Simon & Schuster Australia
20 Barcoo Street, East Roseville NSW 2069

Second Edition December 1995
Third Edition (Totally Revised) June 1997

Viacom International
Sydney New York London Toronto Tokyo Singapore

Copyright © Noel Whittaker Holdings Pty Ltd

National Library of Australia
Cataloguing-in-Publication data

Whittaker, Noel, 1940-
  Living well in retirement

  Includes index.
  ISBN 0/7318/0671/9

  1. Finance/personal - Australia. 2. Investments -
  Australia. I. Title.

Cover design by Sharon Felschow
Typeset in Australia by Ocean Graphics Pty Ltd, Bundall,
Gold Coast, Queensland, 4217
Printed by McPhersons Printing Group, Victoria
Cartoons by Paul Lennon

Acknowledgements

As you read this book and notice the detailed and technical information it contains you will appreciate the amount of work that went into its production. I am indebted to my wife, Geraldine, and my business partner, Cheryl Macnaught, for spending hours discussing with me various aspects of the contents, and providing much needed moral support.

A big "Thank you" is also due to:

Advance Asset Management
Michael Klug, Ruth Copelin and Paul Callaghan of Clayton Utz
MLC Life
Department of Social Security
Peter Toohey and the staff of the Tricare Group
Ray Connelly and the staff of Connelly Temple
David Smith and the staff of the AM Group
Des Knight; Dr Toby Ford; Max Worthington; Noel Adsett
Amanda Gore; Professor Jon Nussbaum
Professor Bob Norton; Lex Irvine
Christopher Duff of Cannon and Cripps
The Armstrong Jones Group
Commonwealth Bank of Australia
Office of Ageing, Brisbane
Early Planning for Retirement Association
Rothschilds
Janette Whelan for the editing; Paul Lennon for the cartoons
Sharon Felschow for the cover design; Jeff Draney, Noel O'Halloran of Ocean Graphics for the typesetting and McPherson's Printing Group for production

As well, I received invaluable assistance and feedback from Roland Lindenmayer, Alan Gray, Rosemary Kent, John Collins and Karen Elliot-Smith who read the original manuscript before it went to print. Many of their suggestions and comments have been incorporated into the text. Louise Beard helped with the index and, as always, the staff of Whittaker Macnaught provided the ultimate in patience and support.

Contents

Introduction

Thinking about retiring in the next 30 years? You are part of a quickly growing group. Since 1981 the number of people aged 65 and over has grown by a massive 84%, and by 1993 the number of people in Australia aged 65 and over had passed two million. In contrast, the under 15s have grown by only 2% in that time, and those aged 15 to 64 have grown by 42%.[1]

By the year 2001 it is expected that over 2.4 million Australians will be aged 65 and over, and by the year 2025 this is likely to increase to 4.3 million.

Department of Social Security figures released in June 1994 reveal that some 42% of the population of pension age were getting the maximum pension, almost 20.4% of the 65 and over age group were in receipt of a part pension, and 14% were getting a Veterans' Affairs pension. The remaining 24% were self-funded retirees. Over 75% of the 65s and over were on some form of welfare!

Now think about those in work. Because of technology, the number of jobs available is not increasing nearly as fast as the number of people who are turning 65. To make it worse, we have slashed migration. The rate of our total population increase is down to just over 1% per annum.

Ask yourself "How can we continue to pay pensions at the rate of 25% of weekly earnings to 75% of the aged population?"

It's a double whammy for both those who are working and those who are retired. The pressure to restrict access to aged pensions is growing as the numbers of aged increase. Yet those in the workforce are faced with trying to build funds for their own retirement at the same time as they are being called upon to support the growing number of aged.

That's the bad news. The good news is that accumulating wealth for retirement, and then keeping it secure after retirement, is still possible for those who make the effort to learn what to do. Better still, the recent discoveries concerning the ageing process are pointing the way to a long, healthy and fulfilling life after 60. That's why I have called that period "The Years of Fulfilment".

---

1. Source – Australian Bureau of Statistics.

It should be a time of freedom. Freedom from debt, freedom from tight deadlines, and freedom from the demands of children and your workplace. It should also be a time of discovery when you are free to explore the things you have dreamed about.

To help you do all that is the aim of this book, and this is why I have taken a holistic approach and have covered retirement from the psychological angle as well as the financial one. The contents include ways to be healthy in your mind and body, as well as in your pocket.

Living Well in Retirement is intended as a companion to my other books, *Making Money Made Simple, More Money with Noel Whittaker, Golden Rules of Wealth* and *Getting it Together,* and should be read in conjunction with those books. Where possible, I have not repeated material that is covered in the other books. You should also consider buying my *Wealth Creator on CD-ROM* which incorporates a personal budget, a retirement planning tool, and many useful calculators.Details are in the back of this book.

The problem with reading a book on a complex issue like retirement is knowing where to start. To understand a topic like superannuation you should know about tax, but to understand tax you should know about superannuation. It's like trying to eat a giant circular pie. To make it easier for you, I have divided the book into eight separate divisions so you can start at any one that interests you. However, the best way to approach it may be to read the whole book quickly from the start and then focus on the sections that apply most to you.

The fact that you are reading this book shows you are serious about living well in retirement. Congratulations. Now join me as we plan your approach to "The Years of Fulfilment".

NOEL WHITTAKER

1

RETIRING – SOME FUNDAMENTAL PRINCIPLES

Nature is an endless combination and repetition of a very few laws.

RALPH WALDO EMERSON

Long life, good health, prosperity and happiness! What better goals could you have, and what better age could you be living in to achieve them? The astounding advances in medical technology, coupled with the rapidly increasing knowledge of the way our minds work, have given us advantages our forefathers could have only dreamed about. To make it even better, Australia is a stable and relatively prosperous country with a generous social welfare system.

However, a long life, good health, prosperity and happiness are not things that just happen. You have to work at achieving them, and to do that you have to understand some fundamental principles. Because this book is mainly about money, we'll start off by discussing four fundamental principles of building wealth. They are:

1. Understand the miracle of compound interest
2. Practise the guaranteed secret of wealth
3. Use the power of dollar cost averaging.
4. Go for growth

Before we look at each of these, let me give you a tip. Approach this chapter with a positive attitude and don't start thinking "the rates mentioned here are not available today" or "what about the impact of tax?" Certainly they are important issues, but this chapter is not the place to raise them. Here you are learning universal fundamental principles that will stand you in good stead for the rest of your life; they do not change. Tax rates vary among individuals and countries, and earning rates vary with inflation and the economy generally. What you learn in this chapter will **stand good in any country and for any rate of inflation.**

The Miracle Of Compound Interest

The principle of compound interest is that you do not withdraw earnings or growth from an investment, but leave them intact to be added to the principal. Thus the interest becomes merged, or "compounded", with the principal.

> **EXAMPLE:** *You have $10 000 in a bank account. If the interest rate is 10%, you earn $1000 in a year. You have the choice of spending the money or letting it stay in the bank. If you leave it intact, you will start the second year with a balance of $11 000. That is the way interest compounds. Your second-year earnings will be $1100 if the rate stays at 10% and you will start the third year with a balance of $12 100. The third year's interest will be $1210.*

Notice that the amount you have working for you grows at a faster and faster rate. Look how the earnings rapidly increase. The earnings of $1100 in the second year are 10% more than the earnings in the first year. The earnings of $1210 in the third year are 21% more than the earnings in the first year. By year seven, at 10% per annum compounded, the principal has doubled and with it the earnings. Now you have $20 000, on which the next year's earnings will be $2000.

Next we'll look at the effect of rate of return.

> **EXAMPLE:** *Both X and Y are aged 40 and wish to retire at age 65 with an indexed income of $2000 a month. Neither has any money now. If inflation is 3% over the period, that $2000 a month in today's dollars will be equal to $4200 a month when they turn 65. Suppose X is a conservative investor and keeps his money in low-paying term deposits which give a long-term average of 6%. He will need to invest $1100 a month to reach his goal. Y is a more educated investor and prefers growth investments. If they produce 9% per annum she will have to invest only $534 a month to reach her goal[1].*

---

1 The figures were produced by the *Noel Whittaker Wealth Creator on CD-ROM*. Details are in the back of the book.

The wiser asset choice led to a higher long-term return, but it had other benefits too. Because Y has to invest less for the future, she has more money to spend today.

By now you should be convinced of the need to start the investment program as quickly as possible and of the importance of gaining the best rate of return that is consistent with the risks you are prepared to accept. Now let's move on to the most important financial discovery I have ever made.

The Guaranteed Secret Of Wealth

I stumbled across a concept that I called the "guaranteed secret of wealth" in late 1992 when I was reflecting on what investments had worked for me and what had gone wrong. It suddenly became obvious that money is like time; you can either use it wisely or fritter it away. Most jobs are completed right on the deadline, and you must have gone through the panic in the household when an assignment is due "tomorrow".

Think back to 1980 when I appeared on national television showing people how much interest they could save by repaying their mortgages fortnightly instead of monthly. The banks laughed at the idea then because they failed to see how changing the payment frequency could affect the outcome when the interest was still being charged on monthly balances. They had missed the point.

If you repay a loan at $600 a month you pay back $7200 (12 x $600) in a year. If you repay $300 a fortnight you repay $7800 (26 x $300) in a year. Just changing the frequency of the payments has enabled you to pay back $600 a year more – that's $12 a week. The fascinating part about it is that in almost every case the borrowers pay back that $12 a week without effort. Why is this? Remember I said money is like time, you spend what you have.

Most of us go through the same process:
• We get paid.
• We pay our bills.
• We spend what's left over.

When the borrowers were repaying $600 a month they paid it happily, spent the rest, and were broke by next pay day. When they changed the payments to $300 a fortnight they still paid that, spent the rest and finished the fortnight broke. Their spending behaviour didn't change, but they found the extra $12 a week without pain. If you can understand that, you have grasped one of the most important financial principles in the world.

> KEY POINT: Most people get paid, pay their bills and spend what's left over.

Your reaction might be that $12 a week is not much. True, but another major principle is that little things can add up to a huge sum over time. Think again about that $12 a week. It will shorten the term of the loan so much that it could easily chop $100 000 off the interest bill. Now we're talking bigger sums. But wait! Interest on a home loan is not tax-deductible, therefore any savings of interest come from after-tax dollars.

Thus a **saving** of $100 000 of after-tax money could be the equivalent of **earning** nearly $200 000 before tax is taken out. The small action of changing the frequency of the loan payments has given the borrowers the equivalent of a pay rise of $20 000 a year for 10 years.

The power and the simplicity of this led me to the "guaranteed secret of wealth":

To become wealthy you must commit a substantial amount of investment money as the first item spent out of your pay packet, and continue to invest it without fail.

If you want another example think of our PAYE tax system whereby all employers deduct taxes out of their employees' pay. Most people arrive at pay day broke, yet, not one person who is paid under the PAYE system has any trouble paying their group tax at the end of each year. It's those high-income earners who are not on the PAYE system that have problems. If taxes rose by 20%, or fell by 20%, most PAYE taxpayers would still live on their after tax income and greet each pay day with an empty pocket.

Time and time again when giving seminars I say to the audience, "Put your hands up if you have paid your house off." Usually plenty of hands are raised. Then I put the clincher, "Leave them up if you have invested every payment that you no longer needed to make since the loan has been paid off." The arms all drop and there are sheepish grins everywhere. Yes, they intended to invest the payments but somehow they never got around to it. Now three or four years might have passed by, and the $600 a month they were investing without fail has vanished. Possibly $30 000 or more has slipped through their fingers.

That sounds like nearly everybody's savings and investment plan. They promise they will start "next week" but something keeps cropping up. Then, as if in a twinkling, 10 years have flashed by and the retirement date is getting to be a reality. Then they get into a panic about having enough to live on in their retirement years.

You should now understand this fundamental principle of building wealth, but how do you use it once the family home is paid off? That's simple. Keep up the investment process by some negative gearing, or some regular saving, or a combination of both. Just make sure you keep investing the money you no longer need for the mortgage payments.

Now I'll explain how to achieve success in a regular investment program using one of the most exciting concepts you will ever hear about – the technique of "dollar-cost averaging". It's a way to guarantee profits.

Dollar-Cost Averaging

Dollar-cost averaging is a strategy whereby you place a fixed sum at regular intervals into the same investment. Consequently it is perfect to use in conjunction with the "guaranteed secret of wealth" and "the miracle of compound interest". Provided you pick the right investment vehicle, you cannot lose – your profits are guaranteed.

All you do is decide how much a week, fortnight or month you can afford to invest. The best way to do this it to choose a frequency that coincides with when you get paid. For example, if you are paid fortnightly, make a fortnightly commitment. If possible, have the money taken from your pay automatically so you won't be tempted to spend it. It can be credited straight to a special account that is kept just for savings, or invested directly into a vehicle such as a balanced trust or a growth trust[2]. What is most important is that you **keep it up**. You see, human beings are strange creatures – they love to buy in boom and sell in gloom.

Let me tell you how it happens in real life. A share boom starts and the papers are full of stories of fortunes being made on the stock market. A couple visit their financial adviser who tells them about compound interest and convinces them about the merits of

---

2 These are discussed later in the book.

regular investment. They agree that regular investment is right for them, but their real motivation stems from the 35% per annum the investment has returned over the last year. They happily sign up to invest $500 a month into a share trust but, after six months, the market takes a dive and their initial investment of $3000 falls to $2200.

The couple are shell-shocked and, after talking to some of their negative friends or relatives, decide share trusts are a waste of money and advisers are useless. They stop the program, forever disillusioned about shares, share trusts and regular investment. Their next step is to buy an investment house because "you can't go wrong with real estate". Famous last words!

Why does dollar-cost averaging work? Because, if you keep up your regular investment in a falling market, you get a larger number of units as the price falls. Thus you buy your biggest parcel at the bottom of the market, and when the market eventually rises you will make your first profit on the largest number of units.

Here is something you must note carefully. This technique will work only if the value of your chosen investment eventually recovers. This is why I recommend it only for top-quality unit trusts that have a connection with the share market. Based on history, you can be sure the share market will always recover to a position greater than its previous best.

KEY POINT: Dollar-cost averaging is a superb strategy if you are certain the price will eventually recover as you are buying the largest volume at the lowest price. Do not use it for speculative investments.

Now we'll look at an example to show the combined effect of compound interest, time and dollar-cost averaging. Let's assume you started a regular investment plan of $500 a month into an investment that matched the All Ordinaries Accumulation Index, which takes into account dividends as well as capital growth. If you started investing your $500 a month in January 1994, you would have invested $18 000 by December 1996, and the value of your investment would now be $22 000. Even though you did achieve 13.5% per annum compound, and the value of your capital has grown by 22% overall, this is not going to excite you too much.

However, if you had started the program in January 1990 you would have had more time on your side. You would still have achieved better than 13% per annum compound, and your investment would have been worth $67 000. But, it's still not dramatic when you consider that you invested a total of $42 000 over those seven years. Your total capital invested has grown by 60%.

Now comes the exhilarating part. If you had started investing that $500 a month in January 1980, you would have had 17 years of investing. The compound return is 13.9% per annum, little different, but your investment is now worth $374 000 for an outlay of $102 000. That's more than three and a half times times your investment. The extra time made all the difference. Best of all, it may now be growing by $48 000 a year, eight times as much as you are contributing. You have achieved a critical mass of capital that is exploding into life.

Go For Growth

Rapidly increasing life expectancies mean that many people will spend nearly as much time retired as they did at work. For them, this raises the problem of trying to accumulate enough money while they work to keep themselves when they don't. To put it simply, one of the main investment risks now is that people will live longer than their money.

Overcoming this challenge is going to require a complete re-think of the way we view investing. The line of reasoning for many is still: "I've worked hard all my life to build up these assets. I can't afford to take a risk with them as there is no time to start again." That's a logical view, but usually their next step is to move to cash-type investments such as term deposits and debentures, to avoid any chance of their capital falling if the market crashes. Unfortunately they expose themselves to a greater risk, which is illustrated by the chart below.

It tracks the fortunes of two people we'll call Mr Brown and Ms Green. They retired in 1979 with $100 000, which was a hefty sum in those days. Mr Brown figured he couldn't take any "risks", so placed it all in term deposits which, then, paid him about $9000 a year.

Ms Green had come from a family where owning shares was the norm. She decided to place the whole lot in an industrial share trust. The dividends were only about $6000 a year in 1979, but she

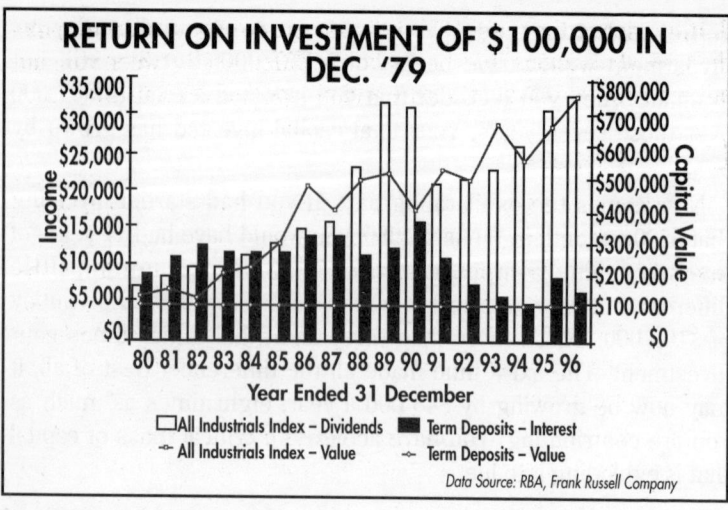

RETURN ON INVESTMENT OF $100,000 IN DEC. '79

Year Ended 31 December

☐ All Industrials Index – Dividends   ■ Term Deposits – Interest
◦ All Industrials Index – Value   ◦ Term Deposits – Value

Data Source: RBA, Frank Russell Company

was a long-term thinker, and knew that share dividends tended to grow with time.

If you cast your eyes along the graph you can follow the fortunes of both our retirees. Mr Brown has had no capital growth, and his interest cheques have fluctuated between $16 000 a year and $6000 a year In fact, over the last few years, he has had a double whammy – his nominal returns have been dwindling at the same time as the purchasing power of his money was steadily being eroded by inflation. In contrast Ms Green has enjoyed a steadily growing income which, from 1 July, 1987 consisted mainly of franked dividends. Thanks to the imputation system, her present income of $30 000 a year is tax free. She has also benefited from rising values in the share market; by the end of 1996 her original $100 000 had grown to nearly $800 000.

Note that the sharemarket falls of 1987, 1990 and 1994 have had little long-term impact on her capital, and none at all on her income. The only income "blip" is an upward one that happened because of the particularly high dividend payments in 1989 and 1990, which were the result of companies paying out special dividends after the change in company tax rates. Ms Green has enjoyed a steadily growing, tax-free income.

The lesson here is that it behoves all investors to get even a few dollars in share-based investments at an early age as possible, so they can become comfortable with share-based investments, and get accustomed to the normal movements of the market. Failure to do this means they approach retirement age ill-prepared to make the critical decisions that can make the difference between running out of money and living a secure and prosperous retirement.

Conclusion

I hope by now I have sold you on the necessity of starting a regular savings program. However, there are many insurance-based savings plans being peddled that do more good for the salesperson than the investor. They sign up unwary investors for savings contracts for 10 years or more, and if the investor stops contributions within two or three years of starting off the plan has almost no cash value.

When you commence a regular savings program the best way to do it is to have a sum deducted from your pay and sent by bank authority to the fund manager of a growth trust. There is no contract, normally no exit fees and you can raise, lower or suspend your payments at will without penalty. Usually the only cost to acquire the investment is a 5% entry fee on all new money.

The other warning is not to put it off. Find an adviser and start now. Time passes faster and faster as we get older, and putting it off means that two years or more will pass while you "think about it". You now know that compound interest takes time to work. Those two years could cost you nearly half your growth over the long term.

Summing Up

- Small increases in rate or in the length of time invested make huge increases in the amount of money we get back.
- Compound interest is slow to start its work but, like the rock rolling down the hill, gets faster and faster as time passes. Unfortunately, many people give up and don't give it time to work its magic.
- It is human nature to pay our commitments and live on what's left over. By including investment in the commitments, we guarantee the future gets priority over the present.
- Dollar-cost averaging is a "no fail" process provided you choose an investment that will eventually recover if the value falls after you invest.
- Go for growth so you won't outlive your money.

2

HOW LONG WILL THE MONEY LAST?

It is easier to keep up than catch up.

LEO D. BARDSLEY

"Can we afford to retire?" is one of the questions a financial planner hears most. Ironically, it usually comes from those to whom the answer is a resounding "yes", but who down in their hearts want some reassurance. The other question is "When can we afford to retire?" This often comes from a much younger couple who have had the good sense to start planning for retirement well in advance.

In either case it is simple to calculate if you can afford to retire, and when you can afford to retire. The process goes like this:

1. Work out how much a year you will spend when you are retired.
2. Decide when you would like to retire.
3. List what resources are available to provide for those needs.
4. Calculate the retirement income your present resources will provide.

We'll now work on these step by step. The method of doing it may appear complicated at first glance, but if you follow it through slowly it is not nearly as hard as it looks. Just remember to complete one stage, and make sure you understand it, before moving to the next one.

Calculating Your Retirement Spending

First prepare a budget using the principles in the chapter on budgeting in *Making Money Made Simple*[1]. Use your present pattern of spending as a guide but adjust it for retirement by eliminating such items as loan payments, school fees, fares to work, bought lunches, work clothes, union fees and superannuation.

Even though you will be free of many expenses when you retire, it is sensible to allocate a sum for contingincies, for many of our retired clients have faced many unexpected expenses. The main ones seem to be medical expenses or costs that arise as a result of wanting to do things for their children.

Most of the other expenses are common to almost everybody, but there are four big items that vary widely between people. These are travel, clothes, alcohol and dining out. You will have to make your own assessment of these. When you do the calculations remember that the body seems to lose its tolerance for big meals and alcohol as you get older.

Also list the big "one off" items that are likely to occur when you stop work. These may include replacing the car, buying a caravan or a boat, paying off any outstanding debts, and having the big trip. Don't be frightened to put them on your list even if you feel they are out of reach. This book is all about helping you make your dreams come true, and you will be amazed what you can achieve once you start to write down your goals. Seldom a day passes that I don't receive letters from readers saying my books have helped them achieve goals they had never dreamed would be possible until they started some serious goal planning.

The dilemma

When you are trying to formulate a retirement plan you strike some major problems when you think about which numbers to use. It's like preparing a budget for a business. There are some items about which you can make a reasonable estimate; there are others that at best are a good guess, because the final outcome will be known only in retrospect.

The factors over which you have **some control** are:

1. how much you will spend each year

---

1   The easiest way of all is to use the Budget calculator in my *Wealth Creator on CD-ROM*. Details are in the back of this book.

2. how much of your capital you intend to leave to your beneficiaries.

The factors which are **uncertain** are:

1. how long you will live
2. what will be the state of your health and the amount of your health costs
3. how much government assistance will be available for you
4. what rate of return your investments will provide.

These might be difficult questions but it is better to face up to them as soon as possible. Therefore, let's tackle them head on, and try to make some reasonable "guesstimates".

When thinking about these calculations, see yourself as a traveller on a long trip. Even though you have carefully planned the route, storms may happen with little notice, and other unplanned incidents are certain to occur. Therefore, you have to monitor your progress continually and make adjustments when necessary. All we can do now is show you how to put a plan in place. Once that is done, you and your adviser will have to look at it at least once a year and take whatever action has become necessary to keep you on course.

> KEY POINT: Your retirement plan needs to be looked at carefully at least once a year and adjustments made if necessary.

Doing Your Own Budget

Your budget will have given you a good idea of what it will cost you to live, and we have found that most retirees stick to their budget well. They have developed the habit of "cutting the coat to fit the cloth" and are prepared to live for a month or two on a shoestring if a lot of heavy expenses suddenly crop up.

We'll now do a retirement plan together, and for this exercise we'll assume your spending budget in retirement is $20 000 a year in today's dollars. Once you know how to do the exercise you can do your own figures, but if it all gets too difficult seek help from your adviser, who can do this on computer in a few minutes. You don't have to worry about being stuck on your own.

Now we don't know what inflation will be between now and when you retire, so we have to make some assumptions about it. However, before we start trying to adjust the figures for inflation we have to find out what you will need when you retire, expressed in the dollars of today.

Spending in the year you retire might be:

Overseas trip	$25 000
Change over car	$15 000
Renovate house	$10 000
Total cash outlays	$50 000

That's the "one off" expenses. In addition, you will need to have accumulated sufficient resources to provide an income of $20 000 a year until you die. Now it's getting harder because we don't know the date of your death. Therefore, all we can do is take a guess based on your present health and your family history, although family history sometimes doesn't help much. For example, my mother died at age 54, but her father lived till 93. My father died at 64 yet had two brothers who lived till nearly 90.

We could look up the life-expectancy tables and discover that a male aged 60 should live to 77, and a woman aged 60 to 82. But life expectancy rises as age rises. A male aged 65 should live to 79 and a woman aged 65 to 83. Once you get very old they seem to just add two years. For example, a person aged 92 has a life expectancy of 94.

Don't get too hung up on this life-expectancy business. Some people will die before their life expectancy and some will live far beyond it. Nevertheless, we have to arrive at some figure for this exercise so, to keep it simple, I have assumed age 80 as the time of your death, and 60 as the date of your retirement. This brings us to an assumption of 20 years as the time you will spend in retirement.

The next assumption is that you are prepared to consume your investment capital during your lifetime, but that you will leave the family home to your beneficiaries. I appreciate this is somewhat unrealistic because, under the present rules, the level of the aged pension rises as your assets decrease. This has a self-compensating effect because the rising aged pension reduces your need to spend capital. Unfortunately we can't guarantee the present aged pensions rules will still be in force when you retire, and I would rather err on the conservative side when helping you set a goal of how much you will need when you stop work. If you get an unexpected bonus, so much the better.

How Long Will The Money Last?

To calculate the amount of capital you will need to produce the income necessary, you will have to take a guess at a **real rate of return**. This is an important concept and you will need to understand it for the rest of this exercise. The real rate of return is the return you get on your money after inflation. For example, you are achieving a real rate of 5% if inflation is 2% and you earn 7%. You are also getting a real rate of 5% if inflation is 8% and you earn 13%.

KEY POINT: The real rate of return is the difference between the rate of inflation, and the return you are getting on your investments.

Here's a fascinating bit of information for you. If the **real** rate does not change the time taken to spend the capital will be about the same. It doesn't matter what the inflation rate is, or what the earning rate is. In the Table 2.1 you can see what happens if we start with an opening balance of $300 000, make withdrawals from it at the rate of $20 000 a year, and increase those drawings so they keep pace with inflation. In other words the drawings remain a constant $20 000 in today's dollars.

The example gives two scenarios. One where the earning rate is 6% when inflation is 1%, and another where the earning rate is 10% and inflation 5%. In both examples the real rate of return is 5%. Notice the time to spend the money is fairly similar even though the figures are different. This is because we are speeding up the size of the withdrawals to keep pace with inflation so, even though the earnings are greater, the withdrawals make up for it.

As you will see in Table 2.1 it took 28 years for the money to be expended when the return was 6% and inflation was 1%, and 30 years when the return was 10% and inflation was 5%. In reality the rates of return and inflation will vary each year; they will not stay fixed for 30 years. This is why it is important to focus on the real rate of return and not allow yourself to be side-tracked by high nominal rates of return when inflation is also high.

Conclusion

Now you should understand the difficulties of trying to budget for retirement, but at the same time appreciate the importance of making an attempt to do it. In the next chapter we'll work through a case study.

TABLE 2.1

Opening capital $300 000. Earning Rate 6% per annum.
Annual withdrawals of $20 000 indexed for inflation at 1%.

Year	Starting balance	Withdrawals increasing by 1%	Earnings p.a at 6%
1	300 000	20 000	18 000
5	288 888	20 606	16 773
10	265 008	21 657	15 311
15	222 851	22 762	12 992
20	169 208	23 923	9 505
25	85 359	25 143	4 437
28	18 647	18 647	0

Opening capital $300 000. Earning Rate 10% per annum.
Annual withdrawals of $20 000 indexed for inflation at 5%.

Year	Starting Balance	Withdrawals increasing By 5%	Earnings p.a at 10%
1	300 000	20 000	30 000
5	340 136	23 153	32 971
10	386 057	29 549	37 275
15	415 328	37 713	39 834
20	405 439	48 132	38 376
25	316 727	61 430	28 906
30	80 959	78 403	4 564

Summing Up

- When doing a retirement budget leave out items such as superannuation and other work expenses, but add items such as travel.
- The real rate of return is more important than the nominal rate.
- Many people live longer than the life expectancy tables indicate.
- Monitor your retirement plans regularly.

3

WHEN CAN I AFFORD TO RETIRE?

Life is like playing a violin solo in public and learning the instrument as you go along.

SAMUEL BUTLER

Now that have done a budget we can move on to a very important section – how to work out the sum needed to produce your retirement income. First we will need to look at two vital tables that tell us how fast we will use our money up.

Tables 3.1 and 3.2 indicate approximately how long it will take to spend $100 000 given a real rate of return coupled with a range of annual drawings. Notice I have used real rates of return again. This is so the tables will be valid in any investment climate.

TABLE 3.1

How long it takes to use up $100 000 at a real rate of 5%.

Years	Real Rate	Annual Drawings
25	5%	$ 7 000
20	5%	$ 8 000
15	5%	$10 000
12	5%	$11 000
11	5%	$12 000
10	5%	$13 000

TABLE 3.2

How long it takes to use up $100 000 at a real rate of 3%.

Years	Real Rate	Annual Drawings
24	3%	$ 6 000
16	3%	$ 8 000
12	3%	$10 000
11	3%	$11 000
10	3%	$12 000
9	3%	$13 000

Now let's work through an example. Assume you have decided that 20 years is the length of time you will live in retirement and that $20 000 a year in today's dollars is what you will spend. If you can achieve a real rate of return of 5% per annum on your money you will need $250 000 to invest on the day you retire to provide you with $20 000 indexed for inflation for the next 20 years. That is $250 000 in today's money of course. **How did we calculate it?**

From Table 3.1 on the previous page we can see that $100 000 invested at a real rate of 5% is used up in 20 years if we withdraw $8000 a year. $20 000 is 2.5 times $8000 so a withdrawal of $20 000 a year will require 2.5 times the amount of capital if it is last for 20 years too. $100 000 multiplied by 2.5 times is $250 000.

You can see now that we have finally arrived at a specific goal – that is to accumulate $300 000 in today's dollars by the time you retire. We arrived at this figure by adding the $50 000 for the special items such as the car and trip to the $250 000 needed to provide the income.

The reason some of the years are in odd numbers is that I tried, when compiling these tables, to keep the annual drawings in even thousands. The figures are not meant to be precise because the real rate of return is continually varying. What the tables do is enable you to take a broad-brush approach to your affairs and say to yourself, "If I intend to spend $24 000 a year in today's dollars when I retire, and I'm so cautious I believe a real rate of 3% is the best I can achieve, I will need to have $300 000 in today's dollars if I live for 16 years after I stop work."

Adjusting The Figures

Now that you have the basics we can move to the area that really counts – setting specific goals. You have already set yourself a concrete figure in today's dollars that you need to accumulate on the day you retire. Now let's go a step further and convert that figure to the dollars of the year in which you want to retire. The process is simple; what's hard is forecasting the inflation rate.

Obviously it's going to be a guess but you've got to start somewhere. If you have your yearly appraisal with your adviser you will be able to make adjustments and recalculate your figures as necessary. In any event, there is a strong link between inflation and what you will earn on your investments.

Now, using the table below, you have to convert that $300 000 to dollars in the year you retire.

TABLE 3.3

Today's dollar adjusted for inflation.

Years until retirement	Expected annual rate of inflation			
	4%	6%	8%	10%
5	1.22	1.35	1.50	1.60
10	1.50	1.80	2.16	2.59
15	1.80	2.40	3.17	4.18
20	2.20	3.21	4.66	6.73
25	2.70	4.29	6.85	10.30
30	3.20	5.74	10.06	17.50

To convert today's dollars to the dollars of the year you retire select the inflation rate you believe will be appropriate and then run your eyes down that column until you come to the number of years to your retirement. The junction is the factor for you to use. Multiply today's dollars by that factor to produce the equivalent amount in future dollars.

EXAMPLE: *You need $300 000 in today's dollars when you retire in 10 years' time. You guess inflation will be 6% per annum. The factor is 1.80, therefore you will have to accumulate $540 000 (1.80 x $300 000) by the year you retire to achieve your goal.*

The table is in five-year steps. However, if the number of years till retirement falls in between these five-year steps, make a guess at what the factor is by taking a midway point between the number on each side. For example if you had 17 years to retirement, and chose 4% as the inflation rate, you could pick 2.00 as the factor. These tables are no more than a rough guide to help you develop specific goals, and you must reassess your situation every year.

Notice the effect of **time** and **rate.** As the time to retirement lengthens, so the amount of physical dollars needed grows faster and faster.

Valuing Your Resources

We have made much progress. We now know how much we will have to accumulate by our retirement date and that is now expressed in the dollars of that day. I'll now take you through a case study to further develop your ability so you can do your own calculations.

CASE STUDY: *Bill and Donna are aged 40. He earns $45 000 a year and she has the chance of some part-time work. Their house is worth $250 000 and is paid off. They have an investment house worth $125 000 that returns $100 a week after all expenses except interest. There is a mortgage of $50 000 on that house which will be repaid in 10 years at their present rate of repayments.*

Bill is in a superannuation fund at work and its present value is $44 000. They have few other assets and both Bill's parents are dead. Mary has a brother and a sister. Her mother is a widow and lives in a house worth $120 000. Mary can realistically expect to receive a third of her mother's estate when she dies.

They would like to retire at 60 and will need $40 000 for a trip and to buy a new car. They calculate their cost of living when they retire at $25 000 a year. All figures are expressed in today's dollars.

The calculations are done as follows:

1. Estimate the inflation rate till retirement. We'll use 4%.

2. Guess the life expectancy. They choose 85.

3. Choose the real rate of return they will obtain on their investments. They select 5%.

4. Calculate the sum needed at retirement to provide $25 000 a year. From table 3.1 we work out that $357 000 will provide $25 000 year for 25 years at a real rate of 5% (3.57 x $7000 = $25 000). We'll round it off at $360 000.

5. Add this figure to the other planned expenditure. The $40 000 for the car and trip, and the $360 000 we have just calculated, makes a total of $400 000 in today's dollars.

6. Convert that to the dollars of their planned retirement date 20 years away. From table 3.3 we look up the 4%, 20 year column, and find the factor is 2.20. Therefore, they need $880 000 (2.20 x $400 000) in the dollars of the year they retire.

Pause here, and make sure you understand how we got to this point. It may be easiest to take a pencil and paper and go through it step by step.

Bill and Donna now have a specific goal of accumulating $880 000 in future dollars. Now we can move on to analysing their present assets.

Own home. It is now worth $250 000 but they will sell it in retirement and buy a unit for $175 000 in today's dollars. This provides an additional **$75 000** that will be available in retirement.

Investment home. It is now worth **$125 000**. We'll assume they sell it when they retire and it keeps pace with inflation in the meantime.

Share of mother's estate. Assume the house keeps pace with inflation but that, after costs, Donna's share is **$30 000** in today's dollars.

From these three sources they have found $230 000 ($75 000 + $125 000 + $30 000) in today's dollars or $506 000 in future dollars. They are now only $374 000 short of their target. Let's check up on Bill's superannuation.

Superannuation. It is now worth $44 000. If we assume it will grow at a real rate of 5%, we can give it a gross earning rate of 9% for the next 20 years. Punch the numbers into a financial calculator, or use my *Wealth Creator on CD-ROM*, and we discover its value in 20 years should be almost $250 000.

Bill and Donna have total expected assets of $756 000 ($506 000 + $250 000) in the year of retirement. Now they are only $124 000 short of target.

How much to invest?

Look at what has been achieved so far. After doing a few calculations Bill and Donna have managed to reduce the fairly general aim of financial independence by age 60 down to a much more specific goal – that is, to accumulate around $880 000 in the next 20 years. The vague dream is now in sight and by realistically valuing their resources they find it is not nearly as impossible as it first appeared. Bill and Donna's present repayments will pay off the investment home by the time they retire but they also need to build the missing link. This is the $124 000 they are short of meeting their retirement target.

Let's do some more figuring. Table 3.4 will tell us how much Bill and Donna will need to invest every year at a given rate of return to achieve a stated amount in a set time.

We shall continue to use our 5% real rate with inflation at 4%. Therefore 9%, the sum of these two figures, is the forecasted earning rate. From table 3.4 we can see they will have to invest $1793 a year for each $100 000 they need. The target is $124 000, so the yearly investment will be $2233 (1.24 x $1793).

TABLE 3.4

Amount to invest every year to return $100 000 at retirement.

Compound Rate	Years to retirement						
	40	30	25	20	15	10	5
7%	$468	$989	$1 478	$2 280	$3 719	$6 764	$16 251
8%	$357	$817	$1 267	$2 023	$3 410	$6 392	$15 783
9%	$272	$673	$1 083	$1 793	$3 125	$6 039	$15 330
10%	$205	$553	$924	$1 587	$2 861	$5 704	$14 891
12%	$116	$370	$670	$1 239	$2 395	$5 088	$14 054
14%	$65	$246	$482	$964	$2 001	$4 536	$13 270
16%	$37	$163	$346	$747	$1 669	$4 043	$12 535
18%	$20	$107	$247	$578	$1 390	$3 603	$11 846
20%	$11	$71	$177	$466	$1 157	$3 210	$11 198

How do they find that? Remember, we have not taken the value of any future superannuation contributions that will be made by Bill or his boss. After making enquiries we find that Bill contributes 5% of salary and the boss contributes 10% of salary. The total yearly contributions are $6750 (Bill's salary of $45 000 x

15%) so, even after taxes and fees, Bill is well in excess of the yearly target of $2233 we worked our before. Bill and Donna are right on track to retire at 60 as planned.

They are also well placed to retire at 55 if Donna goes back to work. Obviously, an earlier retirement would depend on how much Bill enjoyed his job.

Conclusion

This may have been an involved process but work through until you understand it. If it is till too hard after you have done that, don't despair; your financial adviser should be able to do it for you. Just appreciate that it is one of the most significant exercises anybody who is serious about planning their retirement can do. However, life is a long journey and unexpected events, both good and bad, will happen. Sickness or loss of a job can shatter your income, and divorce or a business failure can cause you to lose most of your assets. There are few serious investors who have not lost money when an investment failed to live up to expectations, and often you will find your children will have their hands out for money when they have their own problems.

However, there are lottery wins and maybe business successes, to counter the bad news, and sometimes an investment will produce returns far in excess of your wildest dreams. It's a dynamic world and you will have to adjust your strategy and your expectations in the light of your own circumstances.

This is why accumulating sufficient money for your retirement is a three-step process:

1. Prepare a plan using the technique I described above.
2. Review it with your adviser at least once a year in the light of changing circumstances.
3. Adjust the strategy as necessary.

Now you know how to set your goals, let's move on to discussing the investment options that are available to help you achieve them.

Summing Up

- The earlier you start the easier it is.
- It is not as difficult as it may first appear.
- Don't take the figures literally. Use them as a guide.
- Review it with your adviser at least once a year.

4

WHERE WILL YOU INVEST YOUR MONEY?

I made a resolution to let my money work instead of me!

JOHN D. ROCKEFELLER

By now you should have a good idea of how much money you will need to retire when you choose, and you should understand the major principles of building wealth. Let's now consider the best places to invest your money so you will be able to achieve your financial goals.

When you are deciding where to invest your money, first think about your major goal. This will almost certainly be so big that the very thought of it may overwhelm you, but remember the words of American writer and broadcaster Richard L. Evans: "Everyone who got where he is, had to begin where he was."

Think of it as climbing up a ladder, and tackle one rung at a time. Divide the major goal into smaller sub-goals that are all compatible with the major one. For example, your major goal may be to accumulate $500 000 by the time you retire. To do that you may set three immediate sub-goals you can tackle simultaneously:

1. Pay your house off as quickly as possible.
2. Earn a good rate of return on the $5000 you like to keep as emergency cash.
3. Investigate ways for family members to earn extra money.

None of these are as daunting as accumulating half a million dollars, yet if you do them successfully, you will be well on the way to a secure retirement. After you retire, a major goal might be to live well while retaining the buying power of your money. Sub-goals may be to minimise tax, keep up a fitness program, and to have a secure regular income.

Unfortunately, life has its complications. The problem with setting several goals is that they may be incompatible. Your objectives may be as diverse as:

1. achieving maximum income
2. minimising tax
3. making the money grow
4. having complete security.

The dilemma is that a high income return usually means nil or low growth, and high expected growth may be coupled with nil or low income. Wherever there is a chance of capital gain, there is a chance of capital loss, and to create tax savings you may have to place some of your money in volatile[1] stock market-based investments. If you place it in superannuation you lose access to it, and if you start a negative gearing plan it may cause you worries if you lose your job. There is no such thing as a free lunch.

This leads us to one of the least understood principles of investment planning. **There is no perfect investment** – every investment you make has advantages and disadvantages.

KEY POINT: Every time you are considering an investment option, write down the advantages and disadvantages of what you propose to do. If you can't think of any disadvantages you don't know enough about the investment.

Temper that with common sense. Obviously, putting the money for your holiday next month into the bank is your best course of action, but a disadvantage may be that you could earn a higher effective rate if you paid it off your credit card, and then charged the holiday to the credit card. I'm not suggesting you do that, for it may get you further in debt if you have a wild holiday, but I use the example to illustrate the importance of thinking about all your options.

What you have to do is match the investment to your goal and understand that the strategies you adopt will depend on that goal. Investments fall into two categories:

---

1. In financial circles "Volatile" means that the price is always fluctuating.

1. income investments
2. capital growth investments.

Income investments are meant to produce a secure income with little or no capital gain. Their returns are predictable, but over time you lose out to inflation. We call these short-term investments.

Capital growth investments are in areas such as good property and good shares that should show a steady increase in value as the years pass. However, growth investments can fall in value. The October 1987 stock market crash showed us how quickly, and how far, shares can fall, and during the 1990 property crash Australia saw non-residential property prices tumble. Residential property investors know house prices can lie dormant for years, and then suddenly spurt up.

Investments in growth areas may be made by buying shares and property directly, or by using equity and property trusts. In each case there are costs to acquire the investment and often costs to cash it in. These costs, coupled with the volatile nature of shares and sluggish nature of property, should make you cautious about investing in these areas unless you have **at least** a five-year term in mind.

Here is an example of the folly of investing short-term money in long-term areas:

EXAMPLE: *A couple in their late fifties decided they could make a quick buck in the property market and bought an investment house for $140 000, using their savings of $30 000 as a deposit. The acquisition and loan costs were $5000. They had to borrow $105 000 but believed the capital gain would more than make up for the annual shortfall caused by the interest being more than the rents. The husband expected a superannuation payout of $175 000 when he retired, and they saw this as their safety buffer. If necessary, they could repay the loan with part of this.*

This was their first experience at owning rental property and they soon found themselves frustrated with maintenance. The gardens of the property deteriorated quickly, and by the time retirement came they had lost all interest in being landlords. The market had not taken off in that time, and all they received for the house was $130 000 after selling costs and repairs were paid for. They had lost $15 000, which was half of the nest egg they had started with, as well as the earnings they could have made on the deposit.

This example shows the folly of going into an investment without a full appreciation of the possible risks as well as the potential gains. Probably a better investment for them would have been to top up his superannuation, or place the money in her name in a debenture or mortgage trust. Then there would have been no loss of capital because of the costs of buying and selling, or because the market did not move as they expected.

A major lesson here is that it is better to gain your experience in the share and property market at a young age. Then you have time to start again if you suffer the inevitable failure.

> KEY POINT: Assets that produce capital gain can also give you a capital loss. Therefore, it is better to gain "hands on" experience with them at as young an age as possible.

The Major Investment Decisions

Whenever I make a speech at a Money Show I start by asking "Are you confused by the vast range of options that appear to be available?" Most of the people in the audience have spent the day wandering from booth to booth, and the response is invariably an overwhelming "yes". I then remind them that, despite all the changes to the rules and the plethora of investment products available, there are still only three areas where the bulk of their funds can be invested – cash, property and shares. In *Making Money Made Simple* I called it the "investment menu".

Once you understand that "menu" concept, you will appreciate why you have three major decisions when you are considering where to invest:

1. **Asset allocation.** What percentage of your total assets should you invest in each of the three areas of cash, property and shares?

2. **Investment vehicle.** Do you invest in these areas directly, or do you use managed funds such as unit trusts, insurance bonds and friendly society bonds?

3. **The best owner.** In whose name will each asset be held for ease of estate planning and to minimise tax?

In this chapter we'll look at asset allocation and discuss the good and bad points of most types of assets. In later chapters we'll discuss the other factors.

Asset Allocation

All professional money managers and financial advisers focus on **asset allocation** – the term given to the way your investments are spread. They usually look for a spread over the following sectors:

Australian cash   Australian fixed interest
Australian shares   Australian property
International fixed interest   International shares

It is the percentage of assets in each category that determines the risk[2] of the portfolio, and ultimately its overall performance. In practice, most financial advisers regularly receive suggested asset allocation models from their research sources. These are different for each type of client and vary with the research analysts' views of the market.

Therefore, if the share market was considered high, interest rates in Australia seemed to be on the rise, and our dollar looked weak, a suggested asset allocation might be:

	Low-risk client	*Higher-risk client*
	%	%
Australian cash	45	20
Australian fixed interest	15	15
Australian shares	10	25
Australian property	10	10
International fixed interest	15	20
International shares	5	10
Total	100	100

As you can see, the allocation is still spread over the entire range of assets, but the investor with the higher-risk profile has a greater percentage of the assets in shares. Furthermore, there is a greater emphasis on international investments to take advantage of a weaker dollar.

The term for increasing the assets in a particular sector is "overweighting", and the term for decreasing the assets is

---

2. Risk is discussed in detail in a later chapter.

"underweighting". Thus, if the standard asset allocation model for a conservative investor was Australian cash 35% and Australian shares 20%, the research bulletin might suggest a move to overweight in Australian cash, and underweight in Australian shares to achieve the low-risk asset allocation shown above.

> KEY POINT: You "overweight" to an asset sector by favouring it. You "underweight" by reducing the exposure to it.

The asset allocations above are those used by fund managers and professional investors. However, all investors should get used to the idea of listing their investable assets in sectors, and trying to achieve eventually a spread across all sectors. This is because it is almost impossible for all asset classes to do well at the same time. By spreading your assets, you have a better chance of achieving good overall returns.

One of the main reasons to watch your asset allocation is to prevent the sectors getting out of kilter. Let's assume you have decided that about 25% of your investable money is an appropriate amount to have in Australian shares. You will see from the example below that a steep rise in the market may push this up to 35%, or even more.

	Balance before share boom			Balance one year later	
Property	$90 000	60%		$90 000	53%
Bonds	$21 000	14%		$21 000	12%
Shares	$39 000	26%		$59 000	35%
Total	$150 000	100%		$170 000	100%

Regular monitoring of your asset allocation alerts you to the need to consider taking profits once any sector starts growing above your own benchmark. This is not to say you must take profits; it is to alert you to start doing some strategic thinking. The investors who own the portfolio in the example above should ask themselves "Are we happy with shares making up 35% of our portfolio?"

We'll now look briefly at the major asset classes and consider the advantages and disadvantages of each. They are discussed in more depth in *More Money with Noel Whittaker* and in *Making*

Money Made Simple. What follows here is more in the nature of an overview. Fixed-interest investments, such as bonds and debentures, are covered in depth in the next chapter.

Your own home

I have always recommended the first goal be the purchase and paying off of your own home. This is because it is an investment that is almost foolproof, and enables you to build a substantial asset base quickly while providing free rent along the way.

The disadvantages of holding the bulk of your assets in your own home are:

1. You miss out on the tax benefits available from negative gearing because interest on your home loan is not tax-deductible.
2. You have no exposure to other asset classes such as shares that usually produce higher returns.
3. You have no liquidity if you need money quickly. For example, you can't sell the back steps if you need $2000 to help out one of your children who needs money desperately.
4. You do not gain the experience that investing elsewhere gives you.

Despite these disadvantages, your own home remains your castle. Just remember that the quicker you pay it off the quicker you can start to invest the money that is no longer needed for mortgage payments.

Interest-bearing accounts

Money is kept in interest-bearing accounts so it will be readily accessible when you need it, or because you do not want to risk the normal market fluctuations of growth assets such as property and shares. The advantages are that there are no entry or exit fees and the $1000 you invest should be worth at least as much as when you deposited it. Of course, if you leave it there for five years it will not buy nearly as much when you withdraw it as it did when you deposited it.

The disadvantages are:

1. There is no capital gain.
2. The income from the investment carries no tax advantages.

3. Its value erodes slowly with inflation.
4. It will produce a lower return in the long term than property and shares, and therefore you lose the gains you may have made in other areas.

The serious investor will always keep adequate funds in interest-bearing investments to provide money for daily expenses, and to provide a buffer in case of an emergency. However, if you keep too much in this area, you are not making the best use of your assets.

Residential investment property

Houses and units are the favoured investment for most Australians because they feel safe with them. So often I hear, "My goal is to have five or six houses paid off when I retire and make that my superannuation."

The good points are that it is hard to lose heavily on residential property, at least some capital gain is likely, and you are forced to invest money because you are committed to keeping up the loan repayments. Also the combination of negative gearing and building/depreciation allowances give you some good tax breaks, particularly if you are a higher-income earner.

The disadvantages are:

1. It takes fairly large sums to buy property and you may not feel confident in borrowing $100 000 or more.
2. It is often difficult to find a good buy unless you spend many hours doing the research.
3. Vacancies, tenant damage, and large repair bills are a possibility and could play havoc with your budget, particularly as the property gets older.
4. You may not want the responsibility and worry of managing your tenants.
5. Property is not liquid.
6. Selling the property at a reasonable price may be difficult if you are an absentee landlord.

Residential real estate has been a good investment in Australia since World War II but there are two other factors now that should make you approach residential property with caution. The post-war housing boom that was fuelled by the baby boomers and migration from overseas is coming to an end. The baby boomers are at an age when most of them have bought a house, and migration has been severely curtailed because of high unemployment here. As well, there is a general belief that we have entered a long-term era of low inflation. If this is true, most property prices will rise only slowly.

Shares

Shares are a "must" for the investor who wants to build wealth. When you invest in shares you hitch part of your financial future to the fortunes of those companies whose shares you have bought. If they prosper, you should too; if they fall into financial difficulties you may lose much, or even all, of your money.

Because shares can be bought and sold in small parcels, they have great flexibility and liquidity. Contrast those attributes with property. If you have an investment house and need $10 000 in a hurry you cannot sell a bedroom or two. However, if you own shares you can ring your broker, order a sale of some or all of them, and have the money in your bank account in less than a week.

Furthermore, there is conclusive proof that a good portfolio of shares or equity trusts held over the long term has been a superb investment, and it is a pity that the majority of Australians are still wary of shares, and regard investing in them as akin to having a flutter at the races.

The disadvantages of shares are:

1. Down markets can last for five years or more.
2. You have probably lost the entire investment if the company in which you invest goes broke.
3. The value of shares is outside your control. In contrast, you can improve the value of an investment property by superior management.
4. Share prices can be volatile; the average movement between the low point and the high point of the All Ordinaries Index is around 35% a year.

Despite these disadvantages, shares and share-based investments offer liquidity, tax advantages and good potential for capital gain. Those who stay away from share-based investments may pay a high price in loss of potential earnings.

International shares

Similar comments apply to international shares except that an extra factor comes into play. Because they are expressed in overseas currency, they gain in value when our dollar weakens and fall in value when our dollar rises. Consequently, international investments are seen as a hedge against a falling Australian dollar. This makes them a good investment for anybody whose income is mainly derived from exporting, or for those who travel overseas a lot.

> **EXAMPLE:** *You have $10 000 in shares that are listed on the American market and priced in American dollars. If the value of our dollar drops by 10% against the American dollar, the value of the shares in Australian dollar terms will rise 10%. Similarly the price of a holiday that is expressed in American dollars will rise 10%.*

Our stock market represents about 2% of the total of the world stock markets and we do not have industries such as heavy engineering, aerospace or pharmaceuticals. If you restrict your share exposure to Australian shares you miss out on 98% of the opportunities that are available.

Another factor is that stock markets throughout the world are in different phases of the economic cycle. International investment enables you to place your money where it appears to have the best potential for growth at any time.

Non-residential property

The term non-residential property covers buildings such as shops, offices, warehouses and industrial sheds. At first glance they seem a most attractive investment because in most cases they have a higher yield than houses and units, and tenants usually sign a lease for at least three years. A long lease means you do not have those vacancies every six months that are possible with flats and houses. Damage should be minimal because the tenants use the property as business premises, and your outgoings are often low because the bulk of them is paid by the tenants. If you are well experienced in this field, I suggest this might be a good investment for you.

This can be a superb investment for anybody in business. If you buy your own premises you do not have any worry about vacancies, and when the property is paid off you have secured your business premises for life. This then gives you the opportunity of selling the business when you retire, but retaining the freehold to give you income.

However, if you are not an owner-occupier, remember the old adage "the higher the return, the higher the risk". The disadvantages of non-residential property are:

1. It often costs more than residential property, so you may have more money tied up in one property.
2. It may be very hard to lease when a vacancy occurs. In fact vacancies of **two years or more** are not uncommon. This can wreak havoc with your budget if you have incurred heavy borrowings.
3. If you try to sell this type of property when it is vacant, you will have to drop the price to rock bottom. The agents will say, "If you had a tenant we could find a buyer", not understanding that if you had a tenant you wouldn't want to sell the property.
4. Highly specialised buildings, such as drive-in takeaway food outlets or banks, may be hard to lease if they become vacant because they are suitable for only a certain type of tenant.
5. It is especially vulnerable to economic downturns because many small businesses go broke when times get tough. If this happens, the buildings are even harder to re-lease.

I'll sum it up by saying that non-residential real estate offers great opportunities for the experienced, and great traps for the unwary. Approach it with great caution.

Vacant land

The problem with vacant land is that it produces no income, and therefore you do not get an immediate tax deduction for any interest you spend in buying it. The interest is capitalised and reduces the capital gains tax bill when you sell.

If vacant land is your "thing" you are probably better off buying a block with some form of income-producing structure on it. Then you can claim the interest each year and enjoy capital gain on both the land and the building.

Specialised investments

In this category I include such items as paintings, coins, stamps and antiques. They are not suitable for negative gearing because they produce no income and they are hard to value unless you are an expert. Also forgeries are common, and there can be high commission taken if you have to sell them.

Certainly the ownership of them can give you many hours of pleasure, as well as the opportunity to expand your knowledge, and I have no doubt there are good profits for the few who have the skill to become experts in the field. The rest of us are better off in the more conventional areas of real estate and shares.

Summing Up

- There is no clear-cut path that must be followed – every investment has advantages and disadvantages.
- When you understand the good and bad points, it will be easier for you to decide upon an appropriate asset allocation.
- If you buy real estate or shares, see the purchase as a long-term project, preferably for 10 years.
- Laws can change. That is why all investments need regular monitoring.
- Growth investments will produce the best results over the long term.

5

FIXED-INTEREST INVESTMENTS

No one would remember the Good Samaritan if he had only good intentions. He had money as well.

MARGARET THATCHER

Fixed-interest investments have a significant role in any retiree's portfolio, for in most cases they provide a regular and secure income. However, they are generally misunderstood investments, and many investors are not aware that they do carry some dangers.

A simple definition is that a fixed-interest investment pays a set rate of interest to the holder for the term of the investment. For example, you might place $10 000 in a term deposit, or a debenture, for a two-year period at 8%. As the interest payments fall due, the interest is either paid to you, or compounded by being added to the principal.

The interest rate offered depends on how often the interest is paid. For example, if it is paid monthly you will get a lower rate of interest than if it is paid yearly, or even at the end of the period. This is because of the extra administration costs of processing a more frequent payment, and because the institution has the use of the interest if it does not have to pay it to you for six months or so.

There are two main types of fixed-interest investment:

1. term deposits, bank bills, debentures, unsecured notes and mortgages
2. government and semi-government bonds.

Remember that the two critical points in fixed-interest investing are the credit rating of the borrower (the institution which borrows it from you) and the term of the investment. Never forget

35

you are lending your money to somebody else and you want to make sure you get it back.

Term Deposits, Bank Bills, Debentures Etc.

A **term deposit** is an interest-bearing account with a bank or other lending institution. Usually the rate is fixed for the term of the investment, and the term will vary from one month to two years.

A **bank bill** is a document issued by a bank, or by a customer of the bank, which bears the bank's guarantee of repayment on a set date. The interest rate is fixed for the term of the bill, which is usually from one month to twelve months. Interest is payable to you when the bill matures.

A **debenture** is a loan by you to an institution such as a finance company or a major public company. As security, you and the other debenture holders are given a charge (mortgage) over the issuing company's assets, but this is of little value if the company goes broke. Generally the term is two to five years.

An **unsecured note** is similar to a debenture except that it is not secured by a charge over the company's assets. If the issuing company gets into strife, the debenture holders get paid before the unsecured note holders.

A **mortgage** is often taken out through a solicitor. The investor lends money to one of the solicitor's clients and this loan is secured by a first mortgage over property owned by the borrower. The term may range from two to five years.

EXAMPLE: *You have $75 000 to invest and are happy to leave it untouched for three years if it can earn 8% per annum. The local solicitor advises you he has a client of good character who wants to borrow $75 000 on these terms. As security, the solicitor prepares a first mortgage over one of the client's properties and you then lend the money to the solicitor's client who pays you interest every month. At the end of the three years you may be happy to continue the arrangement at a mutually agreed interest rate, or you may ask for your money to be repaid. If you ask for your money back the client usually pays you out by borrowing from somebody else.*

This may be a mutually beneficial transaction if all goes well, but it can be a worrying one if the borrower is always late with the payments or if the value of the security at a forced sale proves to be less than the loan. There are also dangers if the documentation is not prepared properly.

What term deposits, bank bills, debentures, unsecured notes and mortgages have in common is that they are usually taken for terms of five years or less, and are not regularly traded in the financial markets. If you put, say, $50 000 into one of these investments, your intention would be to leave it untouched till the end of the term when, we hope, you get all your money back after having received interest during the term of the investment.

The advantages are that there are normally no fees, and in most cases the investment is secure. An advantage, or a disadvantage, is that you lock in the rate for the term of the investment. This is great if rates fall, but unfortunate if rates rise.

However, there is no chance of capital gain, no tax benefits attach to the income stream and your capital is depreciated by inflation when your investment matures. Certainly the interest you have received may have compensated for the lack of capital gain, but the benefits of this depend on your tax bracket. There is also the risk of losing your money if you pick a doubtful institution to invest with.

These investments are normally not liquid ones and you may have difficulty getting your money back before the end of the set term. However, some debentures, bank bills and unsecured notes can be traded through stockbrokers, and a lending institution will often let you withdraw some money from a term deposit before its due date in return for paying you a lower rate. Mortgages can be sold, but there may be fairly heavy costs involved.

Let's think about two basic factors that influence fixed-interest investments. These are:

1. **The standing of the borrower.** Most institutions that borrow from the public have a credit rating. Those with the highest credit rating can ask investors to place money with them at the lowest rates because they are offering the highest security. Borrowers with less than the highest rating have to offer a better rate of interest to attract funds.

What would you do if you had $100 000 to invest and had a choice of investing it with two institutions who were both offering to pay you the same rate of interest? If one had a AAA rating, and one had a BB rating, you would invest with the AAA-rated company. The only way the BB-rated company has a chance of getting your money is to offer a higher rate.

> KEY POINT: Borrowers with a high credit rating are able to offer lower rates of interest than those with a lower credit rating. As always, the higher the return, the higher the risk.

This raises a dilemma for investors. Do you take a chance on the higher rate of return or do you stick with the highest-rated company? Obviously, you must be guided by your adviser, but be particularly wary of companies paying rates that are out of line with the market. For example, the now defunct Estate Mortgage Group were offering 18%, when the general market was offering 14%.

2. **The term of the investment.** The term of the investment affects the value of it – the longer the term, the greater the effect.

If prime debentures are offering 10% for five years, I have a valuable investment if I place $50 000 into one when rates are moving downward. However, if rates are moving up when I fix my interest for five years, my investment will become less valuable as rates climb.

There are two reasons for this. First, there is a big connection between inflation and interest rates. If rates are high and rising you can bet that inflation is raging too. This means the $50 000 I get back in five years will not buy nearly as much as the $50 000 I originally invested. Second, my debenture becomes relatively less attractive as prime debentures may now be available paying a safe 13%.

You now know the factors that influence the value of a fixed-interest investment – the credit rating of the borrower, the term of the investment and the prevailing economic climate. Let's see how this works in the exciting bond market.

> KEY POINT: The three main factors that affect the value of a fixed-interest investment are the security of the borrower, the term and the interest rate.

The Bond Market

The term "bond" has several meanings. These include a deposit paid by a tenant, a single-premium insurance policy (an "insurance bond") and some term deposits issued by banks and finance companies. However, in financial markets the term "bond" is used to mean loan documents issued by the Commonwealth Government, State governments and semi-government bodies such as water boards and electricity authorities. These bonds are traded in large amounts daily on the fixed-interest market.

There are both primary and secondary markets for bonds. The primary market is where the bonds first join the market when they are issued by tender to large institutions such as banks, insurance companies and fund managers. The secondary market is where the bond dealers trade bonds, mainly through bond brokers. The Government encourages the secondary market because it provides liquidity for the bond market.

Now the confusing thing about bonds is that they **fall in price** as **interest rates rise**. Therefore you may see headlines such as "Bond market in chaos as yields jump" and read that "bond prices fell as interest rates moved higher on inflationary fears". To understand why this happens, you must appreciate that a bond offers:

1. a regular fixed income until maturity.

2. a capital sum payable at a fixed future date.

Be aware that inflation will erode the value of the bond's income, as well as the principal that is repaid on maturity. Therefore the bond yield will have to be sufficient to compensate the holder for the loss in purchasing power. The problem is that if inflation rises, and yields rise too, a greater part of the income from the bond is taken by income tax.

EXAMPLE: *You buy a 9% $100 000 government bond with 10 years to maturity. This means that it carries a guarantee from the Government that it will be redeemed for $100 000 in 10 years' time, and will pay you interest at 9% per annum (the coupon rate) until then. If inflation runs at 4% per annum the value of that $100 000 you will receive in 10 years is only $67 600 in today's dollars. Furthermore, the real value of the income will also reduce by 4% a year.*

Let's learn three important definitions.

Coupon rate. The interest rate paid by the bond. It is 9% in the previous example.

Nominal yield. The return to a buyer at the price of the bond today. For example, if that $100 000 bond from the above example is worth $100 000 today, the nominal yield is the same as the coupon rate. This is because an investor who paid $100 000 for it would receive $9000 a year income or 9%. However, if bond prices rise, the bond might be worth $110 000. Then the nominal yield drops to 8.18% per annum because an investor who paid $110 000 for that bond today would receive $9000 a year income for an outlay of $110 000 – a return of 8.18%.

Real yield. This is the difference between the nominal rate and the rate of inflation. In the example above, if we assume that bond is worth $100 000 today, the real yield is 5%, made up of the nominal rate of 9% less the inflation rate of 4%.

If inflation starts to fall, interest rates should also start falling, and when this happens the nominal yield of our bond will fall in line with rates generally, and the bond will rise in price. It has become more valuable because neither its income stream nor the capital sum are losing value so quickly through inflation. Also its fixed 9% coupon rate becomes relatively more attractive compared with other investments because rates generally have dropped.

Conversely, if there are expectations of higher inflation, investors wishing to buy bonds will seek a higher nominal yield. Because the coupon rate cannot change (being fixed), the price of the bond must fall to produce a higher yield.

> KEY POINT: Falling interest rates make fixed-interest securities more valuable – rising rates make them less valuable.

You can now see why bonds can rise and fall in value. We'll now move on to showing you how to work out a bond's value. As you read what follows keep in mind there is almost certainly going to be a difference between the yield received by an investor and the original coupon rate.

EXAMPLE: *A $100 000 bond, issued at 9%, will pay $9000 a year until maturity irrespective of what price it trades at between its issue date and its maturity date. However, if you paid $200 000 for that bond on the secondary market, the return to you is $9000 on your investment of $200 000. This is 4.5%.*

By now you should understand that the total return, positive or negative, from a bond is made up of:

1. the income stream – that is, the interest it pays
2. any capital gain or loss made by the holder.

The income stream is simply the coupon rate. The capital gain, or loss, depends on the price I paid for the bond. Remember there are two ways I can get my principal back – sell the bond prior to its maturity date for its market price, or wait till maturity and accept its face value. If I bought that $100 000 bond for $100 000 I know I will get $100 000 on its maturity date because that is what the Government has guaranteed. However, if I paid $110 000 for it, I have locked in a capital loss of $10 000 unless I sell it for more than $110 000 prior to its maturity date. How can I do this? Only if nominal yields fall and the bond rises in value still further.

Notice that as the maturity date of the bond get closer the value of the bond comes more into line with the face value. On the maturity date it must equal the face value.

KEY POINT: The longer time there is to maturity the more a bond's market value may differ from its face value.

If you are confused by now, take heart in the knowledge that bonds are one of the least understood investments – even by some financial advisers. Let's now work through a simple example of valuing a bond. This may help you to understand the subject better.

CASE STUDY

Suppose a relative died and left you a Commonwealth Government bond with a face value of $100 000, a coupon rate of 10% and a maturity date of exactly one year. What you have is a promise from the Government that it will pay you $100 000 on maturity (in this case in one year) and give you 10% a year interest until maturity. Therefore the bond you hold entitles you to receive $110 000 in the forthcoming year. This is made up of the $100 000 capital, plus $10 000 interest for the year.

How do we value this bond? By discovering how attractive it is compared with other investments offering. If interest rates generally are 10%, the market would be prepared to pay $100 000 for the bond because it is offering a similar return to a one-year term deposit.

However, it is more valuable if interest rates for prime one-year securities were only 5%. In that case, a person with $100 000 to invest would get back only $105 000 in 12 months if they invested in the money market. Our bond is worth more. How much more? To calculate the value of our bond we have to figure out what sum invested at 5% today would pay back $110 000 in 12 months. We calculate this as follows:

$110 000 = initial principal + 5% initial principal

= (1 + 0.05) initial principal

Initial principal = $\dfrac{110\ 000}{1.05}$

= $104,762

We have just worked out that a person who wanted to get back $110 000 in 12 months would have to invest $104 762 today. To check the calculations, work backwards:

Initial principal	$104 762
Interest on $104 762 at 5%	$5 238
Total due at maturity	$110 000

As you can see, our bond is worth $104 762 even though its face value is $100 000. We have an unrealised capital gain of $4762 on its issue price of $100 000 and can choose to sell the bond and take the capital gain, or leave it run to maturity and enjoy higher interest than could be obtained elsewhere.

Another important point to notice is that the capital gain or loss is magnified as the time to maturity gets longer. Let's look at the example above again and calculate the value of the bond today if interest rates generally were 5%, and it was **two** years to maturity.

To make it simple we'll assume the value of the bond in two years is $120 500. This is calculated:

Principal sum	$100 000
Interest paid in Year 1	10 000
Interest paid in Year 2	10 000
Interest on $10 000 for a year @ 5%	500
Total value	$120 500

By using a financial calculator we can quickly work out that we would need to invest $109 297 at 5% per annum to grow to $120 500 in two years. Therefore our bond is worth $109 297 and is carrying a capital profit of $9297.

You will also notice that, if interest rates were on the rise, our bond would fall in value as soon as comparable rates generally fell below its nominal yield.

KEY POINT: The time to maturity is a significant factor in the amount of capital gain, or capital loss, that may be made by the holder of a bond.

Adding value

The job of the fund manager is to add value to the client's portfolio. Those bond fund managers adjust their portfolios to minimise losses and maximise gains. They do this by changing the mix of long-dated and short-dated bonds in line with changing economic conditions, and also by changing the nature of the bonds held.

For example, the fund manager will prefer long-dated bonds if the real yields on long-dated bonds are high relative to appropriate historical levels of interest and to real yields on short-dated securities. What's that again? It is a fancy way of saying "if interest rates are high now, and appear to be at or near the top, the fund manager should lock in the good long-term yield by buying long-dated bonds". On the other hand, if interest rates are low and look like rising, the fund manager would prefer short-dated bonds to minimise the risk of capital loss. As we saw before, any capital loss is magnified if rates rise and the bonds are long-dated.

The other factor that determines the price of a bond is **sovereign risk**, which is a factor that is added to the yield to compensate for the bond not being issued by a AAA lender such as the Commonwealth Government. Bond owners who decide a lender has been excessively downgraded by credit rating organisations such as Moodys can make extra profits if they follow their judgement and a re-rating to a better level occurs. As soon as the re-rating happens, the bond becomes more valuable. Some bond funds did well out of bonds issued by the Victorian State Government by buying after the state received its worst credit downgrading, and then selling after the credit rating was revised upwards and the value of the bonds rose with it.

Indexed bonds

These are a recent innovation and are growing in popularity. The lender issues the bond at a fixed rate of interest, but the capital value of the bond grows in line with inflation. If a normal bond was issued at 7%, made up of inflation 2% and real yield 5%, the indexed bond may be issued at 3% plus inflation. If the issue price was $100 000 the value at the end of the first year would be $102 000 and it would have paid $3000 to the holder as well. To put

it simply, you could say that 3% has been paid to you and 2% has been compounded. This is good for you because you get the benefit of compounding, and good for the issuing body who does not have to pay out the compounded interest until the bond matures in 10 or 15 years' time.

The issuers of indexed bonds can offer a lower real yield because the investor has a guarantee that the principal will keep pace with inflation. The owners of normal bonds have no such guarantee, and have to hope that inflation will not suddenly take off. If it does, they face heavy capital losses.

The best way to have an interest in indexed bonds is to invest in a bond trust that holds them, because they are issued in large denominations that are outside the resources of most individual investors. There is also at least one company offering allocated pensions where all or part of the capital sum is invested in indexed bonds. This gives the retiree an income stream that is guaranteed to keep pace with inflation.

International bonds

We are now part of the global village and may invest in bonds in foreign currencies issued by both foreign governments and large foreign companies. These bonds rise and fall in value in line with interest rate fluctuations in exactly the same way as do Australian bonds. However, there is another element in the game. Because international bonds are expressed in foreign currencies, they also fluctuate in line with movements in the Australian dollar.

EXAMPLE: *You have a bond with a market value of 100 000 Swiss Francs. If one Swiss Franc is worth one Australian dollar the bond is worth $100 000. However, if the Australian dollar fell so that 0.90 Swiss Francs equalled $1 the value of the bond would rise to $111 111. Conversely, if our dollar rose in value against the Swiss Franc, our bond would fall in value. Naturally the rise and fall of interest rates would also change the value and you could have a situation when the bond price suffered downwards pressure as overseas interest rates rose, yet faced upward pressure because our dollar was weakening.*

International bonds are like all international investments. We invest in them to get diversification, as well as protection against our dollar dropping. This may be of special importance if you had planned a lot of overseas travel.

Conclusion

By now you should have a general idea of the way fixed-interest markets work and the dangers inherent in them in a time of rising interest rates. Unfortunately, markets sometimes exhibit unpredictable behaviour and the best way to handle this is to have a well-spread portfolio, and to prefer cash, mortgage trusts and short-term fixed interest when rates appear to be rising. You can also have an "each way" bet by having some of your income investments in longer-term securities, and the balance in shorter-term securities, provided you are aware that the price of these securities can rise and fall until their maturity date.

Summing Up

- Your expectation of inflation is a major factor in deciding how much of your money should be in fixed interest.
- The greater the returns offered, the greater the risk.
- Higher rates seldom compensate for loss of capital.
- Fixed-interest securities rise in value when rates fall and fall in value when rates rise.

- If a fixed-interest security has a long time to maturity, its value is more affected by interest rate fluctuations than a shorter-dated security.
- Inflation, and with it interest rates, tends to fall as we enter a recession. That is a time when it is appropriate to prefer fixed-interest investments and hold longer-dated bonds, as a capital gain will occur as rates drop.
- Inflation, and with it interest rates, tends to rise as we come out of recession. Then it is best to prefer growth assets such as shares and lighten the amount in fixed interest while switching to shorter-dated bonds to minimise capital losses.

6

ARE MANAGED FUNDS FOR YOU?

Money is a wonderful commodity to have, but the more you possess, the more involved and complicated becomes your dealings and relationships with other people.

JOHN PAUL GETTY

In this chapter we shall focus on one of the most important decisions you have to make in your investment strategy – are you a do-it-yourself investor or do you prefer other people to do most of the work for you? Don't start feeling inferior at the thought of not being able to do it yourself. We now live in an age of specialisation because most jobs have become so complicated. It makes sense to do what you enjoy doing, and are good at, and leave the rest to experts.

I don't cut my own hair, do my own car maintenance, or clean my own carpets. Furthermore, much to the surprise of many of my friends, I don't "play" the share market, or trade in real estate. The bulk of my invested capital is in managed funds because that leaves me free to do the things I prefer to do.

A long time before retirement comes along, you should set aside a few quiet hours and ponder the following questions:

1. What are the activities I enjoy most?
2. What is my experience in handling investments?

When you are doing that you might think about some research done by American businesswoman Kathy Kolbe. In her book *The Conative Connection*[1] she points out that every human being is born with a bias towards, or away from, four instinctive traits. They can be summed up as:

---

1. *The Conative Connection: Uncovering the Link Between Who You Are and How You Perform* is published in America by Addison Wesley.

1. the need for new and different events in life
2. the need to complete a task
3. the need to seek detailed information before making a decision
4. the need to physically work with our hands.

Depending on our make-up, we may favour some of these and avoid others. My pattern is to prefer the first and third and to avoid the second and last. I enjoy new and different things happening around me and I seldom make decisions without seeking as much data as is available. However, I run a mile if one of our children is given a toy that requires assembly, and I tend to have a lot of unfinished projects on the go.

What about you? Think about your own likes and dislikes. Do you love pottery, knitting, or making furniture? Are you the type who thrives on adventure, or do you prefer life to be predictable? Are you meticulous with your personal records, or are they tossed willy-nilly in a drawer? Do you love group activities, or do you prefer pottering away happily on your own? These are important questions because it is most unlikely you are going to change. It may well be that you and your partner have a bias towards different activities. If this is the case, make sure you respect each other's natural gifts and encourage each other to enjoy what gives each of you fulfilment.

My favourite pastimes are writing, reading biographies and autobiographies, walking, music, dining out, travel and playing golf. With all those things to do, I certainly don't want to have to spend too much time in my retirement dealing with a huge portfolio of shares, or coping with the management of a string of rental properties. Managed funds give me the time to do what I enjoy. On the other hand, if you love buying rundown properties and working on them, or trading the options market, there is no reason you shouldn't keep on doing that when you retire.

> KEY POINT: Make retirement a time to do what you want to do, not what you feel you should do.

The next key point to consider is your investment experience. It's sad but true that much of our investment knowledge comes from painful experiences, but at retirement age you do not have the time or the future earning ability to recover from major mistakes. This is why you should start your investment program, and form a relationship with a financial adviser, at an early age. This will give you time to recover from your inevitable mistakes, and time to build trust with your adviser. If the adviser is not the right one for you, it will become apparent before you have placed too much money through that person's company.

Unfortunately, most retirees have no idea of what is involved in managing an investment portfolio. Our company sees far too many people who believe they will have no difficulty in looking after a retirement lump sum of $300 000 or more, though their investment experience is limited to paying off a house and buying a few Commonwealth Bank shares. They just don't know what traps may lie ahead.

In contrast, I have a retired client who has spent most of her life managing her parents' rental properties, and eventually her own. She does a first-rate job and boasts about her fine record. She would never entrust her properties to anybody else and has the bulk of her capital tied up in those properties. She also has some capital in shares, but this is invested in managed funds because she understands her knowledge of the share market is limited.

> KEY POINT: Be wary about do-it-yourself investment if you have reached retirement age without doing much of it.

What Is A Managed Investment?

I have covered managed investments in great detail in *More Money with Noel Whittaker*, but I will summarise the main points here. Managed funds are vehicles in which your money is pooled with that of thousands of other investors under the control of a fund manager. This fund manager makes the investment decisions and charges an annual fee for doing so. Provided the manager does a good job, the investors are happy. If the manager loses their money, or produces inadequate returns, the investors are unhappy and rightly point out they may have managed their money better on their own.

You will find that almost all managed funds are run by large fund managers such as Bankers Trust, Perpetual, Rothschild and County Natwest, by most banks, or by major life offices such as MLC or Colonial. To make it more confusing, some life offices may offer unit trusts, and some of the other fund managers offer life insurance products such as insurance bonds.

A unit trust is not an entity for tax purposes and therefore pays no tax itself. It is merely a "funnel" that sends the taxable income to the unit holders by way of distributions. Life insurance products, such as insurance bonds and superannuation policies, are tax-paid investments and bonuses are declared only after the fund itself has paid its tax. You do not receive any income from life insurance products (unless you have an annuity or allocated pension), but almost all unit trusts will pay at least a small income, which should be included in your tax return.

In *Making Money Made Simple* I introduced readers to the idea of the investment menu. Just as people going out to dinner may choose between poultry, seafood or red meat, investors have to choose between cash, property and shares. If they choose to do it themselves they may opt for bank accounts, debentures, government bonds, shares and rental houses. If they choose managed funds they may consider such investments as cash management trusts, bond trusts, equity trusts, mortgage trusts, insurance bonds, friendly society bonds and property trusts.

The do-it-yourself investor controls the investments and makes all the decisions. Those who opt for managed funds choose the type of investments they require and then let the fund managers make all the investment decisions.

Investors who use managed funds do so because they realise they do not have the skills and/or the time to do it on their own and because managed funds are such a convenient vehicle for investing money. However, like all investments, managed funds have their advantages and disadvantages. To illustrate them, let's compare investing in an equity trust with investing directly in shares.

1. **Share selection.** If you invest in an equity trust you have no say about which shares are bought and sold by the trust. That is the manager's job. Hence it is a passive investment and one that requires no effort on your part. In contrast, direct share investors select the shares they wish to buy, usually with guidance from their stockbroker, and then decide when to sell or when to buy more.

   Obviously, if you wish to pick your own stocks you are likely to prefer direct investment; if you know nothing about the market you may be more comfortable with the equity trust.

2. **Management fees.** Direct share investment has a time cost, but it is hard to put a value on it. If you have your own business, or are a member of a profession such as law or medicine, you would know that time expended in your

business has the biggest dollar return. Certainly time spent on a favourite hobby may have a much more pleasurable return, but the time spent in your business is the one that produces the dollars.

The equity trust fund manager charges a management fee that I'll cover later in the chapter. It usually ranges from 1% to 3% a year. But the test is not what it costs, but what it is worth. If the fund manager can protect you from bad decisions involving a large loss of capital, or produce a better outcome than you may have achieved, the management fee will be well spent.

3. **Flexibility.** The great benefit of an equity trust is flexibility. Imagine your best friend has $100 000 in equity trusts and you have $100 000 in direct shares. The share market has been roaring along and both of you have made a packet. You decide the market has topped and it's time to get out. To exit the market, you have to sell your shares and pay both brokerage and capital gains tax on the sale.

Your friend decides to get out too, but for her it is easier and cheaper. The equity trust managers will almost certainly give her the option to switch, free of charge, into a range of their other managed funds such as cash funds and bond trusts. Her only cost is capital gains tax.

The inevitable crash comes and you feel it's time to re-enter the market. You have to pay brokerage and stamp duty again. Your friend does not have these costs. When she wants to go back into the share market she simply completes a switch form and moves back in with no entry costs.

A major feature of the equity trust is that it makes it so easy for the investor to fine-tune the portfolio. Suppose, in the example above, both of you decided to reduce your exposure to the market by 20% instead of selling out. Your friend can reduce her portfolio across the board by switching, say, 20% of her holding to a less market-linked area. If you have 20 stocks with a value of $5000 each it is probably not practical to sell $1000 worth of each one.

4. **Profit/loss limiting.** Equity trust managers usually spread your money over shares in at least fifty different companies with the result that your overall loss is minimised if one or two of these shares goes bad. The other side of the coin is that you will not make a huge profit if the trust manager picks a star performer because that share may represent only a small percentage of the portfolio.

5. **Trading.** Equity trusts are not suitable for share trading. A major element of trading is setting a "stop loss" order, which is an instruction to the broker to sell immediately the price drops to a certain figure. This is to protect profits already made, or to keep losses within a predetermined figure. You cannot ask a fund manager to put a stop loss on a unit trust.

6. **Liquidity.** Equity trusts are highly liquid, but you don't have access to your money as quickly as you do with direct share investment. If you own shares, and the market takes a sudden plunge one day, you can phone your stockbroker to find out the latest prices. If you decide to sell you can place an order immediately, and the transaction may be consummated in a minute or so if there are buyers available.

If you decide to withdraw money from your equity trust, you cannot phone the fund manager's office and sell your units immediately. You will have to lodge a redemption form with the fund manager and you will not know the redemption price until it is announced next day. In two or three weeks you will have your cheque, just as if you had sold shares.

You should now understand that managed funds such as equity trusts are designed to be long-term passive investments – they are not for those with a trading mentality. Which is best for you? That is your decision. There will always be those who prefer to battle the market on their own; there will always be others who prefer to leave all that stuff to the fund managers. In the end it gets back to your own comfort level and how you want to spend your spare time.

> KEY POINT: Managed funds such as equity trusts are designed for long-term passive investment. They are not trading vehicles.

Measuring The Manager

The idea of using managed funds is that the fund managers, because of their skills, can add value to your investment. In other words, they will have to do better than you could do yourself if they are to justify their management fees. How do you measure the success of the manager? By comparing the manager's performance with that of other managers or by comparing it with a benchmark.

To find out how any investment compares with other investments, you can ask your adviser to prepare comparative graphs for you, or you can look up the tables that are in publications such as *Money Management*. When you do this, make sure you compare "apples" with "apples" and don't fall into the trap of comparing "apples" with "tomatoes". For example, an industrial share fund is different from a resources share fund, and a "balanced" fund is different from a "growth" fund.

Be wary of comparing performances between funds. There are two main reasons for this. First, the risk levels of the funds may be quite different, which makes comparisons invalid. Second, a certain fund may show the best performance figures over five or ten years because of some spectacular performances five or six years ago that still affect the figures. Another fund may have been a far better performer over the last three years.

To illustrate this, let's pretend I gave you the choice of investing in Fund A or Fund B and told you that Fund A had averaged 13.6% per annum over five years and Fund B had averaged 10% per annum over the same period. Which do you choose?

The correct answer is that you could not pick the best one on the basis of the figures I gave you because a major factor in your decision is what the figures were for each year. They are as follows:

	Year 1 (five years ago)	Year 2	Year 3	Year 4	Year 5 (most recent)
Fund A	20%	25%	10%	8%	6%
Fund B	6%	8%	10%	12%	14%

Naturally you would have to look at the reasons each fund has performed as it has, but the year-by-year figures show Fund A has been far more volatile than Fund B and its returns are declining. In contrast, Fund B's performance is consistent and steadily getting better.

Another test is to use a benchmark, and the most commonly used one is the relative index. There is a wealth of information about index construction in *More Money with Noel Whittaker,* but to put it simply it is a measure of a market as a whole. For example, the All Ordinaries Index is a measure of value of the main companies listed on the Australian Stock Exchange; the Morgan Stanley Capital Index is a measure of leading international shares.

The best a fund manager can hope to do is outperform the appropriate index. If you have an equity trust that falls 5% when the market, as measured by the All Ordinaries Index, has fallen 10%, your manager has done well. Once again make sure you compare the fund with the appropriate index. For example, your industrial share fund should be measured against the industrial index, and if you wish to include income as well as growth you should measure against the appropriate accumulation index. Accumulation indices include all income or dividends and assume they have been reinvested.

For some reason you will often see claims that most managers don't do better than the index. I find that surprising because it is not true, but don't take my word for it. It is something you can check easily for yourself. Find a list of comparative tables such as are published each fortnight in *Money Management* and look up an index fund. Now look at the total number of funds in that category and look where the index fund is placed. You will almost invariably find the index fund ranks halfway. Therefore, just as many managers beat it as there are those who fail to beat it.

That is where your financial adviser should be able to guide you. It is the adviser's job to guide you into funds that will consistently outperform the index, and by ongoing monitoring of your affairs keep you in those funds.

> KEY POINT: When comparing a fund with its peers, or with an index, make sure you compare it with a similar fund or with the relevant index.

Fees Of Managed Funds

We all know that you get only what you pay for, and can expect nothing for nothing. If you invest in a managed fund, such as a unit trust or an insurance bond, the fund pays certain fees to the managers, the people who run it. Let's look at these fees in detail.

Entry fees

Most managed funds charge an entry fee and it is this fee on which most new investors focus their attention. The fee varies with the time that a new investor could reasonably be expected to stay in the fund, but you will find that funds whose main objective is to produce income have a lower fee than those that are expected to produce capital gain.

For example, a cash management trust or a debenture has no entry or exit fees, income trusts may have a 2% or 3% entry fee, and growth trusts such as equity trusts and property trusts have entry fees that usually range from 3% to 5%. Friendly society bonds and insurance bonds may charge a 4% or a 5% entry fee. Usually, the fund manager uses part of the entry fee to pay brokerage to the licensed dealer who recommended the client place the business with the particular fund.

Investment products are continually evolving and many fund managers are now offering "no entry fee" products. In most of these the lack of entry fee is made up by charging higher management fees for the first three to five years.

EXAMPLE: *The XYZ Fund might offer investors the choice of a 4% entry fee payable at the start, or no entry fee coupled with an additional management charge of 1.33% for the first three years.*

Which do you choose? Some clients like the no-entry-fee option because the whole of their money is working from the first day; others prefer to pay the 4% and get it over with. When you choose the management fee option, the fee is deducted from your earnings in the first three years. In effect, you are getting it as a tax deduction.

In the long run it probably matters little. However, if you are a high-income earner now, who will be retired when you redeem the investments, you can gain tax advantages by using the no-entry-fee option. This is because you will be getting the entry fees as an effective 47% tax deduction when you invest, because they are effectively deducted from the first three years' income that is paid to you. When you eventually withdraw money from the fund, you should be in a lower tax bracket and may pay capital gains tax at 20% at most.

The point is to be aware of the entry fees and to understand the reasons for choosing one option or the other.

There are also some funds that have no entry or exit fees yet which do not charge additional management fees to compensate for the absence of entry fee. These usually fall into two categories:

1. **Income trusts** such as cash management trusts, where an entry fee would not be appropriate

2. **Other trusts** where the manager is not charging an entry fee so as to attract business. If you are considering using one of these, the main factor to consider is the ability of the manager, and your adviser is the best person to guide you. There is no point in jumping into a no-entry-fee fund just to save fees and then having to pay the price in below-average performance.

Exit fees

There are usually no exit fees for managed funds that charge an entry fee, but many no-entry-fee funds charge an exit fee if you withdraw from the fund before a specified time has elapsed. This normally varies from three to five years and may be charged on a sliding scale depending on the length of time you have been in the fund.

Your adviser and the prospectus will explain these fees for you. The main factors to remember are:

1. Don't use a fund with entry or exit fees as a short-term investment.

2. Check out if the lack of entry fee is made up for by higher management charges for the first few years.

Internal fees

The fees you should note carefully at the start are the ongoing management fees, for these are the ones that you never notice after you invest. This is because all returns are quoted net of fees.

When your quarterly statement arrives from the XYZ Fund it may state the distribution is "1.6 cents a unit" and it may tell you the fund has "returned 15.8% for the half-year". However, the statement is unlikely to mention the annual management fees.

The prospectus will state the fees clearly, but they are often more readable in the information sheet most advisers include with their recommendations. The fees are usually expressed as a percentage of the asset value of the fund. For example, the management fees of a cash management trust might be 0.75% per annum of the fund value, and for an equity trust 1.85% per annum of the fund value. These fees are ongoing and pay the manager for the cost of running the fund.

The assets of investors in unit trusts have to be held by a recognised trustee company. Therefore, unit trusts have trustee's fees in addition to manager's fees. These generally range from 0.077% per annum to 0.125% per annum. Insurance company funds are not required to have a trustee, so their products have no trustee fees. Their annual management fees are similar to those charged by unit trusts.

As well as the above fees some managers charge an incentive fee, which may be as much as 10% of any increase in asset values. Is this too much? To judge it objectively you have to look at the fund's performance compared with other funds that charge lower fees. Believe me, we in the industry are extremely conscious of managers' fees and soon notice if the funds that are charging above-average fees do not put in an above-average performance.

The term for the sum of the fees charged by a managed fund is MER (manager's expense ratio) – all the fees charged by the manager expressed as a percentage of the assets of the fund. It is the best and simplest guide to the fees of the fund and is usually between 1% and 3%. Obviously, a lower MER means a better result for the investor if the fund performance is adequate. The information provided by your adviser should always state the MER for any fund recommended.

As you can see the fees are substantial. However, don't be put off by that. Think of the old saying "Don't ask what it costs – ask what it's worth". When you invest in a managed fund, such as a unit trust, all the work is done for you. There are no repair bills to find, no rates to pay, no land tax returns to fill in, no long conferences with your stockbroker, no credit checks to carry out, and no advertising or interviewing of tenants. The fund manager will even pay the money straight into your bank account for you.

> KEY POINT: Don't ask "Are the fees too high?" Ask "Am I getting value for the fees?"

Listed Investment Companies

The managed funds mentioned in this chapter so far have one thing in common – if you wish to redeem your money you have to make application to the fund manager who will calculate the value of investment based on the value of the assets in the trust. These funds are not listed on the Australian Stock Exchange but, if the managed fund is an equity trust, it will invest your money in listed shares so we can say it is an unlisted vehicle that invests in listed investments.

There is another class of managed funds known as "listed investment companies" (LICs) that I'll discuss now as an appreciation of the differences will help you to a much better understanding of the subject of managed funds in general. The two best-known LICs are ARGO Investments Ltd and Australian Foundation Investment Ltd, but there are also ones managed by such leading fund managers as Bankers Trust and Rothschild. They are **listed** investment vehicles that invest in listed shares, and thus are different to a normal equity trust that is an **unlisted** vehicle that invests in listed shares. Your first reaction may be "there can't be much difference", but stay with me and I'll show you that there are significant differences. They relate mainly to pricing and fees.

Valuation. The price of an equity trust unit is found by adding up the value of the assets in that trust and dividing the total by the number of units. Hence the value of the unit is always equal to the sum of the parts. An LIC is not valued by the manager; it is valued by the stock market. Obviously, investors will take notice of the underlying assets owned by the LIC, but the price will rarely equal the sum of the parts. Usually LICs trade at a discount or premium to their net asset backing, but historically they have traded more at a discount than at a premium. Therefore, an investor who is keen on LICs usually has the chance to buy a basket of assets for less than it would cost to buy the assets if they were bought individually.

That sounds great but there is always the disadvantage. If the stock market tumbles the discount usually gets bigger. Those who wish to sell will find themselves disposing of a basket of assets at a price that is now well short of the value of the individual assets.

I'll use an oversimplified example to explain what I mean.

EXAMPLE: *Let's assume the total assets of the ACE unlisted trust were:*

1000 XYZ shares at $10 each	*$10 000*
2000 MNO shares at $5 each	*$10 000*
Total value	*$20 000*

ACE has 20 000 units on issue so the value of each unit in ACE is $1. If the XYZ and the MNO shares rise by 10%, the portfolio owned by ACE is now worth $22 000 and each unit in ACE is worth $1.10. The units have increased by 10%, which exactly reflects the increase in value of the underlying assets.

If ACE became a listed investment company, a rise in asset backing of 10% is likely to cause a rise in the price of the shares in the LIC but it may be more or less than 10%. If the LIC shares rose to only $1.05, sellers would not get back the true asset value.

> KEY POINT: Shares in an equity trust are valued by the fund manager and will always represent net asset backing. Shares in a listed investment company are valued by the stock market and hence will usually be at a discount or premium to net asset backing.

Closed or open-ended. An equity trust is an open-ended fund, which means it is usually open for new subscription so the inflow of funds is theoretically unlimited. A deluge of new funds may dilute future returns for existing unit holders if the trust has difficulty investing all this new money wisely. Furthermore, if the trust gets bad publicity and suffers a flood of redemptions, it may be forced to sacrifice assets to meet these redemptions to the detriment of the remaining unit holders. This happened in 1990 to the unlisted property trusts and the problem was solved only when they became listed vehicles similar to LICs.

An LIC is a closed vehicle and accepts new funds only when it chooses. It goes about its business of investing, and is untroubled about investing new money or paying redemptions. It lets the market fix the selling price for its shares, and if there are no sellers there can be no buyers.

Liquidity. Equity trusts and LICs both invest in listed shares so both can be regarded as liquid investments. There is one major difference and I hinted at it in the previous paragraph. Equity trusts are redeemed by the fund manager at net tangible asset backing and the investor will always be able to withdraw funds provided the trust can sell assets to meet redemptions. As the assets of the major equity trusts are mainly blue-chip shares, it is unlikely they could not be sold.

In order to sell shares in an LIC you have to find a buyer. Certainly there are usually buyers around, but in the event of a stock market crash you may have to give a hefty discount to find one.

Fees. Most equity trusts have entry fees of around 5% and no exit fees. LICs incur normal brokerage and stamp duty, which is about 2.5% on buying and 2.5% on exit. Thus there is little overall difference in total buying and selling costs. Managed investments tend to have higher internal charges than LICs for they have far more administrative work to do.

How Safe Are Managed Funds?

In this chapter we are discussing advantages and limitations of managed funds, but don't be concerned if it takes you a while to grasp it. Few investors seem to comprehend them completely, and it is common to hear questions like "Is a trust a safe thing to invest in?" This question shows a lack of understanding, for anybody who appreciated the managed fund concept would understand the proper question to ask is "What type of risk and volatility is involved with this particular investment?"

A managed fund is not some complex device, but is merely a legal structure that enables investors with relatively small investment funds to participate in the kind of investment that may be beyond the capacity of them as individuals. The main elements for any investor to think about are the skill and reputation of the trust manager, together with the area in which the trust assets will be invested.

Because trusts normally keep a cash reserve to meet redemptions, it has become customary to treat investments in them as fairly liquid, and unit holders have become used to being able to cash in all or part of their investment within two or three weeks. This flexibility of being able to withdraw part of the investment at short notice is one of the outstanding features of unit trusts.

However, this ready cashability cannot be guaranteed if the trust is investing in assets such as property or mortgages that are

not capable of fast realisation. In July 1990, several unlisted property trusts were forced to place a freeze on redemptions following the investor panic that arose after the Estate Mortgage collapse and the public airing of the problems of OST and Pyramid Building Society.

This should not be a cause for alarm, but investors should be aware that managed funds are merely providing an avenue that enables some investors to do the same thing that others are doing, by themselves, without using a fund manager. The investor who invests directly in assets such as mortgages, debentures, government bonds or property has no guarantee that these investments may be quickly cashed at face value. The direct investor is no better off than the indirect investor. Once this fact is understood the mystique surrounding trusts should vanish.

A managed fund has no magical power to gild an investment such as shares, mortgages or property with qualities that direct investment in the same areas does not possess. Therefore, investors in all managed funds should study the underlying assets before becoming involved with them. This is of particular importance in a depressed market.

Think about two top-flight property or equity trusts. One is fully invested, and the other is holding at least 40% of its assets in cash. If the market slumps, the one with the cash is beautifully placed to snap up any bargains that come on the market. It will also fall in value much less than the fully invested fund if the market crashes, because a large part of its assets are in cash, which has not fallen in value. For example:

	Equity Fund A	Equity Fund B
Cash	400 000	50 000
Shares	600 000	950 000
Total	1 000 000	1 000 000

If the sharemarket falls 30%, the position becomes:

	Equity Fund A	Equity Fund B
Cash	400 000	50 000
Shares	420 000	665 000
Total	820 000	715 000

On the other hand, the fully invested fund will benefit most from a sudden market upsurge, because all its money is in the market.

Conclusion

Only you can decide whether you prefer direct investment, managed funds or a combination of both. After reading this book and discussing it all with your adviser, you should be better placed to make an educated decision.

The main risks in managed funds are:

1. **Loss of value because of share market fluctuations.** This will happen whether you invest in managed funds or on your own. If you can't handle that, and you are not prepared to take a long-term view, stay out of the share market.

2. **Loss of capital because a "lender" fund (mortgage trust or debenture) has suffered bad debts.** This risk is handled by spreading your money around different funds, and choosing only the ones that have been approved by the research source of your adviser.

3. **Loss of capital because the managed fund was a highly speculative one** such as a film scheme or an agricultural scheme. Be aware that you should not invest in these areas with money you cannot afford to lose.

4. **Loss of capital, because of our dollar falling in value,** when you invest in a trust with international exposure such as an international equity trust or a resource trust. This risk is everpresent with direct or indirect investment in these areas.

By now you should have a better understanding of managed funds and do-it-yourself investing and know which one you prefer. Remember, it is not a question of one being better than the other, but of one being better for you. We'll now go a step further and look at simplifying investment through master trusts, and saving fees through wholesale funds.

Summing Up

- When you invest in managed funds you are paying fund managers to do most of the work for you. If they do this well you are probably better off than trying to do it yourself.
- The more investment experience you have had in your lifetime the better placed you are to do it yourself.
- Be wary of comparing performance figures.
- A managed fund should behave the same as the assets in which it invests.
- You can be experienced in one area and not in another. In that situation you can use a combination of do-it-yourself investing and managed funds.

7

MASTER TRUSTS AND WHOLESALE FUNDS

Money is like an arm or a leg – use it or lose it.

HENRY FORD

There has been so much publicity about the ageing of our population that most of you now realise the need to accumulate money for retirement or for unexpected incidents. However, the growing complexity of financial matters has made it a difficult task to do on your own.

Consequently the managed funds such as equity trusts that I discussed in the last chapter have been increasing in popularity as investment vehicles. Yet, despite their growing acceptance, surveys show that less than 10% of investors really understand how they work. I hope, after reading the previous chapter, you are now in the informed 10%.

The benefits of investing in managed funds are obvious. They enable you to place your money in a wide range of areas and gain a diversification that would not be possible on your own unless you were a millionaire. A single investment in a balanced trust can spread your investment over fixed-interest securities, property and shares throughout the world.

Trusts also free you from the daily management of your affairs. You do not have to cope with difficult tenants, or make decisions about a large portfolio of shares. You can go for a six-month holiday hiking in Europe and know your affairs will be looked after by your fund manager while you are away. Furthermore, you do not have that barrage of paper that keeps coming if you have rental properties or a large share portfolio.

If you have ever owned a few rental properties you know about the inspection reports, land tax returns, agent's statements, body corporate fees, insurance policies, and the never-ending bills for maintenance. If you have shares you will be inundated with reports, rights issues, notices of special meetings, take-over offers, top-up offers, and of course dividend cheques to bank and record.

However, although trusts do eliminate the day-to-day management of your portfolio and also substantially reduce the paperwork, you may still have bookkeeping problems if you spread your money over several trusts. These can be exacerbated if there is foreign income, franking credits, capital gains tax, or tax-free and tax-deferred income involved. Many of my clients have complained to me about the amount of paperwork that even a modest investment across four or five trusts can generate, and they often arrive with folders of stuff for me to sort out. Much of it goes straight into the wastepaper basket.

The other problem with having a lot of different investments is the cost of moving from one to another if you change your investment strategy.

How do you solve the problem of too much paperwork and the cost of changing investments? Enter the **master trust.** It is a fairly new concept that is designed to simplify the investment process still further, and reduce much of the paperwork and personal record-keeping that investors in managed funds have to cope with.

TABLE 7.1

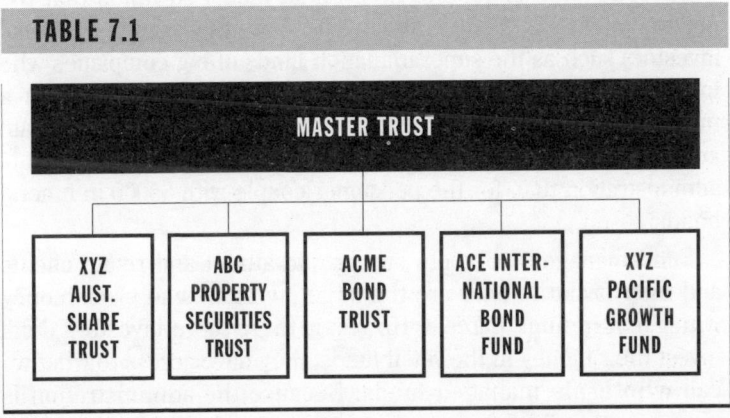

A master trust is a vehicle that lets you spread your investment over a range of trusts by using one more trust – the master trust. You invest all your money in the master trust and it, in turn, invests in a range of other trusts that are called the "sub-trusts". This simplifies your record-keeping because all the income flows through the master trust and, in effect, you have only one trust to keep track of.

The cost of moving investments becomes negligible too. Investors in a master trust can usually switch between the underlying trusts at minimal cost if their investment strategy changes.

Master trusts are growing in popularity and are likely to play a major role in your retirement strategy, but to understand them you will have to know about wholesale funds and pre-mixed funds. Let's talk about these now and then I'll show you how it all fits together.

Retail And Wholesale Funds

In the previous chapter I discussed managed funds and the entry, exit and management fees involved. The funds mentioned in that chapter were **retail funds** – the ones the average investor deals with. Typical investors might be Mr Jones with his $75 000 rollover, Ms Smith with her $20 000 insurance bond, the Brown family with the $10 000 put away for their children's education, or Mr and Mrs Green with a $5000 funeral bond. Each investor has a separate account and looks forward to regular reports and, where appropriate, income distributions. All this involves a lot of costly administration work for the fund.

There is another type of investor in managed funds that the general public knows little about. These are the large institutional investors such as the superannuation funds of big companies who invest millions every year, and wealthy individuals with over a million dollars to invest. These large investors also have separate accounts with the fund, but it costs little more for their administration than for the pensioner couple with $5000 in funeral bonds.

Fund managers compete strongly to attract and retain clients and their favourite ones are the large investors who place money with them in huge parcels. However, these large investors don't invest their money in the retail funds; they have access to what we call **wholesale** managed funds. Because the administration is minimal in relation to the large sums invested, these wholesale funds have far lower management fees than the retail funds I mentioned in the last chapter. Often their management fees are as low as 0.5% per annum, a full 1% cheaper than a retail fund.

You may be thinking "Why is he telling me this? I haven't got hundreds of thousands of dollars to invest!"

This is where master trusts come to the fore. *You* may not have a large sum to invest but, if you combine your money with that of many other investors through a master trust, the master trust can invest in the wholesale fund on your behalf and pass on the benefit of the lower fees to you.

KEY POINT: Wholesale funds are available only to people and institutions with large sums to invest. The management fees of wholesale funds are much lower than those charged by retail funds.

You now know that master trusts can give you access to wholesale funds with lower management fees, but be aware the master trust itself is usually run by a different fund manager from the ones who run the sub-trusts. You are still liable for the fees charged by the master trust. These will vary between master trusts and are clearly stated in the prospectus, but in most cases they range from 1% to 2% per annum. Add these to the 0.5% or so charged by the wholesale sub-funds and you get total fees of between 1.5% and 2.5% per annum.

As you can see, the combined fees of the master trusts and the underlying wholesale trusts are usually no more than those incurred by people who invest directly in retail trusts. Consequently, investors in master trusts can enjoy the benefits of the master trust at minimal extra cost.

Watch The Administration

Should you use a master trust? I believe they are the best vehicle for most investors because of the simplified paperwork and the ease of switching. However, as well as being conscious of the overall total of fees charged, you should focus on the quality of the master trust's administration.

The main job of the master trust manager is to receive the money from investors, place it in the various sub-trusts, keep accurate records and arrange for prompt withdrawals when required. As you can imagine, the quality of the administration of the master trust is critical. If the manager of the master trust cannot cope with the paperwork you may be unable to withdraw money when you want it, or find that switch requests have not been acted upon. This could cause hardship or even loss.

We have already had one case in Australia where a master trust manager suffered a breakdown in his computer systems and the hapless investors were left in limbo for months while the mess was sorted out. They did not lose their money and there was no suggestion of malpractice; it was a simple matter of the computer system being unable to cope with the demands placed on it. Retirees can do without those worries, which is why you should ensure that any organisation offering a master trust has the resources to run it properly. Your adviser can guide you.

Pre-Mixed Funds

Now that you understand managed funds, wholesale funds and master trusts, let's go one step further and examine "pre-mixed funds" that have names like **Capital Stable, Capital Secure, Balanced** and **Growth.** Before we take that step, let's step back in time to the early days[1] of the financial advisory industry in the 1970s. It started with specialist property trusts, and as the industry evolved we saw the introduction of bond trusts and equity trusts. In the early 1980s, because of deregulation of the financial system and the boom that accompanied it, a plethora of trusts flooded the market. We saw a huge range of specialist trusts such as resources trusts, smaller companies trusts, Japanese trusts and trading trusts.

To get an appropriate asset allocation, an adviser sometimes had to suggest clients spread their money over ten or more trusts. This was confusing for many investors but also required continual monitoring by the adviser to ensure the asset allocation stayed on track, and that the individual funds were all performing as hoped. Many advisers did not have the resources to do this and, in any event, each time an investment was switched there was capital gains tax to worry about. There also may have been exit or entry costs on the switch.

---

1. This history is discussed over several chapters in *More Money with Noel Whittaker.*

The solution was to offer "pre-mixed" funds. Instead of having your money in ten different funds, you could choose the risk level that suited you, and the fund manager would blend a fund from his existing range of trusts. Probably one of the first of these was the "managed" rollover fund.

Most "managed" rollover funds prior to the 1987 crash were pre-mixed trusts that were supposed to provide a secure investment with a degree of risk that would be acceptable to most retirees. However, when the crash came, investors learnt that many managed funds should have carried a title like "aggressive share fund" as they saw the value of their money drop by 40% and more. The fund managers had become carried away in the race to be the best monthly performer and had lost sight of their primary aim - to protect the investors' capital.

The New Blends

Much has happened in the industry since 1987 and now almost all fund managers are offering investors the choice of individual funds or blended funds. A favourite among retirees has become the capital stable fund, which came into being to provide the performance that the managed rollover funds had promised, but failed, to do. Capital stable funds stayed away from speculative assets and carried a high percentage of cash and fixed-interest investments as well as possibly 25% to 30% in shares. They paid high returns in 1993 when bonds and shares were booming because of falling interest rates, but some fell in value by nearly 5% in early 1994 when bond prices and share prices fell in value.

If you are investing in rollover funds now, you will find most managers are offering three basic options ranging from highly conservative to aggressive. The funds have a range of names depending on the providers, but common terms are capital secure, capital stable and market-linked. The aim of each fund is to maximise returns that are consistent with the risk of each asset class but within different time frames.

For example, the aim of a capital secure fund might be no negative returns over any one-month period, and for a capital stable fund no negative returns over any 12-month period. A goal for the more volatile market-linked or growth funds might be no negative returns in any rolling 36-month period.

TABLE 7.2

Comparison of asset allocation of a capital secure fund and a market linked fund.

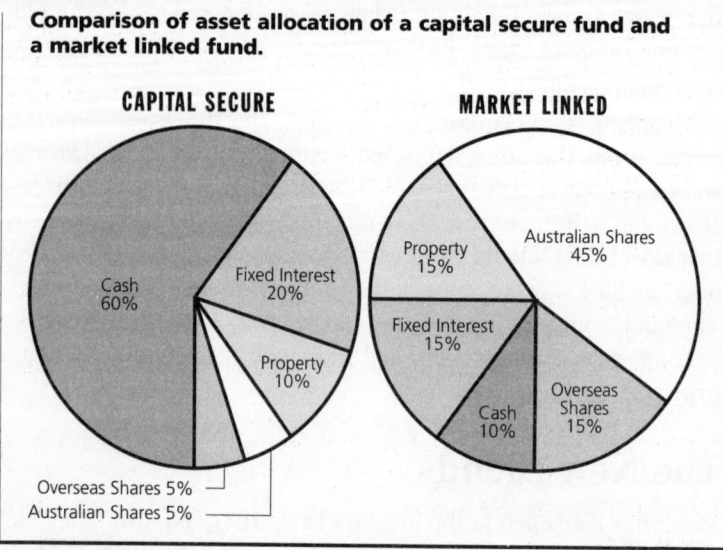

CAPITAL SECURE

Cash 60%
Fixed Interest 20%
Property 10%
Overseas Shares 5%
Australian Shares 5%

MARKET LINKED

Property 15%
Australian Shares 45%
Fixed Interest 15%
Overseas Shares 15%
Cash 10%

Most of the leading fund managers offer pre-mixed trusts for non-rollover money. These have names like growth fund if it is highly weighted to shares, balanced fund if it has a more conservative asset mix, and monthly income fund if it has only a small percentage of shares in the asset mix.

The Catch 22 for retirees is that they stand between a rock and a hard place. If they refuse to accept a portfolio where the values can fall as well as rise they condemn themselves to a life of poverty unless they are extremely wealthy now. The only investments suitable for them are low-yielding capital guaranteed funds and cash.

This is obviously not acceptable for most retirees, but the only way to achieve the returns necessary for a secure retirement is to include volatile assets in the mix. Once you include volatile assets such as fixed-interest investments, shares, property and international funds you open the investor to fluctuation in the overall values of the portfolio.

The solution is to take the time to understand the nature of the assets in your investment mix and know how each asset class is likely to behave. Then you, and your adviser, can construct a mix of capital secure, capital stable and market-linked funds that is appropriate for you.

As an example, let's assume you have $300 000 in an allocated pension fund and are drawing a pension of $20 000 a year. A mix of 20% capital secure, 60% capital stable and 20% market-linked might suit if you are drawing all your pension from the capital secure fund. This would see your next three years of pension taken care of because it is all coming from the capital secure area. While this is happening, the other two sectors have time to grow in the way that is appropriate for that mix of assets.

Conclusion

You should now appreciate how the master trust concept offers you a wide variety of choices that may be summed up as:

- Invest in a range of individual trusts that are part of the master trust menu.
- Invest in one pre-mixed fund such as a capital stable or a balanced fund.
- Invest in a range of pre-mixed funds in proportions that match your goals.

As you can see, master trusts offer the flexibility of reduced paperwork and cheap switching facilities. Some have only pre-mixed funds and some offer both pre-mixed funds and the do-it-yourself option. If you choose the former, you can opt for categories such as capital stable option, balanced or growth. If you prefer the latter, you can design your own asset allocation.

Now that you are an expert on managed funds we shall move to everybody's favourite topic – how to save tax.

Summing Up

- A master trust is a vehicle through which you invest in other trusts.
- Wholesale funds have lower management fees than retail funds.
- Often the combined fees of the master trust and the wholesale trusts in which it invests are no more than the fees for equivalent retail trusts.
- In a pre-mixed fund the fund manager determines the asset allocation.
- Good administration is vital if you are using master trusts.

8

SAVING INCOME TAX IN RETIREMENT

No one ever went broke saving money.

ANON

It doesn't matter whether you are trying to build assets for your retirement, or making them last after you have retired; a knowledge of legal ways to save tax is a must. Despite the undeniable truth of this, we find that most people who come into our office are not using their assets and income in the most tax-effective way. They are wasting some of their precious resources. Therefore in this chapter, and the following four chapters, I'll teach you the fundamentals. Then, if you want more specific information about tax-saving techniques you can speak to your accountant or your financial adviser as well as referring to my other books.

First, understand there are many inconsistencies in the way the Tax Act is interpreted. Because the Act is unclear, your adviser often may be unable to say with certainty that a course of action you are considering will pass Tax Office scrutiny. Suppose you owned an investment property that was originally bought for negative gearing purposes but over time the combination of a reduced principal, rising rents and falling interest rates meant you were now paying tax on the net rents. A solution may be to transfer the house to your spouse if the spouse was a low-income earner and this would probably be acceptable to the Tax Office. However, there is a section in the Tax Act called Part IV A which has the power to disallow any action done with the motive of avoiding tax. Therefore, it is possible that the act of transferring part of a property to a spouse just to save tax may be attacked by the Tax Office under Part IV A.

Furthermore, when dealing with your tax adviser, you have to decide what overall approach you will take. Some people are aggressive and will have a go at anything that has even a slight chance of getting through. If you feel this is appropriate for you, an aggressive adviser may suit you best. There are others, like myself, who bend the other way. As far as I am concerned, if there is even a chance a strategy might be disallowed I will not touch it. As you can imagine, the solicitor who advises me on tax is one of the most conservative in the country but I sleep well at night.

Another danger is that our tax system now works on self-assessment. This is a process whereby the Tax Office no longer checks your return, but relies on your honesty. Now, instead of giving all tax returns a cursory check, they select a sample for a detailed audit every year. Naturally if any errors are found you may be liable for back tax and penalties. The danger is that you may think you have got away with something when in reality you have not yet been chosen for the dreaded audit. A client once told me it was possible to claim the cost of building a carport on an investment home as a tax-deduction. When I told her it wasn't, she replied "Well I put it on the tax return and they passed it." In reality they hadn't looked at her return – yet!

> KEY POINT: Our tax system now works on self-assessment. Don't imagine you have got away with an illegal deduction just because your return isn't queried in the year it is lodged.

Tax affects your assets and income in two ways:

1. By taxing the income you receive – this is called income tax. It is discussed in this chapter.
2. By taxing any profits on sale when you dispose of an asset. This is called capital gains tax and is discussed in a later chapter.

There are also a host of hidden taxes such as sales tax, payroll tax and fringe benefits tax, but we will ignore them here because there is little we can do about them. They are part of the broadening of the tax base which is continually happening. Governments throughout the world realise that high marginal tax rates are a disincentive to working harder and are trying to make the tax-take less painful by reducing the direct personal rates of tax and increasing the indirect taxes.

Under our progressive tax system the *rate* of income tax increases as our income increases. Since 15 November 1993 the rates of tax for private individuals are:

TAX BAND SCALE

Taxable income	Tax payable and marginal rate
$0 – $5 400	Nil
$5 401 – $20 700	Nil + 20% on the balance above $5 400
$20 701 – $38 000	$3 060 + 34% on the balance above $20 700
$38 001 – $50 000	$8 942 + 43% on the balance above $38 000
Above $50 000	$14 102 + 47% on the balance above $50 000

In addition, Medicare levy is added to the tax income, but for simplicity I have ignored it in this chapter. The rates for children and companies are different from the above, but I will not go into them here as the aim of this section is to consider ways retirees can save tax.

You can reduce your overall income tax bill if you can arrange your affairs so that some of your income is earned by a person, company or investment vehicle that pays less tax than you do. You can also save tax if some of your income includes tax credits or rebates or if you have some allowable deductions. We shall focus on these strategies now.

Marginal Rate versus Average Rate

To appreciate this chapter you will have to understand the difference between marginal rate and average rate. They are terms that are bandied around continually but often incorrectly.

Think first about the **marginal rate.** This is the rate at which you are taxed on the highest portion of your income. You will notice the tax is levied in "bands". The first band is the tax-free band and runs from nil to $5400. Provided your total taxable income stays in this band, you have no tax to pay. Then we come to the 20% band, which is for incomes between $5401 and $20 700. Once you earn over $20 700, you enter the 34% band where every extra dollar is taxed at 34% until your income rises to $38 000. At this point, every extra dollar earned over $38 000 is taxed at 43% until $50 000 is reached and the rate increases to 47%. It is this 34% or 43% or 47% that is referred to as the marginal rate.

> KEY POINT: Your marginal tax rate is the tax you pay on the last dollar you earn.

Now think about the **average rate.** Let's consider a taxpayer earning $28 000 per annum. From the table above we can work out that the tax bill for the year will be $5542 ($3060 on the first $20 700 and 34% on the balance of $7300). If we divide this into $28 000 we can see that tax is being paid at an average rate of 19.8 cents in the dollar or 19.8%.

As you can see the average rate covers the **whole** of the income, whereas the marginal rate affects only any **extra** dollars earned. It is the management of the marginal rate that is the major concern in financial planning. You may ask what is the importance of the average rate. It's a good question but I don't have a good answer. To me it is of academic interest only because, in practice, in financial planning we use the marginal rate. For example, if people are earning $20 700 a year from their investments and want more income, they must realise that tax will take 34% of any extra income generated. What this does to the average rate is irrelevant.

You should now understand that people minimise tax by staying in the lowest tax bracket that is consistent with the income level they need. We have found that few retiree couples need more than $35 000 a year after tax to live on, so most individual retiree's income should fall into the $5400 to $20 700 band. That is the 20% marginal band. Provided both stay in the same band, it doesn't matter what the individual incomes are.

EXAMPLE: *Ted and Mary earn $15 000 a year each while Tony and Sue earn $20 000 and $10 000 respectively. The tax due is:*

Ted	$1920	Tony	$2920
Mary	$1920	Sue	$ 920
Total tax	$3840		$3840

Because all parties have a marginal tax rate of 20% the tax for each family is the same provided the total income is also the same.

> KEY POINT: You don't need to equalise your incomes to
> save tax as long as you both stay in the same tax band.

Split Your Income

Rearranging your affairs so that you or your spouse can move to a
lower tax bracket is known as income splitting. This means the
income is apportioned between family members instead of being
all heaped on one person. In the example above, if Sue earned
$30 000 and Tony earned nothing, the tax payable by Sue would
have been $6222. Income splitting reduces it to $3840.

As the tendency for people to choose an income stream instead
of a lump sum when they stop work grows, it will become more
common for the main breadwinner to receive the largest income in
retirement by way of an allocated pension or work-related pension.
If this happens it is even more important that the spouse holds the
balance of investments to ensure that both parties stay in the same
tax bracket. This will not affect aged pension entitlements. When
assessing your eligibility for an aged pension, the Department of
Social Security looks at the overall position, so it does not matter
in whose name income is derived or assets are held.

If you have substantial assets and your affairs are diverse you
will probably find that family trusts are good vehicles for income
splitting. These are covered later.

Minimise The Non-Deductible Items

When you can arrange your affairs so that an item is tax-
deductible, the Tax Office effectively subsidises the cost at your
marginal rate.

EXAMPLE: *John and Karen both earn $60 000 a year. John
is paying 9% interest on the loan for his own home while Karen
is paying 10% interest on the loan for her investment property.
Who is paying the highest effective rate of interest? The answer
is John, because Karen can claim hers as a tax deduction. His
effective rate is 10% but she receives an effective subsidy of
48.5% (47% + Medicare Levy). This reduces her effective rate
to 5.15%.*

As you can see, non-deductible interest on home loans and,
worse still, on credit cards and personal loans, is one of our
biggest costs. However, look on the bright side – every dollar you

invest in paying back that non-deductible interest is earning you the equivalent of the interest rate you are being charged after tax and with no fees and no risk. Look at the example above again. Every dollar that John invests in reducing his mortgage is earning him 9% after tax. He would have to earn nearly 18% in an interest-bearing account to beat it.

Building wealth for retirement, and living well in retirement, demands that you make the best use of your financial resources. One of the most tax-effective areas in which to invest your money is getting rid of non-deductible debt.

> KEY POINT: A sound retirement strategy is to eliminate all non-tax-deductible debt as a major priority.

Provisional Tax

This term scares a lot of people who think wrongly that provisional tax is some fierce **penalty** tax that comes about when you earn even a little extra money.

If you are a wage or salary earner you will be used to having your tax deducted each pay day by your employer who then sends it to the Tax Office. This is called PAYE (pay as you earn) tax or group tax. But there are other cases where taxable income is earned, and tax is not taken out of it. Some common cases are interest and dividends received, and income received from running your own business. If this income exceeds $1000 a year it is subject to provisional tax.

Provisional tax is tax payable in advance, based upon an estimate of the expected other income of the taxpayer that has not already had tax deducted from it. The object of this tax is to put taxpayers who are not subject to PAYE tax on an equal footing with those who are.

EXAMPLE: *Mary retired on 1 July 1996 and for the year ended 30 June 1997 earned $20 700 from her investments. As you can see from the table of tax rates, the tax due on $20 700 is $3060. Her accountant will lodge her tax return before 31 October 1997 and she should receive a tax bill of $6683. This is made up as follows:*

Tax due for the year ended 30 June 1997	*$3060*
Provisional tax for the year ended 30 June 1998	*$3623*
	$6683

The provisional tax is based on the assumption that Mary will earn 8% more in the second year and is calculated on an expected taxable income of $22 356.

If Mary and her accountant work out that her income in the 1997-98 year will be less than the $22 356 automatically calculated by the Tax Office, she can apply for a variation of provisional tax. This will be granted by the Tax Office without any fuss and the provisional tax bill reduced in line with the estimate of income Mary has provided. However, if she has made an error of more than 15% in calculating her income for the next year she will face penalties from the Tax Office.

Provisional tax is paid in April for the financial year to end in the following June (two months later). When the actual income is known after the tax year ends that June, the actual income is included in the tax return. Tax is then assessed on the actual figure, and the amount of provisional tax already paid is credited.

Let's assume that Mary's income stayed at $20 700 for three years and that she lodged variation forms each time. Thus in the second year her primary tax bill is $3060 and her provisional tax bill is $3060 to make a total tax bill of $6120. In the third year the tax bill will look like this:

Tax for second year	$3060
Provisional tax for third year	$3060
Total tax due	$6120
Less Provisional tax paid previous year	$3060
Tax due	$3060

So you can see that provisional tax is not an extra tax – it is merely an advance tax. Once you get past that frightening first year where you pay two years' tax at once it is easy to manage. Did you notice why Mary had to pay two years' tax at once? Because she went through the whole 1995-96 year and paid no tax at all.

Since 1 July 1987 taxpayers liable to pay over $8000 per annum provisional tax have had to pay it in quarterly instalments. This has taken them much closer to being on the same footing as the PAYE taxpayer. Pensioners who receive even a part pension tax rebate are also free from provisional tax.

The easy way to handle provisional tax is to have your financial adviser or your accountant estimate your income in the first year of retirement, and then calculate the tax on that income. When you know that figure, make sure enough money is put away in a separate account to cover it. If you do that you come to the end of the first year with the tax for that year in the bank.

Another way to handle it is to estimate your average tax rate and then deduct that from all monies you spend. It works like this.

EXAMPLE: *A couple have a taxable income of $15 400 each from their investments. The tax on this is $2000 or 13% of $15 400. They bank all their investment income in a special account for ease of record keeping. When they need money to spend they transfer the amount needed to their working account, and also transfer 13% of this sum to a special tax account. If they needed $2000 to spend they would also place $260 in the tax account. At the end of the year the tax is provided for in that special account.*

KEY POINT: If you are subject to provisional tax when you retire, you should open a separate bank account and put money for tax in it regularly.

Tax Deductions For Retirees

What investment expenses can you claim as tax deductions? The test is "was this expense necessarily incurred in producing assessable income?" It is a complex subject, but for most retirees there are not many items that can be claimed. Certainly the cost of preparing your tax return is a tax deduction, and if you own investment property you can claim such items as rates, management fees and repairs. There are also possible claims for investment advice and the cost of magazines and other services that you may need to keep your investment portfolio in good shape. These include portfolio management fees, annual review fees, bank charges, accounting fees, and reasonable travelling expenses to inspect your investments. At all times the expenses must be reasonable in relation to the size of the portfolio. A person with a total investment portfolio of 100 shares worth a few hundred dollars that is returning $20 a year in dividends would be hard-pressed to claim much in expenses.

If you buy shares, property or managed funds, the costs of acquiring these assets are not tax-deductible. They are added to the base cost of the asset and reduce any profit on sale. This results in a saving in capital gains tax so you are getting some tax relief even though you may have to wait for it until you sell the asset.

Conclusion

It's amazing how many people focus on the problem and not on the solution. I know that almost nobody likes paying tax, but far too many people worry so much about paying tax that they ignore the importance of making money, adopting a smart tax-effective investment strategy and sound financial planning. There are even some who complain if their income increases because they see it as putting up their tax bill. Even though income tax is here to stay, and illegal avoidance carries huge penalties, a good strategy will save you paying unnecessary tax. The best advice I can give is to plan your affairs properly, and consult your adviser **before** buying or selling any investments.

Summing Up

- Try to arrange your affairs so you and your partner stay in the same tax band.
- Our tax system works on self-assessment. It may be years before an incorrect claim is discovered, but it will be discovered, sooner or later.
- The marginal rate is the most important when planning your affairs.
- Pay off all non-tax-deductible debt as a first priority.
- Make provision, in a separate account, for tax on income that is not subject to PAYE tax.
- Always seek expert advice before buying or selling.

9

TAX-EFFECTIVE INCOME

The taxpayer – a person who works for the administration without having to pass an entrance exam.

RONALD REAGAN

In the last chapter we discussed ways to structure your affairs to save tax. Now we'll go a step further and consider investments that have a tax advantage because of their nature. Let's start by making sure you understand the difference between a tax rebate and a tax deduction.

A **tax rebate,** or **tax credit,** is an amount that is used to reduce the amount of tax you owe. For example, if you earned $20 700 the tax payable would be $3060; if you were entitled to a rebate of $1000 the tax due would drop to $2060.

In contrast, a **tax deduction** reduces the amount of tax you have to pay by reducing your taxable income. If you earned $20 700 and were entitled to a tax deduction of $1000, your taxable income would drop to $19 700 and your tax bill would be reduced by $200, being the $1000 deduction applied at your marginal rate of 20%. See how the rebate of $1000 reduces your tax bill to $2060, whereas the deduction of $1000 reduces it to $2860. If your marginal rate was 38% the tax deduction would save $380 of tax.

Notice two important points. First, a tax rebate is worth more than a tax deduction because your tax is reduced by the full amount of it. Second, rebates treat all taxpayers equally, whereas a tax deduction favours higher-income earners. In the example above, a $1000 deduction would be worth $470 to a top marginal-rate taxpayer. This is why the Government would rather give a tax rebate instead of a tax deduction where it is practicable to do so.

> KEY POINT: A tax rebate treats all taxpayers equally. A tax
> deduction is worth more to those on higher incomes.

Now that's clear, let's move on to one of the best known, but
least understood, tax-saving devices – dividend imputation.

Dividend Imputation

For many years Australian shareholders suffered double taxation
on company profits. First the companies paid tax on any profits
they made, then the shareholders were taxed again when they
received these tax-paid profits as dividends. As the top marginal
tax rates then were over 60% it meant the total tax-take could be as
high as 78%. Is it any wonder that many turned to "bottom of the
harbour" schemes to try to reduce the tax burden?

Now those dark days have gone and, since 1 July 1987,
dividends from companies that have borne the Australian
corporate tax rate carry imputation credits. The word "impute"
means to "give credit for" and this is exactly what the imputation
system does. It enables shareholders to get credit for the tax paid
by the companies in which they hold shares. This has had the
effect of making dividends from most Australian companies tax-
free to many shareholders. Better still, in the case of low-income
shareholders the imputation credits **reduce their tax payable on
income from other sources.**

The system works like this:

Suppose a company made $1 000 000 profit, paid tax of $360 000,
and distributed the balance of $640 000 to its shareholders. The
$360 000 of tax paid entitles the shareholders to $360 000 of
imputation credits. Notice that for every $64 distributed to
shareholders the company has paid tax of $36.

Assume a shareholder has 10 000 shares in the company and
the company paid a dividend of 6.4 cents a share. The dividend
paid to that shareholder is $640 and it would carry with it
imputation credits of $360 as a result of the tax paid by the
company. Because the imputation credit can be used to help that
shareholder's tax, it is nearly as good as a cash bonus. Therefore **it
is treated as taxable income** (the technical word is "grossed
up") and has to be added to the taxpayer's other income. Does that
sound unfair? Look how it works in practice:

Personal tax is calculated as follows:

Dividend paid to shareholder	$ 640
Add Imputation credit (grossed up)	360
Income to be included in taxpayer's return	1000
Tax on this $1000 at 20%	200
Less Credit for tax paid by company	360
Net credit available	$ 160

Notice how the imputation credit as well as the dividend is included in the tax return, and how this imputation credit is available to pay the tax due. In this example the shareholder has done **better** than receive the dividend tax-free – in effect there is a tax-free cash bonus of $160 accompanying it.

Remember I said the imputation credit was available to be used to pay the shareholder's tax from all sources. This surplus of $160 is available to be offset against **other income** of the taxpayer.

Contrast the tax treatment of interest of $640 earned in a bank account. If the depositor had a 20% marginal rate, she would pay $128 tax on the bank interest and certainly have no excess tax credits to use to reduce tax on income from other sources. This is what makes shares paying franked dividends so popular with experienced investors, and why shares are such a great investment for retirees who can handle their volatility.

Now we'll consider the effect on the income of a higher-income earner. With a 47% marginal rate she would pay $300 tax on the bank interest and only $110 on the dividend. This is calculated:

Dividend paid to shareholder	$ 640
Add Imputation credit (grossed up)	360
Income to be included in taxpayer's return	1000
Tax on this $1000 at 47%[1]	470
Less Credit for tax paid by company	360
Balance of tax payable	$ 110

The tax payable on the dividend of $640 is $110. This is an effective rate after tax of 17.2%, far lower than the 47% that the investor would pay on the bank interest.

Be aware that imputation credits will be available only on dividends paid out of profits of a company that have borne

---

1. Excluding Medicare Levy.

Australian company tax. These are called **franked dividends.**
Profits that have not borne Australian company tax will not carry
imputation credits, and dividends from these sources are taxed in
the same way as bank interest. Non-franked dividends arise if the
company is not paying company tax because it is using up tax
losses. Partly franked dividends occur when some of the
company's profits are derived from overseas and not subject to
Australian tax.

As you can see on the copy of a dividend advice below,
companies advise shareholders which dividends are "franked" and
which are not.

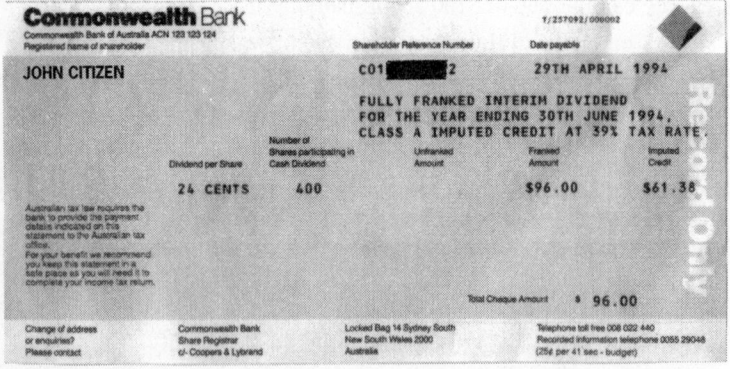

KEY POINT: The dividend imputation system makes
dividends effectively tax-free for lower-income taxpayers.

Property Income

Property income can also be tax-effective whether you own the
investment property directly or invest in property trusts.
Irrespective of the size of the property, the principles are the
same. There are some items that give rise to a tax deduction but
do not require an immediate outlay of cash. These are borrowing
expenses that are being written off over several years, depreciation
and building allowance. When the owners of an investment
property are preparing their tax return the income and
expenditure for tax purposes might look like this:

As you can see, this property is negatively geared and has made
a loss of $5300. This loss is transferred into the taxpayers' current

Income		
Rents	$10 000	

Expenditure		
Agents fees	$800	
Borrowing expenses	1000	
Building allowance	4000	
Depreciation	1500	
Insurance	400	
Interest	7000	
Maintenance	600	
Rates	900	$15 300
Loss carried into body of tax return		$ 5 300

tax return and deducted from their taxable income for that year. Look at the profit and loss statement again and notice that the borrowing expenses, the building allowance and the depreciation expense, which total $6500, have not required any cash outlay in this present financial year.

The borrowing expense represents a one-third share of the $3000 costs of arranging a three-year interest-only loan, the depreciation[2] is a tax deduction for wear and tear on items bought several years ago, and the building allowance is a special factor that we will consider next. The taxpayers are entitled to claim a tax loss of $5300 yet have made a "cash" profit of $1200 when the allowable expenses of $6500 that did not require an outlay of cash this financial year are taken into account. A further bonus is the refund of nearly $2500 that will come back to them from the Tax Office because of the negative gearing.

Building allowance

In 1982 the Federal Government brought in a 2.5% per annum depreciation allowance for **non**-residential buildings on which construction started after 19 July 1982[3]. This was later extended to 4% for **non**-residential buildings started after 21 August 1984. When the rules relating to negative gearing were changed on 17

---

2. A detailed explanation of depreciation is given in *More Money with Noel Whittaker*.
3. The starting date is regarded as the date the footings were poured.

July 1985, this 4% depreciation was extended to cover residential buildings **used for investment** for which construction began after 17 July 1985. When negative gearing was brought back in the September 1987 Budget, the depreciation allowance was reduced to 2.5% for eligible buildings begun after 15 September 1987.

This allowance is calculated on the building component only so it is important, when purchasing investment properties, to apportion the sale price to maximise the building component at the expense of the land component. Obviously, the amount placed on the land must be reasonable, but if you were buying an investment house for $150 000 it may not be unrealistic to put $50 000 on the land and $100 000 on the building.

Provided construction of this investment house began after 17 July 1985 and before 15 September 1987 the owners could claim, for the next 25 years, a tax deduction of $4000 (4% on $100 000) from their income **from any source.** The rules regarding building a house changed in the 13 May 1997 Budget. Properties bought after 7.30 pm on that date will still qualify for the building allowance, but when such properties are sold, the sellers will have to pay increased Capital Gains Tax. For such properties, the amount of building allowance claimed will have to be added back to any capital profit made. The tax treatment remains unchanged for properties brought before May 1997.

Allocated Pensions And Annuities

When you are reading about superannuation in this book you will notice that allocated pensions and some annuities provide an income stream that entitles the investor to a tax rebate of 15%. Better still, in many cases part of the income is tax-free. Retirees who can combine the rebate and the tax-free portion often end up paying no tax whatsoever.

> **EXAMPLE:** *Mr and Mrs Jones are retired. He has an allocated pension of $17 000 a year that carries with it a rebate of 15% or $2550. The tax on $17 000 is $2320, but it is completely eliminated by the rebate. Mrs Jones receives interest income of $11 000 a year and franked dividends of $6000 a year. Her tax position is:*
>
> | | |
> |---|---:|
> | *Interest income* | *$11 000* |
> | *Franked dividend* | *6 000* |
> | Add *Imputation credits (grossed up)* | *3 375* |

Taxable income	*20 375*
Tax on this sum	*2 995*
Less *Imputation credit*	*3 375*
Tax due	*Nil*

As you can see, both Mr and Mrs Jones are enjoying a tax-free retirement.

Make The Rebates Count

You will notice how I have stressed the importance of getting good advice before you make investments. That is particularly important when rebates and credits are involved because they are wasted if you don't use them in the year you become entitled to them. They cannot be carried forward to use in subsequent years.

EXAMPLE: *Merv has a taxable income of $20 000 made up of income from part-time salary, debentures and term deposits. His wife, Daisy, has income of $14 000 that comes from franked dividends from the large share portfolio her mother left her. Merv has an annual tax bill of $2920 but Daisy's tax return shows:*

Income from dividends	*$14 000*
Add *Imputation credits*	*7 800*
Taxable income	*21 800*
Tax payable	*3 434*
Tax credits	*7 800*
Credits wasted	*$ 4 366*

If the assets were held for maximum tax effectiveness some of the shares would be held in Merv's name. Then the imputation credits that are now wasted could be used to eliminate Merv's tax.

A similar situation occurs with the rebate that comes from allocated pensions. In many cases it is better to have husband and wife drawing a pension each than having all the income being generated by just one of them.

Conclusion

By now you should understand that tax need not be a burden in retirement and that a couple should be able to earn between

$30 000 and $40 000 a year between them free of tax. However, to do this you have to invest in vehicles such as allocated pensions and share-based investments. This is why it is important to build up your superannuation prior to retirement so you will have a tax-effective income stream through an allocated pension, and why you should get used to share-based investments at a relatively young age. Once people reach retirement age they are generally reluctant to be involved in share-based investments if they have never had them before.

We'll now continue gaining knowledge about ways to save tax by discussing ways to invest in tax-advantaged areas.

Summing Up

- A tax deduction is worth more to a high-income earner than a low-income earner.
- Rebates treat all taxpayers equally.
- The imputation system ended double taxation of company dividends and made dividends effectively tax-free for lower-income earners.
- Allowable deductions that do not require an expenditure of cash are highly tax-effective.
- Make sure your investments are held in the name of the person who takes the most advantage from a tax rebate, tax credit or tax deduction.

10

TAX-FREE AND TAX-PAID INVESTMENTS

The major inconvenience of being poor is that it takes up all your time.

WILLIAM DE KOONING

You can save thousands of dollars in tax if you choose the right structure, but regrettably many people are still unwittingly paying far too much tax. Do you know why? Because they let themselves be talked into what they understand are tax-**free** investments when in reality they are tax-**paid** investments. Let's examine them more closely.

There are two investment structures:

1. Those that pass the income and the income tax and capital gains tax **to** you. These include unit trusts, allocated pensions, and investments such as shares and rental houses.
2. Those that pay you no income, but pay the tax **for** you. These include superannuation funds, rollover funds, insurance bonds and friendly society bonds.

Which one is best? That depends on how the rate of tax paid by the investment fund compares with your own marginal tax rate. Obviously it is a good idea to have money in a 15% tax-paid investment such as superannuation if your marginal tax rate is 47%. It makes no sense to have money in insurance bonds paying 39% tax if you are retired and your marginal rate is 20%.

Income-Generating Investments

If you own income-producing investments the income flows through to you and must be included in your tax return. The rate of tax payable on this income will depend on your marginal tax rate, so it will be less for a lower-income taxpayer than a higher-income taxpayer. It may also be reduced if the income is earned by a company, because the company tax rate is 36%.

Many income-producing assets give you a combination of income and growth. For example, a rental house will produce rents that must be included in your taxable income each year, and the house should also increase in value to give you a capital gain. No tax is payable on this capital gain until you dispose of the property, but nevertheless it is still payable at some time. Shares are similar. They pay dividends to you and also give you capital gain.

The key factor here is that both the income and the capital gain are returns from the property or shares and you will pay tax on them at some stage – the income now, the capital gain later.

Tax-Paid Investments

In contrast, any money you place in a tax-paid investment goes into a fund. The fund pays the appropriate rate of tax on your behalf, and credits you with bonuses or earnings that are calculated after the tax paid by the fund is taken into account. Notice that no income is paid to you directly, it accumulates in the fund and is reflected in the growing value of your share of that fund.

The main investment structures that pay tax for you are superannuation and rollover funds (15% per annum), friendly society bonds (33%[1] per annum), and insurance bonds (39% per annum). Funeral bonds are best of all because they are exempt from tax, and allocated pension funds are a bit of a hybrid. The fund itself is a tax-free fund, but you pay tax on the income you draw from the fund even though it does enjoy generous tax concessions. You'll learn about allocated pensions in depth soon.

To help you understand how tax-paid investments work, let's invest a mythical $1000 in a range of investments that all return a gross 10% and observe what happens to the net return to the investor when the fund pays tax. Don't worry if you think 10% is unrealistic – the aim of the exercise is to give you an understanding of the system.

---

1. This rate is being progressively raised to 39%.

HOW TAX PAID INVESTMENTS WORK

Based on an investment of $1 000.

Investment Type	Gross return	Tax paid by fund	Net return	
Bank account	$100	nil	$100	10.0%
Allocated pension fund	$100	nil	$100	10.0%
Funeral bond	$100	nil	$100	10.0%
Superannuation Fund	$100	$15	$ 85	8.5%
Rollover fund	$100	$15	$ 85	8.5%
Friendly society bond	$100	$33	$ 67	6.7%
Insurance bond	$100	$39	$ 61	6.1%

Notice how the net return drops as the tax rate rises.

Now let's compare two investors, a retiree who earns $16 000 a year and who is in the 20% marginal tax bracket, and an executive who earns $80 000 a year and who is in the 47% marginal tax bracket.

If they both left that $1000 in the bank at 10% the interest would be $100. However, the position after tax is:

	Retiree		**Executive**	
Income	$100		$100	
Tax	20		47	
Net return	$ 80	8%	$ 53	5.3%

The net return for the retiree is 8% and for the executive 5.3%.

Now look what would happen if both invested that money in insurance bonds. From the table above you can see their net return each would be 6.1%.

Obviously, the lower-income earner is better off leaving the money in the bank and the higher income-earner is better served having it in insurance bonds. This is because of the difference in the marginal tax rates of the two investors. If the money was invested in superannuation instead, both would earn $85 or 8.5% and thus enjoy better returns than if they had left it in interest-bearing accounts. The superannuation fund's tax rate of 15% is lower than either taxpayers' marginal rate.

> KEY POINT: A tax-paid investment is worth having only if the rate paid by the fund is less than your own marginal rate.

Now we must consider any other taxes or restrictions we might incur by being in tax-paid funds. The Tax Office is not so generous that it will allow funds to pay tax at rates that are lower than individual marginal tax rates without imposing some conditions.

Friendly society bonds and insurance bonds

The proceeds of these are exempt from any further tax in the hands of the investor provided they are held for at least 10 years. Contrary to popular belief your money is not tied up and can be withdrawn in whole or part at any time, but if you do withdraw your money early some tax **may** be payable. If you withdraw all or part of your money before seven years have passed since you made the original investment, the accrued earnings that relate to the amount you withdraw are taxable. However, you become entitled to a rebate to compensate for the tax paid by the fund. If the withdrawal is made between the seventh and the tenth year, tax applies on a pro rata basis.

> **EXAMPLE:** *Tess earns $40 000 a year so her marginal tax rate is 43%. She invested $20 000 in an insurance bond four years ago and its value is now $25 000. She decides to cash it in and use the proceeds to reduce her housing loan because she believes the effective after-tax return will be greater. The bond is paying 5.5% a year after taxes and charges, and her mortgage rate is 10%. The tax on withdrawal is calculated by adding the $5000 profit on the bond to her taxable income, which results in additional tax payable of $2150 (5000 × 43%). However, Tess may claim a rebate of $1950 (39% of the $5000 profit) to compensate for tax paid by the bond fund on her behalf.*

As you can see, the total additional tax payable by her is only $200.

I must stress that the money is not tied up for 10 years so any money invested in friendly society bonds and insurance bonds may be accessed at will. Better still, investors in lower tax brackets can often save tax by cashing in insurance bonds before the 10 years have passed.

> **EXAMPLE:** *Mavis earns $13 000 a year and has an insurance bond she bought six years ago for $10 000. It has*

grown to $15 000 and she wants to cash it in to buy a new car.
Tax on the profit of $5000 will be $1000 because it is taxable at
20%, her marginal tax rate. However, she is entitled to a rebate
of $1950, being 39% of the $5000 taxable profit. This $1950
not only pays the tax of $1000 on the profit, but also provides
$950 of tax credits to pay the tax on part of her other income.

As you can see, it is similar to the way imputation credits work
to reduce tax for low-income earners.

Superannuation

Money in superannuation suffers a tax of 15% before your returns
are declared, which makes it one of the most tax-effective
structures available. However, in most cases you lose access to the
funds until you are at least 55 and have retired. Furthermore, you
may pay a lump sum tax when you withdraw money from
superannuation. More details are given in later chapters.

Tax-Free Bonds

The only tax-free investment is a funeral bond. As these bonds are
discussed in detail in the section on estate planning I will mention
them here only briefly. They are a superb investment for
pensioners because the fund earnings are tax exempt, and neither
the asset nor the earnings count for income- or asset-test
purposes. However, the proceeds of these bonds must be used
only for your funeral and they are inaccessible until you die.
Therefore, only small amounts of money, possibly $2500 for each
investor, should be placed in this area.

A Common Fallacy

Many retirees, and I regret to say their advisers too, get the
average tax rate confused with the marginal tax rate when they are
working out the best way to handle rollover funds. Remember,
rollover funds and superannuation funds pay tax at 15% from the
first dollar earned, but for an individual the first $5400 is tax-free. If
a retiree has $300 000 in rollovers, and his wife has no income, it
may make good sense to withdraw enough from the rollover fund
to invest in such a way that it will give her an income of $5400 a
year. Then she generates $5400 of income in the tax-free area, and
he has the balance in the 15% tax-paid area.

Unfortunately some advisers recommend withdrawing half of the rollover fund and putting it in her name. If the amount withdrawn was $150 000, and it was invested at 8%, the income would be $12 000 a year on which the tax is $1320. This is certainly an average rate of 11% and some argue that she is better off to have an average rate of tax of 11% than to have the money in a rollover fund at 15%. The truth is that she is paying no tax on the first $5400, but 20% tax on the balance. A better strategy is to withdraw enough to give her an income of $5400 and leave the balance in the rollover area where the tax rate is 15%. Naturally, as we mentioned in the previous chapter, if she had tax-effective income in that $5400 a year, it would be appropriate to increase the amount held in her name until a level was reached where the credits eliminated the tax.

Naturally, any withdrawals from rollover funds should not be done without considering the impact of lump sum tax.

Conclusion

Congratulations, your knowledge of tax is now way above the average. You should understand the difference between tax-paid and tax-free investments, and be able to discuss any proposed strategies with your adviser intelligently. We'll now move to a more complex but vitally important area – capital gains tax. It's an area where careful planning can often save you a lot of tax.

Summing Up

- Tax-paid investments are appropriate investments in situations when the tax paid by the fund is lower than your marginal tax rate.
- Always compare the tax paid by the fund with your own marginal rate.
- If an adviser suggests you use insurance bonds or friendly society bonds, ask him or her what is the purpose of the recommendation.
- Money in friendly society bonds and insurance bonds is not tied up for 10 years.
- Withdrawing money from friendly society bonds and insurance bonds before 10 years have passed may save you tax.
- Appreciate the importance of the marginal rate when assessing investment strategies.

11

CAPITAL GAINS TAX

Taxation has made more Americans into liars than golf.

WILL ROGERS

You are certain to face capital gains tax at some time and the aim of this chapter is to give you a brief summary of how it works. Just remember it can be a complex topic and the information here can do no more than alert you to some of the traps involved. You should always consult your accountant **before** you buy or sell any assets, as your situation may be only slightly different from the examples given here, but that difference may have important ramifications. Remember, too, that capital gains tax is an emotive phrase, but for most of you it should not be nearly as severe as you may think. Like most taxes it can often be reduced by careful planning.

Capital gains tax (CGT) may be payable when you dispose of certain assets, but you should understand:

1. no CGT is due until disposal of an asset you acquired on or after 20 September 1985 takes place

2. any profit is adjusted for inflation

3. the family home is exempt from CGT provided it is held in your own name

4. how much CGT you pay depends on your marginal tax rate in the year of sale

5. careful planning can help you to minimise CGT or even eliminate it

6. no CGT is payable on motor cars, personal belongings worth less than $5000 each, and any asset acquired before 20 September 1985.

I'll start by explaining the basic principles and then we'll move on to some examples that many affect you.

The introduction of CGT was part of a review of the Australian tax system in the 1980s that included a substantial reduction in personal tax rates, and a broadening of the tax base that gave us such nasties as the fringe benefits tax. There is a growing realisation throughout the world that high marginal tax rates simply encourage tax evasion and that it is simpler to collect revenue with excise duties, sales taxes, and goods and services taxes. In 1967 the top marginal rate in Australia was 66.7% (plus a levy of 2.5%), which cut in once income reached $32 000 a year. Nobody would tolerate that today.

Since the introduction of a capital gains tax, profit on sale of most assets acquired after 20 September 1985 is taxable. There are a few exceptions, but the main one is the family home, provided it is held in the name of the taxpayers personally.

> KEY POINT: To be exempt from capital gains tax your family home must be in your personal name. It cannot be held in the name of another entity such as your family company, your family trust or your superannuation fund.

To calculate the figure on which the capital gains tax is levied, you work out the net profit on the transaction, and then adjust it for inflation. That's not as difficult as it sounds, and the following example will help you understand it.

EXAMPLE: *Tony and Marie pay $96 000 for an investment property in 1988. The costs of purchase are $4000, which brings the total cost of the property for CGT purposes to $100 000. This is called the base cost. They sell it 10 years later for $173 000.*

The profit on which CGT is payable is the difference between the "base cost" adjusted for inflation and the net selling cost. The base cost is simply the amount paid for the asset, including purchase costs, plus any money spent on the property for capital improvements such as adding a garage or a patio.

In this example, to keep it simple we'll assume they made no capital improvements to the property after they bought it. Therefore, to work out the profit after adjustment for inflation, we take the base purchase price of $100 000 and translate it into the dollar value at date of sale. The Tax Office publishes tables to help you calculate the inflation-adjusted figure, but in this case I'll do it for you.

If we suppose that inflation has averaged 4% over that 10 years, the factor is 1.48. In other words, $148 000 today is equivalent to $100 000 10 years ago if inflation is 4% per annum. If there had been improvements carried out their value is adjusted separately, unless they were done at the time of acquisition.

Purchase price	$ 96 000
Costs	4 000
Base purchase price	$100 000
Base price after adjustment for 4% inflation =	$148 000
Sale price	$173 000
less Selling costs	5 000
Net proceeds	$168 000
Less Inflation-adjusted purchase price	148 000
Profit liable for capital gains tax	$20 000

After we have taken into account that the $100 000 used to purchase the property has a value today of $148 000 because of inflation, the real profit is only $20 000.

The first step is over – now comes the tricky part. We have to go through what is called a "notional averaging process" to calculate how much capital gains tax is payable. It involves taking a sample of the capital profit and then assessing capital gains tax on that sample. The aim of this is to reduce CGT for lower-income earners by trying to assess the CGT at their marginal tax rate. This might sound complicated, but work the example through and think about why it is done.

Let's assume Tony is now retired and earned $18 000 in that financial year, and Marie's affairs were arranged so her other income was $3000. Therefore, Tony is in the 20% bracket and Marie is in the zero bracket.

Notice how we took a "sample" of the profit by dividing it by 5. We then used that sample to calculate the increase in taxable income and multiplied it by 5 to find the CGT payable. If we had not done this the impact of the capital gains tax may have forced them into higher marginal tax brackets. Without that change,

	Tony	Marie
Share of adjusted profit	$10 000	$10 000
Divide by 5 (the sample)	2 000	2 000
Add the sample to taxable income so their new taxable incomes are	20 000	5 000
Increase in their tax so caused	400	Nil
Multiply increased tax by 5 to arrive at capital gains tax	$2 000	Nil
CGT payable	$ 2 000	Nil

Tony's extra $10 000 of income would have pushed him into the 34 cents in the dollar tax bracket and Marie's would have pushed her into the 20% bracket. Capital gains tax would have been higher for both of them. In this case, Tony's CGT was levied at 20%, his marginal rate, and Marie's was levied at nil, her marginal rate.

Nobody likes any sort of tax, but things aren't too tough when taxpayers can buy a property for $96 000, sell it ten years later for $173 000, and pay capital gains tax of only $2000.

Tony was a $90 000 a year executive when they bought the property but was retired when they sold it. If it had been sold while he worked, the CGT on his share would have been 47% of $10 000. This is why it is important, if at all possible, to defer a disposal until a year of low taxable income.

KEY POINT: Your taxable income in the year of sale may affect the amount of CGT you pay. Try to defer the timing of any sale until a year when you have a low taxable income.

The Date Of The Contract

CGT is calculated by using the **dates** of the purchase and sale contracts and it does not matter on what date the money changed hands. For example, in *More Money with Noel Whittaker* I discussed mandatory agreements that are often drawn up by two or more business partners. These set out the terms on which the estate of a dead partner will sell that person's share of the business to the surviving partner. The documents are usually drawn up when the partners are all in good health and often the purchase price is large, $500 000 or more. Many business people do not realise that CGT is payable **immediately the document is drawn up,** not when somebody dies.

You now know the amount of capital gains tax depends on how long the asset is held, and the income of the owner in the year of sale. Be aware that **no indexation adjustment** takes place until you have owned the asset a year. Furthermore, the indexation is calculated in practice by using quarterly numbers obtained by the Tax Office from the Bureau of Statistics. This is highly relevant in a time of high inflation but not so important when inflation is low.

The inflation adjustment works in quarterly periods that begin 1 January, 1 April, 1 July and 1 October. Therefore, it makes no difference if a contract is dated 1 January or 31 March, the inflation adjustment is the same.

EXAMPLE: *On 1 July a person buys shares for $100 000 (including costs) and sells them for a net price of $110 000 on the following 30 June. No indexation is allowable, and capital gains tax is payable on the whole $10 000 profit. For a top marginal rate taxpayer this would be 47% of $10 000 or $4700.*

If sale is deferred by just a couple of days to 2 July, indexation is available. If we assume that inflation is 4% in the above example, the adjusted cost base becomes $104 000. Then capital gains tax is payable only on $6000. That simple act of deferring signing the sale contract for a couple of days will reduce the capital gains tax by nearly $2000 if the owner is in the highest tax bracket. The same figures would apply as long as the contract was signed at any time during the quarter ending 30 September.

Another year's inflation adjustment is available if the sale was deferred to the following 1 July. If inflation rose to 6% in that financial year the adjustment would take the indexed base cost to $110 000 leaving no liability for capital gains tax.

Notice how the capital gains tax varies from almost $5000 to nothing depending on the date the contract was signed.

KEY POINT: The date of the contract affects the amount of inflation adjustment available to you. No inflation adjustment is available if you have not held the asset for at least a year.

Tax-Free Capital Gains In Retirement

Capital gains tax applies to **realised** profits on all investments so you should arrange your affairs with great care to minimise it. We have seen how a person with no income can make a capital gain, and pay no capital gains tax, provided that one-fifth of that gain does not take them over the level under which no income tax is payable. When cashing units in equity and property trusts, some could be cashed in the last part of the financial year, and others could be cashed early in July to minimise the tax.

CGT is linked to the personal tax scales. As the first $5400 of personal income is tax-free, it follows that a person with no taxable income could have a taxable **capital** gain of $27 000 per annum and pay no capital gains tax. This is because one-fifth of that amount would attract no tax, and tax is calculated by multiplying one-fifth of the tax payable by 5. Thus a one-income family could have investments in the name of the non-earning spouse, make a profit of $54 000 (2 × $27 000) and, by taking half of the income on 30 June and the other half next day, pay no capital gains tax at all! This would be achieved by cashing in half the units on 30 June, and the other half in the next financial year, which starts one day later.

This approach is highly relevant to retirees who are drawing down on capital. Obviously you have no need to draw down on capital until your bank account is nearly depleted and your interest-earning assets are almost used up. By working with your adviser, and timing your asset sales, you could well pay no capital gains tax on the assets you have built up for retirement. Remember, it is only the inflation-adjusted profit that is liable for CGT.

> **EXAMPLE:** *You own $100 000 of units in the XYZ Balanced Fund that you bought in 1988. After you adjust the purchase cost for inflation the indexed base cost of the entire parcel for CGT purposes is $70 000. You wish to withdraw $10 000 so the base cost of this portion is $7000. Therefore, the profit for CGT purposes on the disposal of that $10 000 worth of units is $3000. One-fifth of $3000 is $600, therefore, provided you can keep your other income under $4800 in the year of realisation, you have no CGT to pay. This is because $4800 + $600 = $5400 – the tax-free threshold.*

The ability to do this is one of the great advantages of investment in unit trusts or shares, as partial encashment is easy. It is virtually impossible with direct investment in property.

KEY POINT: You can often eliminate capital gains tax by cashing in relatively small amounts of shares and unit trusts and doing so in a year when your other taxable income is less than $5400.

Now you understand the mechanics of CGT we'll consider some common situations where CGT may apply.

Sale Of The Family Home

No CGT is payable provided the home is in the names of one or more of the occupiers personally. If it is held by a family trust or a company it is not exempt and the normal rules apply.

Sale of a home that has been rented out and also has been the family home

The profit is adjusted on a pro rata basis according to the time you lived in it. Suppose you owned a beach house for a total of eight years. For five years it was the holiday home, and for three years after you retired you lived in it as your principal place of residence. Five-eighths of the inflation-adjusted profit is subject to CGT.

Living on a large block

The land around your own home is free of CGT if it is used mainly for private and domestic purposes and **does not exceed two hectares.** If the total area is more than two hectares any profit on the balance is liable to CGT.

> **EXAMPLE:** *You buy a house on three hectares in 1988 for $200 000. At that time you apportion the purchase as:*
>
> | | | |
> |---|---|---|
> | *Land* | *$120 000* | *3 hectares @ $40 000 each* |
> | *Improvements* | *80 000* | |
> | *Purchase price* | *$200 000* | |
>
> *You sell 10 years later for $500 000 and apportion the sale:*
>
> | | | |
> |---|---|---|
> | *Land* | *$300 000* | *3 hectares @ $100 000 each* |
> | *Improvements* | *200 000* | |
> | *Selling price* | *$500 000* | |

You are liable for CGT on the extra one hectare. The cost is $40 000 plus inflation adjustment and the selling price is $100 000 less a proportion of the selling expenses.

Temporary absence from the family home

In some cases it is possible to leave your own home and still maintain full exemption from CGT. To do this you have to apply for a principal place of residence exemption. The exemption will apply indefinitely if you leave your house vacant, and do not rent it out, and will cease only when you sell the property or if you nominate another property as your principal place of residence.

If you rent your home out and then return to live in it the CGT exemption lasts for six years only. Consequently, if you return after seven years, some CGT is payable if you eventually sell the house.

> **EXAMPLE:** *You buy a house in 1987, live in it for one year, rent it out for seven years and then live in it again for two years before selling it. Thus, out of a total of 10 years, the house has been rented out for seven years, but the CGT exemption is only six years. This leaves one year out of the 10 subject to CGT, so a tenth of the inflation-adjusted profit is subject to CGT.*

You cannot nominate more than one principal place of residence, therefore it is possible you may own two houses and be claiming an exemption on the house you are now renting out, even though you are living in another. In that case, the rental house you own is exempt from CGT, but your other house is not.

Capital Gains Tax And Death

No CGT is payable by a deceased estate unless the assets are bequeathed to a tax-exempt body such as a charity or a church – it is those who **receive** the assets through the will that may suffer CGT. Let's go through the basic principles first and then we'll look at some specific examples.

For CGT purposes, the deceased's assets are deemed to be acquired by the beneficiaries as at date of death, so CGT may be payable by the beneficiaries when they dispose of them. If the deceased acquired the assets prior to 20 September 1985, the beneficiary's cost base is **market value** at date of death. If the deceased acquired the assets after 20 September 1985, the beneficiary's cost base is the **indexed cost** as at date of death. This is the original cost adjusted for inflation.

To help you understand how it works, let's imagine that you have been left an investment by your mother who has recently died. We'll assume it's a parcel of units in an equity trust.

Your first job is to find out when she acquired it.

If she bought the investment **before** 20 September 1985 you will have been deemed to have acquired it on the date of her death at the market value on that day. CGT may then be payable by you when you sell it. Suppose she paid $20 000 for the investment in August 1985 and she died on 1 September 1998 when it was worth $80 000. You are now deemed to have acquired it for $80 000 on 1 September 1998. When you dispose of it you will have to calculate a new indexed cost based on your "cost" of $80 000. You will be liable for CGT if a profit results after inflation adjustment. As you can see the situation is no different from your buying an asset for $80 000 on 1 September 1998.

If the investment was acquired by her **after** 20 September 1985 any capital gain (or loss) is effectively transferred to you. The Tax Office assumes you acquired it on the date of her death at its indexed cost base then.

Let's use the same figures as above but assume she bought the $20 000 investment in October 1985, instead of August 1985, and that the base cost adjusted for inflation was $40 000 when she died. You are now deemed to have acquired it for $40 000 on 1 September 1998.

Notice how her CGT liability has been transferred to you.

> KEY POINT: Usually a deceased estate is free from capital gains tax. The liability is transferred to the beneficiaries.

Inheriting The Family Home

This is probably the most common occurrence. In the following examples I shall assume the property was your parents' principal residence, and that both parents have died leaving it to you.

Acquired by the deceased before 20 September 1985

If the home was acquired before 20 September 1985 it would have been exempt from CGT if they had sold it before they died, irrespective of whether it was used as their own home or for investment. You will be exempt from CGT if you satisfy any **one** of the following:

1. You dispose of it within two years of their deaths. Watch this one carefully because estates can take quite a while to wind up. If the date of the sale contract by you is even one day more than two years from date of death, CGT is liable from the date of death. This could be costly in a raging real estate market.
2. You sell the home as executor and in the period between death and sale a person nominated in the will lived in the house.

During that time it cannot have been used for producing income. This may happen if a child of the deceased lived in the house in terms of the will as happens when one child has stayed at home for years looking after the parents. In this case the will often leaves the house to all the children but gives rights of occupancy to one child for as long as that person wants to live in the home.

3. You sell the house as a beneficiary, at no time after death was it used for producing income, and you or a person nominated in the will lived in it until sale.

Acquired by the deceased after 20 September 1985

The rules are similar if the home was acquired after 20 September 1985, provided the property was used by the deceased as their home from the date they acquired it. If it was rented out for part of that time, CGT may apply on a pro rata basis.

As executor or beneficiary you will be exempt from CGT on disposal of the house if **both** the following conditions are satisfied:

1. The deceased used the house solely as their principal residence.
2. You satisfy any **one** of the three conditions in the previous section (acquired by the deceased before 20 September 1985).

We can sum up the situation of inheriting the family home as follows. You can:

1. **Live in it.** Then it will be your principal place of residence and free of CGT when you sell it.
2. **Sell it.** Depending on the timing of the sale, CGT may be payable if the price you receive exceeds the price for which it was transferred to you from the deceased estate. You can get around this by ensuring it is transferred from the estate to you at market value.
3. **Rent it out.** If this happens your cost base is the price for which the estate transferred it to you. If you sell it you will pay CGT on any profit after inflation adjustment.

Watch The Purchase Price

You now understand that the base cost has a major effect on the amount of CGT you pay. Therefore, you should be alert to any opportunities to boost the base cost. For example, if you are buying a home on over two hectares, try to get an apportionment that puts a high value on the land and a low one on the house.

Similarly, when property is being transferred from an estate, try to get the valuer to go for a high valuation. I am not suggesting you be dishonest but when property is being valued there are low "forced sale" valuations and higher "normal course of business" valuations. Ask the valuer for the highest one he feels it is honest and ethical to give.

If the deceased had substantial assets that were acquired before 20 September 1985, have proper valuations done as soon as possible after the date of death. This provides the beneficiary with clear evidence of market value in the event of a sale that may take place many years in the future.

Capital Improvements

Take care if you are adding to a property you bought before September 1985, because any improvements that are effected after that date are regarded as a separate asset if the indexed cost base exceeds the amount set out in the Tax Act. This was $80 756 for the 1993-94 income year and increases annually. The improvements are subject to capital gains tax even though the original asset is not.

> **EXAMPLE:** *The Wilsons bought a property in a good area in 1980 in the name of their family trust. In 1987 they carried out renovations to the value of $90 000. If they sell the property the land and house will be exempt from CGT because they were bought before 1985, but the extensions have to be separately apportioned and CGT paid on any profit after inflation adjustment. The house is their residence, but there is no exemption from CGT because it is in the name of the family trust, not their personal names.*

This shows the importance of liaising with your accountant before selling any assets. By negotiating an apportionment on the contract that was favourable for CGT purposes, the Wilsons may manage to eliminate CGT altogether.

Think About Borrowing Before Selling

Where possible, borrow for investment purposes instead of selling an asset and paying CGT. This enables you to defer CGT, have more assets working for you, and also claim a tax deduction for the interest on the loan.

EXAMPLE: *John has a property worth $200 000 for which he paid $120 000 several years ago. It returns him a net $12 000 a year and he owes $100 000 on it. He wants to buy another property for $200 000 but works out he will be liable for CGT of $30 000 if he sells the first property. His present position is:*

Property income	*$12 000*
Interest	*11 000*
Taxable surplus	*$ 1 000*
Less *Tax*	*470*
Net return	*$ 530*

If he sells the property he will pay $30 000 in CGT and have $70 000 left over for a deposit on the next property. If he keeps the present property and borrows the whole purchase price of the new property his position is:

Property income	*$24 000*	
Interest	*33 000*	
Taxable loss	*9 000*	
Less *Tax saved*	*4 230*	*(47% of the $9000 loss)*
Net cost	*$ 4 770*	

It would cost him only $92 a week ($4770 a year) to retain the old property and also buy the new one. It would take him six years of paying that $4770 a year shortfall to equal the $30 000 he would have to pay in CGT immediately. It is reasonable to assume the first property would gain in value by at least $100 000 in that time.

This is a graphic illustration of how a smart strategy and a basic knowledge of the tax laws can boost your wealth-creation program.

Keeping Good Records

For CGT purposes you must keep accurate records of all assets purchased, as gains are indexed for inflation from date of acquisition. These records must be kept from the date of purchase until five years have passed from the date of disposal. That could be thirty or forty years.

Most unit trusts have facilities whereby investors can switch between various funds run by the same institution for no extra fee.

This enables them to finetune their portfolio in line with recommendations from their adviser. Now the fund might not charge you for a switch but the Tax Office will, because every switch is regarded as a sale and a fresh purchase for CGT purposes. This is why you should seek advice on the CGT implications every time you think about switching, and try to minimise CGT by switching between funds at a time when it is most suitable for tax planning.

Many investors in unit trusts request that their dividends be reinvested in the same trust. This is equivalent to buying more units with the dividends. Every time this is done the unit holder receives additional units in that trust and separate records need to be kept for each transaction. I once discouraged the practice of reinvesting dividends but experience has taught me the benefits of reinvestment far outweigh the accounting complications. Fortunately many fund managers have now upgraded their systems so they can do the capital gains calculations for you. Your adviser will guide you here.

Some Important Tips

1. **Try to keep pre-CGT assets.** If you have a choice of selling pre-CGT assets or post-CGT assets, favour selling the post-CGT assets if possible. Naturally all the circumstances have to be carefully taken into account and these include your taxable income in the year of sale, and the potential of one asset compared with another. Nevertheless, if you hold the pre-CGT asset it will continue to enjoy tax-free capital growth. Once the asset is sold this benefit is lost forever.

2. **Offset losses if possible.** If you are faced with a capital profit on which CGT is payable, try to find an asset that is carrying a capital loss and sell it in the same financial year. Maybe it's the dud shares you bought, or those unlisted property trusts that sank in value in 1990. Remember, you can only offset capital losses against capital profits, and it would be a shame to pay CGT on capital profits this year and then realise a capital loss next year and have nothing to set it off against in that year.

EXAMPLE: *Robin earns $80 000 a year and has made a capital profit after inflation adjustment of $20 000. CGT will be almost $10 000 because she is in the top tax bracket. She meets with her adviser to discuss the potential of her investment* *portfolio and decides to sell her units in an unlisted property trust that cost $30 000 and are now worth $10 000. This creates a capital loss of $20 000 that wipes out her entire CGT liability. If she had deferred taking action until after 30 June she would have to wait to make some more capital profits to use up the capital losses.*

This concept is explored in detail in *More Money with Noel Whittaker.*

3. **Beware of gifts.** Many people are not aware that an asset does not have to be sold to create a CGT liability. Any type of disposal, including giving it away, may trigger it.

   EXAMPLE: *The Blacks decided to go into partnership with their son, Luke, in the purchase of an investment house. He was a university student and they figured it would give him a commitment and some stability. It was bought in joint names, rented out, and the Blacks picked up the shortfall between the interest and the rent. Luke did his bit by mowing and attending to the general maintenance and the project worked well.*

   A few years later he wanted to move into the house so he and his new wife would have a place of their own. His parents were happy to give him their share of it. Unfortunately, or fortunately (?), there had been a property boom and the value had nearly doubled. The parents received a huge bill for CGT.

   The problem could have been solved with foresight. All the parents had to do when the house was purchased was to put it in Luke's name with themselves as guarantor.

4. **Defer a sale if possible.** Try to defer sale of an asset for as long as possible if CGT will be payable on sale. This enables you to have the use of the money that you would pay in CGT. Waiting till 1 July to sell an asset gives you an extra 12 months use of the money that has to be paid in CGT because the transaction does not have to be reported until you lodge your tax return the following June.

5. **Be aware of rollover relief.** Rollover relief does not have a thing to do with the rollover funds you use when you leave a job. A rollover is said to occur when an asset is transferred from one owner to another but the CGT status is preserved. Thus in certain cases an asset can be transferred without an immediate CGT liability being created. It enables a person to whom an asset is transferred to elect to maintain a pre-CGT asset as a tax-free asset or to defer CGT liability of a post-CGT asset.

The main applications are when a business is being reorganised and in marital separations, and if you are involved in either you should seek expert guidance. Rollover relief is given automatically when assets are transferred between spouses complying with a court order. For example, assets acquired jointly after 20 September 1985 can have rollover relief if transferred to one or the other and this can defer CGT for years.

Conclusion

You are probably feeling confused by now, but you have done a great job to get to the end of the chapter. It's a complex issue and I have only scratched the surface of it here, but the most important point is that it is imperative you take advice about CGT implications before buying or selling any asset or when making your will. In the next chapter we'll stretch you some more and discuss saving tax through trusts and companies.

Summing Up

- Capital gains tax is levied on the sale of almost all assets acquired since 20 September 1985.
- The family home must be in the name of the residents' personal names to be exempt from CGT.
- CGT depends on the taxable income of the owner in the year of sale.
- On death, any capital gains tax liability is transferred to the beneficiaries.
- The dates of disposal are critical.
- CGT can often be cut down by forward planning.
- Retain pre-September 1985 assets if possible.
- Always seek expert advice before you buy and sell an asset.

12

FAMILY COMPANIES AND FAMILY TRUSTS

No just man ever became rich suddenly.

MENANDER (342-292 BC)

For higher-earning retirees, family trusts and family companies can be effective tax-saving devices. They enable you to divert income to other taxpayers such as people and companies who may be in lower tax brackets than you would be in yourself if all the income came to you.

First, appreciate the main difference between a trust and a company. A trust does *not pay tax*; it is a device that diverts income to people or companies who pay the tax. In contrast, a company is a taxpayer in its own right and is liable for tax in the same way as you might be. However, company tax is only 36% and there is no Medicare levy.

Notice that companies pay tax at 36% from the *first* dollar earned whereas, for a person, the first $5400 is tax-free, the next $15 300 is at 20% and so on up the scale. For example, company tax on an income of $40 000 is $14 400. Personal tax on the same income is just over $10 000. It is not until you reach an income of $85 000 a year that the total company tax payable becomes lower than the overall personal tax.

Companies

Companies evolved many years ago to solve the problems of raising capital for enterprises. Before companies came into use, most capital was raised by investors who had to form partnerships because they had no other choice. This was an unattractive option and many investors were reluctant to become involved because any member of a partnership is personally liable for all the partnership debts. To solve this problem business people formed "limited" companies in which the liabilities of the shareholders were limited to the amount of uncalled capital on their shares.

The main benefits of a company are:

1. some protection against liability
2. the ability to employ the owners of the business and thus have the benefit of group taxed wages and full tax-deductibility of superannuation, provided it is paid by the company
3. a lower rate of tax once the 43% marginal rate band is reached.

Let's work through an example to help you understand the principles. This exercise is directed mainly to people in business who are directing their energies to building wealth for retirement. It would seldom be appropriate for retirees unless their affairs were very complicated.

EXAMPLE: *Bob and Mary have a total income of $200 000 a year from their business. If they operate as a partnership and split the income $100 000 each, their total tax bill is $75 204 (2 × $37 602). This leaves them with an after-tax income of almost $125 000. If it was their first year in business they would face a combined tax and provisional tax bill of almost $160 000 in the following April.*

If they had operated as a company instead of a partnership their figures for the year ended 30 June 1994 may have been:

Profit	*$200 000*
Less *Salaries ($35 000 to each)*	*70 000*
Less *Superannuation ($20 000 each)*	*40 000*
Profit earnt by company	*90 000*
Tax thereon (@ 36%)	*$ 32 400*

Look where Bob and Mary are on 30 June of that financial year. They have no further personal tax to pay because they received a group taxed salary from their company who is their employer. Furthermore, they have salted $40 000 away in superannuation where it is safe from creditors if the business gets into trouble. Instead of struggling to pay a joint $160 000 tax bill next April there is only a $32 400 company tax to be paid.

Naturally there are disadvantages:

1. The amount of wages that can be paid to a family member as an employee of the company has to be reasonable for the work done. If Mary was working solely as a typist for the company it could not pay her a $35 000 a year salary.

2. It is bad practice to hold assets in a company name unless these assets are trading assets. The reasons are detailed in full in *More Money with Noel Whittaker* but have to do with capital gains tax on sale of any company assets. For example, a company may buy a building for $100 000 and sell it 10 years later for $200 000. If the inflation-adjusted cost base was $160 000 there would be capital gains tax payable on only $40 000 in the year of sale but there would remain a liability for tax on the balance of the $60 000 capital profit. This is payable in the event of the winding-up of the company.

3. Bob and Mary's after-tax profit of $60 300 can only be withdrawn by paying it as a dividend to the shareholders. This may cause further tax to be paid, depending on the tax bracket of the shareholder. However, as dividends do not have to be distributed every year, the after-tax profits can build up, giving an effective deferral of tax.

As you can see, companies are a highly effective tax-saving tool if your income is sufficient to warrant using them. Next we'll discuss discretionary trusts and unit trusts, which I believe are the best structures for most people in business.

Trusts

Even though a trust is a separate legal entity it does not pay tax. Instead it acts as a conduit or funnel and distributes the income down to its beneficiaries to pay. Thus it has characteristics of both a company and a partnership. However, a trust can employ its beneficiaries provided the wages are reasonable for the work done, deduct group tax from their salaries and eliminate provisional tax. You cannot do this with a partnership.

There are two main types of trusts:

1. discretionary trusts

2. unit trusts.

You will find that discretionary trusts are mainly used for a family's affairs, whereas unit trusts are used when a range of unrelated people have an interest in the same investment.

Discretionary trusts

A discretionary family trust has the greatest flexibility of all. This is because the trustees have absolute discretion to pay the income where it will be most tax-effective.

Let's look at the business owned by Bob and Mary, but this time we'll assume it's run through a discretionary trust. The income can be split:

Profit	$200 000
Less Salaries ($35 000 to each)	70 000
Superannuation ($20 000 each)	40 000
Profit available for distribution to beneficiaries	$ 90 000

They have two children – Mark, their 18-year-old son, who is at university, and Kim, their 16-year-old daughter, who is at high school. As well as the two children, the trust beneficiaries include Bob's mother and a family company that was set up when they formed the trust. Now all this may sound complicated but take the time to work through it. The knowledge gained may be worth many thousands of dollars in tax savings to you.

After discussion with their accountant Bob and Mary decided the $90 000 profit should be distributed as follows:

	Distribution	*Tax payable*
Mark aged 18	*$20 700*	*$3 060*
Kim aged 16	*416*	*nil*
Bob's mother	*20 700*	*3 060*
Family company	*48 184*	*17 346*
Total	*$90 000*	*$23 466*

If Bob and Mary had been trading as a partnership the tax on that extra $90 000 would have been $42 300 because it is all liable at 47%, the top marginal rate. By the use of a trust, whose beneficiaries include a company, it drops by over $20 000 to $23 466.

You may wish to reread the chapter on children's tax in *Making Money Made Simple* now. As you can see, Mark is treated as an adult because he is 18 but Kim is allowed to earn no more than $416 of "unearned income" tax-free before moving to the 66% bracket. The trust distribution is termed "unearned income" because she has not physically worked for it. If she did work in the business, which is probable, that earned income is treated separately and comes out of the business as wages, not as a profit distribution. Thus she may earn a further $5 400 as wages tax-free.

A special benefit of a family trust is that the beneficiaries do not have to work for their distributions of income. Contrast this with the case of family members who work for a company where the wages must be reasonable for the duties performed.

TABLE 12.1

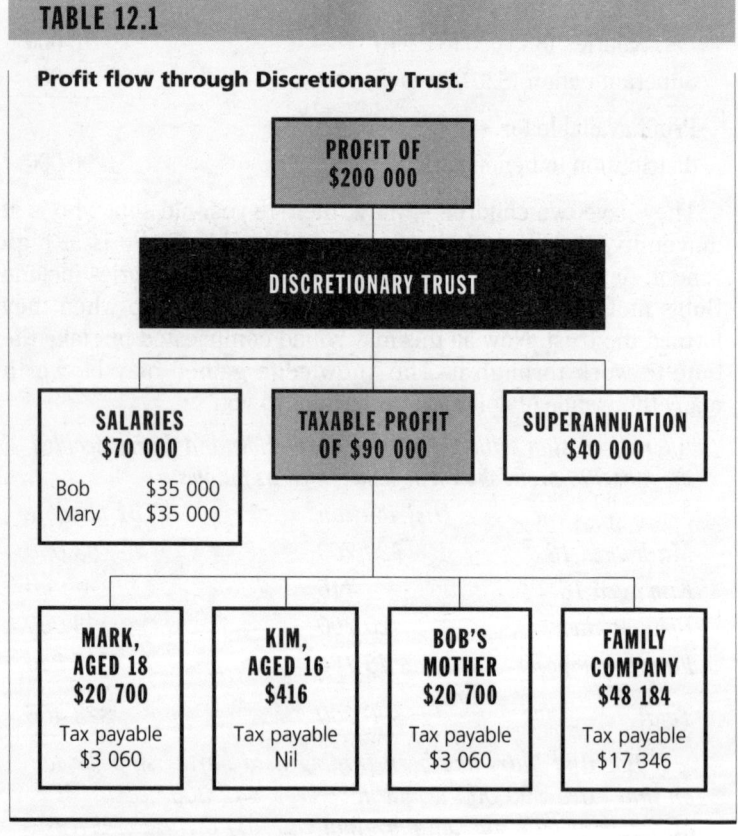

Profit flow through Discretionary Trust.

Unit trusts

Unit trusts are also income-splitting devices but lack the flexibility of the discretionary family trust. They are used when you desire to keep the interests of the beneficiaries separate. This may be because the investors are unrelated, or because different members of the same family are involved as investors.

Let's suppose that Bob decided to buy a block of flats in partnership with his two brothers, Terry and James. They may have different amounts of money to contribute and in any event want to safeguard the asset for their families. If the building cost $250 000 the contributions may be:

A total of $150 000 as deposit contributed as: Bob $80 000, Terry $40 000, and James $30 000. The other $100 000 is borrowed.

After talking to their accountant they may decide to set up a unit trust that contained 15 × $10 000 units and issue them in proportion to the funds of $150 000 contributed. Bob will have an 8/15 share, Terry will have a 4/15 share and James will have a 3/15 share.

TABLE 12.2

Ownership of Trust.

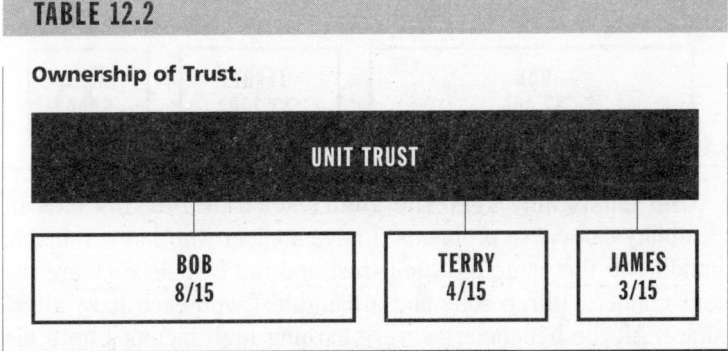

The main point to realise is that there is *no discretion* here at all. Suppose the net rents of that building are $14 500 and the interest is $10 000 leaving a taxable profit of $4 500. This $4 500 has to be distributed to all the unit holders in proportion to their unit holding as follows:

Bob	$2 400
Terry	1200
James	900
Total	$4 500

As you can see, the figures all work out neatly but the result may not be the best for tax-saving purposes. For example, it may not suit Bob if he is already in the top tax bracket for he will lose 47% of his share in tax.

It would have been a better strategy for Bob to buy the eight units in the unit trust in the name of his discretionary family trust. Certainly the unit trust would still have to distribute the $2 400 of income, but this time the beneficiary is the discretionary family trust, which can pass the income down to its own beneficiaries as it wishes.

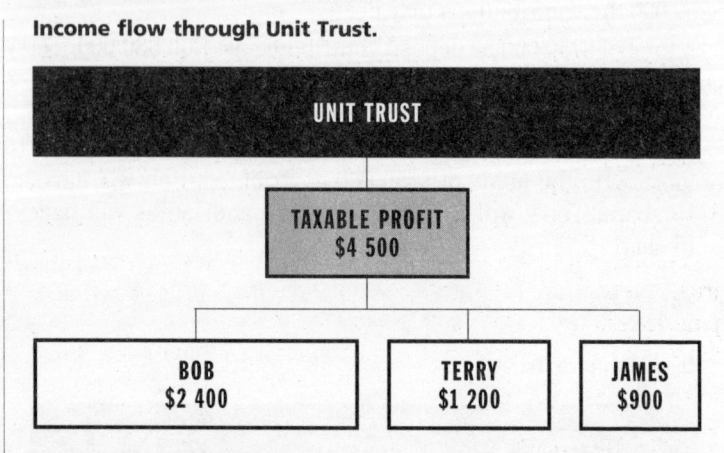

TABLE 12.3

Income flow through Unit Trust.

Unit trusts may keep the affairs separate but this lack of flexibility can cause problems. I have a client who has a valuable building in the name of a unit trust and the beneficiaries are his four children (three sons and a daughter) who each have a 25% share. All the beneficiaries were earning high incomes until his daughter's husband had a serious accident and was unable to work. Since the accident the daughter and her husband have had little income and the perfect solution would be to divert 100% of the income from the trust to them. This could be easily done with a discretionary trust but cannot be done through a unit trust.

A way to prevent the problem in advance would have been to have four discretionary family trusts as the unit holders and have each family as beneficiaries of each other's trust. Then the income would have flowed down through the unit trust to each family discretionary trust, which could have redistributed it to the daughter.

Unit trusts are also the vehicle for many managed funds because they best serve the interests of the individual investors. They were covered in detail in chapter 6.

Testamentary Trusts

To reduce tax, and to keep some control of family assets, many people are now inserting a testamentary trust clause into their will. The effect is that the nominated assets are left to the trust instead of the children. The following example will make it clearer:

CASE STUDY:*Grandad and Grandma Davies have a substantial investment portfolio that includes commercial property and a quality share portfolio. Their two children are successful, married and earn high incomes. There are five grandchildren who are aged between 9 and 21. The grandparents realise that nearly half of the income would be lost in tax, if they left all their assets to the two children. By leaving the investment portfolio to a testamentary trust with the two children as trustees, and the five grandchildren as beneficiaries, the income can flow directly to the grandchildren.*

As this is a testamentary trust, and not a normal discretionary trust, there is no $416 limit on what can be distributed before the punitive children's tax hits; the grandchildren are taxed at normal adult tax rates. Hence, they can each earn an initial $5 400 free of tax, the next $15 300 at only 20%, and so on up the tax scales.

Conclusion

Companies and trusts are normally used by high-income earners who are in business for themselves, and I realise you may not be in this category. Nevertheless, a good knowledge of broad tax principles is no burden to carry and this chapter should have made you aware of the other income-splitting opportunities that exist. If you still find it confusing, work through each example slowly and it will eventually come together. Then, if you feel your affairs can be improved, discuss the position with your accountant and possibly with a lawyer who specialises in tax matters.

Summing Up

- Companies are separate taxpayers in their own right and pay tax at 36% from the first dollar earned.
- Trusts don't pay tax. They distribute profits to the beneficiaries who pay the tax.
- Using companies and trusts can eliminate provisional tax.
- Discretionary trusts are more flexible than unit trusts.
- A company may be a beneficiary of a trust.

13

YOU AND YOUR ADVISER

Advice is seldom welcome; and those who want it the most always like it the least.

LORD CHESTERFIELD (Letters, 29 January 1748)

"Where can I find a good financial adviser?" This is the one question that is asked more than any other whenever I do a radio program or give a speech. I have a stock answer that goes as follows: "That is no different from your asking me how to find a good doctor, accountant or motor mechanic. I really don't know."

Now that may sound like a cop-out, but the truth is that there is no way you can be sure any person is competent in their chosen profession. How do you know your doctor, accountant or motor mechanic is skilled at what they do? How do you know they are not ripping you off? Certainly there are some clues that I will discuss later, but these are just indicators. The reality is that only time will tell.

I am closely involved in the financial advisory business but it is almost impossible for me to pass judgement on the ability of the people who work in our industry in my own city. I hardly ever get to see the portfolios they write and therefore the only gauge I have is their reputation, and the kind of remarks they make, or questions they ask, at industry functions. This highlights the problems for a lay person in trying to assess any professional person's ability.

Nevertheless, a financial adviser is almost certain to play an important role in your future and in this chapter I will give you some pointers to guide you on your search. You should certainly seek an adviser with a good reputation, and who has been through the 1987 share crash and the 1990 property crash. In general, I believe the longer they have been in business the better, and the best indication of competence is recommendations from satisfied clients. In short, if they are well established in the industry, and come highly recommended, you are off to a good start.

Licensed Securities Dealers

First you should understand the difference between a licensed securities dealer who operates under strict rules regulated by the Australian Securities Commission (ASC), and a range of people who call themselves "investment counsellor" or "financial adviser".

You usually find this last-mentioned group selling property or a range of savings plans. They do not operate under ASC regulations and accordingly have far greater freedom to make optimistic statements about the products they are handling. When they say "You can't go wrong if you buy one of these townhouses" you have to regard it as no more than a sales pitch. Maybe what they are selling will turn out to be a great investment, maybe it will be a dud. It is up to you to convince yourself by your own research, because the salespeople who make these claims have no legal duty to ensure their statements are soundly based.

To gain the protection of the ASC rules, you should deal with a licensed securities dealer or a person who is a "proper authority holder" for a licensed securities dealer. The term "securities" includes shares, debentures, most managed funds such as equity trusts, option contracts and ventures such as time share and agricultural schemes. A dealer may have an unrestricted licence and deal in all securities, or he may have a restricted licence and prefer to specialise in just some of them. If you ask the staff at your first interview they will advise you of the firm's area of expertise.

In most cases, the company that runs the financial advisory business is the licensed securities dealer, and the members of its advisory staff are proper authority holders for the dealer. The term "proper authority" means the dealer has given the staff member full authority to give advice on its behalf. The result is that the dealer becomes liable for any wrong advice given by its proper authority holders. As you can imagine, dealers don't issue proper authorities lightly.

KEY POINT: To gain the protection of the Australian Securities Commission regulations you should seek a financial adviser who is a licensed securities dealer, or a proper authority holder for a licensed securities dealer.

Duties Of A Licensed Securities Dealer

To make it less confusing for you, I shall use the word "adviser" in the rest of this chapter to mean a licensed securities dealer or a proper authority holder. In practice, most people giving advice in our industry are proper authority holders.

The ASC rules work from three basic principles:

1. Advisers must have a reasonable basis for making recommendations.
2. Clients should be made aware of any risks involved with the investments or strategy recommended.
3. Advisers must inform clients of all remuneration they will receive from any suggested course of action.

Let's consider the duties of an adviser:

Know the client

To be able to have a reasonable basis for making recommendations, advisers are required to know their clients and to know their products. In other words, advisers have to:

1. Make sure the recommendation is appropriate for the client, taking into account such factors as investment goals, temperament, age, assets, income, type of employment and experience. This is called the "know your client" rule.
2. After thorough research, understand the types of products that should be appropriate for the particular client, and be able to choose ones that fit the needs of that client.

Obviously it takes quite some time for good advisers to do their jobs properly. To fulfil the "know your client" rule they must probe into almost every area of the client's life, and to do this properly most advisers will ask their clients to fill in a detailed form listing information about:

- their ages, income, type of job and health
- their children and what likely expenses will be incurred in educating them
- their assets and liabilities
- their present life, disability and accident insurance
- their superannuation
- their wills and powers of attorney, if any

- when they wish to retire
- how much money they will need in retirement
- any legacies they may receive
- any planned abnormal expenses such as buying a car, paying for a wedding, or going on an overseas trip
- their experience with investments to date; for example, have they suffered losses in the past that have made them nervous now
- any particular likes or dislikes they have: some clients love share-based investments; others are terrified of them

The analysis form usually includes a budget sheet in which the clients record details of their spending. This will indicate the type of lifestyle they now enjoy and will help the adviser and the clients decide together how much there is to spare for an investment program or for extra insurance. It will also help answer that critical question "Can I afford to retire?"

Usually the adviser sends this form to the clients before the interview to give them time to find out all the information required, and to discuss the budget. When they arrive at the interview the clients often hand the form over a little sheepishly with comments such as "That was tough", or "I didn't know we spent so much". In many cases it's obvious this is the first time they have listed their assets or thought about a budget. That in itself may be a major turning point in their lives.

At the first interview, the adviser should discuss each item on the analysis sheet with the clients, but it is likely they will be unsure about some of the items mentioned. Almost certainly they will have only a vague idea of any insurance policies they own, and their work superannuation is probably a mystery to them. The adviser should ask how long they expect to live, and whether leaving money to their estate is important to them. Both these factors are crucial when formulating investment recommendations.

After collecting all this information and discussing it point by point with the clients, the adviser should be well on the way to "knowing the clients". The next step is to decide upon a financial plan based on the information collected and, at this point, the adviser is likely to make a time for another appointment to see the clients and present the recommendations to them. This is to give the clients more time to think about the matters discussed and to give the adviser time to draft the plan.

As you can imagine, to draft the financial plan the adviser will need a sound knowledge of the range of investment products available and the drawbacks and good points of each one.

Know the products

Knowing the client is only a part of the process. The next step for the adviser is to match the investments available with the needs of the client. To do this well the adviser must understand our tax laws, the social security regulations, the superannuation rules, the way each type of investment works, what its risks are, and which are the most appropriate fund managers to use. Here are just a few examples to demonstrate the depth of knowledge required:

1. A person who is not gainfully employed, or who is over 70, cannot join a superannuation fund. This precludes superannuation as an investment for many people.

2. Share trusts may be run conservatively or aggressively. The one to use depends on the client's risk level.

3. The XYZ Fund manager may be noted for its skill in the fixed-interest market but be known to be weak in shares. In contrast the ZYX Fund manager might be a whiz at international equities. The adviser should consult his preferred list and

select a fund manager that is noted for its expertise in the area in which the clients wish to invest.

4. Funeral bonds are a tax-free investment, but the money is tied up until the holder dies and, even then, some fund managers require all the money from the funeral bond to be used for the funeral. Obviously, the use of these is highly selective.

5. Most annuities lock in the earning rate at the time they are taken out for the life of the annuity contract. Therefore, lifetime annuities should be used with caution, particularly in times of low interest rates or if the client is young.

6. International investments give a hedge against our dollar dropping, but the client will lose money if our dollar strengthens.

7. Partially rolling over an Eligible Termination Payment may cause the client to lose valuable tax benefits.

8. Some so-called capital guaranteed investments are a gimmick and the client is far better off in other areas.

As well as these, a good adviser will understand and recommend techniques that can save tax and speed the wealth-building process. Many of these are discussed in this book, but we live in a rapidly changing world and there are always new strategies and products coming on the market. This is why a regular review of your affairs with your adviser is essential.

Research

The ASC expects advisers to carry out their own research and/or to use research sources that are available outside their own firms. As most advisers use external research, the ASC also requires them to "evaluate the overall quality and effectiveness of analyses provided by the research organisation to ensure the reliance placed on that research is reasonable in all the circumstances".[1]

The ASC rules also require advisers to consider economic and accounting information relating to the markets, and to the types of investments recommended.

That's a tall order, and by now you should appreciate how much licensed advisers need to know. But, there's more to it. The adviser has to be able to justify his or her recommendations if ever the ASC does an audit of the file of a particular client. In other words, there should be evidence on the file to indicate the line of

---

1. ASC Practice Note 41.

reasoning the adviser used to arrive at the recommendations. The adviser does this by writing a detailed file note, setting out what was discussed, after each interview with the client. The licensed dealer regards these file notes and other memoranda as being of the utmost importance. The reasons are:

1. It enables the dealer's administration staff to ensure their advisers are giving appropriate advice. Remember, the licensed dealer is responsible for the conduct of its proper authority holders.

2. It is invaluable evidence if the client ever sues the dealer or the proper authority holder for bad advice.

3. It is one of the first things the ASC looks for when they carry out their regular audits on dealers.

4. It helps the adviser to think logically and make sure nothing is overlooked when preparing a financial plan. Many dealers use check lists for this as well.

The problem is that it is human nature to want to buy in boom and sell in gloom. When the stock market is roaring up most clients want to have a piece of it; when it falls into a hole they don't want to touch it. This is bad enough, but many clients also have a change of heart about their original instructions when the market changes. They will often come back to their adviser and insist their instructions were "security above all else" and claim they had no idea the market could fall as much as it just did.

A good adviser will counter this problem in advance. First, the file notes will set out exactly what the clients asked for and also what the adviser recommended and why. Second, the written recommendations to the client will clearly detail any risks associated with the recommendations and expectations of capital growth and income. Third, at the time of making the investments the clients will sign a statement that they clearly understood the risks involved.

If all this is done properly, the client should be well informed and there should be adequate documentation to satisfy the requirements of the ASC and to clarify the position between the adviser and the clients.

How Is The Adviser Paid?

The next matter to consider is how the adviser is paid and what disclosure is necessary. This is a controversial question because the industry evolved from the days when the "advisers" (possibly a better word in the early stages was "salespeople") received their incomes solely from brokerage paid by insurance companies or fund managers.

This laid the industry open to charges of bias and to the oft-quoted line "Advisers will only advise you to put your money in the funds that pay them the most commission". This proposition assumes that all advisers are dishonest, which is nonsense.

Now I have no doubt that some advisers recommend investments purely on the basis of the brokerage the transaction attracts, just as I have no doubt that some motor mechanics overcharge for repairs and that some doctors do unnecessary operations. No profession is free from the odd person who gives the rest a bad name. However, it is wrong to believe that financial advisers are any worse than any other group of professionals.

However, a major difficulty with a system where the adviser is paid only when clients invest money in areas that pay brokerage is that it cannot cater for those people who need financial advice but are not ready to invest money. It is also unsuitable when the appropriate investments are interest-bearing deposits or debentures. Hence the practice evolved of charging an initial consultation fee to pay the adviser for the time spent irrespective of whether money was invested or not. This is why I suggest you steer clear of "free" consultations. Think about it. If the initial consultation is free, how is the adviser going to get paid unless he or she sells you something?

KEY POINT: Beware of free consultations.

By late 1989 some advisers had moved from being brokerage-based to charging an establishment fee on a sliding scale on the investments placed, and other advisers had started to operate on a fee-for-time basis with all brokerage being rebated to their clients. However, this system is also open to abuse and does not stop dishonest advisers from taking advantage of clients. It is not possible for clients to know how many hours were actually spent on their portfolio, and unscrupulous advisers could double their fees by inflating the time spent.

At time of writing, a case came to my notice that concerned a high-profile adviser who proudly works on a fee-for-time basis. The client had gone to this adviser for advice on a superannuation policy and received a bill for $1500 for "10 hours work at $150 an hour". It was only a small superannuation policy, but the adviser claimed it took a lot of time to extract the information from the insurance company. Now I have no idea whether the adviser padded the time spent, but the example does show that clients can get some nasty shocks if they opt for a fee based on the time spent.

Regular surveys carried out on members of the Financial Planning Association show the average brokerage paid is about 2.75% or, to put it simply, $2750 for each $100 000 invested. This comes about because growth investments pay brokerage of between 3% and 4% in most cases, while income investments may pay as little as 1% or even nothing in many cases. If we assume that most people with large sums to invest are over 50, it is reasonable to expect that low-brokerage income investments make up part of their portfolio.

If we use 10 hours as the average time it would take to conduct the initial interview, analyse the data supplied by the client, prepare the written recommendations, and have follow-up consultations to finetune them, we arrive at $1500 as the cost to the client if a charge-out rate of $150 an hour is used. In my experience most clients will seek advice from three advisers before deciding on which one to use, so if all three advisers were fee-based, the client would incur costs of $4500 before the investment was made.

In contrast, an investor can shop around among brokerage-based advisers and pay only initial consultation fees before deciding which adviser is best. If the sum invested was $200 000, and the adviser earned the average brokerage, the cost to the client is $5500. When you consider that many brokerage investors will offer a year's free follow-up service, there is little between them in monetary terms.

You should now appreciate that it is not a perfect system and that proponents of both fee-based advice and brokerage-based advice can make reasonable arguments for their case. In the end the choice is yours, so make sure you are fully informed. The brokerage-paid adviser has to disclose details of all remuneration before you invest. With fee-based advisers you do not have this protection and should therefore demand a reasonable estimate of fees before you agree to deal with them. Many people who have used fee-based advisers tell me they become irritated because they get a bill every time they ring up the adviser with a question, so if you are thinking about using a fee-based adviser you should clarify what will be the cost of follow-up calls.

I suggest the more important consideration is the quality of advice, and I would give this a far higher emphasis when choosing an adviser than deciding on the basis of brokerage or fees.

Ongoing service is also a vital factor in deciding who to entrust with your investments. You will find most advisers are offering some sort of portfolio monitoring service, whereby clients pay an annual fee to the advisory company to have their investment portfolio monitored. There are different levels of ongoing service offered depending on the size and complexity of the portfolio. It may include a regular valuation statement, an annual taxation summary and as many follow-up consultations as are mutually decided to be necessary, at no further cost.

> KEY POINT: The quality of the advice and the cost and extent of ongoing service are more important than whether the adviser is fee-based or brokerage-based.

Discount Brokers

Discount brokers are not financial advisers, they are financial intermediaries who place money for people who believe they need neither advice nor ongoing service. As such they do not have to abide by the "know your client" rule, and do not have any concerns that the investments are appropriate for the client.

Because they do not have to spend the time with the client that is required of a licensed adviser, and do not need to pay for such costly overheads as research or public liability policies, they rebate most of the brokerage to the client. Thus they offer a cheap medium of entry for investors who want to be in managed funds but believe they can look after the portfolio on their own.

I have stressed the importance of building a long-term relationship with an adviser and of having your portfolio regularly monitored. If you ignore this advice and opt for the cheap route via the discount broker you will be on your own. Can you afford to do that?

The Adviser's Dilemma

Unfortunately, giving financial advice is not like giving advice on building a house. A builder works with the laws of physics and, provided the foundations are right and the materials used are sound, the house should be finished on time and last for a lifetime.

In contrast, the financial adviser works with the laws of the markets and real life that tell us:

- if there is a chance of capital gain there is a chance of capital loss
- the Government will always change the laws
- the unexpected such as death, divorce or the need to help children will always happen
- markets will always rise and fall

To make matters worse, there is always a plethora of newsletter writers from all parts of the globe suggesting doomsday is just around the corner, while clients are well known for changing their attitude to money. Against this continually changing background the adviser must try to design a plan that will minimise the chance of loss to the client while maximising the chance of gain.

The sad reality is that the person with the most money is the hardest to advise. If a 21-year-old couple ask for advice you know it is almost impossible to go wrong if they buy a well-located home and pay it off and then invest the money every month that is not then needed for the mortgage payments. That's easy.

Contrast this with the couple in their late fifties who have struggled all their lives, and who have never had an investment other than a term deposit. Suddenly they are about to receive a superannuation payout of over $300 000. They know this is their one and only chance at financial security and are terrified of getting it wrong.

If they are going to live well in retirement they should place part of it in shares and bonds, but if they do this they will suffer volatility. They will probably find the investment options hard to handle and their adviser will equally have difficulty formulating an appropriate plan for them. Almost certainly they will have been to several seminars, been hounded by people trying to get their business, and have received heaps of half-true advice from well-meaning friends.

Although the adviser may have his or her own opinion about whether the share and bond markets are going to go up or down, and this may be backed up by top research, the outcome is still not guaranteed. The adviser can produce graphs and performance figures, but chances are the couple may not understand what they are being told. The result of this confusion is that the clients may be seduced by past performance figures and jump into a bull market just before the top, or decide to keep their money in cash and miss out on the next jump up. Either way they lose.

> KEY POINT: An adviser cannot guarantee to protect a client against changing markets unless the client is prepared to accept a much lower overall return as the consequence.

Understand Projected Figures

I once had the experience of losing a potential client to another adviser who was recommending exactly the same investments as I was. What made the difference? The other adviser, in his financial plan, had used higher projected earning rates than I did. Consequently this client believed the same investment would produce a higher rate if it was placed through another intermediary!

Past performance figures quoted about investments should be correct, but understand that figures about **future** growth used in financial plans are estimates of what the adviser's research sources believe will happen. Estimates of future income distributions from investments such as mortgage trusts and income funds should be fairly accurate, but growth estimates are purely a guess and are meant to be long-term illustrations. The fact that a growth estimate is 8% does not mean the investment should grow 8% next year; it means the adviser expects that growth should **average** 8% a year over the next five years.

The biggest danger is when capital growth has been exceptionally high over the previous year or two. It is human nature to want to get in as quickly as possible when you see figures showing past growth of 20% or 30% a year, but no investment can sustain that pace in the long term. It is almost certain to be followed by low, or even negative, figures.

> KEY POINT: An exceptionally strong performance from a growth investment over the past two or three years is often an indicator that the performance for the next year or two may be mediocre.

Bad Advice

In the next chapter I'll cover the major complaints I have heard from people who claim they were victims of bad advice. Bad advice will normally fall into two areas. The first is not really "advice" because it is nothing more than a hard sales pitch disguised as advice. The second is simply incompetent advice.

You can usually identify the first by the approach. It may be a door-to-door or telephone canvasser "taking a survey" or wanting to make a time to talk to you about ways to save tax, or it may be by way of a mailed glossy brochure full of extravagant claims. In any event the next step is a request that one of their "advisers", "client liaison officers", "consultants" or "representatives" call around to see you at home. If they do, I suggest you lock up your purse and unleash the dog.

Probably the best way to dodge the hard-sell merchants is to see financial advisers at their office, not your home, and deal only with people who:

1. are licensed as proper authority holders
2. offer independent advice
3. have a genuine range of investments to offer. How can a person claim to be giving advice when they have only one brand on their shelves?
4. are members of the Financial Planning Association.

Incompetent advice is caused by lack of knowledge, lack of experience, or lack of information about the client's needs. A document[2] issued by the ASC lists the following as examples of inappropriate advice:

1. A recommendation was made that a client invest in securities as a short-term investment where the entry fees and other charges were high relative to any short-term returns that might have been expected.
2. Recommendation to take up highly speculative shares where the client had a nervous temperament.
3. Recommendations to borrow for share-based investments when the risks were not clearly explained.
4. Recommendations to place money in low-return income-generating investments when the client required capital growth.

That last one is worth thinking about because it shows that a nervous adviser who is worried about a market crash cannot duck responsibility by recommending a capital guaranteed or a fixed-

---

2. ASC Practice Note 41.

interest investment when the appropriate investment is one that has the potential for growth. However, if the adviser had good grounds for believing a certain market was overpriced, he would not be guilty of bad advice if he communicated his beliefs to the client and let the client make the final decision.

The following are three specific examples I have encountered:

1. A stockbroker suggested an investor redeem his units in a well-known property securities fund and use the proceeds to buy some listed property trusts. This was ridiculous advice because the property securities fund invested in Australia's leading listed property trusts. Why incur costs to move?

2. A single woman, in her late sixties, worked as a cook in a church hostel. She had no commercial experience. An adviser recommended she form a family trust, start her own self-managed superannuation fund, sell her house to the superannuation fund and then rent it back. When you come to the section on superannuation in this book, you will understand why this was an inappropriate recommendation for a person of her age with no business experience and limited resources. The adviser, who was fee-based, claimed he was trying to get her a bigger aged pension, but I believe he was only trying to generate fees for himself.

Some Pointers

Here are some ideas that should help you in your search for a good adviser.

- Look for a stable company with a good research source and with a substantial length of time in the industry (bear in mind it is a very young industry that did not get going properly till the early 1980s). Find out the number of staff they have and what resources are available for client service. I am not knocking sole operators, but it is important that you receive continuing service and not be disadvantaged if your normal adviser is on holidays for a month.

- Prefer a person who has been through the crash of 1987 and who has a healthy cynicism about projected returns and the claims made in all the glossy brochures and the large advertisements. An experienced adviser knows that "no tree grows for ever" and the star performer of today may be at the bottom of the heap tomorrow.

- Be wary of overconfidence on the part of the adviser. It is extraordinarily difficult to achieve the right portfolio balance in this modern era of rapid change, a volatile stock market and an uncertain property market. Good advisers have a fine appreciation of their own fallibility. If anybody tells you they will ring you up the day before the next crash and get you out of the market, run a mile.

- The reception area of the adviser's office is a good indicator of the attitude of the business. Does it look smart and well run? Does the receptionist appear efficient and interested in you? Is there a friendly and caring attitude prevailing?

- One of the best ways to find a good adviser is to rely on recommendations from satisfied clients, particularly if they are clients of long standing. Good advisers value their reputation and make every effort to keep their clients happy.

- General reputation in the industry and membership of the industry self-regulatory body – the Financial Planners Association – are other factors to note. Details of this institution are given in *Making Money Made Simple*.

- Ask about the level of service that the advisory company will provide **after** you have invested your money. For the serious investor there should be a portfolio monitoring service of some kind. If so, what does it cost and what does it cover?

I suggest you look for an air of permanence in the office appearance. If you are entrusting the investment of your life savings to somebody, it's important that you be able to find them when you need them. If the whole place has a cheap and grotty appearance you had better be careful.

Conclusion

The financial industry planning is at last coming of age, but it is still a young industry and like all emerging industries will still suffer growing pains. Fortunately the commitment by people in the industry to continual improvement is ongoing and is getting better and better. Provided investors realise that they are ultimately responsible for their destiny and must understand fully their decisions, the financial planning industry will benefit all of us.

Summing Up

- Take the time to understand the difference between a licensed securities dealer and salespeople who call themselves "financial consultants".
- A licensed adviser must "know the client" before making any recommendations.
- The quality of the advice should be your main consideration.
- No adviser can guarantee capital growth.
- The client should feel comfortable with the adviser, otherwise inhibitions may prevent frankness.
- Seek a well-established adviser with a good reputation.

14

BAD EXPERIENCES WITH ADVISERS

The greatest error a person can make is to be afraid to make one.

ELBERT HUBBARD

I don't want to introduce a negative note into this book, but I do believe a good adviser will play a vital role in your wealth-creation process. However, I know that some people have had, or will have in the future, unhappy experiences in their dealings with financial advisers, just as they may have had bad experiences with doctors, solicitors, accountants or members of any other profession. This is to be expected whenever people interact.

To help you understand how an unsatisfactory relationship can develop, I will discuss in this chapter the main reasons people have felt dissatisfied with advisers. It may help you achieve a happy and fulfilling relationship with the one you choose.

Let's go through the main complaints.

1. **I invested a large sum of money and never heard from my adviser again.**

Good advisers appreciate the value of an ongoing relationship, for it is in the interest of both adviser and client. Satisfied clients refer friends, which enables the adviser's business to grow. Clients' affairs need regular monitoring to ensure the investments are appropriate in the light of everchanging laws and market conditions.

Solution: Before you invest a dollar through any adviser find out what the ongoing service will be and what it will cost. Ask if they produce a newsletter and whether they send out regular bulletins in the event of a major change in the laws in such areas as superannuation and aged pensions. If there is no ongoing service, or if it is promised as a "free" service, go elsewhere. Nobody can give you free service for the rest of your life.

2. **I invested money prior to the 1987 share crash and it dropped by over 50% when the crash happened.**

You cannot avoid the possibility of capital loss if you invest in any assets that have the potential for capital gain. Possibly you were in aggressive equity trusts or in so-called growth funds where the potential for loss was not emphasised.

Solution: Take heart in the knowledge that the laws have become stricter, and since 1987 the financial planning industry has become more aware of the need for checking that funds are "true to label". Make sure your adviser clearly advises you of the downside risk of growth investments and, if possible, invest a set sum each month, as I mentioned in chapter 1 in the section about wealth-building principles. This will enable you to take advantage of dollar-cost averaging, which works best when the markets are falling.

3. **My investments fell in value and after years I have still not got back what I put in.**

This shows the importance of regular monitoring of your investments. Each type of investment has its good and bad cycles but, as well, there are fund managers who specialise in bull or bear markets (not both) or in certain types of assets. For example, Manager A might be best at international bonds, and Manager B might shine in Australian equities.

Solution: Have your investments regularly monitored and don't be frightened to ask your adviser for a look at his preferred investment list. If he hasn't got one, change advisers.

4. *My adviser recommended I invest in unlisted property trusts. I made heavy losses.*

Until the 1990 property crash most advisers, including myself, regarded unlisted property trusts as a sound investment vehicle. They invested in prime properties that were highly regarded by the banks, who lent huge sums on the security of them. The type of property they owned was sought after by large institutions such as insurance companies, and I believed most small investors were better off owning a tiny part of a giant inner city building, or a shopping centre occupying an irreplaceable site, than trying to cope with the problems of rental houses. This view was shared by the major research houses who provide advice to the financial planning industry.

The 1990 crash, in the wake of the massive recession of that time, saw billions of dollars wiped from the values of prime property. Banks incurred billions of dollars of bad debts as a result. The crash also exposed the lack of liquidity in unlisted property trusts as being a fatal flaw and, to make matters worse, the directors of at least one major property trust manager are facing criminal charges.

Solution: Investors who lost money in unlisted property trusts can take some consolation in the knowledge that the buildings are still in existence and value may eventually be restored to the investments. Also the effect of the loss is lessened somewhat because capital losses once realised can be used to offset capital gains made from other investments. Most of the unlisted property trusts have now listed, and have thus become listed property trusts, which are more like share assets than property assets. This creates a dilemma that the financial planning industry is still trying to solve. How do you provide property in a portfolio for a person who does not have the resources to buy a rental property yet is nervous of shares?

It is a question to which nobody has yet given a satisfactory answer.

5. **A financial adviser advised me to take out a savings scheme with a major life insurance company. After two years of payments I find the surrender value is far less than I have contributed.**

This is a common complaint and often arises because the "adviser" is a salesperson for a life company using the title "financial adviser". As I explained in chapter 1 I am a great believer in a regular savings program, but it is unwise to enter into a contract for it because of the hidden fees that are often involved.

Solution: Stay right away from insurance company savings plans and make sure you take financial advice only from a proper authority holder for a licensed dealer in securities. By doing this you will have the protection of the laws I mentioned in the previous chapter.

6. **I went to a licensed securities dealer to find out if buying a rental property was a good idea. I felt the advice given was too general, and that my main questions were not addressed.**

Many people are confused about the true role of a licensed financial adviser and become concerned when the adviser does not appear to have all the answers at his or her fingertips. Buying property is always difficult because of the time it takes to do the research, but few people will put in the time and effort to study the market properly. There are far too many who want to do it the easy way and hope there is somebody, somewhere, who can wave a magic wand and find them a bargain. Believe me, there is no magic wand.

Solution: Understand there are limits to what a licensed financial adviser can do. In this case, it would probably amount to no more than helping you prepare a budget, making sure your insurance and superannuation is in order and explaining the differences between investment in managed funds and direct investment in property. Only you can decide if the real estate market is about to boom and the type of property you should buy. Your accountant is probably the most appropriate person to consult for detailed information about the tax implications of buying property.

I must add that for every success story I hear in property I hear a corresponding one about failure and frustration. Retirees should be well aware of the dangers of property as well as its merits.

7. **A friend of mine gave some money to an adviser to invest and the adviser vanished with the money.**

Unfortunately these stories do happen – luckily they don't happen too often.

Solution: If you are investing money in a prospectus-based investment through a licensed securities dealer, don't issue cheques in favour of the dealer. Draw your cheques in favour of the trustee company and mark it for account of the fund manager. Full instructions are given in the prospectus, but the normal payee would read something like "Solid Trustees Pty Ltd for account of XYZ Growth Fund". Make sure the cheques are crossed "Not negotiable – account payee only". The dealer will then forward the cheques to the fund manager. If you have not received acknowledgement from the fund manager within 10 working days, phone the fund manager, not the dealer, to make sure your money has been received.

These instructions may seem basic, but many investors have lost money by not following them. Make sure you are not one of them.

8. **We invested money in Estate Mortgage on the recommendation of an adviser and have now lost most of it.**

Sadly, this has happened to many investors. The problem with any mortgage trust is that it may be difficult for researchers to find out the real value of the properties held as security for the loan, particularly if these properties are buildings under construction. Some research houses recommended Estate Mortgage, others did not. Our firm never recommended Estate Mortgage because we felt their newspaper advertisements were misleading and therefore unethical.

Solution: Beware of any lending institution offering higher-than-average returns, and always spread your money about if you are using mortgage trusts.

Conclusion

If you think about the matters raised in this chapter you will notice they relate to faulty advice, bad follow-up service, dishonesty, or the markets not doing what the adviser and the client expected them too. Bad service can often be avoided if you choose an adviser with a good reputation and who has been recommended by your friends, and the information in my books will help keep you away from the other traps. The world is becoming a more complicated place – a good adviser will be an invaluable guide to facing its challenges.

We'll take the education process a step further now by showing you how to read a prospectus.

Summing Up

- Most people will need a good adviser to help them before and during retirement.
- Problems can often be prevented, or solved quickly, if clients immediately tell their adviser about any concerns they have.
- Don't expect advisers to tell you what type of property you should buy.
- Look for quality ongoing service when you are choosing an adviser.
- It is the nature of markets to rise and fall.

15

HOW TO READ A PROSPECTUS

*A single idea – the sudden flash of a thought – may be worth
a million dollars.*

ROBERT COLLIER

No doubt you have read many of the advertisements for
investment products. Naturally, being advertisements, they focus
on the attractive features about the products and possibly quote
good past returns. However, you may have noticed two small
sentences at the bottom of each advertisement: "Future returns
are not guaranteed", and "Applications can be made only on the
form contained in the relevant prospectus".

Both these phrases are there to protect you. The first warns you
not to be seduced into thinking that past capital growth is any
guarantee of future growth; the second is to ensure that you have
access to a prospectus before you part with your money.

If you are going to be a serious investor you should take the
time to learn how to read a prospectus. We now live in an age of
consumer protection, and a prospectus is a document that is
designed to give you that protection. It is a document issued under
the control of the Australian Securities Commission and must be
issued by anybody who seeks money from the public for
investment in securities.

There are some occasions when a prospectus is not required.
For example, if you want to start a little business and ask a couple
of friends to invest money in it you do not need a prospectus, and
your employers don't have to give you a prospectus when they ask
you to join the company superannuation fund. You are not offered
a prospectus when you are considering insurance company

products because they are not securities and are regulated by different laws. However, in general terms we can say that almost anybody seeking money from the general public has to issue a prospectus.

Section 1022 of the Corporations Law states a prospectus shall:

> "Contain all such information as investors and their professional advisers would reasonably require, and reasonably expect to find in the prospectus, for the purpose of making an informed assessment of:
>
> (a) the assets and liabilities, financial position, profits and losses, and prospects of the corporation; and
>
> (b) the rights attaching to the securities."

As you can see, it's a wide-ranging obligation, but think again about the purpose of a prospectus. It is to protect investors, by providing them with enough material to enable them to make an informed decision.

At least that's the theory of it, and I admit a prospectus certainly keeps a lot of the "shonks" from picking your pocket. However, in real life there is still a multitude of things that can go wrong with an investment no matter how much is disclosed at the time you invest.

KEY POINT: A prospectus is a document issued under Australian Securities Commission regulations. The aim of a prospectus is to give investors sufficient information about the product to enable them to make an informed decision about investing money in it.

Before we had adequate prospectus laws, company promoters tried all sorts of tricks. A notable one was to start up a business and then sell it to the public at a figure way above its true value. Another was to raise money to start enterprises that had little chance of making a profit – all the cream was raked off in management fees. That's harder to do now. Full disclosure is required in the prospectus and any dealings or conflict of interest the directors or officers of the company may have must be brought to the attention of a potential investor.

The problem is that the ASC walks the tightrope of trying to make the prospectus comprehensible to the average investor while also trying to make it meaningful to the professional analyst. The difficulties are compounded by many of the new sophisticated accounting practices that have produced accounting statements that have confused even experienced company directors.

As well as regulations concerning the information given in the prospectus, there are restrictions on the way it may be used. For example, most prospectuses expire after six months from date of issue. This is to try to ensure the material in them is up to date.

Furthermore, if you are investing in a prospectus-based investment, it is now law that the adviser cannot tear the application form out of the prospectus until you have filled it in. This is to prevent an unscrupulous securities dealer from stopping you reading a prospectus by getting you to fill in a blank form that has been torn from it. By making you fill in the form while it is attached to the prospectus there is at least a presumption that you had the opportunity to read it before you invested your money.

All these rules are fine in theory, but in practice I have found that few people take the time to read right through a prospectus, and those who do seldom understand it. Sure, there is a small minority who read all the fine print and come back with a long list of questions, but these questions are seldom relevant to the issue; they tend to get bogged down in the detail and ignore the really important bits. It reminds me of a couple considering buying a certain house who spend hours talking about the type of paint used on the outside and never get around to looking at the foundations, or thinking if the design of the house fits their needs.

So be aware that, although a prospectus is there to inform you, there is still more information you should seek before you make a decision to invest.

If you are reading a prospectus, it is most likely because you are thinking of investing in:

1. a new "float" of an established business or a "float" of a promising business concept
2. the privatisation of an existing body such as a State-owned insurance company
3. a speculative venture such as a film scheme or an agricultural scheme
4. a managed fund such as an equity trust, cash management trust, bond trust, or approved deposit fund.

Later in this chapter I shall give you some guidelines for each of the above.

The School Of Irreverent Logic

"The school of irreverent logic" is a term coined by Australian broadcaster John Laws to describe the way he looks at the world – an approach that uses simple logic despite any evidence that may be put up. Many experienced people in the financial field look at a prospectus in a similar way. Here are some examples:

- "Who are the directors of this new company?" demanded the chairman of a leading stockbroking firm. When told, he replied, "If those people are on the board we won't be touching it."

   All he needed to get from the prospectus was the names of the directors. While the chairman was making those observations, the "man in the street" may have been trying to read the glossy brochure that was the prospectus and been mightily impressed by the photographs and the projections of future growth.

- I know from experience that most new films don't make money and that most agricultural schemes end up being disasters. I also know that all the prospectuses make them look like the best investment you will ever find.

   Based on that experience I used the following reasoning when deciding not to invest in Paul Hogan's fourth film,

Lightning Jack. Hogan had a winner with *Crocodile Dundee,* but the sequel, *Crocodile Dundee Two,* had only moderate success. The third film, *Almost an Angel,* was a flop. To my mind Hogan's record as a film maker was not proven and there was nothing to indicate *Lightning Jack* would do anything spectacular. The fact that my judgment proved to be correct is only of secondary importance here – the main point is that my decision not to invest had nothing to do with what was in the prospectus.

When writing the original edition of *Living Well in Retirement* in 1994 I asked my stockbroker for a prospectus for a new float to browse through as I was writing. He gave me one for a casino in a tourist area. It is a handsome document printed on quality paper and full of superb photographs of the area in question, few of which are relevant to the project, and an artist's impressions of what the buildings will look like on completion. It contains forecasts of the profit the company hopes to make, details of the operator's expertise, graphs of the number of tourists who visit the area and 50 pages of small print that few people would be able to understand.

I wrote then "Is it a good investment? The broker certainly thinks it will be a winner; I have no idea. The prospectus would be useful to a person who has the skills to analyse the operation of casinos, but probably all a prospective investor can do is seek advice from an expert in that field." The property was the Cairns casino, which subsequently got into financial strife.

I am not knocking the idea of prospectuses; they have done much to thin the ranks of the corporate crooks. Just understand their limitations.

KEY POINT: A prospectus may give you information, but there are many other aspects of the performance of an investment that depend on the skill of the management and general economic conditions. These are highly variable.

Let me now give you some simple points about the way to approach a prospectus.

A new "float" of an established business or a "float" of a promising business concept

Think first of what you are trying to achieve. Unfortunately too many people regard buying shares as a punt, and taking up shares in a new issue as a super punt. In fact, buying most shares is not like having a bet, it's a method of investing your money. Whether you place part of your money in the "float" instead of somewhere else depends on what you want your money to do.

Certainly the company may be a sound one and an investment in it may be rewarding in the long term. However, as there are hundreds of other companies in which you can buy shares, ask yourself:

1. Do I wish to invest in shares?
2. If I want to invest in shares, am I better off to use a managed fund such as an equity trust?
3. Do I wish to invest particularly in this float?

What you have covered in this book so far will help you decide the answers to the first two questions; the prospectus will help you decide about the last one. Once you have read the prospectus, and read all the articles in the papers about the issue, you will be well placed to discuss your involvement with your stockbroker or your financial adviser.

The privatisation of an existing body such as a State-owned bank or insurance company

In this case the Government is selling all or part of the enterprise to the public. We all know that governments are perpetually strapped for cash so it follows that they will be seeking to extract the highest price the market will bear. If the float is a high-profile one, such as the GIO or the Commonwealth Bank issues, there will be loads of publicity and the papers will be full of commentary, some of it expert.

You will have to approach this in the same way as you would approach the new float I mentioned before. Just remember the Government will be after the highest price so the new issue is unlikely to be a bargain.

A speculative venture such as a film scheme or an agricultural scheme

The prospectus will always look good but "speculative" is the operative word here. Many of these ventures, being tax schemes, carry a guarantee that all or part of your initial investment will be returned to you eventually. Often people with tax problems, lured by the guaranteed returns, fall into the trap of borrowing for schemes in order to get an immediate tax deduction. In many cases the chickens come home to roost a few years later because any profits or guaranteed returns come back as taxable income.

When this happens the proceeds are insufficient to clear the debt and the investor is worse off than before.

I dislike these investments but, if you have your heart set on going into one, talk to your accountant and your adviser about the strength of the guarantees, the viability of the project, and the effect the returns will have on your budget.

A managed fund such as an equity trust, cash management trust, bond trust, or approved deposit fund

These are the investments that are most likely to hold the bulk of your retirement assets, which is why so much space has been devoted to them in this book. In the chapter on dealing with your financial adviser I pointed out that these were offered mainly by licensed securities dealers who by law have an obligation to find out all about your financial situation and then make a recommendation to you in writing that is appropriate in all the circumstances.

Notice you have a protection here that you do not get if you are participating in a new float or buying shares direct. Your adviser is required by law to know your situation, know the investments recommended and then draft a proposal to you in language you can understand. This is probably of much greater value than having a prospectus. Also, the adviser is likely to give you information sheets on each of the investments recommended. These are virtually a summary of the prospectus and contain such vital information as the aims of the fund, the fees charged by the fund manager, the assets in which the fund invests, and the size of the fund.

You should read the information sheet in conjunction with the prospectus and the recommendations from your adviser. Make sure you understand it all and jot down any questions you have so you won't forget them at your next interview with your adviser.

When reading a prospectus for a managed fund, pay particular attention to the following sections:

Who should invest? Are you in this category?

The objective of the fund. Does this match your goals?

The time horizon. Is this suitable for you?

Acquisition fees. Are there entry or exit fees? If there is an exit fee, but no entry fee, does the fund charge a higher management fee for the first three or four years to compensate for the lack of an entry fee?

Management fees. All funds charge management fees. Are they reasonable when compared with industry standards and in the light of the fund's performance?

The asset allocation. Usually there is a chart or pie graph showing the types of assets in which the fund invests. Is this where you want your money to be?

Security of capital. Does the prospectus state that the value of the investment can rise and fall? If so, can you cope with volatility?

The fund manager. What is the track record of the manager? How does the manager rate with respect to its peers?

Conclusion

You should now know the purpose of having prospectuses and their limitations. I suggest you approach prospectuses as you would the instructions you are likely to find with the medicine the doctor gives you. Read them by all means, do your best to understand them, and make sure you ask about anything that concerns you. However, for most people it is the recommendation of their professional adviser that should carry the most weight.

Summing Up

- The aim of a prospectus is to ensure investors are fully informed about securities in which they may invest.
- A prospectus cannot disclose all relevant information.
- If possible, obtain an information sheet and other relevant documents besides the prospectus.
- Learn to pick out the important points covered in a prospectus.

16

UNDERSTANDING RISK

Life is a succession of lessons that must be lived to be understood.

RALPH WALDO EMERSON

Risk is a simple word, yet it can be one of the most difficult concepts you will ever have to set your mind to. This is because the word itself has dual meanings in the investment world, and even in the context of its common meaning of loss, there are several ways that this loss can happen. Furthermore, by taking action to avoid one type of risk, you may leave yourself open to suffering another type of risk.

The simple way to avoid financial risk may seem to be to place your money in the bank, where there are no entry or exit fees and you have a high certainty of getting it all back when you ask for it. This may eliminate one kind of risk – credit risk – but it still leaves you vulnerable to all the other risks.

Think about "Joe" who died in his late 50's nearly 30 years ago. In those days women weren't supposed to know about much about money or business so, to protect his wife "Gracie" from all the "risks" of investment, his will provided that his two investment houses be sold upon his death, and the money placed in the bank. The reasoning seemed flawless. Gracie could live on the interest, while the capital would remain intact for the children after she died.

It turned out there was a flaw in the logic. Gracie is still alive. Sure, the original $14 000 is still in the bank, but the interest certainly isn't enough for her to live on. She has been deprived of a good living, and the children have been cheated of their inheritance. All because Joe was trying to avoid risk.

147

The reality is that life is inherently risky. In fact, it is so risky that the only certainty we have is that we are going to die one day. There's risk in getting married, risk in having children, risk in starting a business and, these days, even risk in walking down the street. But to try to dodge risk by locking yourself in a cocoon is to pay the highest price of all. You miss everything.

The way to handle risk is to live your life on the balance of probabilities. This means you combine what you know to be true, with what is likely to happen.

Apply this to investing and the conclusions are that you will probably live to at least 85, and that growth investments will give the highest and most tax effective returns. Therefore the least risky strategy for you is to have a substantial part of your assets in growth investments.

Look at the chart that shows the British experience. It contrasts the fortunes of three investors who, during the period 1963 to 1995, put 10% of their gross income into a pension fund that let them choose the type of asset into which the fund invested their money. One chose the cash option, one chose the bonds option and one chose the shares option.

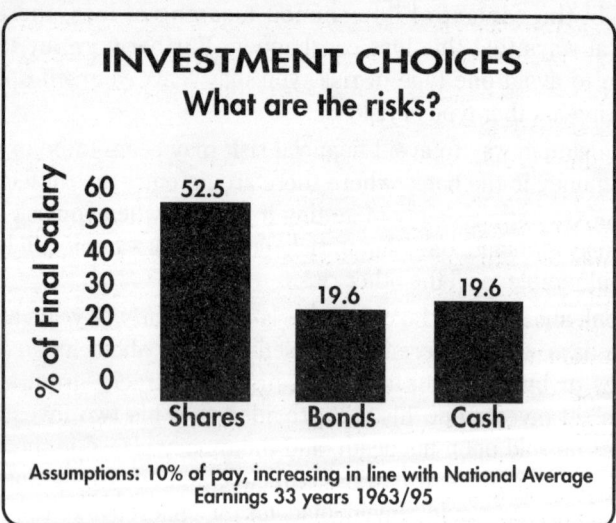

INVESTMENT CHOICES
What are the risks?

Assumptions: 10% of pay, increasing in line with National Average Earnings 33 years 1963/95

The result shows how much pension they received, expressed as a percentage of their salary when they stopped work. Notice bonds fared the worst with 19.6% and cash did little better with 22.3%. The share-based fund produced a pension of 52.5% of their retiring salary.

Those who went to cash or bonds to avoid risk paid a huge price; a reduction in their standard of living at retirement of nearly 60%.

Let's now briefly discuss the other types of risks.

Credit Risk

Credit risk is the chance that the institution to whom you lend money will be unable to pay it back. This may be caused by dishonesty, bad management or because one or more of their borrowers have defaulted and the underlying value of the security is insufficient to discharge the debt. Leading examples of losses because of credit risk are Cambridge Credit and Estate Mortgage. Cambridge Credit had its money tied up in unsaleable vacant land and Estate Mortgage had too many non-performing loans.

The cure for credit risk is to use substantial corporations that have been recommended, in writing, by your investment adviser and to spread your money between different companies so that if one does get into trouble it doesn't take all your money with it. I am amazed how often the television stations feature people who have lost their life savings by investing the whole lot with one institution. By asking your adviser to put all recommendations in writing you put yourself into a position to take legal action if you lose money in a "capital guaranteed" investment, or if a "safe" mortgage trust goes broke.

Lending bodies make their profit by borrowing money from one group of people and lending it out to others. Naturally they want to borrow it as cheaply as possible, and lend it out at the highest rate the market will bear. The rates being offered to borrowers increase as the standing of the lending body decreases. Therefore the better the reputation and credit rating of the lending institution, the less they have to offer to depositors.

Consequently the lower rated institutions have to charge more and their borrowers are more likely to be those who are forced to pay a higher rate as they have trouble borrowing from the higher-ranked organisations. This is why the chance of your losing your money increases as the rate of return rises.

Market Risk

This relates to a situation where you have bought an asset and its value drops. The asset may be anything from a bar of gold to shares in BHP; the nature of it makes it subject to the ebb and flow of market forces.

You protect yourself against market risk by first recognising that any asset that has the potential to rise in value may also fall in value. Once you appreciate this, you should know not to put all your funds into one area, or to invest in "growth" investments when the time frame is a short one. However, you must also be aware that while investments like shares and property have the potential to suffer falls in value, these areas have historically shown the best returns over the medium to long term. This is what the term "risk versus reward" means. If the best returns were available in prime fixed-interest investments, there would be no point in taking a higher risk by going into property and shares.

The major danger in placing money in quality property and share trusts is that you will be forced by circumstances to sell the assets during a time when the market is depressed. This must be avoided at all cost, and is simply done by keeping sufficient money in the cash area for your foreseeable requirements.

Opportunity Risk

Mr Smith buys $70 000 of shares, and Mrs Jones buys a block of land for the same price. After two years the shares are worth $90 000 and the land is still worth $70 000. Mrs Jones has lost the opportunity to achieve two years earnings on her $70 000, and has thus suffered opportunity risk.

It is difficult to eliminate opportunity risk as capital gain cannot be guaranteed. Thorough research before making the commitment may help to prevent the problem, and on-going monitoring of the performance may help you to say "enough" after a decent period and act to withdraw your funds and look for greener pastures. A good tip is to write down the reasons for buying each asset at the time you do it. This may help you later when you are trying to decide to retain or sell.

Legislative Risk

Governments are continually changing the rules and today's perfect financial plan may be obsolete on Budget night. Luckily our Government seems to have learned the lesson about the folly of retrospective legislation, which is why we now have such a range of confusing transitional measures.

About the only way to guard against legislative risk is to stay as flexible as is possible, always seek expert advice about your affairs and make sure your investments are monitored on a regular basis. This applies particularly in the areas of superannuation and roll over funds, which are discussed in depth later.

Re-investment Risk

This is the risk faced by people who place money in long-term debentures when interest rates are relatively high. They enjoy several years of good returns, but then find to their horror that interest rates have dropped substantially when the debentures come due for renewal. They then face the dilemma of locking into lower rates to protect themselves from further falls, or staying in short-term interest-bearing accounts in cases rates start to rise. In any event their income is greatly reduced and they may be forced to spend capital just to get by.

The solution to the problem is to prepare for it in advance and try to have a major part of your retirement income coming from income from growth investments. As the example in Chapter 1 showed, this tends to grow steadily with time and does not suffer the same fluctuations as income from interest-bearing investments.

Risk Or Volatility

In the investment world, the word risk can have another meaning – volatility. This is the degree that the price of a share moves around. There is a term "beta factor" used in investment circles which indicates the degree that a given share's prices move against the index. The index, by definition, has a beta factor of 1.0, so if a share has a beta factor of 2.0 we know that it is twice as volatile as the market.

In theory the higher-risk (more volatile) portfolios should show higher returns than low-risk portfolios but look at the following "risk/reward" table which shows that a low-risk manager can be a high performer and a high-risk manager can be a poor performer.

The left-hand vertical column measures return and the bottom horizontal column records volatility. Fund Manager C is the worst performer because he has achieved the worst return while taking the most risk. Contrast C's performance with that of Fund

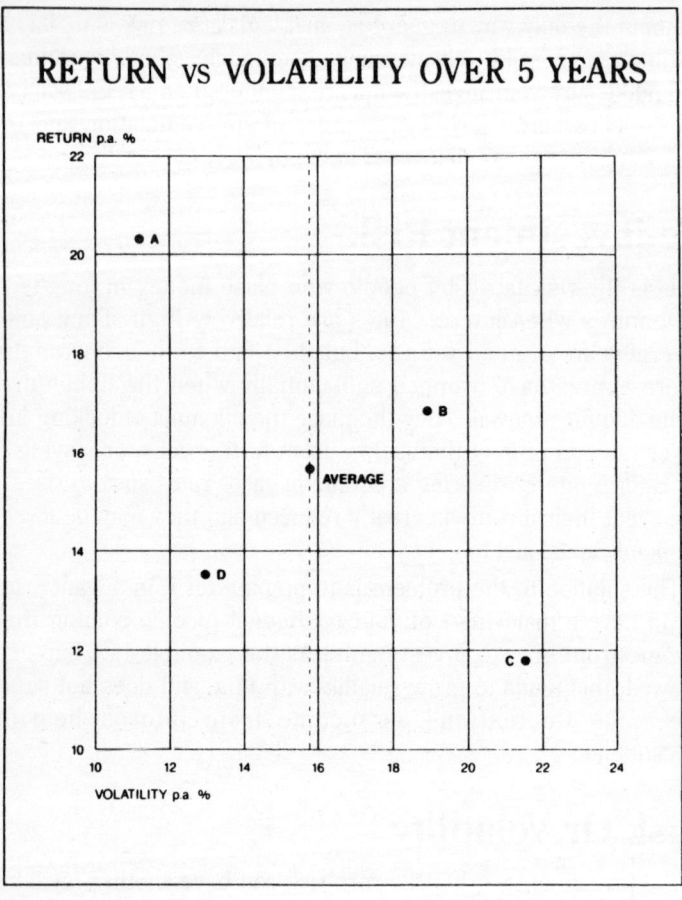

RETURN vs VOLATILITY OVER 5 YEARS

Manager A who has managed to pull off the jackpot – the highest return coupled with lowest risk!

Depending on market timing a low-risk manager may also achieve better cash results than a high-risk manager. Compare a conservative fund which earned 20% in the first year and minus 4% in the second, with an aggressive one that earned 100% in the first year and minus 50% in the second. On first glance you may think the second one would do best, but if you invested $1 000 with each at the beginning of the first year you would now have $1 152 in the first fund and $1 000 in the second.

This is not a recommendation that you avoid high-risk (volatile) investments but rather an effort to show you that a high-risk investment need not outperform a low-risk one.

Risk Of Non-Diversification

Reams have been written about the need to diversify and not have all your eggs on the one basket, but many investors end up with no diversification because all they have is a lot of similar baskets. Examples are people whose whole investment portfolio consists of suburban rental houses, or who are entirely invested in industrial shares, or who have cash-type deposits with at least four different banks and building societies. It is also common to see investment advisers spread a client's money over four equity trusts who have precisely the same approach to investment. This is not diversification.

The only true diversification is to spread your assets between various types of investments as well as between various markets. This is why it is vital that investors in managed funds clearly understand the nature of the underlying assets that make up the portfolio.

Capital guaranteed?

The crash of 1987 led many investors to flee to the security of "capital guaranteed" investments and away from "market linked" ones where values could rise and fall in line with the stock market. The size of the rush to capital guaranteed is indicated by the fact that in 1987 just over two billion dollars went into this area, but for 1989 it was almost seven billion dollars. As a result, the Insurance and Superannuation Commissioner issued stringent guide-lines (Circular 273) to take effect from June 30, 1989 to ensure the solvency of life offices issuing capital guarantees.

Previously there was a broad requirement that assets must exceed liabilities, but the new provisions put such a strain on reserves that many life offices closed their capital guaranteed funds to the entry of new money. In lieu they started "capital stable" or "capital secure" funds where the money was invested in areas such as fixed-interest securities, the money market, and possibly a few prime shares. Although there was no guarantee from the life office, the nature of the investments meant that the policy holder was much less subject to market risk.

Clients regularly say to us "I want everything to be capital guaranteed" and then often find it hard to understand that few investments can be capital guaranteed.

There is no guarantee if you buy property or shares, either directly or through property and equity trusts, and the only guarantee carried by government bonds is that you will receive the face value at maturity and the scheduled interest along the way. The main investments left are interest-bearing deposits with highly regarded institutions, or insurance products that carry a guarantee from a major life office.

Certainly the term "capital guarantee" gives investors a warm feeling that they will not lose any of their capital but the question to ask is "Is the price worth paying?". The irony is that the capital guaranteed funds are backed by the same cash, property and shares that back the market-linked funds so should give a similar return over a long period. The rates declared on the capital guaranteed funds are calculated by deducting a premium from the market-linked returns. Thus by their very nature, market-linked funds must provide better returns over time than capital stable funds, which in turn should outperform capital guaranteed ones.

Conclusion

I hope by now you realise why few investments can be described as "capital guaranteed" and why investors pay a high price for investing in capital guaranteed areas. It is impossible to eliminate risk but by taking the trouble to understand the underlying characteristics of investments you can choose a risk that is appropriate for your own situation. In the next chapter I'll show you some specific examples of risk.

Summing Up

- You cannot eliminate all types of risk
- By avoiding one type of risk you may leave yourself open to another
- The higher the return the higher the risk
- Growth investments will do better than cash investments in the long term
- Spread your investments

17

HAZARDS AND RISKY INVESTMENTS

It's no good saying "Hold it" to a moment in real life.

LORD SNOWDON (Royal photographer)

You can work hard to build wealth for a secure retirement and see your carefully laid plans torn apart by an incident you never imagined could happen. Occasionally a tragic accident will happen that nothing could have prevented. However, in the majority of cases incidents causing financial problems can be prevented or minimised if you have the knowledge, and in this chapter I will give you a few pointers that may help to prevent the loss of your hard-earned money. There is also a lot of other material in *More Money with Noel Whittaker* and you should take the time to read that too. This chapter is more in the nature of an overview.

Avoid Higher-Than-Average Returns

You are bound to come across advertisements offering returns that are way over what can be obtained elsewhere. You may also find seminars where self-styled gurus will teach you how to play the options market or the stock market.

If you are tempted by these, remember that in any pool of money where some players make huge gains, others must make huge losses to pay for those gains. Also ask yourself why anybody who had found the secret of wealth by knowing the right time to enter and exit markets would bother to charge a couple of hundred dollars to let anybody else into the secret.

Beware Guarantees

It starts out so easily. One of your children, or even a friend, might ask you for a few minutes of your time. They tell you that they have just approached the bank for a loan for a worthwhile purpose but the stuffy old bank has refused them. However, *if* they can get a guarantor the loan will be approved and everybody will live happily ever after. Naturally you are the person they hope will become the guarantor.

They will probably assure you it's only a matter of putting your signature on a piece of paper to keep the bank happy. Don't you believe it. In reality it means **if they can't repay the loan you do!**

...I had the most awful dream last night

There is a wise saying in legal circles that goes "There are no secrets kept, and there are no guarantees that are not called up." It might be extreme, but the harsh reality is that the bank, with its vast experience, believes the applicant is somewhat doubtful as a credit risk. If you go guarantor you are gambling with your money; backing your judgement that the bank is wrong.

Now I am not telling you to avoid guarantees in all circumstances. However, think carefully about the nature of the transaction, and the extent of the total possible liability. Suppose your daughter is an industrious and sensible person who is going to university and getting by with casual jobs. If she wants to buy a car I see no problem with your going guarantor if she does not yet have a credit record, or if the bank believes her income is insufficient to meet the payments. At least you know her character, and your liability is limited to the amount she borrows.

The great danger is when the borrower is engaged in a development project and wants you to sign papers that mortgage your home for the project. Development projects are high-risk ventures, and it may be two years or more before the sales proceeds start rolling in. During that time the economy may go from boom to bust and interest rates may go through the roof. You are the one in danger of losing your home.

Continuing guarantees are the greatest trap of all as the following story will illustrate:

EXAMPLE: *The Browns had just retired at age 55 when they were approached by their daughter Helen who was married to Tom. Tom had an entrepreneurial nature and after much research had found a small block that he considered was perfect for subdivision. He was working for a finance company and did not have the capital to finance the project. Helen saw this as Tom's big chance to prove himself and begged her parents to go guarantor. They were hesitant about doing it but finally gave in. The project was a stunning success and within 18 months they were all having a celebratory drink together. The Browns then slept easily again, knowing they did not have to worry about the guarantee.*

Spurred on by the success, Tom and Helen took on a bigger project using the same lending institution. As the lending institution did not ask for any fresh guarantees, Helen did not discuss the fine details with her parents. The new project went badly wrong and the Browns were shocked to find the guarantee that they thought had lapsed was still effective, because it was still held by the lender and had not been released. The Browns lost their home.

Salting It Away

Because of the way the income and assets tests for the aged pension work, many people have found it beneficial to "gift" money to members of their family. Even though it is technically a gift, in reality the money is being held by the family member in the role of unofficial trustee. There is a clear understanding that the money is to be "gifted" back to the parents if they need it.

Provided this gifting is done five years before the parents apply for the pension, or is limited to $10 000 per year, the parents may receive a higher pension. There is also little likelihood of the money being recalled by the parents.

Problems may arise if marital strife raises its ugly head in the family to whom the money has been given.

EXAMPLE: *Mr and Mrs White wanted to divest themselves of some assets to get the aged pension. However, there was a problem because their two sons earned high incomes and income tax would take nearly half of any earnings on money if it were placed in either son's name. After a family conference, they decided to "gift" the money to the wife of one of the sons because she did not work. After all, what could go wrong; they were happily married and seemed to be the perfect couple.*

Circumstances change. A few years later the son's wife caught him having an affair, which radically changed their relationship. Then, as far as she was concerned, the money was a genuine gift and she had no intention of giving it back.

That story may have had a different ending if the White's had invested the money in the son's name in an insurance bond or a friendly society bond. There would have been no annual taxable earnings to worry about, and after 10 years the son could have withdrawn the money free of tax if the parents wanted it back.

However, other problems can occur. If one of your children is holding a large amount of your money, and then gets into financial problems, there may be considerable tension if it becomes a choice of solving the problem with your money or losing his home. If he left your money untouched, and then went bankrupt, the money may still be taken by the Trustee in Bankruptcy to pay the creditors.

Buying Off The Plan

You intend to retire in five years and have been looking around for a unit at the beach. One Saturday morning you notice an advertisement for a building that will be completed in 18 months. You make enquiries and discover that you can "buy off the plan", which involves putting down a deposit of 5% on the purchase price of $250 000, and paying the balance when the building is completed. The real estate agent assures you that you can't go wrong as property values are booming, and the unit should be worth at least $300 000 by the time you have to pay for it.

You are somewhat reluctant, particularly about buying a place that is not completed, but you let yourself be seduced by the salesman's spiel and finally sign the contract.

The 18 months pass quickly, but when the time comes to pay the balance the finish is not quite as you had expected. To make matters worse, the property boom has now entered one of its regular slumps, and the developer has slashed the prices of the unsold units to $225 000 for a quick sale.

You consult your solicitor about getting out of the contract on the grounds of the unsatisfactory finish. She tells you this is a "grey" area and, while you may have a case, there is no guarantee you will win. If you take the developer to court, and lose, it may cost $50 000 for his costs and yours and you would still be forced to buy the unit. Sensibly you decide that you do not want the mental strain of court action, nor the possible costs, at this time in your life and you go ahead with the purchase of an overpriced unit that you don't like.

Maybe I've painted a gloomy picture of the worst that can happen, but every year many people are caught by buying off the plan. I'm not saying don't do it, for I know some people who have made good profits using this strategy. However, I am warning you to do your homework thoroughly, be aware of the pitfalls, and try to avoid it if possible. Think about it – if the rise in price was a certainty the developers would be unlikely to sell off the plan; they would wait as long as possible.

Lending Money On Mortgage

Earlier in this book I discussed lending money out on private mortgage through a solicitor. While this is a common form of investment you should be aware that recent amendments to the law have placed onerous duties on lenders. These laws require all sorts of documentation to be signed by the borrowers, and if this is not done properly the borrowers may have the right to deny owing the money.

If the borrowers can substantiate their claim that the lender did not complete the required documentation you may never get your money back.

The lesson here is if you lend money out on mortgage use only solicitors who are experienced in this field, and insist on a certificate from them that the borrowers have signed all forms that are necessary under the appropriate laws. This will enable you to take action against the solicitors if they fail to complete the documentation.

Borrowing With No Repayments

I am often asked by older people about borrowing money against the value of their home, and having the debt repaid from their estate. The institutions who make these loans usually secure them by a first mortgage over the house property and require no repayments until the house is sold. Then the loan, plus all accrued interest, falls due for payment.

The danger here is the effect of compounding. If the interest rate is 12% the debt doubles every six years, so a 65-year-old person who borrowed $10 000 today would owe $20 000 in six years, $40 000 in twelve years and $80 000 by the time they reach age 83. By then they could still be strong and healthy.

The best course of action depends on what the prospective borrowers perceive as their life expectancy, and whether they wish to leave any money to their estate. If possible, it is better to borrow the money from their children interest-free. The children would be better off to help now, and to receive the property when their parents die, than to force the parents to borrow and possibly see the value of the house lost in a rising debt.

If borrowing is the only course of action, wait as long as is practicable before taking up the loan, and borrow as little as possible.

Conclusion

This chapter has given you insight into the way financial problems can sneak up on you, but unfortunately it usually takes experience to spot the potential problems. Often this experience can be very costly. The best advice I can give is to learn from the experiences of others and don't be afraid to ask for expert advice when it is appropriate to do so.

That completes the first three sections of the book. Your knowledge should now be greatly expanded and you may be able to toss around terms like "master trusts", "capital gains tax" and "dollar-cost averaging" like an expert. Now it's time to change course and help you to embark on a voyage of discovery of our superannuation system. The importance of it in your retirement plans may be gauged by the fact that I have devoted the next 14 chapters to it. If you are like almost everybody I talk to, you will be confused about the subject and somewhat distrustful of it. That's a natural reaction, but stick with me – it is not so difficult once you get into it.

Summing Up

- Avoid higher-than-average returns.
- Be very careful of giving a guarantee.
- Understand the nature of continuing guarantees.
- Beware of putting assets in other people's names.
- If you lend money on mortgage, insist on a letter from the solicitor stating all requirements have been met.
- Buying off the plan can be dangerous.

18

SUPERANNUATION – WHAT'S IT ALL ABOUT?

Nothing is less worthy of honour than an old man who has no other evidence of having lived long except his age.

SENECA (De Tranquillitate)

Mention the word "superannuation" and most people will act as if you are about to launch into a discussion on nuclear science. They think it's too complicated, they don't understand it, and the continual changes have made them wary about using it.

Now I admit there have been many changes, and some parts of superannuation are complex indeed, but it is a superb investment vehicle when used properly. Furthermore, the whole focus of our retirement program is based on the premise that superannuation will gradually replace the aged pension for almost everybody; we cannot afford to keep paying pensions. This is why superannuation is likely to figure prominently in your retirement planning, and why nearly a quarter of this book has been devoted to superannuation and all the bits and pieces, such as allocated pensions and annuities, that go with it.

As you read the chapters in this section for the first time, try to focus on the broad principles and leave the detail for further study. Don't be concerned if you have some difficulty with the fine details – even though the principles are simple, there are still many transitional rules and some of the mechanics are quite complex. Remember, too, that much of the complex material affects less than 5% of our population, so don't let it put you off.

The best way to think about superannuation is to regard it a process whereby you deprive yourself of money to spend now, so it will be available to spend when you retire. You will find the rules relate mainly to tax concessions to encourage you to invest in superannuation, tax penalties if you try to squirrel too much away, and rules to stop you withdrawing it too soon.

By now you will realise the population of Australia is ageing and there are fewer and fewer workers to support the growing number receiving some kind of government assistance. To solve these problems the Federal Government is trying to:

1. encourage and compel people to provide for their own retirement through superannuation

2. reduce the number of people eligible for pensions by tightening the guidelines for pension eligibility.

3. encourage retirees to take their superannuation as an income stream (private pension) instead of a lump sum.

How Superannuation Evolved

The present concept of superannuation is that your employers, and possibly you, place money in a fund that enjoys tax concessions. It is left to grow in this fund, or in other superannuation funds, until you are ready to retire. Then you may enjoy further tax concessions if you use vehicles such as rollover funds and allocated pensions. Your contributions come from your after-tax dollars and your employer's contributions come, in part at least, from wage rises you didn't get. As you can see, you are the one paying for it in the long run.

It wasn't always like that. Until the early 1980s legitimate superannuation was generally available for government employees, and male white-collar workers only. After working at the same job for a year or two, an employee might be invited to join the company's superannuation scheme to which the employer contributed an amount equal to a percentage of the employee's salary. Usually the employee contributed something as well. The money was invested in fixed-interest securities and shares with the aim of providing a fund for the employee's retirement. Often, when retirement came along the employee took a pension from the fund. That was the forerunner of the allocated pensions that are so popular now.

Problems arose when people started changing jobs regularly. The funds used then were "defined benefit" funds, which I'll discuss in the next chapter, and usually the only money the resigning employee got out of the superannuation fund was a refund of his contributions plus 4% per annum interest. In most cases, the amount was so small that it was quickly frittered away.

As well as the problems with frequent job changes, there were abuses of the system. Unfortunately, there were many employers who used superannuation purely as a tax-saving device and many of the schemes that were set up in the 1970s were designed to minimise tax rather than provide benefits to employees. Typically, the employers would make a large tax-deductible contribution to their superannuation fund, then lend it back immediately to the employing company at minimal interest.

Ringing in the changes

The Hawke Labor Government totally changed the way superannuation worked. They legitimatised it by stamping out all the rorts that had crept in; they helped to make it universal by extending cover to all employees; and last, but certainly not least, they used it as a huge and quickly growing source of tax revenue. This growth in tax is discussed in the next chapter. They also made numerous changes regarding the amount you could have in superannuation when you retired. This is called your reasonable benefit limit (RBL) and will be covered later.

Because there have been so many "patch ups", as well as changes to the system, most people are wondering if it's all worthwhile, particularly as there is so much fear of more changes. However, although the changes have been continual, no retrospective laws have been passed and there has been a consistency in direction amid all the turmoil. The trends are:

1. to raise the taxes paid by the superannuation system
2. to limit the amount you can have in superannuation
3. to encourage you to take the benefit as a private pension, and not a lump sum, when you retire
4. to encourage "preservation"[1] of the money you have in superannuation till you retire.

Taxing the fund is short-sighted, as well as self-defeating, because the tax reduces the end benefits considerably. However, the other principles are logical. To limit the amount anybody can have in a low-taxed area is fair, preservation to retirement age is essential, and most retirees are better served with an income in

---

1   Preservation means that you cannot withdraw the money till you retire.

retirement instead of a lump sum. Let's look now at the finer details.

Who may contribute to super?

Only people who are gainfully employed, and are aged less than 70, may contribute to superannuation. However, if you are a member of a superannuation fund you may make further contributions to that fund for up to two years after you left your last job provided you are not permanently retired. The definition of "gainfully employed" is working 10 hours a week. No minimum amount of wage is specified.

KEY POINT: You must be gainfully employed and aged less than 70 to join a superannuation fund. "Gainfully employed" is a somewhat loose definition.

From 1 July 1997 a working spouse may make non-deductible contributions of up to $3000 a year for a non-working spouse, or for a spouse whose income is less than $10 800 per annum. Instead of a tax deduction, the working spouse will be able to claim a rebate of 18% for these contributions, so the maximum rebate able to be claimed will be $540. This may be of some use to people who have substantial sums in interest-bearing accounts, but when you consider that a person earning $10 800 a year is in the 20% bracket already, moving to a 15% bracket is not going to make a huge saving in tax.

Reasonable Benefit Limits

Reasonable benefit limits (RBLs) can be a complex topic for higher-income earners and a later chapter is devoted to it. To put it very simply, your RBL is the amount you may have in superannuation when you retire without being liable for excess benefits tax. Since 1 July 1994, almost everybody has a lump sum RBL of $400 000 (in 1994 dollars) and a pension RBL of $800 000.

KEY POINT: Your RBL is the amount you may have in superannuation without being liable for excess benefits tax.

How Much Can Be Contributed?

There is a limit to the amount that can be contributed in any one year as a **tax deduction**, but **no limit** on what you can contribute as an undeducted contribution. If you end up with more superannuation than the normal tax rules allow, you are said to be in an "excess benefit" situation, which may result in severe tax penalties. Undeducted contributions are not included when your RBL is worked out.

From 1 July 1994 the total amount of tax-deductible contributions from any source in a financial year is based on the member's age at tax-year end: At 1 July 1996 the figures were:

Age of member	Maximum deductible contribution
Under 35	$ 9 782
35 but under 50	$27 170
50 and over	$67 382

These limits are indexed to AWOTE^2 each 1 July.

KEY POINT: There is a limit to how much can be contributed as a tax deduction. It depends on your age. There is no limit for undeducted contributions.

Moving To A Lower Taxed Area

One of the greatest benefits of superannuation is that it enables you to move funds to an area where the tax is lower than if you paid it yourself. Our lowest marginal tax rate is 20%, which cuts in at $5400 a year; then the tax rates increase progressively until they reach 47% once you earn more than $50 000. Medicare levy is added to all these tax rates.

Suppose you were in the top tax bracket and earned $10 000 a year from your investments of $100 000. Tax plus Medicare levy would take 48.5% or $4850 from your earnings leaving you with $5150 or 5.15%. If that $100 000 earned $10 000 in your superannuation fund, tax would be 15% leaving you with $8500 or 8.5%. That's a huge difference in favour of the superannuation fund, and there's no Medicare levy.

KEY POINT: Superannuation enables you to move funds to an area where the tax may be lower than you would pay if the funds were held in your own name outside the superannuation system.

---

2 Average weekly ordinary time earnings.

Furthermore, the presence of franked dividends in the superannuation fund's income can reduce the effective rate considerably.

EXAMPLE: *You have $150 000 in superannuation and your fund has income of $11 000 for the year, which includes fully franked dividends of $4000. The imputation credits on the $4000 of dividend income are $1920. Tax is calculated thus:*

Total income	$11 000
Imputation credits grossed up	$ 1 920
Taxable income	$12 920
Tax thereon @ 15%	$ 1 938
Less *Imputation credits*	$ 1 920
Tax payable	$ 18

You can see that the franked dividend income has wiped out almost all the tax, and the fund income for that year is virtually tax-free. The tax benefits are substantial, but obviously the higher your marginal rate the more worthwhile it is to have funds in a lower-taxed environment. Just be aware that the price you pay is loss of access. However, for many this is an advantage because they cannot dip into it.

Tax-Deductibility Of Contributions

Superannuation contributions are a tax deduction to the employer who makes them, but there is no tax deduction allowed for any contributions made by employees. This may seem illogical, but you will find that logic is not one of the outstanding features of our superannuation and aged pension policy. Superannuation contributions may give rise to a partial tax deduction if made by a person who is self-employed. An example is given later in this chapter.

From 1 July 1998 all non-deductible contributions to superannuation will qualify the contributor for a rebate of 15% with a maximum of $3000.

EXAMPLE: *Geraldine pays $77 a fortnight ($2000 a year) into her employer's fund. Her tax rebate is 15% of $2000 or $300.*

Those who are not members of an employer-sponsored fund (these are mainly self-employed people) may claim a tax deduction of $3000 plus 75% of the balance of the contribution. This gives rise to great scope for tax planning.

EXAMPLE: *Dr Drake, aged 56, is expecting a taxable income of $70 000 this year and also has to pay tax this year on a realised capital gain of $20 000 after inflation adjustment. He has little superannuation and plenty of cash in the bank. He makes a contribution of $79 000, which entitles him to a tax deduction of $60 000 ($3000 + 75% of $76 000). This cuts his taxable income down to $10 000 and allows him also to slash his capital gains tax bill from 47% to 20%.*

As you can see there is no logic in the present system whereby employers get a full deduction, self-employed get a part deduction and employees get a rebate instead of a deduction. Self-employed people who want a full deduction can get it by forming themselves into a trust or a company, and higher-level employees can have their superannuation contributions paid from pre-tax dollars by using salary-sacrifice schemes.

A *salary-sacrifice scheme* occurs when staff negotiate a remuneration package containing a reduced actual salary coupled with high superannuation contributions paid by the employer. This suits the employer, who still gets the tax deduction (just like paying a higher salary), but does not have the other costs such as workers' compensation premiums and holiday pay that are normally added on to the cost of paying salaries.

The employees benefit because they get a higher after-tax income, part of which is invested at low tax rates. This will show how it works:

EXAMPLE: *Kevin and Marcia are 50 years of age, and intend to retire at 60. During their remuneration negotiations it is agreed that both will receive a rise of $10 000 a year. Marcia requests a salary increase of $10 000 to $60 000 per annum, but Kevin asks that he be paid a salary of $50 000 per annum plus $10 000 per annum paid by the employer into his superannuation fund. This is a tax deduction to the employer.*

Marcia loses $4840 of her $10 000 per annum salary increment in tax so that at the end of the year she has placed only $5160 of the $10 000 in her bank account. There is no group tax deducted from Kevin's $10 000 but the superannuation fund will pay a 15% tax on entry. Thus after a year the fund will hold $8500 where the earnings are taxed at no more than 15%.

Marcia is being taxed at almost 50% (47% plus Medicare) on the interest on her $5160 in the bank. After a year she has earned interest of $310 less tax $150 leaving a balance of $5320. Contrast this to Kevin's position where his share of the superannuation fund may have grown to over $9500 in a year. While Marcia's $10 000 pay rise has shrunk to $5320 in just one year, Kevin's has almost doubled that sum. The maximum lump sum tax that will be taken from that $9500 when the funds are withdrawn is 15% (it may be nil) and Kevin has the whole $9500 working for him at reduced tax rates until retirement. Even with no further contributions it may have grown to $22 000 when he turns 60.

Notice the outcome. Kevin's investment capital will grow faster and faster in a low-tax environment. Marcia is carrying such a tax burden that her money will never get a chance to grow properly.

It is different for those who are young. For example, salary packaging for superannuation may not suit Robin, who is 35. Instead of tying up money for at least 20 years in superannuation she may prefer to take the full salary and use the after-tax dollars to speed up repayments on her home mortgage. Alternatively, if her house is paid off, she may feel the $10 000 is better used to pay interest on a negative gearing project.

> KEY POINT: It is the tax-deductibility of contributions that gives superannuation its great attractiveness as a wealth-creation measure. Try to arrange your affairs so that the contributions come from pre-tax dollars not after-tax dollars.

How long can you stay in superannuation?

You cannot make contributions to superannuation after your 70th birthday, but you can retain money in your superannuation fund after age 70 as long as you are gainfully employed for at least 30 hours a week. Therefore, a person aged 80 who was working could still have funds in superannuation.

Once you reach 65 you are required to exit the fund unless you are working 10 hours a week.

Access to your Superannuation

The Government allows superannuation to have valuable tax concessions so that people who contribute to it will not be relying on welfare when they retire. This is why the laws regarding preservation (access to your superannuation) are continually being tightened. Obviously if we could access our superannuation prior to retirement there would be many who would find a good reason why they "had to have the money now".

From 1 July 1996 almost all superannuation benefits, with the exception of undeducted contributions made since June 1983 and certain resignation and retrenchment benefits, have been preserved. These exceptions will cease on 1 July 1999 when all contributions will be inaccessible till preservation age. The May 1997 Budget tightened the rules on preservation still further. From 1 July 1997, for those leaving Australia permanently benefits cannot be released until the owner has reached preservation age.

Preservation age is being slowly increased with the aim of having all benefits preserved till age 60 by the year 2025. Those aged 32 or more at 1 July 1992 are not affected by the changes. The phase-in schedule is:

Date of birth	Preservation age
After June 1964	60
After June 1963 and before July 1964	59
After June 1962 and before July 1963	58
After June 1961 and before July 1962	57
After June 1960 and before July 1961	56
Before July 1960	55

Those whose preservation age is more than 55 will still be allowed to retire at age 55 and obtain limited access to their lump sum benefits provided the balance of their superannuation benefit is taken as a non-commutable lifetime pension or annuity. From 1 July 1996 the amount of this lump sum benefit has been:

Age	Lump sum limit indexed to AWOTE
55	$30 000
56	40 000
57	50 000
58	60 000
59	70 949

Almost all of you will now have "preserved" benefits that cannot be withdrawn until you are aged 55 at least, and in a following chapter I will show you how to locate them on your superannuation fund statement.

Understanding the preservation rules is most important when you are deciding on your retirement strategy. There is no point in having a goal of retiring at 50 and living off your superannuation, or planning to buy a block of flats when you retire, if the money is locked up until you are at least 57 and a large part of it can then be taken only as an annuity.

> KEY POINT: There is a strong trend to restrict access to your superannuation benefits until you reach age 60 and retire. Make sure you know how much of your benefit is preserved and to what age.

Conclusion

Congratulations, you now have a basic knowledge of superannuation. You know how superannuation evolved to meet society's changing needs, and how the taxes on it grew to help feed the government purse. You understand that money in superannuation enjoys tax concessions so it can grow faster, and that there is a limit to how much you can contribute to this tax-advantaged area.

Next, we'll discuss how the superannuation system is taxed.

Summing Up

- Superannuation is the major plank of our retirement incomes policy.
- It is compulsory for employers to make contributions for their employees.
- Superannuation enables you to hold funds in a low-tax area.
- Contributions made by employers are tax-deductible; contributions made by employees are not tax-deductible.
- There is a limit to how much that can be contributed to superannuation as a tax deduction.
- The preservation age is being gradually raised to age 60.

19

TAXES ON CONTRIBUTIONS AND FUND EARNINGS

One of the greatest pieces of economic wisdom is to know what you do not know.

JOHN KENNETH GALBRAITH

Until the early 1980's superannuation was an investors' haven. There was no tax on contributions or fund earnings, and just a minuscule tax on lump sum payments out of the fund. Obviously there was quite an incentive to place money into superannuation. Then, in a series of revenue-raising exercises, the Hawke Labor Government imposed taxes on various sections of superannuation.

1. In 1983 they raised the tax on retirement payments from less than 3% to 30%, but introduced rollover funds as parking places for retirement monies.

2. In 1988 they raised the tax on the earnings of superannuation funds and rollover funds from nil to 15%.

3. In 1988 they reduced the tax on superannuation lump sums from 30% to 15% but, in lieu, imposed an entry tax of 15% on tax-deductible contributions to superannuation.

The change of government from Labor to Liberal in 1996 did not mean the end of the taxes. The Liberals went to the polls guaranteeing no changes to superannuation, but in the August Budget announced a 15% surcharge on contributions.

This trend to continually increase taxes on the fund is a strong reason to consider alternative investment strategies, but you should be aware that superannuation does still offer substantial tax concessions. Provided you stay in touch with your adviser you should be able to decide on a strategy that is appropriate for your own circumstances.

We'll now look at the taxes in detail.

Tax On Contributions

There was no tax on contributions until 1988. Then the Government slashed the tax on the post-1983 component to 15% from 30%, but in lieu introduced a 15% tax on those contributions for which a tax deduction is claimed.

There is no entry tax on contributions made since 30 June 1983 that have not attracted a tax deduction or a rebate. These are known as **undeducted contributions** and are returned to you free of any exit tax when you retire. Making undeducted contributions can be a vital element of your retirement strategy as they can increase the tax-free component of an allocated pension, as well as enabling you to move assets into the low-taxed superannuation area without an entry tax.

It is important to understand that the entry tax is not levied by deducting a flat 15% from tax-deductible contributions. It is calculated by treating the deductible contributions as taxable income of the fund. Consequently, imputation credits in the fund income can reduce the impact of the entry tax.

EXAMPLE: *You have $250 000 in your self-managed superannuation fund. The fund has investment income of $13 000 for the 1996/7 year, which includes fully franked dividends of $8000. Imputation credits on the $8 000 are $4 500. That year the fund also receives $20 000 of tax-deductible contributions. The tax for the year is calculated:*

Investment income	*$13 000*
Imputation credits grossed up	*4 500*
Deductible Contributions	*20 000*
Taxable Income	*37 500*
Tax on $37 500 @ 15%	*5 625*
Less *imputation credits*	*4 500*
Tax payable	*1 125*

If there had been no franked dividends in the income, and hence no imputation credits, the tax payable on the contributions of $20 000 and the income of $13 000 would have been $4950. The imputation credits wiped out the tax on the investment income and reduced the contributions tax from $3000 to $1125.

> KEY POINT: The 15% entry tax is levied only on contributions for which a tax deduction has been claimed. Franked dividend income in the fund can reduce the impact of it.

Contributions Surcharge

In the 20 August 1996 Budget the Howard Liberal Government announced a surcharge of 15% on future tax-deductible contributions where the member earned $85 000 or more. For surcharge purposes, total income is defined as taxable income plus deductible superannuation contributions. The surcharge is to be levied progressively over the $70,000 to $85,000 income range on the basis of 1% for each $1000 of income over $70 000. For example, if a person earned $70 000 a year and contributions from their employer were $8 000 a year, the income for surcharge purposes would be $78 000 a year, and a surcharge of 8% would apply to the $8000 of contributions. The $70,000 threshold will be indexed.

This surcharge will be in addition to the 15% contributions tax mentioned above. Unfortunately, as the surcharge is a charge and not a tax, franking credits cannot offset it.

> KEY POINT: The surcharge is an additional entry charge on deductible contributions on behalf of higher-income earners. Franking credits cannot reduce it.

Tax On Fund Earnings

Superannuation funds pay tax at 15% per annum on their earnings, which makes them an efficient vehicle in which to hold income-earning assets. Costs of running the fund and insurance premiums are allowable deductions, and imputation credits and depreciation allowances from property-based investments can reduce, or even eliminate, the tax altogether.

Allocated pension funds are tax-free funds so capital gains tax can be avoided if you convert your superannuation fund to an allocated pension fund before you cash in assets that carry a capital gains tax liability.

Tax On the End Benefit

This book contains an entire chapter on tax on the end benefit but I'll mention it briefly now for the sake of completeness. Until the 1983 changes, 5% of your termination payment was added to your taxable income, which meant the effective tax rate on that lump sum could be no more than 3%. The Hawke Government raised the tax on termination payments to 30% (later reduced to 15%) but, to avoid retrospectivity, dated the changes from 1 July 1983. If you started work in 1975, and retired in 1995 with a termination payment of $200 000, the total service period was 20 years divided into 8 years of "pre-1983 service" and 12 years of "post-1983 service". We usually refer to these terms as "pre" and "post".

Therefore the payment is split into 8/20 of pre ($80 000) and 12/20 of post ($120 000). To calculate the lump sum tax on the pre you add 5% of the $80 000 ($4000) to the owner's taxable income in the year the money was paid over. Provided the owner is 55 or over, the first $86 495 of the post is tax-free and the balance is taxed at 15% plus Medicare levy. Higher tax rates apply on the post if you cash in your termination payment before age 55.

Lump sum tax can be deferred if you place the money in a rollover fund or leave it in a superannuation fund. These issues are covered in detail in later chapters.

Conclusion

You should now understand the way the taxes work, and be able to discuss various tax-saving strategies with your adviser. Now we'll consider another major element – access to your money.

Summing Up

- The taxes on the superannuation system have been continually increasing.
- The 15% entry tax is levied only on deductible contributions.
- Superannuation funds pay tax at 15% on their earnings, but this can be offset by imputation credits in the funds' income.
- The surcharge cannot be offset by imputation credits.

20

ANALYSING YOUR OWN SUPERANNUATION

Success is being able to hire someone to mow the grass while you play golf for exercise.

ANON

Now you have an idea of the way superannuation works we can start the important job of analysing the superannuation you have accumulated so far. First understand there are two types of funds – **accumulation funds** and **defined benefit funds.** You are almost certain to have money in an accumulation fund, and there is a chance you may also have money in a defined benefit fund. Let's discuss both to enable you to identify the one you are in.

Types Of Funds

Accumulation funds

Accumulation funds work on the same general principle as bank accounts. Contributions are made, costs and taxes are deducted, and earnings are credited. At any stage, your entitlement is the balance in your account. Therefore, the amount you will have at retirement depends on the amount of contributions made, the earning rate and what costs and taxes were deducted. If you are in an accumulation fund you should receive an annual statement explaining the transactions. You are probably a member now of one of the compulsory superannuation funds that are accumulation funds. There is one major difference between a bank account and your account with an accumulation fund. The bank account cannot fall in value because of market fluctuations, but the balance in your superannuation fund can fall, unless the money is capital guaranteed.

It is a requirement of the superannuation regulations that members are kept well informed and, if you are in an accumulation fund, you should receive an annual statement along the lines of the specimen that follows. The law requires the statement to provide a lot of other information but the specimen statement provides the essential elements. Seek these out and make sure you understand them.

ABC PTY LTD - EMPLOYEES RETIREMENT FUND

Statement for year ended 30 June 1997.

NAME OF MEMBER: John Citizen

DATE OF BIRTH: 20/4/53

DATE JOINED FUND: 01/02/87

Balance at 1 July 1996	$9 312.22
Contributions by employer	$1 000.00
Contributions by employee	$ 500.00
Earnings for year @ 8.5% per annum	$ 865.50
Sub-total	$11 677.72
Less	
Contributions tax	$150.00
Administration fees	$75.00
Cost of life and TPD insurance	$112.50
Balance at 30 June 1997	$11 340.22

That's simple, isn't it – at 30 June 1997 you have $11 340.22 to your credit. This is your money and if you retired or resigned the money could be withdrawn, left to grow or rolled over to another superannuation fund. Which of these actions is appropriate depends on your age and whether the money is preserved. Notice how the contributions from your employer and from yourself have added to the starting balance, and how the fund earnings have made the balance still larger. See how the administration costs, the contributions tax and the life cover included in the fund have been taken from your accumulated balance. The 15% tax on the fund earnings would have been struck before the earning rate

(8.5% in this case) was declared, and the 15% tax on contributions applies only to the employer's contributions because the employees cannot claim a tax deduction for their contributions.

If you are self-employed, or have taken out additional superannuation through other institutions such as life companies and banks, you should still receive an annual statement direct from the fund manager providing similar details. Naturally, if you are an employee taking out extra superannuation, or a sole trader or working in partnership, there will be no employer contributions on this statement. All the money will have come from you.

> KEY POINT: Money in an accumulation fund grows because of contributions and fund earnings and is reduced by taxes, fees and the cost of insurance.

Defined benefit funds

You usually find **defined benefit funds** in career industries such as the Public Service and in large companies. You do not have a growing balance that you can verify each year because a defined benefit fund works on a different principle. Membership of a defined benefit fund carries a promise from your employer that you will receive a set sum on your retirement. This sum is defined by a formula that might read:

You may retire at age 60 with a lump sum of 5.44 times your final average salary over the last three years of your service.

The formula might vary if you leave at some other time such as at age 55 or 65.

Let's look at a defined benefit fund statement and compare it with the one from the accumulation fund shown previously.

The statement shows that the member, John Citizen, may retire at age 55 or after and indicates his lump sum payment as a multiple of his finishing salary. For example, if he chooses to retire at age 58 he will receive 5.8 times his salary for superannuation purposes as a lump sum. The salary for superannuation purposes is usually the average salary for the last three years. His superannuation salary at date of the statement is $35 000, so if he were 60 now he could retire with $203 000 (5.8 × $35 000). It is reasonable to expect salary for superannuation purposes will move somewhat in line with inflation. Therefore, it is fair to assume that members know at any time what their superannuation payout will be in today's dollars. Hence there is built-in inflation protection.

XYZ PTY LTD - EMPLOYEES RETIREMENT FUND

Statement of benefits as at 30 June 1997.

NAME OF MEMBER: John Citizen

DATE OF BIRTH: 20/4/53

DATE JOINED FUND: 01/02/87

SALARY FOR FUND PURPOSES: $35 000 a year

Retirement benefit multiple at age 55	5.2	$182 000
Retirement benefit multiple at age 58	5.8	$203 000
Retirement benefit multiple at age 60	6.1	$213 500
Death benefit at 30 June 1997		$245 000
TPD benefit at 30 June 1997		$245 000
Resignation benefit as at 30 June 1997		$10 625

Usually the employee contributes a percentage of salary and the employer contributes as much as is needed to provide the final benefit. If the fund is performing well, the employer may not have to make any contributions in some years – in depressed times the employer contributions might be substantial.

The point to note is that, apart from your own contributions, you do not have a growing balance as you would in an accumulation fund. Therefore, if you resign, your termination payment will be calculated according to the internal rules of the fund and you may receive little more than your own contributions plus interest. In the statement above you can see the resignation benefit is $10 625.

Comparing a defined benefit fund with an accumulation fund

A **defined benefit fund** is simpler for those employees who intend to stay with their present employers until retirement, for they have a good idea at all times of what their retirement entitlements will be. Also, these entitlements are always expressed in today's dollars.

However, there are possible problems:

1. Your employer might go broke and you may not get all you are entitled to. This is not a common occurrence, but it does happen.

2. You may opt for greener pastures when you go through your mid-life crisis and resign, leaving behind a lot of valuable

entitlements. Worse still, you may keenly desire to leave but, as you believe you cannot afford to resign, you waste a valuable part of your life working at a job you hate.

3. Your final entitlement is expressed as a multiple of your final average salary over a three-year period. If, for some reason, your rise up the corporate ladder slows right down, your final salary may be far less than you hoped. Remember, the final entitlement is a multiple of your salary, so a lower salary means a lower entitlement.

Defined benefit funds are losing popularity because:

1. employees are now much more mobile and few contemplate working for the one employer for their entire working life

2. employers do not like the uncertainty of having to pay large unknown sums in superannuation at some future date. With an accumulation fund their responsibility ends once they make the contributions into the superannuation fund. Then it becomes the responsibility of the trustees of the fund.

In contrast, an **accumulation fund** gives you the security of knowing that the balance in your name can be taken to the next job if you leave. It does have one major drawback; the fund may not produce the final superannuation benefit you had hoped for. This may happen because you, or your employer, chose a badly performing fund or because contributions were insufficient to bring about the outcome you were seeking.

The problem of an insufficient end benefit can be alleviated if you monitor your fund balance closely and "top up" the balance as necessary with extra contributions. I have stressed elsewhere the importance of an annual review of your affairs. Extra contributions may be made by way of salary sacrifice, but if you are not happy with the fund your employer has chosen you can take out additional superannuation through other fund managers.

Naturally the suggestion to increase your superannuation assumes you have the money available to do it.

> KEY POINT: In a defined benefit fund it is the employer's responsibility to ensure there are funds available at retirement to fund the promised benefit. In an accumulation fund there is no such promise. Therefore employees who are members of accumulation funds assume this responsibility.

Award Superannuation Schemes

The award superannuation schemes began when some strong unions got their employers to start making superannuation contributions for their workers in addition to the normal negotiated pay increases. Other unions got into the act and it became common when award negotiations were going on for part of a pay rise to be paid into the employee's superannuation fund instead of going directly to the employee. This caused problems because some employers had workers under many different awards, and some had won negotiated superannuation and others hadn't. You can imagine the confusion. But, to make it worse, many smaller employers refused to pay award superannuation at all. They believed as a matter of principle that employees should pay their own super.

Finally, the Government brought in the Superannuation Guarantee Charge legislation, which requires *all* employers to make superannuation contributions on behalf of their staff. Initially the level of contributions was equivalent to 3% of each employee's salary but it is being progressively raised to 9% of salary. These contributions are being paid by the employer in addition to the employees's salary, but the Government's intention is that future salary rises will be moderated to take into account the compulsory superannuation contributions paid by the employer. There have been strong moves to require employees to contribute a compulsory 3% of salary but, at date of publication, this is not yet law. During the phasing-in period, employers with national payrolls of less than $1 million paid less than larger employers. The rates are as follows:

Year	Payroll $1 million or less	More than $1 million
1994-95	4%	5%
1995-96	5%	6%
1996-97	6%	6%
1997-98	6%	6%
1998-99	7%	7%
1999-2000	7%	7%
2000-01	8%	8%
2001-02	8%	8%
2002-03	9%	9%

As you can see, annual superannuation rises occur until all employers are paying 9% of salary into superannuation for each employee. This is all part of the Government's plan to take people off the aged pension. Obviously a compulsory superannuation scheme must be an accumulation one, and it is now common for employees in defined benefit funds to have money in compulsory accumulation schemes too.

KEY POINT: Compulsory superannuation contributions under the Superannuation Guarantee Charge legislation are placed in accumulation funds.

Unfunded Funds

Many public sector workers are members of unfunded superannuation funds. These are defined benefit funds where the employer, a government body, does not maintain a separate superannuation fund but simply pays retirement benefits from the public purse as each employee leaves. Unfunded funds have become a "hot" issue because at date of writing there was over $60 billion of unfunded liabilities in existence. These liabilities have to be found by future governments from their current revenue.

If you are a member of one of these funds you will pay higher lump sum tax when you receive your benefit. This is because no progressive employer contributions are made on which the 15% entry tax can be levied. This is covered in detail later.

A Project For You

Now that you have a good grasp on the elements of super, let's start the vital task of analysing your present superannuation assets. First you should obtain your latest superannuation statements and decide whether you are a member of an accumulation fund or a defined benefit fund or both. The two examples at the start of this chapter will guide you, but ask your financial adviser if you are unsure. Bear in mind you may well be a member of both types of fund; the defined benefit fund you have been in for years, as well as a small accumulation fund set up for you because of the Superannuation Guarantee Charge.

While you are going through your papers, pull out any personal superannuation plans you may have taken out direct with any of the insurance companies or banks. They are always accumulation funds. Take particular note of the starting date.

If you are in a **defined benefit fund** you should think about the following:

1. What is the earliest age at which I am entitled to a retirement benefit? It is usually at least 55. Do I intend to stay until that age or am I likely to resign earlier? What will I get if I resign?

2. Is there life insurance in the fund? Does it cover me just for death or also for total and permanent disability? Is my state of health such that I can get replacement life assurance if I leave my employer?

3. If I intend to spend my working life with my present employer, can I "buy" additional benefits by making larger contributions or by buying back extra years of service? The amount you receive from a defined benefit fund takes into account length of service because there is a connection between service and total contributions, but some employers will let you make a lump sum contribution or increase your contributions to gain a higher end benefit.

If you are in an **accumulation fund** consider:

1. Who are my fund managers? How does their performance rate against other fund managers? If you are unsure, your financial adviser will be able to give you a list of comparative returns.

2. Have I the right to ask my employer to put my contributions in a different fund, or am I stuck with the one the employer chose? If I wish, can I roll my superannuation monies to another fund without penalty?

3. What is my fund's investment strategy? Remember, it may invest in a range of areas across cash, fixed-interest securities, shares and property. Is it a capital guaranteed fund, a capital stable fund or a market-linked fund? Is this appropriate for me at my age? Can I choose the risk level or must I stay with what everybody else has?

4. What is my estimated benefit at retirement if contributions continue at their present level?

5. Is this sufficient for my needs then?

6. If I increase my contributions will my employers increase theirs too? Some employers will do this.

7. Is there life assurance in the fund? Does it cover me just for death or also for total and permanent disability? What is the

cost of it? Does the cover reduce each year while the premium stays constant, or does the cover drop each year as the fund balance grows? Is my state of health such that I can get replacement life assurance if I leave my employer?

If you are a member of a personal superannuation fund taken out through a life company or a bank ask yourself the same questions. Also find out the yearly contribution, and what penalties you will incur if you stop payments and roll the proceeds over to another fund.

When you have finished doing this you will have acquired a good knowledge of the superannuation you have, and if you analyse it the way I suggested earlier you will know if it is sufficient for your retirement needs.

In the next chapter I'll show you how to decide on your own personal superannuation strategy. Meanwhile, let's discuss the value of having life assurance incorporated in your superannuation.

Life Assurance

The Superannuation Guarantee Charge superannuation does not make life assurance compulsory, but most employers are happy to have it included because it saves a little of the anguish if the breadwinner dies.

However, most of the compulsory schemes contain only a nominal amount of death cover, less than $75 000, and this is paid for out of the contributions. To save administration costs, some of the compulsory schemes simply allocate one dollar a week out of the contributions for life assurance. Because the premium is fixed, the amount of cover gradually drops, but this drop in cover is often made up by the growing value of the fund.

EXAMPLE: *At age 30 Tom has $75 000 of life cover in his fund and a balance of $5000. At age 45 his assurance is down to $50 000 but his accumulated balance has grown to $30 000. In each case $80 000 is available to the estate if he dies, although its real value has decreased as time passes because of inflation.*

A good employer superannuation fund will let employees vary the assurance to suit their individual needs. For example, whenever our firm has installed superannuation schemes for companies, we have tried to give employees the right to choose whether they want life cover and, if so, how much. The reason is that life assurance has a cost that is paid out of your fund balance and accordingly reduces the amount of money you have working for you.

Many superannuation funds will let the employee have up to $150 000 of death and TPD cover without a medical examination. That may still be inadequate, but at least assurance at this level can be a significant help to the surviving spouse with a young family. On the other hand, many single employees with no dependants have no need for life cover, and older working couples with no debts may well believe they can cope without assurance if their partner dies. In these cases it is a waste to spend those precious investment dollars on unnecessary assurance.

Most employer-sponsored superannuation funds include some life assurance for you and you should take it into account when you are calculating your life assurance needs. Remember, it is cheaper overall to include life assurance in superannuation because the funds usually have access to group assurance at cheap rates. Furthermore, if the contributions are being made as a tax deduction to the employer, the true cost of the contributions is much less than if they came from your after-tax dollars.

EXAMPLE: *Jack is aged 45 and earns $60 000 a year. He decides he needs $300 000 of life and total and permanent disability assurance but finds out the annual premiums are $1200. After speaking to his adviser he discovers they can be included in his superannuation policy for only $1100 per annum because the fund manager has access to insurance at wholesale rates. Jack arranges for his employer to increase the employer superannuation contributions by $1100 and reduce his salary by $1100. If it is done this way the cost to Jack in pre-tax dollars is only $1100. If Jack had arranged the cover for $1200 outside of the fund the cost to him in pre-tax dollars would have been over $2300.*

As you will learn later a major advantage is that, provided the superannuation is not in excess benefits, any death benefits paid to a spouse from a superannuation fund are free of lump sum tax.

Top-Up Superannuation

Most employees approaching retirement are going to receive superannuation payouts of far less than the $434 000 or so they may have as their reasonable benefit limit. If you are in this category, and have spare funds available, you should consider putting surplus money into "top-up" superannuation by way of additional contributions into your existing fund or by the purchase of single-premium **superannuation bonds.**

Why leave surplus funds in the bank or building society where you pay tax every year on the interest, or buy ordinary insurance bonds where the fund itself pays tax at up to 39% a year? By topping up your superannuation you transfer assets from an area where tax may be high, into an area where the present tax is no more than 15%. Thus the returns are higher as the superannuation fund pays tax of no more than 15%, and tax on the growth can be deferred until aged 65 by the use of rollover funds and even further if you start an allocated pension.

Conclusion

By now superannuation should be less of a mystery to you, particularly if you have taken the time to look critically at the latest statements from your own fund. Think of it as a strategy whereby you give up income today in order to spend it in retirement. To encourage you to provide for your retirement through superannuation, the Government lets your money enjoy tax advantages while you are working, and gives you further tax benefits when you start to use it. In the next chapter we'll try to discover what your own superannuation strategy should be.

Summing Up

- If you are a member of an accumulation fund you have a balance that you can verify regularly.
- Membership of a defined benefit fund offers you a promise that you will receive a specified sum when you retire after reaching a set age.
- Defined benefit funds are not appropriate for employees who change jobs regularly.
- Take the time to analyse your own superannuation statements to find out the value of your superannuation.
- Include your life cover in your superannuation if possible and have the contributions made from pre-tax dollars.

21

YOUR OWN SUPERANNUATION STRATEGY

Money is only good when you've got something else to do with it. You can lose everything, family, all your dreams, and still have a pocketful of money.

GEORGE FOREMAN

By now you should have a basic understanding of superannuation, know whether you are in a defined benefit fund or an accumulation fund and possibly have an idea if the superannuation you have is adequate. What do you do now? That depends on your age and the amount of money you have accumulated to date. Let me stress there is no set path you must follow, but the following hints may give you a guide for further discussion with your adviser. At all times keep the following in mind:

1. The strategy you adopt must be fairly simple and one that you can stick to.

2. Getting the highest rate of return on your funds is paramount.

3. The sooner you start, the more chance compound interest has to work its magic.

4. It is always better to keep control of your money than to lose access to it.

When you take the above into consideration, I recommend you place a low priority on superannuation if you are under 35. Concentrate on paying your home off, for that is a strategy that is simple and gives a high effective return. When you have achieved that goal you can reassess your plan and work out ways to invest the dollars you no longer have to use for mortgage payments.

Never forget that you lose access to money in superannuation until you are at least 55 or possibly 60. For younger people this may mean the money cannot be touched for 30 years or more. I believe locking up money for 30 years or more is not a wise move and, in any event, your employer will be contributing at least 9% of your wages to superannuation for you. This is quite a considerable sum.

If you are aged between 35 and 55, and have your home paid off, consult a financial adviser who will calculate what money you need to invest each year to retire with the income you require[1]. You will probably find a combination of some superannuation and negative gearing is the best way to go.

If you have a fairly large balance in superannuation now, seek expert advice before you make any more contributions so you don't fall into the excess benefit trap. This is especially important if you were aged under 50 at 30 June 1994. No longer will it be wise to "tip some money into super on 30 June to cut the tax down". Every case is different and must be decided in the light of all the other information.

> KEY POINT: The younger you are the more wary you should be of superannuation because of the loss of access for a long period, and the risk of more changes in the law.

Superannuation Versus Other Strategies

I know the perceived complexity of superannuation has turned many people off it, but don't make the mistake of putting superannuation in the "too-hard basket" because of the complicated rules. Without doubt, superannuation will be most worthwhile for many of you, even though it will not be as attractive for others. How do you know which category you fall into? By understanding a concept called the **doctrine of relative attractiveness.**

When you are dealing with your financial affairs you often have to choose one out of several available options. The major factor

---

1   You could also use the retirement program in my *Wealth Creator on CD-Rom.*

that influences your decision is how **attractive** one option is **compared** with another, which I referred to above as relative attractiveness.

For example, if you had a choice of borrowing money from one bank at 7% and another at 9%, you would choose the lower rate unless there were other factors such as high establishment charges or heavy ongoing fees to be taken into account. However, if the 9% rate was fixed, the 7% rate was variable and interest rates appeared to be on the rise, you may decide a fixed rate of 9% was a more attractive option.

Until 1983, placing money in superannuation was exceptionally attractive because contributions were tax-deductible, there was no tax on entry, no tax on fund earnings and an effective tax of 2% on exit. Now the relative attractiveness of superannuation when compared with other investments has decreased, because there are taxes on entry, taxes on fund earnings and an exit tax.

Your marginal tax rate is a most important factor when you are considering your attitude to superannuation, because making contributions to superannuation transfers money to a low-tax environment. Obviously, the desirability of placing money in superannuation increases as the difference between the tax paid by the fund and your own marginal rate grows.

EXAMPLE: *Dianne earns $60 000 a year and has a marginal tax rate of 47%. A tax-deductible contribution of $1000 through salary sacrifice into super is worth $470 in tax saved as well as giving her the ability to shift the earnings on $1000 from the*

47% bracket to the 15% bracket. If Ken has a marginal rate of 20% a tax-deductible contribution of $1000 saves only $200 and the earnings on the $1000 have been shifted from the 20% bracket to the 15% bracket. It is not nearly as attractive for Ken to make that $1000 contribution as it is for Dianne.

A reason investing outside of the superannuation area might be attractive is because superannuation funds cannot borrow. Borrowing for investment enables you to buy an asset today instead of possibly waiting years till you have the funds available to do it, and is also the best way to boost the rate of return on your funds invested. If you borrow to a level where negative gearing is involved, the potential returns are boosted still further.

This is why readers in the high income bracket are likely to find they can get better returns by borrowing for property and shares than by placing large sums of money into superannuation. There is an added benefit of acquiring assets through borrowing instead of building up funds in superannuation. Your money is not locked up till age 60.

Paradoxically, the more conservative higher-income investors may use a combination of techniques to achieve the best of both worlds. They could use their own self-managed superannuation fund to invest in fixed-interest securities and blue-chip shares without borrowing, but at the same time do some gearing into real estate outside the superannuation system.

EXAMPLE: *A self-managed superannuation fund had $100 000 invested in fixed-interest securities such as bonds returning $10 000 a year, and $100 000 in shares returning a fully franked $5000 a year. Tax-deductible contributions for the year were $20 000. Income tax is calculated thus:*

Income from shares and bonds	*$15 000*
Imputation credits	*$ 3 000*
Contributions	*$20 000*
Taxable income	*$38 000*
Tax @ 15%	*$ 5 700*
Less *Imputation credits*	*$ 3 000*
Total tax payable	*$ 2 700*

If there were no contributions, total tax would have been $2700 (15% × $18 000). This would have been eliminated by the imputation credits, leaving $300 of credits wasted. In the

above example we have used the $300 to reduce the effective tax
on entry to $2700 or 13.5% of the $20 000 contribution. The
overall effect is that the fund's earnings for the year are tax-free,
and the normal 15% entry tax has been reduced.

This may be more attractive than keeping the shares and bonds
outside the superannuation system if the investors are in high
personal tax brackets. They are still free to enjoy the benefits of
negative gearing as well.

The Common Choices

To help you plan your own strategy, let's look at the choices you
face from when you start work. Don't forget, everybody who is an
employee is now in a compulsory superannuation scheme that
may include a small sum of life assurance.

1. **Starting work.** This is when you should be learning money
   management skills and saving for a car and your first house.
   Rely on your compulsory superannuation at work and don't
   take out additional superannuation as you won't be able to
   withdraw it till you are at least 60.
2. **Couple who both work.** The main goal now is to get the
   house paid off as quickly as possible. Any money invested in
   repaying the house mortgage is earning the equivalent of the
   mortgage interest rate in a capital guaranteed environment.
   Superannuation cannot match that. The current preservation
   rules make additional superannuation particularly unattractive
   for women who intend to stop work permanently. Any funds
   they have in superannuation will be inaccessible till age 60 with
   the earnings taxed at 15% a year. If accumulated outside the
   superannuation system in the name of the non-working spouse
   the money can grow in a tax-free area with full access at all
   times. That is a more attractive option.
3. **House paid off.** This is where the choices get interesting. If
   you are on a high income, it is almost certain there will be large
   contributions being made into a superannuation scheme by
   your employer and there is probably no point in your putting in
   extra contributions. You may consider a negative-gearing
   program if you are an aggressive investor, and possibly think
   about putting money away for children's education in unit
   trusts or friendly society bonds. If you earn a moderate income,
   you may not feel comfortable with borrowing a large sum for

an investment property. Possibly a regular saving program into unit trusts or some top-up superannuation may be appropriate for you. At all times the marginal tax rate of your partner must be taken into account.

4. **Nearing retirement.** By now you should be near the peak of your earning capacity. Pouring money into superannuation is probably a good plan because you should not be worried about losing access to your money for a relatively short time. You will need to take expert independent advice about the options open to you, but it is likely that heavy contributions of top-up superannuation will be a good strategy if you are under-funded now. Don't worry if you can't claim a tax deduction for the contributions because non-deductible contributions don't incur a 15% entry tax, nor do they count towards your reasonable benefit limit.

Some Common Questions

Question: How do I know the Government won't change the rules again?

Answer: I have no doubt they will be changed many times in the future. However, all governments are aware of the rapidly ageing population and the growing welfare bill, so there is no reason for any government to make superannuation so unattractive that nobody will want it.

Question: Surely I am better off investing in such areas as my own home and in negative gearing? At least I know they can't get me there.

Answer: You may be right, but see the answer to the previous question – how can you be sure of anything a government will do in the future? There have long been cries to put a wealth tax on family homes over a certain value, to restore death duties and to outlaw negative gearing. I am not saying these will happen but who knows? Maybe these areas, and not superannuation, will be attacked if the pressures continue.

Question: We hear about these millions of dollars that will be coming to us in 40 years' time. Where will the money come from?

Answer: $1 today will be equivalent to $5 in 40 years' time if inflation runs at 4%, so $1 000 000 then will be worth only $200 000 in "real" money. Superannuation funds invest in cash, property and shares and receive money from contributions and earnings. It is paid out in payments to retirees and then to surviving spouses and eventually families. It does not go out of circulation, it just keeps changing hands.

Question: Is it worth starting my own self-managed fund?

Answer: Self-managed funds are covered in detail in the next chapter, but to put it simply you would need to have existing superannuation assets of at least $100 000 to make it a worthwhile proposition because of the costs involved in administration. Then you have to consider if your time would be better spent on improving your business or your skills, or in having more leisure time.

Conclusion

You have now analysed your own superannuation and should be well on the way to formulating your superannuation strategy. If the last three chapters have been heavy going, take a break and then read them again before going any further. The next chapter is about starting your own superannuation fund, but this will not be appropriate for many readers, so if it doesn't affect you, skim through it quickly before proceeding to the chapter on rollover funds that follows it.

Summing Up

- Superannuation enables you to transfer money to a tax-advantaged area and then withdraw it at retirement as a tax-advantaged income stream.
- The continual changes, and the strong possibility of your money being inaccessible till age 60, are strong reasons to consider the relative attractiveness of other investment strategies.
- The older you are now the more attractive is superannuation.
- Superannuation is particularly unattractive for a woman who intends to stop work when she is young, and stay out of the workforce for many years.
- Your marginal tax rate is a major factor when deciding how much money to place in superannuation.

22

STARTING
YOUR OWN
SUPERANNUATION
FUND

The most popular labour saving device is still money.

PHYLLIS GEORGE

On 1 July 1994 a new set of rules came into place for self-managed superannuation funds. The new rules impose tough obligations on those who run the funds and the question asked continually is "Has it become too difficult for me to run my own fund?"

The answer is an unequivocal "no". It is certainly still viable, and in some cases advisable, to have your own self-managed superannuation fund, but there are four major factors that will influence your decision:

1. The amount of assets the fund will hold. If it does not contain at least $100 000 the setting-up costs and the annual expenses are not worth the exercise.

2. You must have an occupation that makes it practicable for you to have your own fund. If you are an employee of a major company it would be unlikely that you would be allowed to transfer your present balance in your employer's fund to your own fund. If your employer's fund is a defined benefits fund, it would not be possible to transfer your balance because, as you now know, defined benefits funds don't work like that. Self-employed people such as doctors and lawyers, as well as those

who run their own businesses or have large amounts rolled over, are perfect candidates to start self-managed funds.

3. You must have the time and the skill to handle it. This need not be as scary as it sounds because it usually involves knowing who to hire to do these tasks. I have my own self-managed superannuation fund and my accountant does all the book work, leaving me to do the investment. As my fund invests mainly in managed funds such as equity trusts, my job consists solely of working out the sectors in which I want the fund's money to go, choosing which fund managers to invest it with, and then writing out cheques as surplus money becomes available to invest.

4. You must be the type of person who understands the importance of carrying out your legal responsibilities. There are many people who run small businesses who are honest in every way and who are efficient in running these businesses but are slack when it comes to their statutory requirements. They mean to have the annual general meeting but forget, they intend to keep better records but spend the time helping one of their clients. If you are like this, don't try to run your own superannuation fund.

> KEY POINT: It may be worthwhile starting your own self-managed superannuation fund if the asset balance is over $100 000 and you have the time and the skill to run it.

In this chapter the term "self-employed" includes people who are employees of their own business. When you are an employee of your own company, instead of trading as a sole trader or a partnership, the employing company is entitled to a full tax deduction for the superannuation contributions it makes on your behalf.

Why Bother?

Self-managed funds are for those who like to take a hands-on approach to investment. I may not get any better returns by running my own fund than I would get if I simply invested in "balanced" or "growth" superannuation bonds with some of the leading fund managers, but I enjoy the fun of planning my own asset allocations, and of moving money around the various sectors and managers.

There are also many people, particularly those who run businesses, who don't like having their affairs in the hands of others. They are happier doing it themselves even if they don't always do it as well. These are the ones who choose their own shares and often put property in their superannuation funds.

Starting Your Fund

The *Superannuation Industry (Supervision) Act 1993,* known as SIS, states that only "regulated" superannuation funds are eligible for tax concessions. As saving tax is the main reason for being in superannuation, it makes sense to ensure your fund complies with the rules. Giving full details of all the rules is beyond the scope of this book, but if you wish to start your own fund you will need to take expert advice from your accountant, financial adviser and possibly your solicitor to make sure you get it right.

The main initial jobs are appointing a trustee for your fund, having a trust deed drawn up, and establishing the necessary records of the fund. There are firms who specialise in doing all this, and it's usually only a matter of contacting them through your accountant. In a day or so a pile of documents will arrive on your desk and your fund is going. The total cost should be around $500, but will be more if you decide to have a company as trustee for you – then you will also have the costs of forming the trustee company.

Most small superannuation funds appoint the proprietors of the business as trustees, but I prefer a company as trustee because you don't then have the problem of what to do if a trustees dies. I run my business through a family trust so, for me, it's a simple matter of using the same company to act as trustee of the family trust as well as the superannuation fund.

Because the Government wishes to ensure superannuation funds are run properly and provide adequate information to their members, the main thrust of the regulations is to lay down rules for the trustees' behaviour and for adequate and regular reports to members. For example, members of all funds must receive detailed statements of their accounts every 12 months, and be advised promptly of any material changes in the funds that may affect their investments. Funds that have fewer than five members have less rigorous reporting requirements than larger superannuation funds.

It is interesting to note the change in approach to breaches of the rules. Under the old system, the Tax Office had the power to take away the tax concessions enjoyed by the superannuation fund in the event of irregularities. However, this approach did not have the desired result, for it punished the members of the fund who may have been innocent victims and who may have already suffered financial loss because their fund had not been properly run. Now it is the trustees, or the directors of the trustee company, who are punished.

KEY POINT: The trustees of the fund are responsible for ensuring the fund complies with the rules. Failure to comply can result in heavy fines and/or gaol sentences.

Once your fund is running it works like a small business. You have a bank account that accepts superannuation contributions as well as income from the fund's investments, and pays out such items as fund expenses and benefits to members. Each year you, or your accountant, will have to prepare a full set of financial statements and prepare and file a tax return. The fund must be audited every year and a report sent to the Insurance and Superannuation Commission, which is the watchdog authority for the superannuation industry.

The bookkeeping is quite simple and there is relatively little administration to do. Once the fund is going, it should be easy to maintain as long as you keep the records up to date and attend to all the duties, such as having regular meetings and sending required reports to members. These jobs are the responsibility of the trustees, who face heavy penalties if they are not done properly.

Which Assets To Buy?

If you are thinking about starting your own fund you must be aware that there are restrictions on what the fund can do and on the type of assets in which it can invest. The trustees must ensure any investment made by the fund is sound, is non-speculative, is producing a demonstrably commercial rate of return and would not prevent the trustee paying benefits as they fall due. Furthermore, the transactions must be at arm's-length, which is an accounting term for saying that the parties cannot be associated. For example, members of the fund cannot sell their own assets to that fund.

The following are just some of the assets that a superannuation fund may *not* invest in:

- undeveloped land
- residential property held for private use such as the family home
- partly paid shares
- futures contracts.

Also, it may not be involved in carrying on a business because this is regarded as being of a speculative nature. A member of the audience at one of my lectures told me he had been advised to get his superannuation fund involved in "spec" building. This seemed a great idea to him, because superannuation funds pay tax at only 15% on their earnings, so he had gone ahead and bought five vacant blocks using the superannuation fund's money. He got a rude shock when I told him what he had done was illegal and he was faced with all the costs of transferring the land to another entity.

> KEY POINT: There are certain assets in which a superannuation fund may not invest, and it may not operate a business.

Furthermore, a superannuation fund is not allowed to borrow money. This is because the regulators believe that borrowing introduces a higher level of risk and a fund that borrows is not as safe as one that doesn't.

You may not agree with this and believe, as I do, that a sound level of gearing is one of the best vehicles around with which to build wealth. Nevertheless, the law must be obeyed, and in any event, the effectiveness of negative gearing depends on a high marginal tax rate to produce the largest possible tax refund from the Tax Office. Even if superannuation funds could borrow, who in their right mind would go into negative gearing using a vehicle that paid 15% tax at most? You would be negating the tax benefits.

Therefore, a sound principle is to refrain from buying property in the name of your superannuation fund. It is better to buy it in your own name, or that of your family trust, and gain the benefits of negative gearing in the names of the taxpayer with the highest marginal tax rate.

KEY POINT: A superannuation fund cannot borrow,
therefore you can usually generate better returns by buying
property outside the fund using gearing.

Setting An Investment Strategy

The rules require that all superannuation funds formulate an
investment strategy in the light of:

- the likely return from the fund's investments, having regard to
  its objectives and the timing of future benefits to members
- the diversification and risk of the investment mix
- the liquidity of the fund's investments
- the ability of the fund to discharge its obligations.

This has to be in writing and is best done in conjunction with
your adviser, who can prepare written recommendations about
your present and proposed investments. Remember, a trustee has
definite obligations to ensure the fund performs well and failure to
take appropriate advice may be a breach of this requirement.

So what do you put in the fund? The following are some of the
assets that are eligible:

- shares in listed companies
- debentures issued under a prospectus
- interest-bearing deposits
- approved unit trusts
- investment property
- life policies
- public securities
- foreign currency accounts in major currencies.

There are others, but the ones I have listed are the main ones.
As you can see the range is broad, but the cardinal rule is that a
superannuation fund must pass the sole-purpose test. That is, the
sole purpose of the fund must be to provide retirement benefits for
its members. Therefore, the trustee of the fund, probably you or a
company controlled by you, has to be able to justify any
investment decision to the world at large. Obviously, buying a little
beach house in the fund's name for the purposes of great
Christmas holidays would not pass the test.

KEY POINT: A superannuation fund must pass the sole-purpose test. That is, it must be run for the sole purpose of providing retirement benefits for its members.

The best strategy is to load your superannuation fund with income-producing assets such as debentures and bond trusts and then add an appropriate amount of shares paying franked dividends. The franking credits that go with the dividends can substantially reduce the tax paid by your fund.

What we are trying to do is to create wealth for you and save tax as well. For an effective strategy, this wealth should be spread over a range of assets in a tax-effective way. Wouldn't it be silly to be paying tax at up to 47%, plus Medicare levy, on the income from interest-bearing accounts, shares, debentures and bonds in your own name when, with the right asset mix, you could let the income from them compound tax-free in your own superannuation fund?

Doesn't it also make sense to gear your property and keep it outside the superannuation fund and enjoy the benefits of negative gearing at the top marginal tax rate?

Reduce Capital Gains Tax

Your superannuation fund can be an important tool in reducing or even eliminating capital gains tax. Maybe you are an investor who likes to try to time the share market and there comes a time when you feel the bull run is ending and it is time to take some profits. The problem is that, if you sell shares and share-based investments in your own name to lock in those profits, you pay up to 47% capital gains tax. It makes the exercise hardly worth it. It is much less painful if those investments are held by your superannuation fund because here you pay no more than 15% capital gains tax.

An even better strategy is to hold your capital profits until you retire and then convert your superannuation fund to an allocated pension fund. Allocated pension funds are tax-exempt, so you can do all the buying and selling you wish in that fund and pay no capital gains tax at all.

Unfortunately, you can lose out on tax advantages by holding shares in your superannuation fund, after it becomes a tax-exempt fund, because you lose the benefit of the imputation credits. How's this for a winning strategy:

You build up your superannuation fund with shares and share-based investments, as well as cash and bonds, during your working life. When you retire you convert the fund to an allocated pension fund, which enables you to sell all the shares free of capital gains tax. If the shares remained in the tax-free allocated pension area, the franking credits would be wasted. You then make a lump sum withdrawal by commuting part of the pension and use that money to buy shares and share-based investments in your own name, or by simply making the lump sum payment by way of a transfer of the shares **in specie.**[1]

This strategy enables you to enjoy tax-free growth in the superannuation fund during your working life, and still retain the asset in your name, or that of your family, when you retire.

Conclusion

After reading this chapter you should appreciate that it is feasible to have your own superannuation fund if you are self-employed, or have large amounts in rollover funds, and are prepared to handle the responsibilities that go with running it. However, I cannot stress too highly that there are heavy penalties for non-compliance with the rules, so don't enter into the responsibility of forming your own fund without seeking expert advice.

Now that you are an expert on superannuation funds, we'll move on to the next stage, rollover funds.

Summing Up

- It is still possible for self-employed people to run their own superannuation funds.
- The trustees of the fund are responsible for running it properly.
- The fund cannot borrow or carry on a business.
- There are certain assets the fund may not buy.
- The fund must have a written investment strategy.
- Superannuation funds are good vehicles for reducing tax.

---

1. *In specie* means that the distribution is made in kind (i.e. by transferring the shares themselves) instead of cash.

23

ROLLOVER FUNDS

There are two classes of forecasters. Those who don't know and those who don't know that they don't know.

JOHN KENNETH GALBRAITH

Rollover funds play a central role in retirement planning for almost everybody, so it is vital that you gain a sound knowledge of them. You won't be short of offers and, if you are nearing retirement, you would have seen advertisements everywhere inviting you to seminars where financial advisers will discuss the advantages of rollovers. It's certainly a good idea for you to go to at least one of these seminars, but I have found that many people come away more confused than ever.

To try to make it easier for you I will explain the history of rollover funds in this chapter and discuss the fundamentals in a simple way. This should give you some basic knowledge, but be aware that the topic can get a little complicated, so don't despair if it doesn't all click on the first reading.

Let's start with a simple definition:

A rollover fund is a place where you may keep some of the money you receive as a result of leaving your job so it will be available for you when you retire.

By "rolling" this money into a special fund, you set it aside where it is kept separate from your other funds. This gives it a much better chance of being kept intact to enable you to spend it in retirement.

It is important to understand that a rollover fund is taxed like a superannuation fund, that is, at 15% per annum on its earnings, so having money in the rollover area is really no different from having it in superannuation. In fact, you will soon learn why superannuation funds are fast becoming the most popular places for your rollover money.

Before rollover funds came into being in 1983, most people did not keep money they received from leaving a job in a separate account. Instead they used it to pay debts, or buy a car, or put it in their everyday bank account where it became mixed up with their other money and was often quickly spent. Consequently, it was never available to help them in retirement. This did not bother most retirees – they knew they had the aged pension to fall back on. Now access to the aged pension is being progressively tightened, and those who don't look after the money they get when they leave a job to go to another might regret it when they finally stop work.

The Birth Of Rollover Funds

Rollover funds came into being as a result of a taxing measure when, in 1983, the Hawke Government took a new approach to superannuation. First, it tried to make superannuation available for everybody in a way that would provide genuine retirement incomes. It did this by encouraging compulsory superannuation and by closing the loopholes that had allowed many small businesses to rort the system.[1]

Second, the Government decided to use superannuation as a major source of extra taxes. Prior to 1983, the tax on termination lump sums was found by adding 5% of the lump sum to your taxable income. If we assume, for simplicity, that the top marginal rate was 50%, it is obvious that the tax on lump sums could then be no more than 2.5%.

EXAMPLE: *You received a termination payment of $100 000 when you left your job. No tax was taken from it when you got it but you had to add 5% of it ($5000) to your taxable income in the tax year that you received it.*

There were no facilities to defer this tax, and there was no encouragement to keep the termination payment intact. That is why it became customary to retire in early July so your taxable income was low for the year in which you had to add 5% of your termination payment to it.

---

1. I covered these in detail in *Making Money Made Simple*.

There was also no tax then on money contributed to superannuation, and no tax on the superannuation fund's earnings. These were introduced in 1988.

The Hawke Government started the pillaging of our superannuation monies by raising the tax on termination payments to 30%. However, to avoid the stigma of retrospectivity the increased tax applied only to that portion that related to "post" 1 July 1983 service. Pre-1983 payments were taxed as before; 5% of the lump sum was added to taxable income.

This is how the terms "pre" and "post" that you hear tossed around in every retirement seminar originated.

EXAMPLE: *Mary started work in her present job in July 1973 and retired in June 1996 with a lump sum of $230 000. She has 10 years of pre-1983 service and 13 years of post-1983 service. Therefore, the lump sum splits into 10/23 pre ($100 000) and 13/23 post ($130 000).*

That hasn't been too difficult, has it? You will come to an entire chapter on the lump sum tax soon. However, we'll now think about the two incentives the Government introduced to encourage people to save their termination money for retirement. Remember the population is ageing and the funds for pensions are shrinking.

1. It introduced rollover funds. If you placed your money in one of these, you could defer paying the lump sum tax until you withdrew monies from the rollover fund. This enabled you to earn money on the taxes you owed the Government. Furthermore, these rollover funds paid no tax prior to 1988, so by leaving your money in them you enjoyed tax-free growth.

2. It introduced an incentive discount. If you left your termination monies intact till after your 55th birthday you paid only half-price tax on the first $55 000 of the post component. Therefore, this first $55 000 was taxed at 15% not 30%. Naturally Medicare levy was added.

That is how the concept started – as a tax-free place to keep your retirement funds.

KEY POINT: A rollover fund is a place to keep a termination payment. You pay less lump sum tax if you leave the money untouched till you are 55.

The Taxes Increase

Governments are always hungry for money, and in 1988 the then Federal Treasurer Paul Keating suddenly realised he had made a dreadful blunder. He had raised taxes on lump sums from 2.5% to 30%, but was unlikely to get much benefit from the measure – we may still be at work while his government may have left office. He had introduced one of the most unpopular taxes since the Boston Tea Tax, but was getting little benefit from it.

To rectify this unhappy situation, he performed another economic miracle. He chopped the 30% exit tax in half, and imposed a 15% entry tax on tax-deductible monies going into superannuation while slashing the exit tax on the post-1983 component to 15%.

Now a tax of 15% at the start of an investment, as well as a tax of 15% on the end benefit, gives an investor the same dollar return as if the whole lot had been taxed 30% at the end. The major difference is that the Government of today receives half of the lump sum tax **now**, instead of waiting for 30 years or more when a future government would get their hands on it. The reduction from 30% was phased in over a five-year period that finished in 1993 and the rates of lump sum tax on the post-1983 component are now:

Aged under 55	20% on the post-1983 component plus Medicare levy
Aged 55 and over	First $86 495[2] Nil
	Balance 15% plus Medicare levy

The tax on the pre-1983 component remains unchanged; 5% of it is added to your taxable income in the financial year it is withdrawn.

The Components of a Termination Payment

Money cannot be placed in a rollover fund unless it originates from an **eligible termination payment (ETP)**. The term ETP

---

2. This sum is indexed to average weekly ordinary times earnings (AWOTE).

refers to monies falling due on "termination" of a job and that are "eligible" to be rolled over. They include all superannuation entitlements, accrued sick leave and severance payments. An employee leaving a job may be entitled to some or all of the above, and they are all eligible to be rolled over. Almost certainly there will be other monies such as accrued long-service leave and accumulated holiday pay that are **not** ETPs, and therefore **cannot** be rolled over.

The superannuation payment may consist of the accumulated balance of both employee and employer contributions together with their earnings. Probably part of the superannuation may have to be "preserved" in a superannuation fund or a rollover fund until the employee retires on or after age 55.

As you can see, only some parts of most termination payments are eligible to be rolled over. It is the parts that can be rolled over that comprise the eligible termination payment (ETP). The ETP can have up to four components and it is vital for effective tax planning that you understand the sequence:

- Component (a) Invalidity component
- Component (b) Pre-1983 component
- Component (c) Undeducted contributions
- Component (d) Post-1983 component.

Until July 1994 there was also a concessional component that arose if there was an early retirement scheme, invalidity or redundancy. It was the difference between what the employer should have paid if there was a voluntary termination on that date and what was actually paid – in other words, a "golden handshake".

EXAMPLE: *A television personality was retrenched – her contract had 24 months left to run at $4000 a month, which totalled $96 000. The station paid her exactly $146 000, being the balance of the contract plus $50 000 as a special payment. Only the $50 000 could be styled "concessional component" because it was the gratuitous payment made by the employer.*

The concessional component still exists where it formed part of monies rolled over prior to 1 July 1994, but its amount does not grow. Any earnings on it become intermingled with the pre- and post-1983 components.

From 1 July 1994 the amount that can be paid as a bona fide redundancy or an early retirement payment has been severely limited. From that date the amount is limited to $4180 plus $2090 for each completed year of service with the present employer. These payments are exempt from tax, but they are *not* ETPs and cannot be rolled over.

Monies in excess of the $4180/$2090 formula are treated as an unfunded **ex gratia** eligible termination payment. Depending on your age, length of service and amount of other superannuation, you could lose up to 31.5% of the payment if you do not roll it over.

Component (a) Invalidity component

This essentially replaces the old concessional component mentioned above. It may occur when people's employment is terminated because of their mental or physical incapacity to engage in their present employment. For example, an airline pilot who failed a medical may qualify for an invalidity payment even though he could do other work. These payments are tax-exempt and they can be rolled over. The amount does not grow and the earnings become part of the pre- and post-1983 components.

Component (b) Pre-1983 component

The pre-1983 component is a proportion of what is left of the ETP once any concessional or invalidity component has been deducted. It is calculated on a pro rata basis in the ratio of pre 1 July 1983 days and post 1 July 1983 days of service.

The "pre-1983" service may carry valuable benefits by minimising the overall tax payable so it is important to maximise it. The commencing date of the pre-1983 component is the date the employee started work with the employer, **provided the employee is a member of the employer-sponsored scheme on retirement.**

> **EXAMPLE:** *Carla started work at Ace Pty Ltd on 1 July 1977 and joined the staff superannuation scheme on 30 September 1989. Her service for lump sum tax purposes is deemed to start from 1 July 1977. When Carla changed jobs in 1994 she rolled over the ETP. This enabled her to retain the original starting date of 1 July 1977 with a subsequent large reduction in eventual lump sum tax.*

Another way to maximise pre-1983 service is to locate a still-current superannuation policy that was started years ago. You are entitled to nominate the commencement date of the policy as the deemed starting date of all eligible service provided the old policy and any subsequent ETPs are rolled into the same fund at some stage.

Component (c) Undeducted contributions

This is the total of employee contributions made since 1 July 1983 for which no tax deductions have been allowed. These are returned to the employee tax-free and their total does not count for reasonable benefit level purposes. In the next chapter we shall see how valuable they can be in saving lump sum tax. Their value does not grow because all their earnings are added to the pre and post components.

Component (d) Post-1983 component

This is merely the balance of the lump sum. Because of the way the calculations work, it may sometimes be a negative amount. If this happens it is reduced to nil and the "pre" is altered accordingly.

Why Roll Your Money Over?

There are five reasons it may be appropriate to roll over your ETP instead of taking the money and investing it elsewhere. They are:

1. To defer payment of your lump sum tax and have the money that is due in lump sum tax working for you.
2. To reduce your lump sum tax by deferring withdrawal until you turn 55 if you are under 55 when you receive the lump sum.
3. To hold funds in a low-taxed area. Rollover funds pay tax at no more than 15% in contrast with the lowest marginal tax rate, which is 20% once you earn more than $5400 a year.
4. Because it is a "preserved" benefit and must be kept in the superannuation rollover area until you turn at least 55 and stop work. Once termination payments did not have to be preserved, but the preservation age is being slowly raised to 60 and the preservation rules are being continually tightened to prevent people spending their termination monies before they retire.
5. To retain money in the superannuation area so you can start an allocated pension and enjoy the tax benefits it gives.

Rolling Over

Let's quickly review what we have learnt so far. A rollover fund is a fund where you can invest an ETP with the result that lump sum tax is deferred until you make a withdrawal. The system works on the "carrot and stick" approach and is designed to encourage you to leave the money intact till retirement. The fund pays tax on its earnings at 15% per annum, but this may be reduced if the fund receives income from franked dividends. Lump sum tax is payable on a pro rata basis on any money withdrawn from the fund.

The money may stay in the rollover area until you are 65 and at that stage must be withdrawn unless you are still working at least 10 hours a week. Withdrawals before your 55th birthday suffer a higher tax than those after that date, and the loss of the earnings on that part of the ETP that represents the lump sum tax due can be considerable. You will read in the next chapter how your money can grow faster if you opt for a part pension and that, by starting an allocated pension or converting your entire lump sum to an annuity, you can escape the lump sum tax altogether.

Leaving Your Job Or Retiring

Your rollover money is created if you receive an ETP when you leave a job or retire. You may also receive an ETP as a beneficiary if somebody dies and leaves certain benefits to you – this situation is covered in chapter 31.

There is always some lump sum payment made when a person leaves a job but the amount of it, and the make-up of it, depend on the circumstances. If you are young, and have been with that employer for a short time, you may get only some accrued holiday pay, in which case there might be only a little superannuation to roll over.

At the date of your resignation, your superannuation entitlements will be held in the employer's own fund, or in an external fund. If they are in the employer's fund you will almost certainly be required to withdraw them and, if they are preserved, to roll them into another fund.

If the money is in an external fund, you should ask your adviser if it should be left there, or rolled elsewhere. The factors in making this decision are your age, the amount involved and the fees and performance of the fund in which your accrued superannuation is presently placed. For many younger people this may be your first experience with an adviser, so take note of the comments I made in chapter 13 and choose one who you believe can guide you well over the long term.

If you are in a high-paid job, or have many years of service, or are retiring or being made redundant, the lump sum may be a large one. In this case, your employer will usually give you prior notice of how much the payment will be and what the expected components are. The payment will probably include such items as accrued long-service leave and accrued annual leave that cannot be rolled over, as well as the ETP, which is eligible to be rolled over.

If your employer does not offer this information before your finishing date, ask for it, for you will need to spend some time planning what to do with it. Once you get this information take it to your adviser so you can explore your options and, if appropriate, have a financial plan drawn up.

If you are 65 and retired, the money cannot be rolled over into an approved deposit fund or deferred annuity. It must be taken in cash and lump sum tax paid, or used to buy an annuity or placed in a superannuation fund and an allocated pension started immediately. If you choose the allocated pension option, no lump sum tax is payable. If you are 65, and not retired, the money can be rolled into a superannuation fund and left there till you finish work.

If you are under 65 your options for the ETP component are:

1. You can take in cash any part of it which is not preserved. If you do this the lump sum tax on the post-1983 component is deducted by the employer and a group certificate issued to you with the cheque. Details of the other components, if there are any, must be included in your next tax return where the appropriate tax will be assessed.

2. You can roll the ETP into an approved deposit fund (ADF) or a deferred annuity (DA).

3. You can roll the ETP into another superannuation fund.

4. You can roll the ETP into an eligible annuity.

If you intend to roll it over, the money must be forwarded by your employer to your new rollover vehicle, or retained in the employer's superannuation fund. Until 1 July 1994, you had 90 days from the date of receiving the money to decide what to do with it, and you could accept it in cash and then roll it over within the 90-day period. Those rules no longer apply.

KEY POINT: The money must be rolled directly from your employer's fund to your own rollover fund. If this is not done, you lose forever the right to place that sum in a rollover vehicle.

By the time your finishing day arrives you should have canvassed all your options with your adviser, who will have forwarded to your employer all paperwork necessary to roll the ETP into the rollover fund or funds you have chosen.

If the lump sum is a large one, and you are still unsure of the best way to invest it at the time of finishing up, instruct your employer to pay the money direct into a no entry fee/no exit fee capital secure approved deposit fund instead of deducting the tax and paying it to you. This gives you time to make considered judgements about where the money should eventually be invested for the long term.

You can often save money if you or your adviser collect the ETP and the supporting documentation from your ex-employer to ensure it is processed speedily. ETPs are often large sums of money and many employers simply put the cheque in the mail with the result that it arrives a week or so later, causing you to miss out on several hundreds of dollars of earnings. There is no point in wasting money needlessly.

Rollover Vehicles

Now that we understand the rollover process, let's look at the vehicles that can hold your rollover funds. Remember, rollover funds originated in 1983 and were similar to superannuation funds in that they were places to hold money that was meant for your retirement. The difference then was that you could continue to add money to your superannuation fund but could not withdraw it, while you could withdraw unpreserved money from your rollover fund but not contribute to the fund. In 1983 neither fund paid tax on its earnings – this was raised to 15% per annum in 1988.

Accordingly, when rollover funds were introduced in 1983 the main ones used were approved deposit funds (ADFs) and deferred annuities (DAs), and there were initially some important differences between them. This is because the development of rollover funds happened in the following way.

The introduction of lump sum tax created the need for rollover funds. Naturally, the securities industry wanted a part of the action and the introduction of the approved deposit fund was perfect. The name was right – an "approved" place in which to "deposit" your "eligible" termination payment. Leave the money in there until 65 if need be, enjoy tax-free growth along the way, withdraw a few thousand dollars whenever you needed money, and if you died before age 65 your spouse was entitled to the balance tax-free.

Then the life insurance industry got into the act. In a time of high interest rates, rolling the money into an annuity may be a good idea. Then why not have a hybrid annuity called a deferred annuity? Roll your money into one of these, enjoy tax-free growth and have the option of starting an annuity when you wished or withdrawing some or all of the balance whenever it seemed the best thing to do. Better still, there was no need to withdraw at age 65; with a DA the money could be left indefinitely in a tax-free environment and then rolled on for the spouse to continue the investment in a tax-free area when you died.

Naturally the ability to invest in a tax-free area for life, and beyond, gave the DA a tremendous advantage over the ADF and, after protests from the ADF lobby, DAs were put on a similar footing to ADFs on 12 January 1987. However, the measure was not made retrospective and there are many retirees aged over 65 with money that has been happily invested in DAs since before 12 January 1987, even though these funds have paid tax at 15% on their earnings since 1988.

If you think about the foregoing you may detect a lack of logic that created a lot of unnecessary work, because you had vehicles styled ADFs and DAs that are almost identical to superannuation funds. In fact, they were all so similar that I often described them to clients as "three jars of Vegemite with different labels on each jar". Yet it was not practical to roll your ETP into a superannuation fund in those early days because the money became inaccessible until you retired. It was far better to invest it in an ADF or a DA where you could make withdrawals from unpreserved money when you wished.

Logic has now prevailed and further changes in the rules that took effect from 1 July 1994 have resulted in superannuation funds fast becoming the preferred rollover option. One of the most significant changes gives you the option to withdraw unpreserved money from your superannuation when you wish. Consequently it seems likely that ADFs and DAs will slowly fade into disuse.

I'll discuss ADFs and DAs first and then move to superannuation as a rollover vehicle.

KEY POINT: Superannuation funds are becoming the preferred rollover vehicle.

Approved deposit funds

An approved deposit fund (ADF) is a security and accordingly is issued under a prospectus with trustee supervision and under the control of the Australian Securities Commission. The prospectus provides more information than a life office brochure, however, that is not likely to influence the performance of the fund.

Originally ADFs tended to invest mainly in interest-bearing securities, but now many are available that invest in property and shares. Several large fund managers have started ADFs that invest directly into their own property and equity trusts.

Upon the death of the owner, the funds are allowed to be paid free of any lump sum tax to a dependant provided there is not a problem with excess benefits. The funds cannot be retained in the ADF by the beneficiary or rolled into another fund.

Deferred annuities

Deferred annuities (DAs) are issued by life offices and are therefore controlled by the Life Insurance Act. Technically a DA is an annuity from which the income has not yet started to flow, in contrast to an ADF, which is merely a receptacle for rollover money. Even though the DA contract will contain provisions for you to eventually start an annuity there is no compulsion to do so, and if you ever wish to start an annuity you do not need to have funds in a DA. This is why DAs are little different from ADFs in practice.

Both ADFs and DAs pay tax at 15% on their earnings and these earnings accrue for the owner's benefit instead of being paid out regularly.

If the owner of a DA dies, the funds in the DA can be rolled over for the benefit of a dependant called the **reversionary annuitant,** provided the DA contract is drawn so as to allow this to happen and the reversionary annuitant was nominated prior to the death of the owner of the DA. Funds can then be left in this rollover area by the new owner until the date on which the **original holder** would have turned 65. Then the new owner has four choices:

1. Convert the funds to an eligible annuity.
2. Withdraw the funds and pay lump sum tax.
3. Roll into a new rollover fund where the money can grow until his or her own 65th birthday.
4. Roll the money into a superannuation fund and start an allocated pension.

If you receive money as the result of the owner of a DA dying, you should speak to your adviser immediately about reasonable benefit limits. Because the money comes to you as an ETP, it could put you in excess benefits if you have other money in superannuation or rollover funds. In this case you may be better off to cash in all or part of it and pay the lump sum tax.

Sometimes a **nominated dependent beneficiary** is named in the DA contract instead of a reversionary annuitant. In this situation, the person or persons named will receive the money tax-free as a lump sum. It cannot be rolled over. However, if a deferred annuity contract provides the beneficiary with the option to continue the policy, the beneficiary is regarded as a reversionary annuitant and must treat the legacy as an ETP as described in the previous paragraphs. The amount cannot be received as a lump sum free of tax.

You should now appreciate how important it is to take good advice when you are considering investing in a DA, and why great care is necessary in deciding whether you wish to nominate a reversionary annuitant or a beneficiary. If you die first, the benefits to the dependant of receiving the proceeds tax-free may outweigh the facility enjoyed by the reversionary annuitant of leaving the money in a low-tax environment. The best strategy depends on the other income and age of the recipient.

Superannuation funds

Now that unpreserved monies can be withdrawn from your superannuation fund when you wish, superannuation funds are becoming the preferred rollover vehicles. They now offer most of the benefits that can be gained by investing in an ADF or a DA, but have some other advantages as well:

1. If you are a member of a superannuation fund, and are happy with the performance of that fund, it saves entry and exit fees if you can leave your ETP in that fund when you change jobs.

2. It makes for good long-term financial planning to have your retirement money in one vehicle, particularly if you change jobs regularly, as it cuts down administration fees. Many employers will pay the compulsory contributions into a fund of your choice, which means you can retain the one superannuation fund no matter where you work. If you have an employer who won't contribute to your fund, you can always roll the money from the employer's fund into your fund regularly. **You don't have to wait till you resign.**

3. You can arrange your life insurance through a superannuation fund, a facility that is not available through a DA or an ADF.

4. When you retire you can stay in the same superannuation fund if it provides allocated pension facilities.

What is clear from the above is that a good superannuation fund is now meant to serve you for a lifetime. You and your employer contribute to it as you work, you leave your ETP in it when you change jobs, and you live out of it by way of an allocated pension when you retire. Naturally this presupposes that the fund is well run, gives you a good return on your money, has reasonable administration fees and has the facility to provide you with competitive life insurance. These are all matters on which your adviser can guide you.

Which Component Should Be Withdrawn First?

This is a matter to consider when you are withdrawing money from the rollover area, but it is a complex question to answer, and all I will do here is give you some pointers to discuss with your adviser.

In general terms, the concessional or invalidity component should be the first part withdrawn because its withdrawal from the rollover does not increase the post-1983 component, as do the undeducted contributions, nor does it affect the ratio of pre/post days.

The part to treat carefully is the undeducted contributions, as their presence in the rollover affects the post component.

Therefore, the effect of withdrawing the undeducted contributions on their own would be to increase the post component. It is generally best to take just enough undeducted contributions to equal the post. Any more would be wasted.

EXAMPLE: *Tom's ETP is $200 000 consisting of 10 years of pre and 10 years of post. The concessional component is $5000 and the undeducted contributions are $20 000. He wishes to withdraw $20 000.*

He should first take the whole $5000 that constitutes the concessional, which leaves $15 000 to apportion between pre and post. The next step is to work out the pre component – 10/20 of $15 000 which is $7500. If he nominates $7500 from the undeducted to make up the balance of the withdrawal there will be no post in this withdrawal to be taxed. This leaves $12 500 of undeducted contributions still to be used.

The withdrawal becomes:

Concessional component	5 000
Undeducted contributions	7 500
Pre component	7 500
	$20 000

The balance of the ETP becomes $180 000 made up as follows:

Pre-1983 component 10/20 × $180 000	= $ 90 000
Undeducted contributions remaining	= $ 12 500
Post-1983 component	= $ 77 500
Total	= $180 000

If $15 000 of the undeducted, as well as the concessional component of $5000, had been withdrawn instead, the balance would be:

Pre-1983 component 10/20 × $180 000	= $ 90 000
Undeducted contributions	= $ 5 000
Post-1983 component	= $ 85 000
Total	= $180 000

Notice how the post has risen with a consequent rise in tax liability. In the next chapter you will learn that it sometimes best to adjust the components to increase the post when the owner is over 55 and the post is under the 1994 tax-free limit of $79 586.

Conclusion

You should now understand why rollover funds came into being and how they are designed to encourage you to keep intact monies you receive when you leave a job. When you place funds in the rollover area you are enjoying valuable tax concessions, as well as helping to ensure you have enough money to live comfortably when you retire. Superannuation funds will be the rollover funds of the future, so make sure you choose a good fund early in your career and stick with it.

In the next chapter I'll explain how ETPs are taxed, and after that we'll move on to reasonable benefit limits, which regulate how much you should have in the tax-advantaged rollover area.

Summing Up

- A rollover fund is a place where you may keep some of the money you receive as a result of leaving your job so it will be available for you when you retire.
- Lump sum tax is deferred when you roll the money over. You thus receive earnings on a higher amount.
- The lump sum tax rates reduce after you turn 55 so you will reduce your tax if you leave it rolled over until then.
- Rollover money is placed in the superannuation area where tax on fund earnings is no more than 15%. This is likely to be lower than your marginal rate.
- Funds you roll over that have not been designated preserved benefits may be withdrawn in whole or part at any time. Lump sum tax is then payable on a pro rata basis.
- Seek expert advice before withdrawing money from a rollover fund in order to use the components that give the best tax advantage.
- Unless the money comes from an untaxed fund, and you are under 55, it is almost impossible to go wrong by rolling your money over. Therefore, if you are unsure about what to do, roll over into a cash-type ADF with no entry or exit fees.

24

TAX ON THE END BENEFIT

I am not interested in this income tax service. Could you please cancel my name in your books . . . I do not know who registered me as one of your customers.

THE RESPONSE OF A NEWLY INDEPENDENT ZIMBABWEAN TO THE
TAX OFFICE OF HARARE WHEN ASKED TO FILE A TAX RETURN

By now you should be much better informed about superannuation funds and rollovers. Let's now expand that knowledge by discussing how they are taxed.

There are three taxes that affect your eligible termination payment (ETP) once it is rolled over.

1. The **tax paid by the rollover fund** on its earnings, which reduces the earnings credited to your account.

2. **Excess benefit tax** that becomes payable when you withdraw more from the fund than is allowed under the reasonable benefit rules.

3. **Tax on the end benefit** when you withdraw.

We'll consider each one in turn.

Tax On The Fund

Rollover funds are almost identical to superannuation funds, and ETPs can be rolled into superannuation funds. As you know a superannuation fund pays tax on its earnings at 15%, but this can be reduced by the presence of franked dividends in the fund's earnings. Obviously, it is desirable to have franked dividends to reduce the fund's tax, but these come only from Australian shares.

This creates a dilemma for anybody with money in rollover funds and superannuation funds. Do you raise your exposure to shares to reduce the tax paid by the fund, or do you stay in the less volatile areas of cash and bonds and suffer a higher tax on your fund? Naturally a lower tax means a higher earning rate, which comes through in faster capital gain.

Excess Benefit Tax

The importance of reasonable benefit limits (RBLs) is discussed in the next chapter. If the money you withdraw from your rollover fund or superannuation fund exceeds your RBL you may be liable for excess benefit tax on the balance. This tax is levied at the highest marginal tax rate plus Medicare levy and in extreme cases could run into hundreds of thousands of dollars.

The following chapter gives the details, but meanwhile be aware that you *must* seek competent advice when handling your rollover.

Tax On The Components (Or Tax On The End Benefit)

An ETP can have up to five components:

1. The **concessional** component, which includes sick leave, golden handshake and redundancy paid before 1 July 1994.
2. The **invalidity** component discussed in the previous chapter.
3. The **pre-*1983*** component, which includes that part of the lump sum that relates to pre-1983 service.
4. **Undeducted contributions,** which is the part that represents contributions since 1 July 1983 for which no tax deduction has been claimed.
5. The **post-*1983*** component, which is that part of it that relates to post-1983 service.

No lump sum tax is payable until the monies leave the superannuation/rollover area, so you can roll your money from one rollover fund to other rollover funds as often as you wish without paying lump sum tax. It is only when you start withdrawing funds that tax is payable. The components are taxed as follows:

1. **The concessional component.** 5% of the amount is added to your taxable income in the financial year it is withdrawn.
2. **The invalidity component.** It is tax-free but its amount does not grow. Its earnings are added to the pre and post components.
3. **The pre-1983 component.** It is taxed the same as the concessional component: 5% of the value is added to taxable income in the year the money is withdrawn.
4. **The undeducted contributions component.** The amount of the undeducted contributions is returned to you free of lump sum tax. However, be aware that the amount of the undeducted contributions component does not grow; the earnings on the undeducted and concessional components are added to the pre and post components.

   EXAMPLE: *You have an ETP of $100 000 consisting of $30 000 undeducted contributions and $70 000 post. After 12 months it grows to $110 000. The proportions will then be undeducted contributions $30 000 and post $80 000. The undeducted amount will stay the same.*

5. **The post-1983 component.** If you withdraw money from your ETP before age 55, the tax on the post-1983 component is 20% plus Medicare levy provided the post is "taxed". "Untaxed" post suffers a higher tax but, as this is less common, I have left it till later in the chapter. Once you reach 55 the first $86 495 of the post is tax-free and the balance is taxed at 15% plus Medicare levy.

KEY POINT: You can save lump sum tax if you leave your superannuation and rollover money untouched until age 55.

Calculating The Components

In order to work out the tax we have to split the ETP into its components. Let's study an example to see how the calculations are done.

EXAMPLE: *Mr Jones, aged 53, finished work because of ill-health on 1 July 1994 after 24 years with his employer and received a lump sum of $200 000. He started work with that employer on 1 July 1970 and had paid in $20 000 of superannuation contributions since 1 July 1983 for which no tax deduction was allowed. The lump sum comprised his superannuation payment of $120 000 and an $80 000 invalidity payment.*

Step 1: **Calculate the invalidity component**

This is the $80 000 paid to him as an invalidity payment. The balance of $120 000 is left to be apportioned between the other three components.

Step 2: **Calculate the pre-1983 component**

His pre-1983 service is 13 years and his post-1983 service is 11 years. Thus the $120 000 is split in the ratio of 13/24 and 11/24. In practice, days would be used, but I have used years to make the example easier to understand. The pre-1983 component is 13/24 of $120 000 = $65 000.

Step 3: **Account for the undeducted contributions**

$120 000 – $65 000 = $55 000. Subtract the undeducted contributions: $55 000 – $20 000= $35 000.

Step 4: **Discover the post-1983 component**

That's simple – it's the $35 000 left over. If the post happened to be a negative figure, it becomes zero and the pre is adjusted accordingly.

Therefore the ETP is made up:

Component (a) Invalidity component	$ 80 000
Component (b) Pre-1983 component	$ 65 000
Component (c) Undeducted contributions	$ 20 000
Component (d) Post-1983 component	$ 35 000
	$200 000

You can see it's not too difficult provided you take it step by step. Now that we know the amount of each component we can calculate the tax due.

Calculating The Tax

Component (a) Invalidity component

$80 000 – this is tax-free.

Component (b) Pre-1983 Component

$65 000 – this is taxed under the old rules – 5% of the total is added to his income in the year the money was received.

Component (c) Undeducted contributions

$20 000 – these are returned to the employee tax-free.

Component (d) Post-1983

$35 000 – this is taxed at 20% because he is under 55. If he was over 55 tax would be nil, because the component is less than the $83 168 threshold.

In practice the whole of the post-1983 component is added to the taxpayer's taxable income, and a rebate is applied to reduce the tax payable in terms of the scale. The taxpayer's marginal rate will apply instead of the scale rate, if it is less than the scale rate.

EXAMPLE: *Consider a person under 55 with a $10 000 post component and only $4000 of other income.*

Post component	*$10 000*
Other income	*$ 4 000*
Total income	*$14 000*

The tax payable on $14 000 is $1720 plus Medicare levy. If there was no post-1983 component, the income would be $4000 on which no tax is payable.

The difference in tax is $1720, which is less than the $2000 (20%) tax that is normally payable on a lump sum of $10 000 for people under 55. Thus the lower rate of tax of $1720 applies.

> KEY POINT: You can sometimes reduce the tax on the post component by reducing your other income in the year of withdrawal.

Untaxed Post

An untaxed post component occurs when all or part of the ETP comes from an unfunded fund. An unfunded fund is one for which the employer does not put money aside in advance to pay benefits as they fall due. Instead, the benefits are funded by direct payments from the employer out of current cash flow when the employee finishes service. Examples are retiring benefits paid direct from consolidated revenue to public servants, and such payments as unused sick leave where it is paid direct by the employer when the employee finishes work.

As there have been no contributions paid during the course of the person's employment there can be no 15% contributions tax levied. Hence the post-1983 component is taxed under the old rules. The tax is:

Rates of tax on untaxed post		
Recipient's age	Untaxed element	Tax rate
Less than 55	All	30%
55 or older	First $86 495	15%
	Excess over $86 495	30%

Medicare levy is added to the above rates.

Beware the unfunded trap!

Because of the way the tax is levied, there is a potential trap for people under 55 who receive an ETP that includes untaxed post. A tax of 15% is deducted **immediately any untaxed post is placed in a rollover fund** and the balance of the payment then becomes normal "taxed" post and is subject to tax as detailed below when the post is withdrawn. Hence the dollar amount of the untaxed post does not grow as it turned into taxed post the moment it was rolled over. Its earnings are apportioned between taxed post and pre if any.

Let's review the rates of lump sum tax on the taxed post component.

Rates of tax on taxed post		
Recipient's age	Taxed element	Tax rate
Less than 55	All	20%
55 or older	First $86 495	Nil
	Excess over $86 495	15%

Now consider someone under 55 with an ETP from an unfunded fund. If she does not roll over the ETP, the untaxed post suffers an immediate tax of 30% plus Medicare levy.

If she does roll the money over, an immediate entry tax of 15% is deducted, and the balance becomes liable for the tax on taxed post as set out above. If she withdraws the money before age 55 she suffers a lump sum tax of 21.5% (20% plus 1.5% Medicare levy). This makes a total tax of 35.5%.

If she had not rolled the untaxed post over in the first place the total tax would have been 31.5% (30% plus Medicare levy).

> KEY POINT: If you are under 55, don't roll over any untaxed post unless you intend to leave it in the rollover area until you reach 55.

Tax-Saving Strategies

Decreasing the post component

As you know, the post is the balancing factor, therefore it can be reduced by increasing the pre-1983 service or the undeducted contributions.

EXAMPLE: *In July 1996 a 58-year-old retiree receives an ETP of $230 000 that relates to service that started in July 1973. There is no concessional component, but undeducted contributions total $30 000. The pre-1983 service is 10 years and the post-1983 component is 13 years.*

Thus 10/23 of $230 000 or $100 000 is the pre component, and $30 000 is the undeducted component. This leaves the balance of $100 000 as the post component.

Suppose he had contributed an extra $70 000 as an undeducted contribution before he retired. The ETP would then be $300 000 and the pre $130 500 (10/23 × $300 000). The undeducted is now $100 000 leaving post of $69 500. Thus all the post is tax-free because it is under $86 495.

Increasing the post component

The post can be increased by taking away part of the pre service or by reducing the undeducted component. Why would you want to **increase** the post? Because the first $86 495 is tax-free whereas the pre is taxed at up to nearly 2.5%.

EXAMPLE: *A person had a service period of 30 years comprising 18 years pre and 12 years post. She received an ETP of $140 000 that included $40 000 undeducted contributions. The components are:*

Pre	$ 84 000	18/30 × $140 000
Undeducted	40 000	
Post	16 000	
Total ETP	$140 000	

Look what happens if she first withdraws the undeducted which can be taken tax-free. The ETP reduces to $100 000 and *becomes:*

Pre	*60 000*	*18/30 × $100 000*
Post	*40 000*	
Total ETP	*$100 000*	

She has reduced the overall tax on the ETP and still kept all the post under the lump sum tax-free threshold. If she leaves the money growing in the rollover, the post will continue to increase with each passing day while the pre days remain constant.

In four years the balance may be $140 000 if growth of 9% a year is achieved. The component breakdown will then be:

Pre	*$ 74 000*	*18/34 × $140 000*
Post	*66 000*	*Balancing item*
Total ETP	*$140 000*	

Notice how the pre has grown by $14 000 and the post by $26 000. All the growth on the post has been free of tax because she is still under the lump sum tax threshold.

> KEY POINT: You can reduce the post by increasing the undeducted contributions. You can increase the post by withdrawing some of the undeducted contributions component.

Increasing the pre component

You can increase the pre component by rolling in another payment that has an earlier service date. The most common source of this is a superannuation policy you took out when you were young, even if you then had a different employer.

EXAMPLE: *Dr Wagner has a service start date of 1 July 1973, therefore his pre service is limited to 10 years. He finds a superannuation policy he took out when he left university and this has a start date of 1 July 1953. Provided he can roll the proceeds of this policy, on maturity, into his present superannuation fund or his rollover fund, he will enjoy 30 years of pre, not 10.*

What if you do not have a current superannuation policy that you commenced before you started with your present employer? Then your pre-1983 service starts from the date you joined your present employer, not the date you joined the superannuation fund. This is especially relevant as many long-term employees have recently been enrolled in work superannuation as a result of the superannuation guarantee charge.

> **EXAMPLE:** *Tom started with his present employer in 1973 but did not join the company superannuation fund until 1992. His service date may be backdated to 1973.*

Watch this one carefully because our consultants regularly see ETP statements where the starting date is wrongly shown as the date of joining the superannuation fund. Such an error could be very costly for a person with a large lump sum payment.

KEY POINT: If you do not have a pre-existing superannuation policy, your service date with your present employer for the purposes of calculating the pre-1983 component commences when your employment started, not when you joined the superannuation fund.

Rolling into an annuity or an allocated pension

You can defer lump sum tax by leaving your money rolled over until you retire. However, if you retire before age 65, you must exit the rollover fund at age 65 by doing one of the following:

1. withdrawing your money and paying any lump sum tax due
2. rolling all or part of the money into an annuity
3. rolling all or part of the money into an allocated pension fund.

Most of you will find it is best to take part of the money as a lump sum, and to start an allocated pension or annuity with the balance. The reasons for taking part as a lump sum are to get some money in the spouse's name, if you have one, and to take advantage of the tax-free threshold of $86 495 that applies to the post component.

Your adviser will calculate the components for you, but be aware that $86 495 is the total tax exemption for the post. Therefore, any withdrawals that have been made before your 65th birthday will be counted towards that figure, and you will only enjoy tax-free withdrawals on the difference between what you have drawn to date and $86 495. The balance will be taxed at 15% plus Medicare levy. Tax on the pre-1983 component is levied by adding 5% of the sum withdrawn to your taxable income, so if you can arrange your affairs to remain in the 20% bracket with the inclusion of that 5% of the pre, the effective tax is 1%.

No lump sum tax is payable if you choose either of the other two options, rolling the remaining funds into an annuity or allocated pension, but tax is payable on the income that comes to you from either of these. Tax on the annuity income or allocated pension income may be eliminated by the tax rebate. We'll discuss annuities and allocated pensions in depth soon.

Conclusion

By now you should understand the way tax is levied on lump sums and how to reduce it and possibly avoid it. You may have noticed how the Government uses the "carrot and stick" approach to encourage you to leave the money untouched till you retire. The lump sum taxes are lower if you leave the money till at least age 55, and if you roll it over to an annuity or allocated pension you may dodge lump sum tax altogether.

Take notice of the way lump sum tax can be reduced by careful planning and by taking steps to adjust the components.

Summing Up

- The five possible components of an ETP are undeducted contributions, concessional, invalidity, pre-1983 and post-1983.
- The amounts of the undeducted, invalidity and concessional components do not increase. The earnings on these components are added to pre and post.
- You can adjust the post by changing the amount of the undeducted component.
- In some cases you can increase the pre component by rolling in an earlier superannuation policy.
- Take advice before rolling over an unfunded ETP if you are under 55.
- You must exit the rollover fund at age 65 if you are retired.
- There is no lump sum tax immediately payable if you roll your money into an allocated pension or an annuity.

25

REASONABLE BENEFIT LIMITS

All action beyond the ordinary limits are subject to sinister interpretation.

MONTAIGNE

Because money in superannuation and rollover funds enjoys tax benefits, the Government has placed a limit on the amount anybody can have in these areas. This figure is called your "reasonable benefit limit" and is generally referred to as your RBL. It governs the amount you can receive from your superannuation fund, and ultimately your rollover fund, before you become liable for excess benefits tax.

Before the system was simplified, your RBL was determined by a complicated formula that took into account your length of service and your income. However, to try to make it easier to understand, the regulators and the superannuation industry worked together to try and agree upon a fair formula for everybody's RBL. Questions arose such as:

- Is it reasonable for a high-income earner to be restricted to the same RBL as a low-income earner?
- What formula is appropriate for those who have been paying into superannuation for many years under the old rules?
- Is it fair to change the rules for people who are nearing retirement?

After much debate, the issues were finally decided, and on 1 July 1994 the simplified rules took over. Everybody was allowed a lump sum RBL of $400 000 and a pension RBL of $800 000. The figures were indexed and, at date of writing, had grown to $434 720 and $869 440 respectively. Special arrangements were put in place for those aged between 45 and 50 with unusually large balances in superannuation on 1 July 1994, and for all people aged 50 at that date.

Standard Reasonable Benefit Limits

The standard RBL rules are simple in the extreme. Your RBL is $400 000 if you take your superannuation as a lump sum, and $800 000 if you take at least half of it as a complying annuity, discussed later in this chapter. These figures increase each year in line with average weekly ordinary time earnings (AWOTE). Therefore, if you were aged 40 in July 1994, and AWOTE averages 3% a year, your lump sum RBL will be about $800 000 when you reach age 64 and your pension RBL will be about $1.6 million. I calculated these figures using the Rule of 72, which is covered in *Making Money Made Simple*.

Now it's a sad fact of life that most Australians have no chance whatsoever of accumulating sums of this magnitude. Compulsory superannuation introduced under the Superannuation Guarantee Charge laws will provide only minimal benefits for most of you who are now aged 35 and over, and wage increases are likely to be restricted because of worldwide competition. Consequently, you may think right now that accumulating a lump sum of $400 000 in 1994 dollars by the time you retire is impossible. If so, you can take comfort from the fact that you will never have an RBL problem, skip the rest of this chapter, and concentrate on the ones that tell you how to speed up the wealth-creation process. But be warned, judging by the mail I keep getting, those wealth-building techniques of mine can have powerful results. Maybe you'll make so much money that you **will** have an RBL problem.

> KEY POINT: Almost everybody has a lump sum RBL of $400 000 and a pension RBL of $800 000 in 1994 dollars. These figures are indexed to AWOTE.

Transitional RBLs

Before simplification your RBL was calculated by a formula – RBM x FAS. RBM stands for your reasonable benefit multiple and FAS is your final average salary over the last three years of employment. Under this formula, members of a superannuation fund could retire at 65 with a lump sum that was no more than seven times their FAS.

Because the Government is encouraging retirees to take an income instead of a lump sum, a person funding for a private pension is allowed to contribute more to superannuation than a person funding for a lump sum. The aims are twofold – to get the majority of people off a social security pension and to steer retirees into taking private pensions instead of lump sums. Lump sums tend to be dissipated or invested in tax-sheltered areas. Private pensions (or annuities as they are called) create a taxable income stream so the Government can extract taxes from you until death.

When the Hawke Government reformed the superannuation system it decided that seven times final average salary might be fine for a person on $40 000 a year who could retire with a lump sum of $280 000, but felt it was too much to allow a high earner on $200 000 a year to retire with a lump sum of $1.4 million and roll it into a tax-advantaged area. Accordingly, they reduced the RBLs for higher-income earners by lowering the RBMs. To avoid retrospectivity, the new RBMs applied only to that part of an employee's service that took place after 30 June 1990.

Further far-reaching reforms were introduced in the August 1989 Budget. The Government recognised that many highly paid professionals, such as barristers and doctors, tended to taper down their work activity in their late fifties. The concept of FAS was seen to be inappropriate and was replaced by highest average salary (HAS) over any three consecutive working years. Thus, the formula for RBL changed from RBM x FAS to RBM x HAS; This was known as your HAS-based RBL.

When RBLs were simplified again in 1994 those over 45 with large superannuation balances, and those who were aged 50 or more at 1 July 1994, were given the choice of the new standard RBL or a transitional RBL based on their RBM and HAS. Applications for transitional RBLs closed in April 1997, so those of you who have not been granted a transitional RBL will have to use the standard one.

EXAMPLE: *Elizabeth was 51 on 1 July 1994 and had a HAS of $100 000, a lump sum RBM of 6.6 and a pension RBM of 10.2. She has a vested[1] balance of $200 000 in her superannuation fund. Her transitional lump sum RBL is $660 000 (HAS x RBM) and her transitional pension RBL is $1 020 000. These figures will be indexed to AWOTE.*

---

1   "Vested" means that you are legally entitled to it. However, it may still be preserved, so you do not have immediate access to it.

KEY POINT: Those who were 50 and over at 1 July 1994 have a choice of using the standard RBLs, or their individual ones, which are found by multiplying their HAS by their RBM.

Which RBL Do You Use?

That's easy. The lump sum RBL applies if more than 50% of the total benefit is taken as a lump sum. The pension RBL applies if at least 50% of the benefit is taken as a complying annuity.

> **EXAMPLE:** *Mary, aged 65, retires in 1997. Her HAS was $50 000 so she did not apply for a transitional RBL. Therefore she falls under the $434 720/$869 440 RBL rules. Her superannuation payment is $480 000. Her choices are to take a lump sum of $240 000 (no more than 50% of the $480 000) and buy a complying annuity with the balance of $240 000 or to take a lump sum of $434 720 and treat the extra $45 280 as excess benefits.*

We'll talk about excess benefits soon, but meanwhile let's explore complying annuities.

Complying Annuities

Annuities are covered in detail in Chapter 28 but, to put it simply, they are private pensions paid to you by an insurance company in exchange for a lump sum. A complying annuity is a special type of annuity that has been designed to receive superannuation payments. Because complying annuities are usually used by people to get them out of excess benefits problems, they are somewhat restricted.

The main features of complying annuities are listed below, but you may find it easier to re-read this after you have studied the next chapter for some of the terms may be unfamiliar to you. Notice that complying annuities are designed to ensure the annuitant receives a large income and increasing income stream so the Government can extract taxes from it. Another aim is to stop the annuitant continuing to hold a large sum in the tax-free annuity area.

1. **It must be a lifetime annuity.** This is to prevent annuitants buying a short-term annuity with no residual value and quickly using up their superannuation.

2. **The guarantee period must not be more than 10 years.** This is to stop annuitants from leaving a large sum to their

estate by choosing an annuity with lower monthly payments and a guaranteed period way beyond their life expectancy.

3. **It cannot have a residual value.** This ensures a larger income stream.

4. **For annuities commenced before 1 July 1998 payments must be indexed, and the minimum indexation is the lesser of 5% or CPI.** They want to get that money flowing out.

5. **It must be non-assignable and cannot be used as security for a loan.** This is to keep it in the hands of the person who received the superannuation in the first place.

From 1 July 1998 complying annuities will include annuities where the term of the contract is fixed and payable for a term of not less that the life expectancy of the investor. Alternatively the contract must be for at least 15 years and commenced after age pension eligibility age. Indexation of payments will no longer be required.

There is no compulsion that the complying annuity revert to another party on the death of the annuitant, but if the income does continue to a reversionary annuitant that person may not receive more than 100% of what the original annuitant was receiving at the date of death.

Also, a complying annuity may be commuted to a lump sum within six months of its commencement date. However, if you do this, lump sum RBLs apply and you may be liable for excess benefits tax again.

Excess Benefits

You are in excess benefits when the balance of your superannuation or rollover funds exceeds your lump sum RBL if you are taking it all as a lump sum or an allocated pension, or if it exceeds your pension RBL if you are taking at least half the benefit as a complying annuity. If you get into an excess benefit situation you have two options:

1. Cash in the excess benefit and pay tax on it at the top marginal rate plus Medicare levy. This is presently 48.5%. Don't confuse this tax with lump sum tax.

2. Use the excess sum to buy a special type of allocated pension or annuity that is designed for this purpose. These products do not have a deductible portion, nor does the income from them carry a tax rebate.

A point to note is that you are not penalised for excess benefits until you have made enough withdrawals that your balance starts getting relatively low. In practice, all eligible termination payments (ETPs) are reported to the Tax Office, which tests for excess benefits every time a benefit is paid. They take into account the benefit being paid, plus the indexed value of all benefits received since 15 February 1990.

EXAMPLE: *Bill retired with an ETP of $420 000 in July 1994. His RBLs then were $400 000/$800 000. He withdrew $100 000 in July 1994 and withdrew the balance, which had grown to $380 000, in July 1996 when he turned 65. If we use an indexation factor of 3%, the approximate calculations are:*

Indexed value of $100 000 withdrawal	$106 000
Value of benefit cashed in July 1996	$380 000
Total benefit received	$486 000
Lump sum RBL $400 000 indexed at 3%	$424 400
Excess benefit	$ 61 600

Bill is liable for excess benefits tax of $29 876, being $61 600 taxed at 48.5% – the top marginal rate of 47% plus Medicare levy of 1.5%.

KEY POINT: Only sums received since 15 February 1990 are taken into account for excess benefit purposes.

Beating Excess Benefit Tax

In the above example, Bill could have lessened the impact of excess benefit tax if he had taken expert advice before cashing out the balance of his rollover fund. He could have eliminated it altogether if he had opted to take $243 000 (50% of the total balance) as a complying annuity but this may not have suited him for reasons you will understand when you read the chapter on annuities.

Alternatively, he and his adviser could have calculated his RBL position, and withdrawn all the funds except the $61 600 excess benefit portion. He could then have rolled the $61 600 excess benefit into an allocated pension fund or bought an annuity with it.

A lifetime annuity would have provided Bill with an extra income of around $7000 a year until his death. If he opted to place the excess benefit of $61 600 into an allocated pension fund he would have had to take a minimum pension of $3730 in the first year and this would increase annually. We'll discuss the fine points of allocated pensions and annuities soon, but surely either option beats paying nearly $30 000 in excess benefits tax.

Remember, the income that flows from excess benefits rolled into an annuity or an allocated pension fund does not give rise to a tax-free portion or a tax rebate. However, if Bill was married he could have withdrawn enough money from the $424 400 to be taken as a lump sum to start a separate investment portfolio in his wife's name. Their overall affairs could then be arranged so that neither earned more than $20 700 a year including the income from his annuity or allocated pension. Then the tax on the income from either of these sources would be taxed at no more than 20%.

KEY POINT: Excess benefits may be used to start a separate allocated pension or annuity. If so, the income that flows from either investment does not carry a deductible portion or a tax rebate.

Some Questions Answered

Question: If I have excess benefits in a superannuation fund, can I roll them over?

Answer: Yes – they can be rolled over now and you can worry about excess benefits tax later. If you eventually decide to take 50% as a complying pension you may not be in excess benefits as the pension RBL is much greater than the lump sum RBL.

Question: If a person withdraws only undeducted contributions and the concessional component, are these indexed when taken into account for RBL purposes?

Answer: Undeducted contributions and concessional components are not subject to RBLs, and do not count as a benefit received.

Question: Is money in an allocated pension fund regarded as a complying annuity for RBL purposes?

Answer: No, the lump sum RBL is applied to it.

Conclusion

As you will now understand, despite the simplification of the system, RBLs can still be complex. However, for many of you, RBLs will be of academic interest only because you will not breach the $400 000/$800 000 limit. Nevertheless, there will be others with large superannuation payments, and this chapter should have alerted you to the importance of monitoring your superannuation closely. Remember, the sooner you become aware of any potential problem the easier it is to solve them.

Summing Up

- There is no limit to the amount of money you may have in your superannuation or rollover fund.
- Any money you withdraw that is more than your RBL will be deemed to be an excess benefit and taxed at the top marginal rate. You can lessen the impact of excess benefits tax by rolling the excess benefit into a special type of allocated pension fund or annuity.
- Undeducted contributions and concessional components are not subject to RBLs and do not count as a benefit received.
- Your RBL is much higher if you take at least 50% of the final sum as a complying annuity.
- People with money in rollover funds should monitor the balance closely to check if they are moving into the excess benefit area.

26

HANDLING REDUNDANCY

Too many people are thinking of security instead of opportunity.

JAMES F. BYRNES

We now live in a rapidly changing world where technology rules our lives, and inflation appears to be set to stay low well into the next century. To understand the connection between these two factors and redundancy, you will have to appreciate the massive structural changes that have taken place since 1945.

The inflation that occurred after World War II was caused mainly by a combination of three factors. A quickly expanding manufacturing base working on a philosophy of continual price increases, strong demand for labour, and government-owned utilities providing services such as power, mail and telephone. The utilities were not required to make a profit and were run on the assumption that public ownership provided access to a "bottomless purse – the endless supply of taxpayers' money or public borrowing".

In most cases they had a monopoly, so consumers had no option but to accept the price rises when they occurred. It was a cosy world where pay/price rises were the norm – the only question was how much your pay, or the price of an item, would rise each year.

Two things changed all that – technology, and the rise of Asia. Competition from Asia forced industry in the Western world to cut costs, and technology gave it the tools to do it. Industry went into a frenzy of "downsizing", and tens of thousands of jobs vanished as cutting costs began to take precedence over increasing sales. But, the cuts were not confined to the private sector. Governments quickly followed suit, and seized upon privatisation as a way to generate money to fund their shrinking coffers.

Once privatisation occurred the job cuts were staggering. For example, British Gas cut its staff from 90 000 to 50 000, and Deutsche Telekom announced plans to sack 60 000 workers (as well as cutting its prices by 50%). The worker who once demanded a pay rise became thankful to have a job.

A major inflationary factor is consumer expectations. If you think something will rise in price you will try to buy it today, knowing it will cost more tomorrow. But now, office equipment prices have tumbled, phone costs are falling, car prices have dropped substantially and even tyres now last twice as long. We are becoming used to prices falling, or getting better value for the same price; which is a price drop in disguise. The psychology has changed totally.

How does business compete if it can't raise its prices? By cutting costs. How does it do that? By cutting staff wherever it can. Now, throughout the Western world, companies are using contract labour wherever possible, or buying machines that will do the work of several employees. To make matters worse, mergers of big institutions such as banks and insurance companies are adding more people to the unemployment queues.

Unfortunately, despite all the promises from the politicians, there is overwhelming evidence that the trend to laying off staff will get worse, not better. Therefore it is not impossible that many of you who are reading this book will face the shock of getting a redundancy notice.

In case this happens to you, I will now give you 10 vital tips about the best way to handle redundancy:

1. **Stay Flexible.** Resist the temptation to cash in the whole termination payment, pay off all your debts, and put the rest in the bank. This might be a natural reaction, but it could result in your losing valuable superannuation concessions. You should be trying to keep your financial situation as flexible as possible, while ensuring you maintain your tax benefits.

2. **Take expert advice.** The laws regarding superannuation and redundancy payments are complex, and the wrong move could cost you dearly. For example, it appears that the superannuation surcharge could hit termination payments in some cases.

3. **Don't pay off all your debts.** At most, make three months' payments off your loans. It is important to keep funds on hand for living expenses, and when you do find another job your age may preclude you from getting a fresh loan on the terms you enjoy at the moment. If you have investment loans leave these as "interest only", so you don't lose the tax benefits when you work again.

4. **Take time out.** Get away from it all for a couple of weeks off to get your head right. Losing a job that has become a part of your life for years is a stressful experience, even if it doesn't feel like it at the time.

5. **Start with a simple rollover fund.** With your adviser, decide what components of your termination payment can be rolled over, and park them first in a "no entry" or "no exit" fee cash-type rollover fund. Such funds are immune from share-market crashes, and give you maximum flexibility with no risk and minimum cost.

6. **Understand the "unfunded' trap.** Beware if your termination payment contains "unfunded" payments. If you are under 55 you can lose money in some cases if you roll the money over and then withdraw it.

7. **Beware of buying a business.** Don't buy a business just to give yourself a job. Small business is tough these days, and many people in small business work long hours for little remuneration. Investigate any business opportunities thoroughly, and with scepticism.

8. **Roll over if possible.** The termination payment will be in two portions – part that can be rolled over, and part that cannot. Unless there is unfunded money involved you are nearly always better to roll over the eligible portion of your payment. The benefits of rolling your money over are that you don't get hit for lump sum tax; (which could be as high as 20% if you are under 55), and you keep your money in a low tax area.

9. **Protect the undeducted contributions.** Resist the temptation to withdraw the undeducted contribution component of your termination payment, particularly if you are over 45. Sure, you can take it out tax free now, but you will be losing major tax benefits when the time comes to start your allocated pension.

10. **Involve your partner.** A sudden job loss affects the whole family, so make sure your partner goes along to the interviews with your financial adviser and knows exactly what is happening. This is also the time to get all the family together to do a budget. They are more likely to help in cutting down on expenses if they are part of the budgeting process.

Conclusion

Above all, realise that you now have one major goal – finding a new job. Put the same time and effort into doing that as you did when you were working. If you don't, you could easily drift into the trap of sleeping later and later, and losing all your drive. Always remember that the secret of life is to endure; the end of one life can be the start of another.

27

SUPERANNUATION AND DIVORCE

Never marry for money, you can borrow it cheaper.

ANON

In 1979 a landmark court decision was made. In the case of *Crapp v. Crapp* the wife became the first Australian to have the value of a spouse's superannuation taken into account when their divorce settlement was being worked out. It was a right that was made law when the *Family Law Act* was introduced in 1975. Now a spouse's superannuation is up for grabs when the property settlement agreement is being negotiated.

Mrs Crapp was the wife of a Qantas pilot whose large superannuation benefit was undoubtedly one of the couple's biggest financial resources after a long marriage. The fact that his lump sum payout was not due for 11 years from the time of the court hearing gives an indication of the problems that arise when trying to place a figure on its worth.

For most families, superannuation has assumed an important role only in the last few years. Part of the reason is that most women were not covered for superannuation in the past because fewer women entered the paid labour market than today, and those who were working were often in low-paid part-time jobs with few benefits. Traditionally they, as well as the blue-collar male workers, were excluded from superannuation.

Another factor was that rollover funds did not appear until late 1983. Until then most employees spent their accrued superannuation whenever they changed jobs and never accumulated a lump sum of any substance.

We now live in the days of equal rights and equal pay and in an age where superannuation is fast becoming the universal investment. Once, when couples parted, the family home was the only material asset worth fighting about. Now, many of the superannuation payouts are large enough to buy two or three houses.

Although the *Family Law Act* has been in force since 1975 the problems of accounting for superannuation in a property settlement still baffle the courts. The major reason is the difficulty of arriving at a fair value for it. Often the husband has spent all his life paying into the scheme while the wife has remained at home, keeping house, rearing the children and expecting that his growing superannuation will provide them with a secure and happy retirement.

Then the marriage breaks down, divorce occurs and the wife finds herself with no job skills and no superannuation. Even if she quickly found a well-paid job it is unlikely that she would have enough years left in employment to build up adequate funds for retirement through superannuation.

The husband's entitlements are impossible to calculate precisely. He may die, lose his job, change jobs or retire early on medical grounds. In each case the payout will differ, yet divorce may occur many years before any of these possibilities eventuate.

The position is further complicated because the court has tended to regard superannuation as a resource of the marriage, not an asset that can be divided. Thus it has found it difficult to make specific orders regarding superannuation but, if possible, will take the presence of superannuation into account when splitting up the other assets. For example, if an investment property owned by the couple was worth $150 000, and the superannuation benefit was worth $150 000, the spouse without superannuation may be awarded the house to balance things up.

The Family Court has been given wide discretion and will consider the length of the marriage, the extent to which the superannuation fund has grown during the marriage, the ability of the wife to contribute to her own financial needs, and the other assets of both parties. It will consider also probable future changes in the situation of either party. For example, one of them may be expecting a large inheritance or may intend to remarry. The age of the parties is carefully considered, for superannuation may have little relevance if both are young, but assume great significance if they are close to retirement.

In *Harrison v Harrison*, a 1996 case that went to appeal, the Full Court confirmed that superannuation could be treated as a resource of the marriage and taken into account when the assets were being divided, and that it could be appropriate to defer making a order about superannuation to a future date if that produced a fairer outcome.

Normally such deferral occurs only close to retirement, but in one extreme case the judge granted an adjournment of 20 years. The husband was a 39-year-old policeman who gave evidence that he intended to work till age 60 when he would collect over half a million dollars in superannuation. His wife was 38 with responsibility for six of the seven children of the marriage. She had little chance of being employed. The only present assets were personal effects worth around $12 000. The judge decided that more harm would be done to the wife by refusing her request for a 20-year deferral than would be done to the husband by granting it.

Another way is to defer the operation of the order as opposed to deferring the making of the order. In *Sharp v. Sharp* the judge made an order against the husband for $20 000 but postponed the operation of it to the date the husband retired.

If a couple have their own self-managed superannuation fund it is likely that the couple are the only members of the fund, and that one party (usually the husband) has a much higher balance in their members' account than the other. In this case the superannuation regulations provide a mechanism whereby the balances in the members' accounts can be re-allocated. This may enable part of the property settlement to be met from the superannuation fund, and avoids the problem of the wife having to wait till the husband retires before her share of the superannuation can be paid to her.

As you can see it's a difficult issue in view of the many factors involved. However, the following words from the judgement of the Full Court in *McLay and McLay* (1996) FLC 92-667 may sum it up.

The accepted approach proceeds on the basis that superannuation is an aspect of the benefits of the employment of the party of the marriage who is employed . . . each party is often taken to have made, during the course of their cohabitation and because of the way they have ordered their lives, equal contributions to (it) . . . and has been treated by both parties as a central part of saving for their support in retirement.

Conclusion

There are still many unanswered questions regarding superannuation and divorce, but there is no doubt it will become an increasingly important topic as the extent of superannuation coverage grows throughout the work force, and as some women start to earn as much as their husbands. Already we are seeing men applying to the courts for maintenance – it won't be long before men as well as women will start asking for a slice of their ex-partner's superannuation.

Summing Up

- Awarding a spouse part of his or her partner's superannuation has been happening only since 1979.
- The method of apportioning it, or taking it into account, is still evolving.
- The superannuation of both parties is now taken into account in property settlements.
- The court may defer a decision in some cases.

28

ANNUITIES

"Tis said that persons living on annuities are longer lived than others, God knows why, Unless to plague the grantors, yet so true it is, That some I really think do never die.

LORD BYRON

As you know there is a growing trend for retirees to accept at least part of their superannuation entitlements as some sort of an income stream. The Government encourages this because:

1. It prevents the few who want to rort the system from taking a lump sum, wasting it, and then going on welfare.

2. It helps to prevent those who are not used to handling money from losing it all through bad investment and then going on welfare.

3. It's a simple fact of life that most of us feel more comfortable with a reliable regular income to enable us to budget.

You can obtain a regular income if you have a large portfolio of property or shares because the rents and the dividends should keep coming in. However, you will be hard-pressed to get much more than 5% a year income from property and shares, so you would need nearly $500 000 in these areas to bring in the $25 000 a year that is the least amount that many couples need in retirement.

Accumulating half a million dollars worth of retirement assets is beyond the reach of most people unless they read *Making Money Made Simple* early enough. In any event, share dividends can be erratic and prices volatile, while a large property portfolio has the nasty habit of continually coming up with repair bills and vacancies.

The solution is to give yourself a regular income by drawing down on your assets or, to put it another way, spending your

244

capital progressively. I know this thought terrifies many of you, but be comforted by three factors:

1. As your capital reduces you are likely to become eligible for at least a part aged pension and all the fringe benefits. This pension income reduces your need to draw down on your capital and the capital drawdown process becomes slower.

2. You can't take it with you. The cynic asked, "How much money did Howard Hughes leave?" The answer: "He left it all!"

3. Wealth is one of the greatest demotivators of children.[1] The paradox is that some people devote so much time to building up wealth for their children that they neglect these same children.

You can spend capital in a willy-nilly fashion by withdrawing money from your rollover funds on a regular basis, or by cashing in investments progressively. This can be quite effective, but you have to exit the rollover area at age 65 unless you are working, and investment decisions can sometimes get more difficult as you get older.

For most of us an alternative and better method is to formalise the process and spend capital using the vehicles of annuities or allocated pensions. A special bonus is that you can get out of paying lump sum tax by converting the money you have in rollover funds to an annuity or an allocated pension. We'll discuss them in this chapter and the next.

Annuities

An annuity is a regular income paid to you by an insurance company in exchange for a lump sum. You pay the company a sum of money up-front and they return it to you, together with its earnings, as a regular income. The old-fashioned types were extremely simple. You handed over your money to the insurance company and they paid you a fixed income until your death.

The amount of the income depended on your life expectancy, so your age was the critical factor in determining the amount you received. When you died the income ceased, and any money left over stayed with the insurance company. It was like a bet. If you lived longer than the life expectancy tables predicted, you won – if you died early, the insurance company won.

---

1. This is discussed in depth in *More Money with Noel Whittaker*.

EXAMPLE: *Miss Jones is 75, is in perfect health, and has substantial assets. According to the tables her life expectancy is 11 years. She is more concerned with receiving a regular and certain income than leaving all her money to her nieces and nephews. She invests $200 000 in a lifetime annuity that will pay her $2000 a month ($24 000 a year) until she dies. If she lives to 110 the insurance company will keep paying her the $2000 a month; if she dies next year they pocket the money. It's as simple as that.*

Now this arrangement might be fine for Miss Jones who is single and of advanced years. However, it may not be suitable for you because:

1. Your spouse and children may say some unkind things about you if you die leaving most of your wealth in the hands of an insurance company.
2. The older-style annuities provided for an income that did not rise. You would be most unhappy if your standard of living declined rapidly once severe inflation hit, and the cost of living rose but your income didn't.
3. The transaction is inflexible. Once you made this contract with the insurance company it was binding till your death. Consequently you couldn't rearrange your investments if circumstances changed.

Fortunately, annuities have evolved with the times and the modern ones can handle most of the above problems. For example, they need not now continue until death – fixed-term annuities are common and may be taken out by people of any age.

EXAMPLE: *A couple divorced and agreed the man should pay his wife $400 a month for each child until they turned 18. The children were aged 12 and 15. He did not want the hassles of giving his wife a cheque every month and she was concerned that he might lose money in his business and be unable to pay.*

She sought a lump sum instead of the income, but he feared she might squander the lump sum and come back at him again for more money. An annuity was the solution. He paid the insurance company a lump sum of $37 000 and it paid the children $400 a month each until their 18th birthdays. The children had a guaranteed income and he had no fears that a lump sum might be frittered away.

Notice what an effective tool an annuity can be in the appropriate circumstances.

> KEY POINT: Annuities are a product that have to be tailored to the situation. They provide the perfect solution to some problems, but they are most inappropriate for others.

Terms To Know

You had better learn the jargon before we start.

Annuitant: The person who buys an annuity.

Capital protection: When the life assured dies the difference (if any) between the capital paid out and the purchase price is returned to the estate.

Complying annuity: An annuity that meets the requirements of the reasonable benefit limit rules for pensions.

Deductible portion: In most cases part of the income stream is a return of the investor's capital. Unless the annuity was purchased with an eligible termination payment (ETP), the part that represents a return of capital is called the "deductible portion" and is not taxed as income. Obviously, an annuity that provided a full return of the purchase price at the end of the annuity contract could not have a deductible portion, as there has been no return of capital with the income payments.

Guaranteed period: If you choose to have a guaranteed period, annuity payments will continue for at least the guaranteed period even if the annuitant dies before the guaranteed period expires.

Lifetime annuity: An annuity purchased for the lifetime of the annuitant.

Purchase price: The sum paid to purchase the annuity.

Residual capital value: The amount (if any) left at the end of the annuity contract.

Reversionary annuitant: A person, usually a spouse, who is named in the original annuity contract and who will continue to receive the annuity payments if the annuitant dies during the term of the annuity contract.

Term-certain annuity: An annuity purchased for a set term. e.g. 25 years.

In this chapter I shall give examples using all the above terms to help you understand them better. Bear in mind that annuity prices change continually and the ones used in this chapter are merely to illustrate the principles.

The Factors That Influence Annuity Payments

Now let's look at the factors that influence the amount paid under an annuity. Remember it's like buying a car; the more options you add the greater the cost.

1. The life expectancy of the annuitant

Obviously, life expectancy is a critical factor in calculating the regular payments if the annuity is paid until the death of the annuitant. As the life expectancy is obtained from actuarial tables, there is no need for a medical examination, because if you are in poor health you are likely to live a shorter time, and the insurance company won't have to pay so much money out. Life annuities tend to be taken out by healthy people who expect to live to a ripe old age.

2. The source of the money

We can break this down to:

(a) eligible termination payments from an unfunded fund where contributions tax has not been paid on the *post-1983* component.

(b) eligible termination payments where contributions tax has been paid on the *post-1983* component.

(c) funds from other sources.

That part of the purchase price of an annuity that is funded by ETP money cannot have a deductible portion unless there is a undeducted component present. This is one way the Government uses to collect some of that lump sum tax you evaded when you rolled the money into the annuity instead of drawing it out. Only the undeducted component will provide a deductible portion.

> **EXAMPLE:** *A man aged 65 takes out a $100 000 annuity over 10 years using an ETP that consisted of $60 000 undeducted contributions and $40 000 post-1983 component. The deductible portion is $6000 a year being one-tenth of the $60 000 undeducted contributions component.*

If he had chosen a life annuity, the deductible portion would have been $4109 a year, being $60 000 divided by his life expectancy of 14.60 years.

3. The residual capital value (RCV) at the end of the contract

There may be a sum returned to the annuitant at the end of an annuity. Naturally, the larger this residual component, the lower the regular payments.

> **EXAMPLE:** *An annuity of $100 000 over 10 years may pay $12 000 a year if the RCV is 50% or $50 000. Reduce the RCV to 20% or $20 000 and the annual payments rise to $13 600. This is because a larger amount of your own capital is being returned with each payment.*

This may suit people who do not want to lock in all their capital for the term of the annuity contract. Choosing an RCV lets you re-examine your situation at the end of the annuity term, though you must appreciate that the purchasing power of the residual capital value depreciates because of inflation during the term of the annuity.

4. The frequency of payments

Usually, payments are made monthly but can be quarterly, half-yearly or annually. The more frequent the payment the less it is, which is similar to interest paid on term deposits where a higher rate is available for less frequent payments. For most people, the aim of an annuity is to provide a regular income, so monthly or quarterly payments are the most common.

> **EXAMPLE:** *An annuity of $100 000 over 10 years with no RCV may produce $15 160 annually if paid monthly, $15 302 if paid quarterly and $15 863 if paid yearly.*

5. Guarantee of term or of return of capital

You can request that payments continue for a guaranteed period such as 10 years. If death occurs before this date, the payments continue to the estate. Alternatively, you may request the capital protection option whereby any unused portion of the annuity is refunded to your estate upon death.

> **EXAMPLE:** *A woman aged 70 buys a $100 000 lifetime annuity with a guaranteed period of 10 years. It will pay her $11 500 a year including a tax-free (deductible) portion of*

$6770 a year being the $100 000 purchase price divided by her life expectancy of 14.77 years. Without the 10-year guarantee she would have received $12 200 a year. The guarantee is costing her $700 a year.

If she had chosen a capital-protected annuity, the payments would have dropped still further to $11 550 a year.

Was she wise to pay the cost of a guaranteed period, or should she have opted for capital protection? If leaving money to her estate was of no importance to her she is correct choosing the guaranteed term; she is better off having an extra $13 a week to spend now. If she wanted to give her estate some protection in the event of her early death, she should have chosen the capital protection option.

6. Any escalation in the amount of the payments

Payments may increase by a set fixed percentage each year or by the consumer price index (CPI). This helps to protect the income stream from inflation, but you pay a high price for it.

EXAMPLE: *A couple aged 70 and 61 took out a lifetime annuity for $100 000 with 85% of the income to be paid to the survivor on the death of either one of them. The annual payments would be $10 107 if there is to be no increase in the payments, $7956 a year if the payments are to rise by 3% a year and only $6282 if the annuity income is to be linked to the CPI. In each case the deductible amount is $4585 per annum as that is based on the life expectancy of the longest life, not on whether the payments are indexed.*

The insurance companies take a pessimistic view of inflation and make long-term life CPI-linked annuities unattractive.

Certainly there is some comfort in choosing an annuity in which the payments increase each year, but thoroughly investigate what you will receive if the payments do not change. If you choose an annuity with escalating payments, it usually takes about 11 years before you start to receive the income you would have had if you had chosen one where the payments remain fixed. Most retirees find their cost of living drops as they get older. Therefore it may be better to take a fixed term and enjoy a higher income in your sixties and seventies.

> KEY POINT: Before you choose an annuity with increasing payments, investigate how much you would get if the payments stayed level.

COMPARISON OF ANNUITY PAYMENTS

Annuitants are offered a choice of level payments, payments increasing each year by the CPI, or payments increasing each year at 3%.

Year	Payments level	Payments increasing by CPI	Payments increasing by 3%
1	10 107	6 282	7 956
2	10 107	6 596	8 194
3	10 107	6 926	8 440
4	10 107	7 272	8 693
5	10 107	7 636	8 954
6	10 107	8 018	9 223
7	10 107	8 419	9 499
8	10 107	8 840	9 784
9	10 107	9 282	10 078
10	10 107	9 746	10 380
11	10 107	10 233	10 692
12	10 107	10 745	11 012
13	10 107	11 282	11 343
14	10 107	11 846	11 683
15	10 107	12 438	12 034
16	10 107	13 060	12 395

7. The amount of income to be paid to a survivor when it is a joint annuity

Obviously, the higher the amount paid to the survivor the lower the amount that will be paid to the couple, and if the survivor is to continue to receive an income from that annuity, calculations will be based on the one who is expected to live the longest.

The percentage of the original annuity income that should be paid to the survivor is a matter for discussion between you and your adviser. The factors to consider are the other financial resources available and the life expectancy of the one who is likely to outlive the other. It was customary for civil service pensions to pay the surviving spouse 66% of the combined rate, but now annuities funded by ETPs may pay 85% to the survivor and still be regarded as complying annuities. Once again it is a choice of more money to enjoy together now, or of leaving a larger income for the surviving partner when one dies.

EXAMPLE: *A man is 65 and his wife is 61. They buy a $100 000 lifetime annuity with no escalation in payments. The man has a life expectancy of 14.60 years and the woman has a life expectancy of 21.81 years. If payments reduce to 66.6% on the death of either one the annuity will pay $10 500 year reducing to $6993 when one dies.*

If it paid the survivor 85% the starting pension would have been $10 100 a year.

Complying Annuities

Complying annuities are usually used by people with an excess benefit problem. The features of a complying annuity can be summarised as:

1. It must be a lifetime annuity.
2. The guarantee period must not be more than 10 years.
3. It cannot have a residual value.
4. There may be a reversion on death, but the reversionary annuitant may not receive more than 100% of what the original annuitant was receiving at the date of death.
5. Payments must be indexed and the minimum indexation is the lesser of 5% or CPI.

EXAMPLE: *An ETP of $200 000 used to buy a complying annuity comprised pre/post $150 000 and undeducted contributions $50 000. The purchaser was a male aged 65, and his wife was 65. His life expectancy is 14.60 years; hers is 18.56 years. The contract provided for a guaranteed period of 10 years, payments escalating by 5% a year and 85% of the income to continue to be paid to the spouse on the death of either party. Starting payments were $1122 a month or $13 462 a year. The deductible portion was $2694 a year, being the undeducted contributions $50 000 divided by the longest life expectancy, 18.56 years.*

A Unique Tax Saver

Because of the way the mathematics work it is possible to have a deductible portion that is greater than the annuity payment, in which case the **entire** annuity pension is tax-free, and none of it is regarded as income for the aged pension income test.

EXAMPLE: *A woman is aged 76 and buys an annuity for $100 000. Her life expectancy is 10.75 years. Because she asks for the payments to increase by 5% a year the first year's payment is $7962. The deductible portion is $9302 ($100 000 divided by 10.75), which is more than her first year's payment. The surplus of the deductible portion over the annuity income is kept in the annuity fund to be applied to future payments. She will therefore enjoy a surplus deductible portion until the annuity is in the eighth year, when the current deductible portion plus the accumulated excess deductible portion will finally become less than the annual payment.*

Notice that the deductible portion available to her in the first year is only $7962 and that the balance of $1340 ($9302 – $7962) is accumulated as a surplus deductible portion. Next year the surplus deductible portion will drop to $942 ($9302 – $8360), but this will be added to the surplus of $1340 from the previous year so that by the end of the second year there will be $2282 of surplus deductible portion accumulated. This surplus deductible portion rises until the fifth year when the yearly deductible portion of $9302 becomes less than the payment. If she lives for longer than her life expectancy she can claim the deductible portion of $9302 each year until death. It does not stop after 10.75 years.

CALCULATING SURPLUS DEDUCTIBLE PORTION

Year	Age	Annuity payment	Deductible portion	Surplus deductible portion
1	76	$7 962	$7 962	$1 340
2	77	$8 360	$8 360	$2 282
3	78	$8 779	$8 779	$2 805
4	79	$9 217	$9 217	$2 890
5	80	$9 678	$9 678	$2 514
6	81	$10 161	$10 161	$1 655
7	82	$10 669	$10 669	$288
8	83	$11 202	$9 590	nil
9	84	$11 762	$9 302	nil
10	85	$12 350	$9 302	nil

The Fifteen Per Cent Rebate

To further encourage retirees to choose income streams instead of lump sums, the Government allows a special tax rebate of 15% to those who use an ETP to buy an annuity. This rebate is equal to 15% of that part of the annuity income that is left after the deductible component created by any undeducted contributions has been taken off.

> **EXAMPLE:** *A woman retires at age 65 on 1 July 1995. Her ETP of $150 000 consists of pre/post $110 000 and undeducted contributions $40 000. If she used the ETP to buy a 15-year annuity with a nil residual capital value, the income stream would be $17 944 a year. Only the undeducted contributions give rise to a deductible portion, which becomes $2667 ($40 000 divided by the term of the annuity, 15 years). She is entitled to a tax rebate of 15% of the balance of the income stream, $15 277. This is $2291.*
>
> *If she had no other income, her tax return would show:*
>
> | | |
> |---|---:|
> | Total income | $17 944 |
> | Less *Deductible portion* | 2 667 |
> | Taxable income | $15 277 |
> | Tax payable on $15 277 | $ 1 976 |
> | Less Rebate | 2 291 |
> | Surplus tax credits available | $ 315 |

Notice how the judicious use of an annuity has given her a tax-free monthly income of $1495 and even left $315 of tax credits over. These excess tax credits could be used to help pay the tax on her other income if she had any.

> KEY POINT: A tax rebate is available only if the annuity is bought with ETP money.

Advantages Of Annuities

In most cases part of the income (the deductible portion) is tax-free. This is great for cutting down your tax.

> **EXAMPLE:** *Keith is 65. As part of his investment portfolio he has $200 000 in debentures, mortgage trusts and interest-bearing accounts and draws down from them at the rate of*

$20 000 a year. If the money earns an average of 8% he will receive $16 000 income in the first year and will have to withdraw $4000 of capital. His taxable income for that year will be $16 000 on which tax is $2120.

As the principal amount reduces because he is withdrawing more than the money is earning, his "income" of $20 000 will progressively become more capital and less interest. It works just like a housing loan – the payments are mostly interest in the early stages and mostly principal in the latter stages.

His friend Tom uses his $200 000 to buy an annuity that will be fully expended after 15 years. The annual income will also be $20 000, but $13 333 will be tax-deductible, leaving Tom with a taxable income of $6667 on which the tax would be $253.

Can you spot the major difference between the two strategies?

Tom has locked in his rate of return for the next 15 years and has also guaranteed himself a fixed income for all that time. However, he is vulnerable to inflation and rising interest rates. Keith will not do as well if rates fall but will do better if rates rise. However, he suffers the risk of making bad investment decisions and losing all or part of his capital as a result of doing so. He is also paying more tax than necessary in the first few years.

Annuities are useful for maximising the pension, as the deductible portion of the payments is not regarded as income for the income test.[2] In the example above, Keith, if he was a pensioner, would be deemed to be earning $10 000 a year more than Tom and his pension would be nearly $100 a week less because of this increased income. Notice the power of the deductible portion.

Disadvantages Of Annuities

The main problem with most types of annuities is their lack of flexibility, and it will cost you heavily if you have a change of heart. Fixed-term annuities can always be sold back to the life company for a negotiated sum, but it's a bit like selling anything second-hand; you don't get nearly what you paid for it. Once a life annuity has been bought, it is difficult, although not impossible, to reverse the transaction and get your money back in the bank. For this

---

2. Full details of the income and assets tests are given in chapter 40.

reason we are loath to let most retirees tie up too much of their money in this area, particularly if the annuity is for life.

An annuity may be fine for single people in their seventies with nobody to leave their money to, but it is a different matter if they are only 60 with possibly 25 years ahead of them. Who knows what heights inflation might reach, or what changes may take place in their lives in that 25 years? Imagine if they found out that they had only a few months to live and wanted to "blow" all their money on travel or gift it immediately to their family. These options are not available with a life annuity.

Beware Of Inflation

A point that needs highlighting is the devastating effect of inflation on annuities. Certainly you can buy an annuity that is indexed for inflation but, as I pointed out earlier in this chapter, the price is high and usually the maximum increase in payments in any one year is limited to 10%. This is irrespective of the rate of inflation.

> **EXAMPLE:** *At date of writing a couple aged 65 could buy a non-indexed annuity for $100 000 paying them a level $10 319 a year until death. Compare this with an inflation-indexed annuity that pays only $6068 a year for the first year but rises each year with the CPI.*

How fast the indexed annuity payments rise depends on the CPI. If we take 5% as a reasonable figure, it will be 11 long years before the indexed annuity payments rise to $9883 a year, and 12 years before they reach $10 378, which just exceeds the level annuity payments of $10 319. If inflation is less than 5% per annum it will take even longer for the CPI-indexed annuity to catch up to the one with level payments. However, if inflation does run at 5%, it will still take over 20 years for the indexed annuity to have returned the same income as the non-indexed one, because after 20 years the non-indexed annuity would have paid $206 380 and the indexed annuity $200 629. The far more expensive indexed annuity does not start to provide any additional benefits until the owners are 85!

Which is best? That depends on the rate of inflation, but you can build protection for inflation into your portfolio by keeping a large percentage of your interest-bearing funds in shorter-term debentures. Then, if inflation rises, interest rates will too, and you can renew your debentures at the higher rates as they fall due.

KEY POINT: It is unwise to place too great a proportion of your money in annuities.

How To Buy An Annuity

Annuities can be purchased through licensed financial planners or life insurance agents who should be able to explain the advantages and drawbacks of them and obtain quotes from life companies for you. In view of their inflexibility, it is important that you do careful research before investing funds in them.

The figures in the examples in this chapter were done using rates that were current at date of writing, but they are shown only to illustrate the principles. As annuity quotes change at least weekly, you will need to obtain up-to-date quotes if you believe annuities are an appropriate investment for you. You will find that most annuity quotes are good for only 14 days, which means delay in making a decision will necessitate your asking for a fresh quote. The new quote may be better for you, or worse, than the previous one, depending on the way rates are moving.

Once you buy the annuity, you will find it is a trouble-free investment, with the payments being deposited directly to your account. At the end of the financial year, you will receive a group certificate showing the gross payment for the year, less the PAYE tax that has been deducted if appropriate.

What Happens When I Die

There is a mistaken belief that the Government gets any unused money from your annuity if you die before your life expectancy. This is not true. Life insurance companies take life expectancy into account when they quote on an annuity contract and they are aware that many people die before their life expectancy and many live way past it. They also know that the type of people who take out annuities tend to be long-livers. Who in their right mind would take out a lifetime annuity if they expected to die young?

To put it simply, those who die before their life expectancy subsidise those who die past it. It is the insurance company who makes any profit or carries any loss. In this respect it is no different from a bookmaker who loses when the favourite wins and wins when a long shot gets up.

Let's now summarise what happens if you die while you are an annuitant.

Term-certain annuity. The payments will continue to be paid until the end of the contracted term. Instead of being paid to you, they will go to your estate or to another person you nominated as reversionary annuitant when you originally bought the annuity.

Lifetime annuity. The payments cease on your death unless there was a guaranteed payment period that has not yet elapsed. If there was a residual capital value, it is payable to your estate on your death.

Lifetime annuity with a reversionary annuitant. The payments will continue to the other party at the rate specified when you bought the annuity. This is often, but not necessarily, 85% of the original payments.

Complying annuity. The payments will cease on death unless there was a guaranteed period of up to 10 years, or you had nominated your spouse as reversionary annuitant.

Conclusion

By now your knowledge of retirement planning should have improved markedly. You understand rollovers, RBLs, lump sum tax and the benefits and the drawbacks of annuities. You appreciate there is a trend towards taking income streams in retirement and that tax benefits can be gained by rolling an ETP into an annuity, but the disadvantage is that annuities are inflexible and lock in today's rates for the term of the annuity contract.

However, annuities have their place. Short-term money-back annuities can minimise lump sum tax by deferring receipt of the sum to a future date and acting like a debenture in the meantime, and small ten-year annuities with no residual value at the end of the term can increase pension entitlements while giving time for growth investments to bloom. People with a relatively short life expectancy and no beneficiaries may be very satisfied with the bulk of their assets in immediate annuities.

However, these are specialised cases and most of you should not tie up too much money in these areas without deep consideration of the ramifications involved.

Now it's time to explore a much more flexible investment that carries similar tax advantages to annuities – the allocated pension.

Summing Up

- An annuity is a regular income paid to you by an insurance company in exchange for a lump sum.
- Annuities provide an opportunity to save lump sum tax while providing an income stream.
- They are a somewhat inflexible investment so don't invest in them without a full understanding of their disadvantages.
- Part of the income is a return of capital and is thus tax-free. This does not apply to annuities bought with the pre and post components of an ETP. In lieu they enjoy a tax rebate.
- Many insurance companies who offer inflation-indexed annuities limit annual rises to 10% irrespective of the rate of inflation.
- What happens to the money when you die depends on the terms of the annuity contract.
- It is often better to take a non-indexed annuity and enjoy a higher income now, than to opt for one where the income rises each year.

29

ALLOCATED PENSIONS

Money is a sixth sense which makes it possible to enjoy the other five.

RICHARD NEY

Now that you are an expert on annuities, let's examine the main alternative to them – allocated pensions or, as they are sometimes called, "rollover pensions".

Allocated pensions are leaping in the popularity stakes because they offer a flexibility that annuities lack. They are also among the most simple investments you could have. The only problem seems to be that many retirees look for complications in them that simply do not exist.

The forerunners of allocated pensions were pensions paid out of some superannuation funds. Maybe Ace Manufacturing Ltd was a good and stable employer who ran a well-established staff superannuation fund. When John Smith the factory foreman retired, the company had three options:

1. Pay to him, as a lump sum, his balance in the superannuation fund. The problem with doing that was that John probably had no financial expertise whatsoever and might have lost it all. Remember, there were no financial advisers or rollover funds in those days.

2. Buy him an annuity with the money in his name in the superannuation fund. This was occasionally done but, as you now know, annuities don't suit everybody and whether it is a good investment depends on the way interest rates move after you buy one.

3. Start paying him a private pension from his account with the superannuation fund. The fund is well managed and providing excellent returns so it makes good sense to keep the financial structure intact and pay his money to him as an income. The fund will credit his account with the "interest" his money makes, and will debit the account with his monthly pension payments. It's a good deal for John because he still receives a regular income and does not have the worry of trying to manage the money himself.

Allocated pension funds are nothing more than an extension of this idea. You have your own account within a superannuation fund and you draw a regular income from it. The balance will rise with earnings and be reduced by fees and withdrawals.

> KEY POINT: An allocated pension is an income paid to you out of an account you have with a superannuation fund. It rises through the money it earns and reduces through fees and the pension you receive.

There is one major difference between having money in a normal superannuation fund and having it in an allocated pension fund. The allocated pension fund is like an annuity fund – it is exempt from tax. Instead, the income paid to you by the fund is taxable, but is eligible for the same 15% rebate that is enjoyed by annuities that emanate from ETP (eligible termination payment) money. Already you should be noticing the similarity between allocated pensions and annuities.

Because an allocated pension allows you to maintain funds in a tax-free area, and draw an income that may be tax-free, the guidelines require that you take a minimum pension each year. The amount is determined by your age and the amount in your allocated pension fund account. Furthermore, to stop you drawing down too quickly on your capital and resorting to welfare, there is also a maximum amount that can be drawn each year. If you wish to draw more than the maximum amount in any year you may cash in part of the capital sum. The term for doing this is called "commutation" of the pension. I'll explain all this in more detail soon.

For the first few years your allocated pension account will rise if its earnings are more than the withdrawals but, as time passes, the money in your account will start to run down, and one of two things will eventually happen:

1. The money will run out.

   or

2. You will die.

Don't they sound like two awful choices – death or poverty! Don't despair, very few people die broke. If you run out of money you will have to fall back on other resources, which will probably be a combination of your other investments or the aged pension. If you die the unused balance is available for your beneficiaries, either as a pension or a lump sum.

The principles are as simple as that and, if you keep them in mind, you should have no problem understanding what follows. Now let's look at a typical allocated pension account and, as you read what follows, keep in mind that the sole aim of this example is to illustrate the way the allocated pension fund works.

The investor is Ms Brown who is aged 60. She has $200 000 in her rollover fund and it contains no undeducted contributions. She has other investments that provide income and has asked to draw the minimum pension. The pension valuation factors are 17.80 and 9.00, which I'll explain soon. To calculate her minimum and maximum pension you divide $200 000 by 17.80 and 9.00 and arrive at $11 236 and $22 222. Her initial pension must be between these two amounts.

The figures in table 29.1 assume that she commences by drawing a pension of $11 280 a year, at the rate of $940 a calendar month, and that this increases by 2% per annum or by an amount sufficient to raise the pension to the minimum required. Fund earnings are 7% after all fees. The "year-end balance" is the balance in the account at the end of each year.

As you can see, in principle it is similar to a bank account. The important factors to understand are:

1. The earnings vary continually in line with current market trends.

2. The balance of the account is what is left each year after earnings have been credited and fees and withdrawals paid.

3. She may vary her pension whenever she wishes as long as she stays within the minimum and maximum figures.

TABLE 29.1

Year	Age	Fund earnings	Pension paid	Year-end Balance
1	60	14 000	11 280	202 720
2	61	13 810	11 650	204 880
3	62	13 960	12 052	206 788
4	63	14 080	12 457	208 412
5	64	14 181	12 865	209 728

Notice how the fund balance is rising because at this early stage she is withdrawing less than the earnings.

Year	Age	Fund earnings	Pension paid	Year-end Balance
6	65	14 258	13 358	210 627
7	66	14 308	13 766	211 168
8	67	14 333	14 172	211 328

Now we have reached the point where the earnings and the pension are almost equal. The fund balance will start to reduce from here. However, she has done well. She has kept $200 000 of assets in a tax-free environment for eight years, drawn from these assets a substantial sum that carried tax concessions, and still has $211 328 left.

Year	Age	Fund earnings	Pension paid	Year-end Balance
9	68	14 328	14 676	210 981
10	69	14 291	15 070	201 584

The rundown of capital has now commenced. From here we'll look at five-year balances only.

Year	Age	Fund earnings	Pension paid	Year-end Balance
15	74	13 565	17 229	177 169
20	79	11 811	18 649	137 725

Maybe now is the time for Ms Brown to consider rolling the balance of the fund into an annuity. She is still in good health and is not worried about leaving the balance in the fund to her estate. Her life expectancy is now nine years and a non-indexed annuity may pay her $25 500 a year until her death. However, if she continues with the allocated pension the fund balance and drawings will go like this:

Year	Age	Fund earnings	Pension paid	Year-end Balance
25	84	9 059	18 363	81 055
30	89	5 038	20 049	66 044

Now you know the fundamentals we will look at the features of allocated pensions in more detail. As we do this, keep comparing them in your mind with the annuities that you learnt about in the previous chapter.

Features Of Allocated Pensions

You can defer or eliminate lump sum tax. No lump sum tax is immediately payable when you roll into the pension fund. This enables you to defer payment of lump sum tax well past the age of 65, which means there is a larger sum working for you. Furthermore, unless you make lump sum withdrawals in addition to your pension, there is never any lump sum tax to pay. You have escaped it altogether.

Tax-free fund. A superannuation fund that pays a pension is not taxed on its earnings; therefore, once you move your money to an allocated pension fund it is in a tax-free area. In contrast, a rollover fund or normal superannuation fund pays tax on your behalf at up to 15%. Therefore, if all other factors are equal, an allocated pension fund must provide higher returns than a superannuation or rollover fund.

EXAMPLE: *Suppose $100 000 invested in an allocated pension fund and a rollover fund produced $10 000 each (after management fees) for a year. The rollover fund would pay tax of 15% leaving earnings of $8500 while the allocated pension fund would pay no tax leaving earnings of $10 000. Thus the after-tax return from the allocated pension fund would be 10%, and the rollover fund 8.5%. The tax payable, if any, on the allocated pension income to the recipient depends on her other income because of the 15% tax rebate.*

Access to funds. You are able to withdraw capital from the pension plan at any time by commuting part of the pension. Obviously, the sum available to fund the pension will then reduce, resulting in a possibly reduced pension depending on the maximum and minimum levels allowable. Lump sum tax is payable on the sum commuted.

Tax-free growth. Because the fund is tax-exempt, any earnings are tax-free. However, it is possible that your assets may grow so fast that you will have to readjust your minimum and maximum pension figures. That may require you to increase your pension, in which case you may pay a little more tax on the income stream. That would be a pleasant problem to have, wouldn't it?

Variable income. Provided the pension you draw always stays between the specified minimum and maximum levels, you can vary it from year to year to suit your changing requirements. However, if the earnings of the fund are greater than the withdrawals, the balance of the pension plan fund will rise and it is possible you may be required to draw a larger pension or make a lump sum withdrawal by commuting some of the balance.

Tax benefits. That part of the pension income that comes from the undeducted component is tax-free. The part that derives from the balance of the funds in the allocated pension account carries a tax rebate. The combination of these often enables a retiree to enjoy a tax-free income stream.

Variable earning rate. Most annuities fix the initial earning rate for the life of the contract. In contrast, an allocated pension fund will earn prevailing market rates and is able to take advantage of rates as they rise.

Funds not lost on death. A spouse is allowed to continue the pension upon the death of the original member; when the spouse dies any unused funds in the pension plan go to the estate. Thus the beneficiaries are not disadvantaged as is the case with a life annuity.

KEY POINT: The unused balance of an allocated pension fund is not lost when the owner dies. It may be taken as a lump sum or the pension may be continued to be paid to the surviving spouse.

The Upper And Lower Limits

The minimum and maximum pension payments are calculated using tables published by the Insurance and Superannuation Commission. The numbers are referred to as pension valuation factors (PVFs) and a sample of them follows:

TABLE 29.2

Allocated Pension Valuation Factors.

Age	Minimum factor	Maximum factor
55	19.8	9.6
60	17.8	9.0
65	15.7	8.1
70	13.5	6.6
75	11.3	4.3

Be aware that these PVFs are not the same as the life expectancy factors, although life expectancy was taken into account when the PVFs were originally worked out.

To calculate the minimum and maximum pensions, you divide the balance in the allocated pension fund by the relevant PVF for the person's age.

EXAMPLE: *A person is 65 and has $200 000 in his or her allocated pension account. The minimum factor is 15.7 and the maximum factor is 8.1. The minimum pension is $12 738 being $200 000 divided by 15.7. The maximum pension is $24 691 being $200 000 divided by 8.1.*

The fund manager will recalculate the minimum and maximum pensions each year, or when a lump sum withdrawal is made, to take into account the changing balance.

Boosting Your Allocated Pension Fund

Because an allocated pension comes from a superannuation fund, anybody who is eligible to contribute to superannuation can fund an allocated pension by making large contributions to super and not claim a tax deduction.

Such contributions are styled "undeducted contributions" and because no tax deduction has been claimed they do not suffer the 15% entry tax. Therefore, the only cost of making the contribution is the fee, if any, charged by the superannuation fund into which it was placed.

This saves tax in three ways:

1. It initially transfers money to an area (superannuation) where the tax on fund earnings is only 15%.

2. The presence of undeducted contributions can reduce the post-1983 component if a pre-1983 component is present. This will reduce lump sum tax if any of the money is taken as a lump sum.

3. When you eventually start an allocated pension you will get a tax deduction.

EXAMPLE: *Jock is aged 60 and will retire at age 65. He earns $50 000 a year and has $80 000 in interest-bearing accounts available for investment. He knows if he leaves it in interest-bearing accounts he will continue to pay 47% tax on the* *interest. He left another job several years ago and his ETP of $200 000 is rolled over in his superannuation fund. It is split $100 000 pre and $100 000 post. If he places that $80 000 he has available into his superannuation fund as an undeducted contribution the components will change to pre $140 000, undeducted contributions $80 000, and post $60 000. This will reduce lump sum tax considerably if he decides to withdraw it all in cash.*

However, if he decided to start an allocated pension at age 65, the presence of the undeducted contributions will give him a tax deduction of $5479 every year for the rest of his life or until the money runs out. The value of this will depend on the extent of his other income.

The tax deduction treatment is similar to that used with annuities. In the above example, Jock was 65 when he started the allocated pension and his life expectancy was then 14.60 years. The deductible portion is $5479 being the undeducted contributions of $80 000 divided by the life expectancy of 14.60.

KEY POINT: Undeducted contributions enable you to hold more funds in the tax-exempt allocated pension area and also give you a tax deduction on part of the income stream.

Putting It All Together

Let's now examine an allocated pension account in detail and see if you can place the factors I mentioned above. We'll assume that Harold has retired at age 60 and has $250 000 in his superannuation fund. Of this amount, $200 000 is pre and post, and $50 000 is undeducted contributions that he added to his superannuation as he neared retirement to take advantage of the tax benefits I mentioned in the previous paragraph. His wife, Alice, is also 60.

As you can see from Table 29.3, after twenty years have passed there is still some money left. If Alice dies at this time the unused balance would form part of her estate to be distributed in accordance with her will.

Now let's examine the tax effectiveness of the allocated pension plan. As Harold's life expectancy is 18.13 years, the undeducted contributions of $50 000 will create an annual tax deduction of $2758 being $50 000 divided by 18.13. This deductible amount of

TABLE 29.3

Year	Age	Fund earnings	Pension paid	Year-end balance
1	60	17 500	16 000	251 500

Notice how the balance rises for the first two years because the earnings are more than the pension. After the first year of retirement they decide that $16 000 is not enough to live on and raise the pension to $17 000 a year.

2	61	17 066	17 000	251 566

They decide to go for a trip and commute $40 000 of the lump sum. The balance drops by $40 000 accordingly.

3	62	17 060	17 340	211 286
4	63	14 230	17 687	207 829
5	64	13 976	18 041	203 765
6	65	13 680	18 401	199 044
7	66	13 338	18 769	193 613
8	67	12 949	19 145	187 417
9	68	12 500	19 528	180 389
10	69	11 996	19 918	172 467
11	70	11 429	20 317	163 579

Harold dies and Alice commutes $10 000 to pay for the funeral costs and other expenses and reduces the pension to $16 000 because she is now living on her own.

12	71	10 243	16 000	147 822
13	72	9 830	16 320	141 332
14	73	9 366	16 646	134 052
15	74	8 845	16 979	125 918
16	75	8 265	17 319	116 864
17	76	7 620	17 665	106 819
18	77	6 906	18 019	95 706
19	78	6 117	18 379	83 444
20	79	5 247	18 747	69 944

As you can see, twenty years have passed and there is still some money left. If Alice dies at this time the unused balance would form part of her estate to be distributed in accordance with her will.

$2758 will remain constant for as long as Harold continues to draw a pension. If he dies, and Alice elects to continue the pension, her deductible portion will be found by dividing the original undeducted contributions component $50 000 by her life expectancy (22.65) at the time Harold started the allocated pension. Consequently her deductible portion will drop to $2207 ($50 000/22.65).

From the illustration we can see that Harold's pension in Year 10 was $19 918. The tax treatment is:

Pension	$19 918
Less Deductible portion	2 758
Assessable pension	$17 160

This sum carries with it a 15% rebate which is $2574 ($17 160 × 15%). If Harold had no other income, the tax on the $17 160 would be $2352, in which case the rebate would pay all the tax and leave Harold with excess credits of $222 that could be applied against other income if he had any. The rebates cannot be carried forward so are lost if Harold does not generate a little other income to use them up.

> KEY POINT: If the original pensioner dies, and the spouse elects to continue the pension, the deductible portion is calculated with respect to the original amount of undeducted contributions and the life expectancy of the reversionary pensioner at the date the original pension commenced.

As you can see, the allocated pension fund is a splendid retirement vehicle. Now, just to confuse you a little, I am now going to introduce you to another product – the allocated annuity.

Allocated Annuities

Allocated annuities have been placed in the allocated pension chapter because they are far more like allocated pensions than annuities. There is no set term, any unused balance goes to your estate, the earning rate varies with prevailing market rates, and you are required to choose an income from them that falls between a minimum and a maximum amount.

The major differences between allocated pensions and allocated annuities are:

1. Allocated pensions are run by various institutions and are subject to the Superannuation Industry Supervision Act. Allocated annuities are payable only by life offices and friendly societies and therefore are subject to the Life Insurance Act.

2. If the originator of an allocated pension does not nominate a reversionary beneficiary, in the event of his death the trustee of the fund paying the allocated pension will usually exercise a discretion to make pension payments to a surviving spouse. If the originator of an allocated annuity does not nominate a "reversionary annuitant" or an "annuity option" to another person, the balance of the account goes to the deceased's estate.

As you can see, there are only slight differences between them. However, it is important to note that the allocated annuity is a contractual investment and the spouse may be required to continue the allocated annuity if the original holder dies. This is why it is more flexible to use the allocated pension whereby the spouse can choose to continue the pension if he or she wishes.

When Should An Allocated Pension Start?

Normally you would start your allocated pension after you retire, although you are allowed to start an allocated pension with unpreserved ETP monies at any time. However, the problem with receiving income from a pension while you earn other income is that your overall taxable income increases and the extra income may be pushed into a higher tax bracket.

Nevertheless, in some cases, it may be worthwhile starting an allocated pension while you are working.

EXAMPLE: *Mick, who is aged 55 and has $200 000 in unpreserved rollover money, is now working on a part-time basis earning $10 000 a year. If he starts to draw the minimum allowable pension of $10 101 a year from his rollover funds, his total income will be $20 101 a year. The tax on this would normally be $2940, but the 15% tax rebate on the $10 101 allocated pension will reduce the total tax payable by $1515 to $1425. This is only $505 more than the $920 tax Mick would have to pay on his wage of $10 000 if he did not have any other income.*

A major benefit in cases like this one is that, by transferring funds from the rollover area to the allocated pension area, the investor moves them from the 15% taxed area to the tax-free area. This should mean higher returns on the ETP money, but the benefits of doing this should be weighed against the tax payable (less the rebate) on the income stream. As other income rises, the advantages of starting the allocated pension reduce.

An allocated pension may not be started with preserved ETP money until the preservation date passes and the money becomes unpreserved.

Annuity Or Allocated Pension?

By now you should be convinced of the merits of having an income stream when you retire. The question you may be thinking is "Should I choose an annuity or an allocated pension?" There is no simple answer and, unfortunately, many approaching retirement think it is a choice of one **or** the other. A popular but dangerous statement is "With an allocated pension I might run out of money, therefore I am better off with an annuity." If you think like that, you don't understand the difference between them, so let's think briefly about the main points of both.

An **annuity** is a contract whereby you receive a fixed income for a certain period. The period may be a set number of years or until death. At the end of the period your original investment is all gone unless you have contracted to have a specified amount refunded to you. For example, the annuity contract may provide that 50% of the original sum you invested comes back to you at the end of the term. The annuity income stream is capital guaranteed and may stay level, be indexed for inflation or rise by a set amount (such as 5%) each year. The earning rate is fixed for the life of the annuity unless you opt for one that carries bonuses. In this case, the guaranteed income is lower.

An **allocated pension** is an account in your name with a superannuation fund. It is debited with the withdrawals (in the form of a pension) you make from it and credited with the earnings made by the money you have in this fund. You must take a minimum pension each year to prevent the balance of your account rising indefinitely and you cannot draw more than a certain maximum pension.

If your allocated pension fund has a large starting balance, and you start with the minimum pension, the balance of your account may rise in the early years. However, once your yearly pension exceeds the yearly earnings, the balance of your account starts to drop. How fast it drops depends on the size of your withdrawals.

Remember that both the annuity fund and the allocated pension fund are tax-exempt, so by holding part of your assets in either one you have a portion of your assets in a tax-free area. But never forget the crucial difference: when you buy an annuity you fix the rate for the term of the contract, often for the rest of your life. Do you want to invest money now in a product that locks in today's interest rates for the next 20 years or more? That is for you to decide.

If you choose an allocated pension the earnings will vary in line with current rates. If they rise, yours do too. Certainly if rates fall, and stay down for the rest of your life, the annuity may be a better proposition.

A simplistic way to think about it is to pretend that both the annuity and the allocated pension fund are a tax-free bank account. With the annuity, the interest rate and the amount you can withdraw each year is fixed when you open the account. In contrast, the allocated pension offers a variable rate and the right to make withdrawals when you wish.

Obviously, each case must be decided on its merits, but often the best strategy for most retirees is to take an allocated pension to start and convert it to an annuity, if appropriate, after age 75. This gives you the best of the benefits of both.

Reasonable Benefit Limits

In chapter 25, when we discussed the pension RBL and the lump sum RBL, I pointed out that the pension RBL was much higher than the lump sum RBL, but to use the pension RBL you had to take at least half of your ETP as a complying annuity. Despite the similarity in terms, neither an allocated pension nor an allocated annuity is a complying annuity, hence the lump sum RBL is applied.

KEY POINT: An allocated pension is not a complying annuity. Money placed in an allocated pension fund is tested against your lump sum RBL not your pension RBL.

TABLE 29.4

Allocated Pensions versus Annuities.

	Allocated pensions	Annuities
EARNING RATE	Varies	Fixed
LUMP SUM WITHDRAWALS	As needed	Normally none
TERM	Till the money runs out	Till death or set term
VARIED PAYMENTS	Yes - between limits	No - unless indexed
ON DEATH	Spouse has choice of income or lump sum	Usually nothing left
COST TO BUY	Not relevant	Varies with buy date
FLEXIBLE	Yes - very	No

Conclusion

By now you should have a good understanding of allocated pensions and how they compare with annuities. They are simple, tax-efficient investments and are growing quickly in popularity because they provide an orderly method of drawing down on your capital. Now we'll move on to discussing whether a lump sum is better to have in retirement than a pension.

Summing Up

- An allocated pension account is similar in principle to a bank account except that the balance can fall because of market movements if the fund contains growth assets.
- It will last until the money runs out.
- The earnings you receive will vary with general market trends.
- You have access to your funds at all time.
- A spouse may continue the pension on the death of the original owner.
- Undeducted contributions have tax advantages.
- When you die the unused balance is available for your estate.

30

LUMP SUM OR PENSION

The key to your universe is that you can choose.

CARL FREDERICK

Most income streams come from aged pensions, allocated pensions or annuities, which are discussed in detail in this book. However, there are some people who are given the option, when they retire, of a part lump sum and a part pension and can often choose between various combinations of the above.

The options for a 65-year-old person might be:

1. lump sum of $300 000 and no pension
2. lump sum of $175 000 and an indexed pension of $10 000 a year
3. lump sum of $60 000 and an indexed pension of $18 000 a year.

Options 2 and 3 include a pension for the spouse if the original pensioner dies. It is set at two-thirds of the pension the other party was receiving at the date of death.

The question is always asked "Which one should I choose?"

There is no simple answer because it depends on so many factors. Certainly, any good financial adviser could run the above figures through a computer and quickly calculate a cash value in today's dollars on each of the options. However, if we did this using the figures in the above example, and assuming the spouse is 65 too, the cash value of each of the three options is almost the same.

If you are faced with choosing between options similar to the above, the factors to consider are:

1. Are you single or married?

A pension is such a simple option for single people, particularly if they have no intention of getting married. It gives them a guaranteed income for life without the worry of losing any capital and, best of all, the pension is indexed for inflation so they never have to worry about the cost of living. It is probably the best choice for a person who lives simply and is security conscious.

2. Is leaving money to your estate important to you?

A pension is much more valuable to a couple than to a single person because the pension will continue until both die. However, when this happens all the money is gone. Premature death of both still means the pension has ended, and it is possible for a couple to die together in an accident just after they retire.

If your main priority is leaving as much as you can to your children you should choose the lump sum, provided you have confidence in your ability to handle it wisely.

3. What is your life expectancy?

Obviously, the value of the pension rises if you have a long life expectancy, and it can be of much greater value if you have a young spouse for it will continue to his or her death. In general terms, the longer your life expectancy the more inclined you should be to take the pension. However, if your health is not good now, especially if you are single, it makes more sense to take the lump sum and enjoy it while you can.

4. What debts or expenses will you have on retirement?

We have found most retirees have few debts when they retire, but certainly there are some who have been scarred by a business investment that went bad, by having to provide funds to get children out of a problem or through suffering a costly divorce. For them, the lump sum may be the only option for they may need it to get their affairs straight. Then, of course, having spent most of the lump sum sorting things out, they can go on the aged pension and still get a substantial income.

5. What is your experience in handling money?

This is one of the key factors. If you have a good track record in handling money, have a good, long-established relationship with an adviser you trust and enjoy looking after your own money, you will probably prefer the lump sum.

However, if you are not used to handling money and, worse still, you tend to believe what you read in the papers and what well-meaning friends and relatives tell you, I suggest you seriously consider the pension option.

Handling money is a little like developing a good relationship with your partner. It takes time and you always make some mistakes as you learn. Unfortunately money is not as forgiving as your partner. When you have lost it that is the end of it.

6. What other assets do you have?

This is a bit of a Catch 22. If you have plenty of assets it might be prudent to take the pension because you probably don't need any more lump sums. However, if you do have substantial assets, it is likely you are experienced at handling money and enjoy it. In any event, you are quite capable of making up your own mind.

7. Is getting some form of social security important to you?

This is one of the paradoxes in our society. People can work hard all their lives, invest all their spare money, and then discover somebody who has never saved a dollar is nearly as well off on the aged pension. In our experience there are some people who will do almost anything to get at least a little bit of pension, there are others who couldn't bear the thought of a handout, and there are some who "Don't want them sticking their nose into our affairs". You will know which category you fall into.

However, if the aged pension is your goal you may be better off with the lump sum. Then you can spend it on travel or give it away. Just remember, eligibility for pensions is being continually tightened.

Conclusion

Experience has shown that most people who have the option of a pension or a lump sum have a good idea of which one will suit them best, and want their adviser to confirm that what they feel is correct. The points made in this chapter may help.

Summing Up

- The longer you and your spouse expect to live, the more you should favour the pension.
- A pension is often better for a single person.
- If you are inexperienced with money, choose either the pension or find a good adviser to help you manage a lump sum.

31

WHAT HAPPENS TO YOUR SUPERANNUATION WHEN YOU DIE?

The chief value of life insurance seems to be that it gives the person insured an increased capacity for meeting the natural and inevitable trials, difficulties and obstacles of life.

ELBERT HUBBARD

We'll now finish the section on superannuation with a discussion on what happens to money you have in superannuation or rollover funds when you die. It sounds a simple subject, but what follows is some of the most complex material in this book.

Don't feel bad if parts of it are beyond you. The main point to remember is that ignorance of the rules could cost you dearly. Therefore, make sure you, or your loved ones, consult your adviser when a death occurs.

There are two important factors to consider:

1. In what circumstances tax is payable.
2. Who is entitled to receive the money.

Lump Sum Tax

You learnt about lump sum tax in a previous section and I can start off with some good news. In certain circumstances, if you are not in excess benefits when you die, your beneficiaries may receive the proceeds free of lump sum tax. The tax treatment depends on whether the funds are left to:

1. one or more of your dependants
2. the trustee of your estate
3. somebody who is neither a trustee nor a dependant.

Payment directly to one or more of your dependants

Until January 1987 the definition "dependant" was mainly confined to your spouse or your children. However, it was seen as a poor definition because it excluded people who were genuinely dependent on you yet were not a spouse or child. It also covered children who were adult and well able to look after themselves. As a result, the laws were changed. Now the term "spouse" includes a de facto spouse and a former spouse, and the term "child" means any child of the deceased under 18 and includes an adopted child, step-child, ex-nuptial child or anybody else who is financially dependent on you. This is the meaning of "dependant" in this chapter.

If you die while you have money in a superannuation fund, or rollover fund, no lump sum tax is payable if the money is paid to a dependant provided you are not in excess of your pension RBL. This is $800 000 in 1994 dollars for most people. The dependant must take the money as a lump sum as it is not eligible to be rolled over.

> KEY POINT: No lump sum tax is payable if the proceeds of your superannuation fund, approved deposit fund or deferred annuity are paid direct to one or more of your dependants on your death and you are not in excess of your pension RBL.

If you are in excess of your pension RBL when you die, the excess benefit will attract the normal excess benefit tax, which is currently 47% plus Medicare levy.

If the lump sum is payment of the capital remaining out of a superannuation pension or complying annuity, the beneficiary may elect to continue the income stream or receive the money as an ETP. If the latter option is chosen, the beneficiary may roll over the ETP or cash it in and pay any lump sum tax due. This will become increasingly common as allocated pensions grow in popularity, because an allocated pension is a superannuation pension. This election must be made within six months from the death of the member, or three months from the date of probate of the will or the issuance of letters of administration, whichever occurs last.

If you are the beneficiary of any ETPs from a deceased estate, it is wise to keep such ETPs separate from your other superannuation and rollover funds so they do not become mixed up together and cause future RBL problems.

Once the time periods specified above have elapsed, the beneficiary loses the ability to exercise a choice. The money will be treated as an ETP, and taxed as an ETP, but will not be eligible to be rolled over. It will be paid to the beneficiary, who will be liable for lump sum tax.

> KEY POINT: If you are eligible to receive an ETP from a deceased estate, watch the time limits carefully.

Payment directly to the trustee of a deceased estate

The tax treatment of lump sum death benefits payable directly to the trustee of a deceased estate depends mainly on the type of death benefit paid, and whether dependent beneficiaries are involved.

The payment may come from any one of the following:

1. an employer payment that arose because the deceased died while still employed
2. a lump sum that was paid from a superannuation fund
3. a lump sum that was paid from an approved deposit fund.

This money will become tax-free in the hands of dependent beneficiaries but cannot be rolled over. In the hands of non-dependants, money from the above sources is taxed in the hands of the trustee of the estate at tax rates according to the deceased's age.

However, if the payment comes from the unused balance of a superannuation pension, allocated pension or the residual capital value of an immediate annuity, the money is assessable as an ETP but cannot be rolled over.

Payment directly to a non-dependant

A non-dependant gets no tax concessions. The payment is regarded as an ETP and is taxed as an ETP. However, it cannot be rolled over by the recipient. An important point is that the definition of a "non-dependant" requires the person to be a non-dependant both at date of death and at the date of receiving the money.

Accordingly, a beneficiary who was under 18 at time of death, but over 18 at the time of payment, is regarded as a dependant.

Excess benefit tax at the highest marginal rate plus Medicare levy is due on any money that is in excess of the dead person's pension RBL.

Death Of A Member Of A Superannuation Fund While Still Working

Many funds carry life assurance. Therefore, the death benefit will often consist of the proceeds of the life assurance policy held by the fund, as well as the member's balance in the fund if it is an accumulation fund. If it is a defined benefit fund, the proceeds will usually be just the proceeds of the assurance policy, but these policies are often equivalent to the retirement payout. Consequently, the estate of a member of a defined benefit fund often receives a much larger payment than a member of an accumulation fund, particularly if the member dies young.

Provided the funds are paid to a dependant and the deceased is not in excess of the pension RBL, which is highly unlikely, the money is paid free of lump sum tax. **In this case it cannot be rolled over. However, if the proceeds are paid to non-dependants, such as the deceased's person's parents, the proceeds become an untaxed ETP.**

Death Of A Person Who Is Receiving An Allocated Pension

If you die while receiving an allocated pension the trustee of the superannuation fund paying the pension has the option of making the pension payments to your spouse, partner or other beneficiary, or allowing them to take the lump sum that is the balance of the account. Should they decide to take the lump sum, the money is paid to them as an ETP and they have the option of rolling it over or paying normal lump sum tax. There are three possible situations if a person, usually the spouse, decides to continue the allocated pension:

1. **Reversionary pensioner named at the time the pension commenced.** When you start the pension you are allowed to

make a declaration to the allocated pension fund nominating your spouse as "reversionary pensioner". If this has been done, the pension will continue but will now be paid to the spouse.

When a reversionary pensioner is nominated at the time the original pension commences, the tax-free portion is based on the longest life expectancy. Accordingly no adjustment is made when one dies – the pension continues as normal.

2. **Nominated beneficiary named at the time the pension commenced.** If a nominated beneficiary, instead of a reversionary pensioner, was named at the outset, the minimum and maximum pension settings are adjusted to take into account the life expectancy of the new pensioner.

   Furthermore, the tax-free portion of the pension payments is recalculated. The figures used to do this are the current original undeducted contributions amount and the current life expectancy of the nominated beneficiary at the date the deceased spouse commenced the pension.

3. **If no reversionary pensioner or nominated beneficiary was named when the pension commenced.** In this case the proceeds are dealt with according to the will, but the trustee of the superannuation fund paying the allocated pension has a discretion to pay the allocated pension to the spouse. The trustees normally agree to this unless the will is contested or the family is in disagreement. If the pension is continued by the spouse, the pension figures are reworked as in the previous example.

If the spouse elects to continue the allocated pension it will continue till all the money is used up, or until the balance is commuted to a lump sum, or until the spouse dies. On the death of the spouse the money will pass to the spouse's beneficiaries in accordance with the treatment of payments from superannuation and rollover funds set out before.

Notice the difference in tax treatment if a reversionary pensioner is named. The following example will show you why it is usually better to have a nominated beneficiary, or to let the trustee of the superannuation fund exercise a discretion enabling the spouse to continue the pension.

EXAMPLE: *Mr R has a ETP of $300 000 that includes $100 000 of undeducted contributions. As he is 65 and Mrs R is 57, their life expectancy is 14.60 and 25.22 respectively. If he lists her as nominated beneficiary when he commences the* *pension, the tax-free portion of the pension will be $6849 ($100 000/14.60) a year. If he lists her as reversionary pensioner, the tax-free portion will drop to $3965 ($100 000/25.22) a year.*

KEY POINT: Naming a nominated beneficiary when you commence an allocated pension gives more flexibility than naming a reversionary pensioner and will often give greater tax benefits.

Conclusion

Congratulations, you have now read a huge amount on superannuation and should be better placed to make some informed decisions about the best way to use superannuation as a tax-saving and wealth-building technique. This chapter is complex in parts, but for the majority of readers the main issues will be what happens when a person dies with money in rollover funds or if he or she is receiving an allocated pension. Provided the money goes to a dependant, the procedure is straightforward.

Summing Up

- A dependant includes spouse, former spouse and de facto as well as any child of the deceased under 18 years at the time the proceeds of the deceased estate were handed over to that dependant.
- Provided you are not in excess of your pension RBL and you have not commenced an income stream from your superannuation fund or rollover fund, no lump sum tax is payable if the proceeds of such fund are paid to one or more of your dependants on your death.
- If you are eligible to receive an ETP from a superannuation fund or a complying annuity, watch the time limits carefully.
- The spouse or partner of a deceased person receiving an allocated pension has the option of continuing the pension or taking a lump sum as an ETP and paying lump sum tax or rolling it over.
- When commencing an allocated pension it is usually better for tax purposes to name a nominated beneficiary and not a reversionary pensioner.

32

RETIREMENT VILLAGES

My philosophy is that I want to travel first class otherwise my children will, at my expense.

A HAPPY RESIDENT OF A RETIREMENT VILLAGE

What springs to mind when you hear the words retirement village? Do you think about a lot of very old people sitting around waiting for the inevitable, or do you see it as a vibrant community of active people who are so busy they hardly have time to take part in all the activities?

I admit I had a negative image of retirement villages once, but then, as part of my job, I started to visit clients who were living in them. Almost without exception they were far happier and healthier there than they had been in their previous home, and most were sorry they had not made the change a few years before. However, most of them admitted they first experienced apprehension at the thought of moving. They felt it was going to be like "being put into a home".

In reality, moving to a retirement village usually turns out to be an exciting and fulfilling experience, so the aim of this chapter is to provide sufficient information for you to explore the prospect of leaving your own home with an informed mind. Then you will be better placed to decide if moving to a retirement village is appropriate for you.

Let's think about the four main levels of retirement living available once you decide to live in a community instead of staying in the family home. They are:

1. independent living at a retirement village
2. serviced apartments, usually at a retirement village

3. hostels

4. nursing homes.

This chapter will focus on retirement villages, which are for active people who can cope well on their own, and serviced apartments, which cater for those who need some assistance with everyday chores.

Both retirement villages and serviced apartments offer a much lower level of care than hostels and nursing homes and are open to all those who can afford the cost of moving into them. In contrast, you require Commonwealth Government approval to gain admission to a nursing home or a hostel; they are covered in detail in the next chapter.

> KEY POINT: Retirement village living is independent living.

Understand first that a retirement village tends to be an option for people in their seventies and it is a choice that may arise suddenly. Certainly there is a traditional belief that people enter a retirement village because of the facilities offered, or the need to live with people of a similar kind, but in reality this is not so.

In Australia you are likely to start thinking about retirement village living when you become tired of looking after your own home, or if you have a health scare. Suddenly you become increasingly aware of your own mortality and start to mull over how you would cope if your partner died or you became disabled. The idea of moving to a retirement village then comes to the fore, because the choice is usually between that or staying in your own home.

Staying in your own home is certainly fine while you are well. But if your spouse dies there can be loneliness to cope with, and if you become disabled it may be necessary to bring in outside help such as the Blue Nurses and Meals on Wheels. These organisations do a fine job, but the nursing care is limited and specific and there is little social activity of any type.

As the years pass, the difficulties may increase. It is unfortunately very common to find a widow in her late seventies staying in the old family home because she is now too frightened to make the next move. As well as loneliness, she has to cope with the worry and cost of ongoing maintenance problems but, worst of all, she will almost certainly feel increasingly vulnerable to intruders. As our society becomes further polarised between the "haves" and the "have nots", the incidence of crime will increase, and the publicity given to burglaries and vicious attacks will worry aged people more and more.

The tragedy is that people alone in the old family home might be clinging to what they see as "independence", but in reality are becoming increasingly dependent on the help and goodwill of others. If they moved to a serviced apartment in a retirement village they have security and freedom of choice. Their meals and laundry are provided and they can take part in activities of their choosing, yet be alone when the mood takes them. That to me is true independence – being master of your own destiny and once again being part of a community.

Therefore, it makes good sense to consider a move to a retirement village before the choice is forced on you. In a retirement village you often enjoy 24-hour emergency call care, facilities such as a bowling green, a recreational hall and a swimming pool and, best of all, you are likely to live in a close-knit community of like-minded active people who can give you support when you face the inevitable crises of life.

> KEY POINT: Consider the move to a retirement village before the choice is forced on you.

If you are retired, these are the factors that may swing your thoughts towards a move to a retirement village:

1. **Maintaining a house.** You may be getting tired of mowing, painting, gardening and attending to items such as rates and insurance.
2. **Social life.** Your children may be scattered throughout the country and you are starting to feel that little bit lonely. You find yourself spending more and more time in front of the television set and realise you are in danger of vegetating.
3. **Sport.** Deep down you may yearn for a game of bowls or a game of cards but don't feel confident enough to take the steps to do it.
4. **Health.** Maybe a close friend has had a health scare and you realise it would be comforting for you to have trained help close by.

If you can recognise yourself in one or more of the above situations, you should start to explore the possibility of retirement village living. Right now you are almost certainly confused by the range of choices, but by the end of this chapter you will understand them much better. We'll start off by discussing totally independent living in a retirement village and then move on to consider how it compares with living in a serviced apartment.

Today's Retirement Village

Independent living in a standard retirement village provides the lowest level of care and differs little from living in your own home. Usually you live in one- or two-bedroom cottages, or in duplex types of accommodation, and the only care offered is emergency care. Most retirement villages have a string of emergency buttons that can be used to summon help quickly. Activities are usually centred around a recreation hall where residents meet for social activities such as lectures and games and, depending on the type of retirement village, there may be other facilities such as a billiard room, library, swimming pool, bowling green and tennis court. The average age of the resident is 74.

The major benefits of living here instead of in your own home are:

1. There is no garden or pool to maintain.
2. You won't be liable for heavy expenditure such as painting your house or replacing the guttering.
3. Emergency assistance facilities are in place.
4. You can enjoy the companionship of like-minded people. This is particularly important if your partner dies because, even though you have lost a major figure in your life, you have not lost the other friends around you. Thus, you still have a major emotional support base at a time in your life when you need it most, and your independence and contact with your friends is not suddenly taken from you. Later in this book you will read that the latest research shows that the network of friends a person has is a major indicator of how long, and how happily, they will live.

In some retirement villages you will now find at least two levels of care, independent units and serviced apartments. A serviced apartment provides a higher level of assistance and here the typical resident is a woman in her early eighties.

It is even better if the retirement village can also combine a nursing home and/or hostel to cater for situations where one party needs nursing or personal care and the other doesn't. In the retirement villages that provide these facilities it is common to find a husband or wife in a serviced apartment and the spouse at the adjacent nursing home. These facilities enable them to be close together, which would not be possible if the retirement village offered independent living only.

When you start looking at different retirement villages you will notice that only a few offer serviced apartments because of the skill and professionalism needed to manage them. As you can imagine, running a block of serviced apartments is something like running a hotel, except that the "guests" need much more attention.

Notwithstanding their relative scarcity now, serviced apartments are set for huge growth as today's generation of independent residents in retirement villages grow older and less able to manage. To try to fill the needs of those who require serviced apartments, some developers have now introduced what they call a "flexi unit". This is a unit in which people live initially as independent residents. However, if their faculties decline, the developer provides meals and some form of housekeeping from outside sources. The resident pays more for this service.

Serviced apartments range widely in price, but the average cost of a unit would be around $100 000. They range from those that may be described as basic, to those that are quite luxurious. When you buy one you gain access to all the other facilities such as hairdressing, swimming pool, the village bus, billiard room, dining room and guest lounges. Usually the operators supply three meals a day, heavy laundry done weekly, weekly housekeeping services and an emergency call system.

To sum up, serviced apartments provide that "in-between" level of care that is required when a person is far too well to go into a nursing home or hostel, but still needs somebody to help with the meals and the housekeeping.

Legal Title

Now you understand about the different levels of care we can move on to the technical stuff. Some of the most important questions are what are you getting for the money you outlay, what will it cost you each week, what happens when you move out and how are your rights protected. In general terms, there are four different types of retirement village title:

1. leasehold
2. licence
3. company title
4. freehold title.

Each of the above gives you secure occupancy of your unit, but I suggest the most important considerations are the philosophy, resources and skill of the developer. You will find most developers offer only one level of care, that is, independent living in a retirement village. However, there are others who have the resources and the foresight to take a longer-term view and who believe they should offer as wide a choice of levels of care as is possible.

Remember the serviced apartments I mentioned above, and the convenience of having a nursing home in proximity to the retirement village. The residents of the independent living units today are likely to be the residents of the serviced apartments and hostels in the future. It makes sense to stay in the one village if at all possible to maintain your friendship network.

Some retirement villages operate purely on a strata title basis and are only interested in selling units. As a result, there may be no on-site care or ongoing management. If you buy into a "retirement village" that runs on this philosophy, you may find life little different from living in a large strata titled apartment block such as you may find at the Gold Coast. This type of strata title retirement village was once popular in Sydney but is becoming less attractive as people realise the problems that can develop when the residents age and become less capable of looking after themselves and the affairs of their village.

What **is** important is that you seek a developer/operator who has the skills to build a first-class retirement complex, and the resources and skill to run it over the long haul – in other words, one who can stay on to deliver what is promised.

Leasehold

This is probably the most common form of title. When you move into the village you pay an agreed sum in exchange for a 99-year lease on the unit. This lease naturally lasts for your lifetime and if a couple take out the lease, and one dies, it continues to the death of the other partner. Your lease is registered on the title deed but **when you die the rights die with you.** You cannot pass the rights under that lease on to your children even if they are approaching retirement age themselves.

Licence

In some villages the right to occupy the unit is granted by a licence instead of a lease. You lend the developer an agreed sum, and in return you are allowed to live in the property. You are still entitled to live in the unit for life but, unlike a lease, the licence is not registered on the title deed. However, your rights under the licence are recognised by law, so effectively you are in the same position as if you had a registered lease.

Company title

Under company title you buy shares in a company that has an interest in the village and your shares give you the right to occupy a certain unit and to use the common property of the village.

Freehold title

If you buy freehold title you become the owner of the property, in strata title or group title, and have the title deed registered in your name. Be aware this is not quite the same as owning your own home, because the developer may restrict the right to sell it to someone who does not meet the developer's guidelines. Furthermore, you may be liable for a deferred management fee when you leave. This topic is covered in detail soon. However, your family have the right to occupy it when you die if they meet the developer's guidelines.

The Two Main Categories

If you think about the above four options you will find they fall into two main categories:

1. **Lease, licence or company title,** which gives you secure rights of occupancy but leaves ownership with the operator/developer of the village. You still pay a sum up-front and you may, or may not, get most if it back when you leave.
2. **Strata title or group title**[2], which gives you absolute ownership of your unit. You pay for it when you move in, and you sell it, if you can, when you leave.

Which is best? That is something you will have to decide for yourself, for neither is clearly better than the other; both have advantages and disadvantages that we'll cover soon. As you read on, keep in mind the most important factors in your decision will be who will manage the village, what will be the ongoing costs and how and when you will recoup your money if you move out. So you can appreciate both sides of the picture, let's now look at it from the developers' point of view.

As The Developers See It

Developers are in business to make a profit and if they are looking to establish and maintain a thriving business they will be trying to give the best service possible. This entails building a unit that is value for money, irrespective of the price range, and then providing ongoing service by way of the running of the village.

The problem with building retirement villages is that they contain far more than just units to live in. There is normally an administration block, security fencing and recreational amenities such as a lounge, pool and tennis court. If serviced apartments are involved, there will also be a central kitchen and laundry facilities. The bigger the complex the more opportunities there are to save money because of economies of scale, but as the complex gets bigger more capital is required to build it.

Furthermore, if developers build a large retirement village in stages, they have to build many of the facilities at the start. This places a huge cost burden on the first units sold as they are carrying the bulk of the infrastructure costs for the entire project. Consequently, in the early stages they do not make a profit.

You may now be starting to understand that developers have two choices – build for a quick sale or build for a long-term relationship. If developers want a quick sale, they may have to

---

2. In any discussion that follows in this chapter the term strata title will include group title.

build the units down to a cost rather than up to a standard. As a result, there have been many instances where developers after a quick dollar have built a shoddy product that looked good on the surface. They formed the body corporate, sold the units quickly, made their profit, and got out. Four or five years later it is the hapless residents who find the faults in the wiring or the plumbing or in the sealing of the bathrooms and are then faced with the costs of trying to rectify them.

In contrast, those developers who see themselves in the business for the long-term build in the knowledge that they have to maintain the village for maybe 75 years or more. With this in mind they try to provide the best quality that is commensurate with the price they expect to get.

Developers with a long-term attitude realise that if they build a quality product it is virtually impossible to recover their costs in the early stages. They build in the expectation that the good reputation of the village will increase the value of the units in the later stages, and they can start making a profit in the fourth or fifth stage.

Before we discuss strata title and leasehold/licence, let's examine the costs of living in a retirement village.

The Costs

There are four main categories of costs:

1. **Entry cost.** This is the price you pay to gain possession of the unit. This will be either the buying price if it is strata title or company title, or the amount of the interest-free loan you make to the developer if it is a lease or licence arrangement.

2. **Service levies.** Irrespective of the method of title held, residents are responsible for the ongoing costs of the village. These include insurance, water rates, general lighting, staff wages, and repairs and maintenance. As these are reimbursable items, the management is not allowed to make a profit on them but can claim only reimbursement of the actual costs. The manager prepares a budget of expenditure for the year and each resident is levied for a proportion of that expenditure.

   The method used is similar to that used in body corporates where a unit entitlement is struck that is often based on the floor area of your unit.

A simple way of looking at these costs is to compare them with the insurance and maintenance costs of your own home. The situation is also similar to the costs of living in your own home if you decide to leave. You, or your estate, are liable for these ongoing costs **until a resale of the unit is finalised.**

To protect the rights of the residents, some States now have laws that require developers to refund any fees that have not been used because the budget was overestimated. However, if developers underestimate the fees it is they, and not the residents, who have to make up the shortfall. As you can see, developers are unable to take a profit out of the service charges.

3. **Internal maintenance.** Naturally residents are responsible for the internal maintenance of their own units and are required to pay for all damage apart from "fair wear and tear". They are also liable for their own electricity and telephone costs as well as insurance of their personal effects. Some villages require outgoing residents to pay the cost of repainting the interior of the unit when they leave. Other villages offer a free repaint every time it changes hands.

4. **Deferred management fee.** This is the cost that causes the most confusion. The deferred management fee (DMF) is also known as a capital replacement fee and in simple terms may be regarded as part of the developers' profit. Many people seem to regard deferred management fees as a "rip-off", but remember, the developers can make no profit from the service levies or the internal maintenance fees, and often make no profit on the development until they reach at least stage four. Certainly, the leasehold or licence fees provide interest-free capital, but in the early stages these may not even cover the cost of the infrastructure.

A good definition of a deferred management fee is: "A fee or part of the original purchase price deferred until resale of the residence. It includes operators' remuneration for providing community facilities, return for the financial risk taken to establish the village and delayed payment for part of the purchase price until resale."[3] Yes, that's a fancy way of saying "profit".

From the developers' point of view the great thing about DMFs is that they are payable every time the unit changes hands. However, on average, independent living units resell every ten

---

3. *The Retirement Village Handbook 1994.* Produced by the Retirement Villages Association.

years and serviced apartments about every four years, so it is clear the developers have to be patient.

All the brochures I studied while researching this chapter disclosed the DMF in detail and in simple terms, but it is an issue that you should look at carefully, so you know exactly what it will cost when you leave the village. Later in the chapter some examples of the way DMF is calculated are listed.

Leasehold And Licence

Leasehold and licence arrangements are common because they enable developers to retain control over the village and spare residents the worry of trying to sell their units when they leave. Furthermore, they are usually based on the value of the unit, which means the developers recoup much of their capital as soon as the unit is occupied.

An important aspect to consider when entering into a leasehold or licence agreement is how the refund of the money, less DMF if any, is arranged when you vacate the property. Is it refunded to you when you leave, or do you have to wait till the manager finds a new occupier? Does the money you get back contain any element of capital gain and, if so, how is it calculated?

Strata Title

Strata title provides the perceived security of letting you own your unit, but you must understand that it will be just one unit in a village that contains many units as well as facilities such as tennis courts and swimming pools. To run such a centre requires money and skill. This brings up the first big question: Who is going to provide the money and the skill to run the village in which you own a unit?

A strata title complex is run by a body corporate comprising a committee of elected representatives from owners of the individual units. If you have ever been involved in a committee, you will be well aware of squabbles and difficulties that can arise when people try to work together. These difficulties may be aggravated when most of the members of the committee are retired with plenty of time on their hands, and who have had no commercial experience. It is even worse if some of them have become difficult to deal with because of their age.

Imagine what may happen if the management of the village is not satisfactory because the body corporate does not do its job properly. Conditions at the village would go from bad to worse, the residents' lives would be nothing but worry and the value of the initial investment in the strata title unit would be greatly reduced.

Now think about it from the developers' point of view. They can do all the work to set up a beautiful development, but then find that they are at loggerheads with a body corporate that is often controlled by a handful of people. If conflict between the body corporate and the developers continues, everybody loses.

Church- And Charity-Run Retirement Villages

Most church and charity-based retirement villages are now little different from those run by private enterprise. They developed through government subsidies on the understanding that they would look after the poorer members of their particular interest group. These subsidies have been cut drastically because in many cases it was the better-off members who were actually getting priority. Initially, retirees preferred church-run or charity-run villages to private enterprise villages because there was a commonality of interest, but now many have long waiting lists and often they do not offer the same standards of accommodation as the modern villages run by private enterprise operators.

Often, villages run by the churches and charities offer a lower entry fee, but sometimes their exit fee is higher than that charged by private enterprise. Make sure you check it out. Some of the church and charity groups will let you in with an interest-free loan of as little as $30 000, but then you lose it all when you leave. This may appear a cheap way to get in but the heavy exit costs make up for it.

Some Examples

Let's look at a few examples to show the different way costs can work.

Village A

This is a highly regarded village run by a public company and offers leasehold title by way of 99-year lease. It has retirement units ranging in price from $75 000 to $250 000 and serviced apartments priced from $72 000 to $222 000.

The weekly costs are split into three categories and the method of apportionment helps to alleviate concerns about the special levies I mentioned before. There is a flat weekly charge for each person of $18.65, a flat charge for each unit of $7.53 and a charge based on the floor area of the unit. This produces a weekly levy that ranges from $37.40 to $68.70 for one person and $56.10 to $87.00 for a couple.

The fees for the serviced apartments range from $124.30 to $133.00 a week for a single person and $234 to $243.00 a week for a couple.

There are four purchase options available:

1. Pay at a fixed price, say $100 000, and pay DMF when you vacate.
2. Pay an additional 10%, say $110 000, and eliminate the DMF. In other words, the developers' profit is being paid up-front.
3. Pay an additional 25%, say $125 000, and pay DMF but have full capital gain.
4. Pay an additional 25% plus 10%, say $135 000, and have no DMF but all capital gain.

Options 1 and 2 give you, or your estate, no capital gain. Options 3 and 4 give you the right to all the capital gain.

Which should you choose? It depends on your pocket and how much you want to leave to your estate. The first option lets you in for the lowest price, the last option gives most to your estate provided, of course, the capital gain is more than the $35 000 you paid to get it. Think again about the quote at the start of the chapter. Would you rather have an extra $35 000 to spend now, or is leaving it to your estate more important?

Village B

This is a middle-range retirement village run by a church. It offers both hostel accommodation (discussed in the next chapter) and independent living in one- and two-bedroom units. Title is by way of 99-year lease in exchange for an interest-free loan of around $95 000 for the one-bedroom units, and $135 000 for the two-bedroom units.

The DMF is 5% a year for the first five years of occupancy, but residents are guaranteed to get back at least 75% of the loan when they leave. The service levies range from $41 to $53 a week. The church states it will refund your money to you, less DMF, when you are ready to leave.

Village C

This is a quality village offering amenities that include a pool, heated spa, bowling and croquet greens and a tennis court. Title is freehold strata title and prices start at $135 000 for a two-bedroom unit and $220 000 for a three-bedroom unit. The weekly levy is $29.50 and DMF is 2.5% per annum for a maximum of 12 years. Apart from the DMF, the resident keeps all the capital gain on resale. The marketing people for this village claim outgoing residents have received an average capital gain of 9.5% a year after DMF has been taken off.

They have no restriction on your reselling the unit and you may sell it through local real estate agents or through the village's own marketing division. Most buyers for this village make enquiries at the marketing division and as a result most resales are effected in that way.

Village D

This is another church-run village and offers 78 independent living apartments, a 52-bed hostel and a 50-bed nursing home.

Your buying cost buys you a licence to live in the unit "until you wish to leave or until you are unable to care for yourself". Two-bedroom units including garages cost $95 000 and the fees are $37.50 a week. The brochure hinted that residents could move to the next level of care when their condition warranted it, but when you read the next chapter you will discover that entry to the hostel or nursing home is still subject to government approval.

Upon resale, the percentage refundable after DMF is worked on a sliding scale, but this is conditional upon the unit being reoccupied under a new agreement. The managers claim there is a long waiting list for places and there has never been any difficulty in finding a new occupant.

Summing Up The Choices

There is no doubt that retirement village living is fast becoming an attractive option for many retirees and it will be one of Australia's major growth industries as the number of people over 65 increases. The years 2000 to 2020 will be peak years for independent living in retirement villages as the baby boomers move into the 70-plus age group.

There are now hundreds of villages clamouring for your attention, and they offer a wide range of housing options and facilities. In general, you tend to get what you pay for, but the main factors to think about are what best suits your lifestyle and how much you can afford.

A difficult decision may be choosing between strata title or one of the licence or leasehold arrangements, but your title is secure no matter which one you choose. The initial costs of either option are fairly similar, but the main differences may occur in the management of the village and the treatment of the asset when you leave or die. With strata title you own and occupy the unit, and when you die the unit is passed on to your beneficiaries less any DMF.

In a leasehold retirement village you actually lease your unit on a long-term basis (usually 99 years) and when you die your beneficiaries receive a proportion of the value of the unit less the amount for DMF. Under a loan arrangement you or your estate receive the amount of the loan less DMF.

Usually strata title owners are entitled to any capital gain, but this entitlement is not there with leasehold or licence arrangements unless it is set out in the contract documents.

But money is not everything, and there are also other important points to consider before deciding on the right choice for you. Management and maintenance of the village are the key elements in how happy you will be living in a retirement village.

With the management of some strata title villages, the developers may, upon the selling of the last unit, move out and leave the management of the village to the residents. This can cause headaches as many elderly people do not have the skills or expertise to make collective decisions about management or the inevitable repairs required as the buildings age.

In addition, there is the matter of ongoing levies if any facilities need repair. In a strata title complex the body corporate tends to underprovide for future maintenance for fear of creating high, unpopular levies. If this happens, the residents have to pay for major repairs as they occur, and they can find themselves faced with increasing repair and maintenance costs. It is a frightening thought to wonder what would happen to an elderly couple if they did not have the money available to meet the levy.

In a leasehold situation the manager stays on. Most leasehold villages have a resident-funded operating arrangement whereby the operating costs of the village are met through a regular fee. The deferred management charge, usually a predetermined percentage of the price of the unit, is paid when the resident leaves the village.

Buyer Beware

By now you should have a much better idea of what independent living in retirement villages is all about. Let's summarise the points to consider when you are thinking about making the move.

1. Are you ready for it?

The vast majority of retirement village residents make the move to the village easily and are happier than they believed possible. However, there are a few who do not mix in well with the other residents, and some who feel they made the transition to the village at too young an age. I suggest, in most cases, 65 is the minimum age to be considering a move.

2. Who is in control of the village?

The developer of a strata title village has full control at the start, but you must think carefully about what will happen when all the development is completed. Will the developer stay on as manager, or will the responsibility of running the village be left to the residents?

3. What ongoing emergency care is provided?

The major reason people move to retirement villages is security – security from robberies and brutal attacks, and security in respect of medical attention. Make sure you clearly understand **exactly** what emergency care is available. In some villages there are trained staff on duty 24 hours a day. There are others who claim to have emergency care facilities, but on investigation you may find the "facility" is nothing more than a promise that the caretaker will ring a local doctor if there is an after-hours emergency.

4. Does the village offer serviced apartments, a hostel and/or a nursing home as well as independent living?

It is rare to find a retirement village resident moving back to a normal dwelling house; most move to serviced apartments, hostels and nursing homes. Check out what will happen to you if you can no longer care for yourself. Does the village have other levels of accommodation or are you on your own?

5. Can you resell the unit?

The danger here is that the management of the village may insist on sole selling rights for a period of a year or more, and then take well over a year to sell your unit. During this time, even though you have moved out, you may be liable for ongoing weekly fees as well as DMF. If several residents vacate at the same time the village may be faced with a surplus of units to resell and the problem may be made worse if the developer is constructing more modern units in a later stage and is concentrating on those. Another factor that may slow up the sale of your unit is a generally depressed property market because most buyers cannot complete the purchase until they sell their own home.

Don't get too excited if the marketing people tell you that you are free to use local real estate agents when you are reselling. Marketing retirement units is a highly specialised business and most buyers inspect retirement villages as a result of advertising or through recommendations. It is unlikely a local agent would have much chance of effecting a sale.

6. Is there a guaranteed repurchase scheme?

At least one company guarantees to repurchase your unit, or refund your loan, after a set time and under certain conditions. For example, if you died while a resident, and the unit remains unsold after nine months, the company will pay your estate the value of the unit based on an independent assessment, less the DMF.

If there is no guaranteed repurchase plan, and the developer is selling new units, your older unit may remain unsold for two years or more. Your estate may be tied up for all that time, and still be paying levies and weekly fees.

Most advertisements use phrases like "the proceeds of your unit, less any deferred management fees, will be paid to you immediately a new resident moves into your unit". That sounds fine but you, or your estate, are still inconvenienced if it takes years for the marketing department to find the new resident to occupy the unit you vacated.

7. What are the criteria for incoming residents?

Most villages have minimum age limits, often age 60, and do not allow units to be sold to investors. However, every industry has its weak links, and an unscrupulous operator may sell a unit to the first willing buyer who comes along with little regard to the suitability of the buyer to fit into the village structure. Such sales can have adverse effects on the value of the investment in the village by the other residents.

You do gain a little more protection if you choose the lease/licence/company title arrangement, because it is usually a requirement of the lease documentation that incoming residents meet certain guidelines.

8. Do you understand the weekly fees and levies?

Be clear what the fees and levies cover, and make sure you inspect a copy of the detailed budget. Discuss it with your accountant or financial adviser if you are unsure what it means.

It is crucial that the whole financial structure of the village is based on reality and that you are not lulled into a false sense of security by going for the cheapest fees offered to you. If you choose the cheapest you may well discover many expenses have not been properly budgeted for and increases will occur rapidly.

Investigate what arrangements are made for a sinking fund, because at some time the village will need major capital works for repairs and replacements. A good sinking fund is kept in a separate trust account and the levies should be enough to ensure that residents in the early stages of the village are paying their share of future costs rather than having them borne by later residents.

9. What are the arrangements with fees if you die or vacate the unit?

One of the main points of contention seems to be the matter of liability for fees and levies long after the resident has died or moved out. Check this factor carefully and find out what happens if you, as a resident of the village, move into a serviced apartment or nursing home run by the same operator who runs the village. Does this entitle you to an immediate refund of the money paid for the retirement unit, or are you on the same footing as somebody who has left or died?

10. How is the deferred management fee levied?

Similar comments apply to those made above about fees, but in addition you must find out if the DMF is levied on the **incoming** price or the **outgoing** price. There may be a big difference if the value of the unit has risen.

11. Have you checked out the facilities?

What you **need** is more important than what is available. For example, a pool in the village is of little value if you don't like swimming in pools. Many villages offer a bus service and this is a factor to consider if you do not have a car. Are the facilities such as pathways, tennis courts and gardens in good order? If not, there could be heavy levies inflicted on you to maintain them.

12. **What about the residents' committee?**

Most villages have a residents' committee and management should welcome the opportunity for you, as a prospective resident, to talk freely to people on the committee. This is a great opportunity to assess the spirit in the village and to discover any issues that are causing friction or worry to the residents.

A Break With Tradition

One of the major problems associated with retirement villages is the Australian tradition that parents should leave their assets for the use of their children. This is culturally different from the attitude in a country like America where there is more of a "user pays" system. In America, those who own a home and want to go into a nursing home have to pledge the equity in their home. When they die the cost of their care is taken from their estate.

In Australia there are often objections from family members who see the interest-free loan and the DMF charge as coming out of the estate they are looking forward to getting. Possibly the parents may leave more behind them if they stayed in the family home, but the move to the retirement village gives them an opportunity to live their final years in dignity and greater health.

Retirement village living is still gaining popularity in Australia, but at present less than 5% of people move to a retirement village. This attitude is changing because retirees are healthier, wealthier, more assertive and more independent than they have ever been before. Now more people are making allowances for the "golden years" of their life and want to have a fuller life and stay in control. The days when parents went to live with the children are gone, and today's parents realise their children's future is harder to predict. They don't know whether their children's marriages are going to survive, or whether their children are going to be transferred interstate or overseas. The retirement village lets them have their own network of support independent of the whims of others.

Case Study

Retirement village living takes up a lot of space in this book because I believe it will figure prominently for many of you, either for yourselves or for your parents. Most of the research for the topic came from my discussions with operators of retirement villages and other people in that industry. However, to round it off I interviewed a couple living in a middle-range retirement village. They were happy to speak frankly for they were friends of my late parents, and have known me since the day I was born. However, they requested their names not be published, so I shall call them Ted and Mary.

Ted and Mary have been married for 58 years and are now aged 86 and 83. They still appear as bright and cheerful as I have always remembered them. They moved from a two-level home when they were 81 and 78 because Mary fell down the back steps and the local doctor advised them to get into a low-set home as soon as possible. Ted was happy to move because he loves to play bowls but had become worried about leaving the house in case Mary had another fall. At 81 he also felt he was getting ready to stop driving his car, although on the day we spoke he said he had decided to give up driving on his 87th birthday!

Mary regards herself as a shy person – "I am not the type to wander into a stranger's house and introduce myself" – and admitted to being scared of moving. Both are very active members of their local church and Mary feared leaving her friends behind her. It was therefore important to them to find a place close to where they lived.

This narrowed down their choices, but luckily they found a retirement village within three kilometres of their house. This enabled them to retain all their friends and stay at the same church. What obviously still excites them about the village is that it is a short walking distance to major facilities. There is a hotel and three huge shopping centres within 500 metres of the village and a cinema complex about to open. Yet, because of the landscaping and the way the village is constructed, their own unit is so quiet they could be in the middle of the desert.

The village offered three types of units. Studio units where a single bedroom and the living are combined, one-bedroom units that consist of a bedroom, living area, laundry and kitchen, and two-bedroom units. Ted and Mary suggest that couples moving into a retirement village go for a two-bedroom unit if possible to gain extra storage space. As Mary said, "That's what I liked least – going from seven wardrobes to just one." They had to take a one-bedroom unit, as no two-bedroom ones were available when they wanted to move.

Mary did not find the move easy and took a few weeks to adjust despite the welcome they both received from the other residents. However, she quickly settled down and soon had no regrets about the move. According to Ted, they should have made the move 10 years before they did. This fits in with the suggestion that the early to mid seventies is the best time to make the move to a retirement village if you are going to do it.

Their tenure is by loan/licence for which they paid $70 000. They found the documentation "not difficult" to understand and the developer quite reasonable to deal with. After moving in, they obtained permission to build a pergola over their patio, which they did in conjunction with the adjoining owner. They shared with their neighbour the cost of a double pergola that covered the patios of both units.

The lease provides that after three years have elapsed outgoing residents, or their estate, receive the original amount loaned less a DMF of 20%. The developer retains sole selling rights and at the time of my visit there were seven vacant units in the village. Ted said these had been vacant for a "few months" but understood this was because there were now a lot more retirement villages competing for residents. I got the impression the units may take quite some time to sell and Ted and Mary were well aware that unit owners, even when they have moved out, continue to be liable for the weekly fees.

Their present fees are $50 a week and they pay nothing else apart from light, telephone and the insurance on the contents of their unit. The village has a swimming pool and an attractive community hall with a billiard table. Residents can obtain a hot midday meal there if they require it, but have to pay the cost of the meal. The operators originally offered three meals a day but discontinued this when they found the residents preferred to cook their own meals. A hairdresser and a doctor visit the retirement village once a week and will call on residents at other times by appointment.

Each unit has an emergency button that triggers an alarm in the office. This is manned 24 hours a day, and the procedure is that a staff member will contact the appropriate unit immediately the buzzer is pressed. If required this staff member will contact the doctor or call an ambulance. My friends thought the system worked quite well.

This village does not offer any other levels of care such as hostels or nursing homes, which Ted and Mary regard as a drawback. It was not a factor they considered when they were looking around, but I feel there were only two main considerations on their mind then in any event: they wanted to stay in the area in which they had lived, and to be near shopping facilities.

There is a residents' committee that my friends believe "works well". They were invited to join but declined because they felt they had done enough work on committees during their working life. They believe the village spirit is a good one even though "you will always find somebody who has a complaint". I guess that's life. Ted stressed that life anywhere is "what you make it" and that anybody who was determined to find fault would find it.

Possibly there are two facets to this. Ted is the kind of person who is used to making the best out of what he has, but there is also no doubt that he is happier because he can now go out and play bowls without worrying about Mary falling down the back steps.

Without doubt Ted and Mary are happy living in the village and are sorry they did not make the move earlier. That might be an important lesson for all of us.

Conclusion

It's a big subject isn't it, but one that will become increasingly topical as the percentage of people over 70 grows. From the research I have done, it seems you will be as happy living in a retirement village as you are living where you are now. As always, it's your attitude that counts.

Next we'll discuss nursing homes and hostels, the next stage of aged care.

Summing Up

- Retirement village living is independent living.
- Consider the move to a retirement village before the choice is forced on you.
- The skills and philosophy of the developer are vital.
- Ensure you clearly understand what ongoing costs and exit costs are involved.
- Outgoing residents are usually liable for weekly maintenance costs until their unit is resold.
- Consider where you will go if you have to leave the retirement village because of ill-health.
- Choose a unit with as much space as you can afford.

33

HOSTELS AND NURSING HOMES

For each of us there comes a moment when death takes us by the hand and says – it is time to rest, you are tired, lie down and sleep.

WILL HAY

If you live long enough you may reach a stage where you need more looking after than that offered by an independent-living retirement unit or a serviced apartment. Then you have to think about moving to the higher level of care provided by hostels and nursing homes. It is common to think of them in the same vein as retirement villages, but they work quite differently.

It may help if you understand that the aged care industry as we know it now had its start in the 1950s when funding from the Commonwealth Government provided the money for churches and other charitable organisations to provide accommodation for aged people. The services provided included self-care accommodation as well as nursing homes. However, the combination of the number of aged people increasing and the pressures on government funding meant that funding was gradually withdrawn for self-care units. It has been retained only for those who can prove to be in need.

The involvement of private enterprise is a recent development and arose because governments realised the need to have outside developers involved. Until this change of heart, private enterprise had found it too difficult to compete with the capital subsidies given to the church and charities by the Government. Now government agencies and free enterprise operators work together to provide high levels of care.

305

Apart from a few unregulated nursing homes that are run by private enterprise, all hostels and nursing homes are government subsidised and you **cannot gain admittance to them without government approval.** Contrast this with retirement villages where all you need is the money, and the ability to pass the age or health requirements.

The main difference is the level of care needed in a nursing home and a hostel. Most occupants of hostels and nursing homes are women aged 80 and over, and those who are residents of nursing homes have severe disabilities and spend most of their time in bed or in wheelchairs. Therefore, a nursing home consists mainly of rooms that contain one, two or four beds, and the main facilities may be a dining room and shared showers. Full nursing facilities are provided.

In contrast, a hostel is for people who are more active. It will often comprise a cluster of smaller buildings that contain small bed-sitting rooms with ensuite and shared lounges and dining rooms. Heavy laundry is washed and meals are provided but there are often appliances such as washing machines and driers so that residents can do their own washing if they wish. Obviously, nursing-home residents would not be capable of doing this.

As you can now appreciate, nursing homes provide **full-time** care, and hostels offer a much lower level. You may also have noticed a similarity between hostels and serviced apartments. The main difference is that hostels are government-subsidised and you need government approval to live in them, whereas serviced apartments are not subsidised and are open to those who can afford them. This is because the Government recognises that hostel residents are not able to get by without some help.

The Resident Classification System

The system works on the broad principle that to qualify for entry into a nursing home a person must be incapable of independent living. The Government has introduced a system of classification, and once eligibility is established all residents are placed in one of five categories. Category 5 is the lowest level of care required and Category 1 is the highest. The assessment takes into account such factors as being able to prepare simple meals, maintain personal hygiene, use public transport and attend to one's own cleaning and laundry. In some circumstances, hostel care may also be made available to a person who may not qualify under the rules above, but is unable to gain access to any social and community support.

You cannot become a resident of a nursing home unless you are assessed by an Aged Care Assessment Team (ACAT) as being eligible. ACAT is funded by the Commonwealth Government and has staff members in all the major hospitals. One of ACAT's functions is to consider people's overall needs and provide information to people about the options open to them.

Often doctors or social workers refer potential candidates for hostel and nursing-home admittance to ACAT staff, who assess the level of care needed by the applicants and decide if they meet the eligibility requirements. Once ACAT assesses a person as requiring nursing-home care it issues an approved admission form (NH5), which enables the nursing home to claim the appropriate subsidy from the Government.

The new patient is admitted initially as a Category 5, but during the first 21 days in the nursing home the staff of the home also conduct detailed assessments. If these tests show the patient should be in a category requiring more care, the patient's category is changed, and the Government raises the subsidy to the nursing home effective from the original admission date. The classification that finally will be allotted to the resident depends on the hours of care needed each day and the amount of money that is required for the facilities that provide the ongoing care.

Hostels have a separate system of classification that ranges from "Personal Care – High" to "Personal Care – Low".

To become a resident of a hostel you must be assessed by ACAT. The aim of the Government is to have all those who are presently in nursing home Categories 4 and 5 in hostels by the year 2000, but Categories 1 to 3 are likely to be always in nursing homes.

It all sounds like a fairly bureaucratic process, but nursing homes and hostels have growing waiting lists and the system is designed to stop people gaining admission to nursing homes and hostels who don't need the level of care provided there. We could sum it up by saying that the subsidy given to the operator of the nursing home or hostel depends on the level of care needed.

KEY POINT: You cannot become a resident of a nursing home or a hostel until you qualify under the admission guidelines set down and administered by the Commonwealth Government.

The Commonwealth Government is currently spending over $1.3 billion a year on nursing homes and hostels, and in order to cut costs has recently introduced even stricter guidelines to limit entry to nursing homes and hostels. It is also encouraging people who may have once qualified for hostels to stay in their own homes, and those who may have qualified for nursing-home admission to stay in hostels.

The funding and admission criteria of hostels and nursing homes revolve around the following guidelines:

1. Aged people should live in their own homes wherever possible.

2. Aged people should be given admittance to residential facilities such as hostels only when their other support systems are not adequate.

3. The atmosphere and the process should encourage a return to independent functioning wherever possible and not create further dependency.

4. For many people a return to a lower level of government support is not only possible but would be welcomed.

As you can see, these are worthwhile aims and are designed to encourage self-esteem.

A major problem for the Government is that admission to hostels and nursing homes is not means tested and thus even the wealthiest may qualify for fully subsidised nursing care. Because of tight budgetary constraints, it is likely that some kind of means test or "user pays" system will soon be announced. The exempt nursing homes mentioned later in this chapter are probably the start of this process.

Cost Of Entry

Most hostels have an entry cost. The average is $26 000, but it can vary from $15 000 to $60 000 depending on the standard of accommodation offered. This is usually paid by way of a loan to the operator, and a deferred management fee (as discussed in the previous chapter) is deducted from the loan balance when the resident leaves. It is a requirement that all hostels keep a percentage of places for those with limited financial resources. For them there is no entry cost.

There is normally no entry cost into a nursing home.

Who Pays The Cost?

The Commonwealth Government pays the bulk of the costs of running nursing homes and hostels and the payment to the operators is calculated using the formula set out below. Residents of nursing homes contribute 87.5% of the full pension and rental subsidy to the operators. Those residents who do not get a full pension because of other assets or income[1] have to make up the difference from those other resources.

The Government pays far less in subsidies to hostel operators than it pays to nursing-home operators and some long-term residents of hostels get no subsidy at all. This is because they were admitted before the assessment process started. Furthermore, the amount of subsidy depends on how many residents of the hostel are in each classification.

The nursing-home fee system that regulates the fees paid by the Government to the operator as a subsidy is made up of the following components:

1. **Care aggregated module (CAM).** This is intended to cover the costs of the nursing care but includes no element of profit for the provider of the services.
2. **Standard aggregated module (SAM).** This is designed to pay for the infrastructure such as plant and equipment and also to provide food, linen, cleaning, etc. This is the only area in which the providers can make a profit, so it is in their interests to perform as efficiently as possible. However, if they try to cut costs they run the risk of providing an inferior service with the resultant loss of their licence.
3. **Other cost reimbursable expenditure (OCRE).** This is for the cost of occupational superannuation, long-service leave for nursing and personal care staff and workers' compensation premiums for all staff.

   Furthermore, the operator is required to spend the entire subsidy for the care of the assessed residents. Failure to spend all the subsidy may result in it being wholly or partly withdrawn by the Government.

Exempt Nursing Homes

These are a new concept and enable residents to get a higher level

---

1. You will learn about the income and assets tests in later chapters.

of service such as better meals, larger rooms and more facilities, provided they pay extra. The residents have to pay special fees as well as the usual percentage of their pensions, but the exempt nursing home is still government-funded and residents still have to be approved by ACAT.

There are also private nursing homes with all costs payable by the residents. These are similar to private hostels inasmuch as they are run by private enterprise operators without the benefit of government subsidies. Obviously they are for the wealthy.

Some Practical Considerations

You must appreciate that moving into a nursing home can be a distressing experience for older people and for their families. It is often a jolt to be forced to live with others when you are used to living on your own, and people who go to live in a nursing home know that it is often a one-way trip.

The nursing-home staff do their best to keep up morale and encourage those residents who are not bedridden to get up for a few hours a day, and there are now diversional therapists who arrange activities such as crafts. Also many nursing homes have special buses that can take wheelchairs to enable the residents to enjoy the occasional outing.

The demand is much stronger for nursing-home accommodation than hostel accommodation and this can cause temporary problems. For example, if a resident of a hostel becomes ill she might have to leave the hostel to go into hospital, but after being in hospital may find she needs the level of care only a nursing home offers. It is possible, and even probable, that there will not be an immediate place in a nursing home for her and she may have to seek some temporary accommodation while waiting for a place in a nursing home to become available. It is a sad reality that this temporary accommodation might be a hospital for the terminally ill.

Conclusion

The last two chapters have given you an insight into retirement living both in independent units and in hostels and nursing homes. It is not a subject to shy away from, and it is certainly one that is likely to play a significant role in your life as life expectancy continues to increase. As in all new fields you will be much more comfortable with it as your knowledge of it grows.

There have been many innovations to try to make the life of the residents as comfortable as possible. For example, a Government scheme known as "Standards Monitoring" is now in operation whereby monitoring teams visit hostels and nursing homes to observe the standards of care being given and to ensure residents' rights are respected and that a home-like environment is encouraged.

We'll now move on to estate planning – a vitally important, but often neglected, task.

Summing Up

- You need government approval to be a resident of most nursing homes and hostels.
- A nursing home provides a much higher level of care than a hostel.
- Most hostels have an entry cost and also charge a service fee.
- The Government is trying to encourage people to live as independently as possible.
- Moving to a hostel or a nursing home can require a lot of adjustment by a person used to independent living.

34

POWERS OF ATTORNEY

Freedom begins as we become conscious of it.

VERNON HOWARD

Have you ever wondered how you would cope if you suddenly broke your arm, or worse still, became seriously ill? Who would withdraw money from your bank account to pay medical expenses and other bills? If you needed to sell your house to buy one that was more suitable, who would sign the contract and the transfer documents?

Suppose you were holidaying overseas when sickness or accident struck. If you needed money quickly, who would be able to withdraw it from your bank accounts at home?

To cover situations like these, you should appoint at least one other person to act on your behalf. This person is often called your agent or, in legal language, your attorney. It doesn't matter how young you are, accident and illness strike without warning and are no respecter of ages. Giving somebody a power of attorney is like drawing up a will – you should do it now.

I'll explain the three main terms used:

1. The **donor** is the person who gives another person the right to act on their behalf.

2. The **attorney,** or **donee,** is the person who is given this right.

3. The **power of attorney** is the document by which the donor appoints the attorney and sets out what the attorney is authorised to do.

There are various levels of authority you can give to another person. They may range from the right to do no more than make withdrawals on a certain specified bank account, to the right to do almost everything you can do yourself. The right to operate a bank account is simply done by signing one of the bank's forms. Full powers are conferred to another when you execute an enduring power of attorney document.

Notice the importance of the word **enduring** – it is a fairly new concept. It came about because there is a basic legal principle that an attorney can do no more than the donor who gives the power of attorney. For example, a power of attorney might have been given to a person many years ago yet today the donor is dead. The attorney does not have the power to sign documents on behalf of the dead person, because dead people cannot sign documents for themselves. If we take that a step further, we could also say that you cannot be an attorney for a person with an unsound mind because a person with unsound mind does not have the power to sign legal documents.

There is a paradox here. Powers of attorney are most used when a person has suffered a mental condition that leaves them incapable of making decisions or signing documents yet, if we go back to legal theory, this is when a normal power of attorney would lapse. The concept of the **enduring** power of attorney arose to solve this problem. The enduring power of attorney lasts for the life of the donor or until revoked by the donor. Provided the donor was of sound mind when the power of attorney document was executed, any later deterioration in the state of mind of the donor is not relevant.

In the rest of this chapter the term "power of attorney" will be used to mean enduring power of attorney.

> KEY POINT: An enduring power of attorney does not lapse if the donor becomes of unsound mind.

You should note that once a person becomes of unsound mind they cannot revoke a power of attorney. However, if the **attorney** becomes of unsound mind, the power of attorney is automatically revoked.

Preparing A Power Of Attorney

A power of attorney is a simple one- or two-page document that sets out the name and address of the donor, the name and address of the attorney and the powers given in the document to the attorney.

It usually contains the following:

- An appointment of one or more persons as attorneys.

- An authority to do anything the donor lawfully authorises the attorney to do.
- A declaration that the power of attorney will continue even if the donor becomes incapable.

There is space for it to be signed by both the donor and the attorney and then witnessed by an appropriate person.

You can obtain a standard form from any legal stationer and do it all yourself, but I suggest you spend $100 or so and have one drawn up by your solicitor. A good time to do it is when you are having your will made out or updated. There are many facets to estate planning, and the signing of do-it-yourself documents can sometimes cause you many problems that may not have occurred if your solicitor had given you guidance when you were preparing them.

For example, when I was researching this chapter, a solicitor told me about a recent case where an enduring power of attorney had been quite properly executed in Queensland in the presence of a justice of the peace. The donor then suffered dementia and her attorney tried to use the document to sell some property in New South Wales. To his dismay the attorney found the power of attorney was unable to be registered with the Titles Office in New South Wales as that State will not accept a justice of the peace as a witness for that document.

> KEY POINT: It is better to have your power of attorney drawn up by a solicitor who can make sure it suits your needs and is properly signed and witnessed.

The document should be kept in a safe place and, if you intend to use it for buying and selling property, a stamped copy should be registered in the Titles Office or Real Property Office or whatever it is called in your State. Your solicitor will do all this for you.

Another point to note is that a power of attorney comes into operation the moment it is signed. Obviously, you want to keep full control over your own affairs if possible, so I suggest you keep the document locked up with your own papers until it is necessary to use it. This should not cause any problems provided your attorney knows how to get access to your papers in need.

Duties Of An Attorney

If you agree to act as an attorney for another, be aware of the following rules:

1. You must at all times exercise your powers diligently and honestly to protect the interests of the donor.

2. Unless there is specific authority in the document, you should not enter into transactions that may involve a conflict of interest between you and the donor.

3. You must keep your own money strictly separate from that of the donor. Don't let the donor's money get into your bank account.

4. You must keep proper accounts and records of how you handle the donor's money because you may be asked to produce them. This is wise, in any case, for your own protection.

5. You may be required to compensate the donor for any loss caused by your failure to perform your duties properly.

All those rules may have scared you a little, but possibly you still think it's a great honour if somebody makes you their attorney. Just remember it is a job that carries great responsibilities, and one that can easily lead you into strife if you do not cover your actions. You see, it can lead to conflict – conflict of interest, and conflict with members of the family.

Let's assume that Mrs Brown is your neighbour. She calls in to talk to you and explains that her four children are interstate or overseas and it is comforting to have you close by. She is a lovely old lady and you have no hesitation in accepting her request that she give you a power of attorney. Some years later she goes into a nursing home and loses her mental capacities. There is no possibility of her returning to her home. How do you handle the following?

1. Two of the children believe her home should be rented out. The other two don't want to see the family home, in which they grew up, "defiled" by tenants.

2. The eldest son, Tom, has a business that is borrowing money for expansion. He asks you to sign documents mortgaging the house as additional security for the loan. He assures you, "Mum promised to help if I needed it."

3. A daughter, Margaret, has just been divorced and is trying to make a new life for herself. Mrs Browns's will states that all her assets should be divided between the four children equally. Margaret feels the house should be sold now and the proceeds split four ways. Naturally this does not suit Tom who needs the entire property to secure his loan. In any event, the other

daughter, Helen, believes the property has great potential and it would be "a shame to sell it now".

Let's look at the worst case scenario. You think Tom is a very decent fellow and have no doubt that Mum promised to mortgage the house for him if necessary. Consequently, as attorney, you sign the documents needed to mortgage the house to secure his loan. Unfortunately, his business fails and the bank forecloses under its mortgage and sells the house at auction to help cover Tom's debts. The other three children sue you on the grounds that your action in permitting the house to be mortgaged was negligent.

Maybe I've painted a gloomy picture and you may say, "This would never happen to me." But, every day our consultants hear the most amazing stories of family feuds and reverses in family fortunes. Perhaps it won't happen to you, but by refusing to accept the role of attorney for friends you can save yourself a lot of heartache.

KEY POINT: Accepting a power of attorney is a highly responsible job and one that may involve you in legal action. Think carefully before you do it.

Also be aware that an attorney must not use the power of attorney to do anything of benefit to the attorney unless the power is specifically authorised in the document. This may lead to pension problems.

EXAMPLE: *You are an only child and your mother (a widow) gives you power of attorney. She becomes unable to look after herself and goes into a nursing home. The problem is her house. She naturally wants to keep the full pension, but after she has moved out of it for a year the Department of Social Security will treat it as an asset and she may lose much of her pension. If you put tenants in the house the rental income will cause a large reduction in her pension.*

The obvious solution is for her to gift the house to you. You are the sole heir and you know this is what she would do if she was capable of doing it. However, she is in no condition to sign documents and you, wearing the hat of attorney, cannot gift the house to yourself. If you sell the house the sale proceeds must go in her name and again she will lose her pension under the income test.

I will discuss similar problems in a later section, but this one could have been simply solved if somebody else, maybe your solicitor, spouse or financial adviser, had also been given a power of attorney. There is no limit to the number of people you can appoint as your attorney.

KEY POINT: It is wise to give a power of attorney to more than one person. One of the attorneys should be a person who is unlikely to receive any money from the donor's estate.

Safeguarding Your Interests

If you decide to accept a power of attorney, keep good records; then if you do find yourself in a dispute, you have evidence to support your actions. We suggest to our clients that they buy an exercise book and write down the date and nature of each transaction done in their role of attorney.

For example, they may write:

25 March 1996. Mr Sharp, the accountant for Mrs Brown, asked for a cheque for $4500 for tax and provisional tax. After sighting the relevant assessment notice I prepared and signed a cheque for $4500 in favour of the Australian Tax Office on Mrs Brown's account with the Commonwealth Bank, Hereville.

4 July 1997. Karen Smith from Ace Realty phoned about Mrs Brown's investment house at 10 Premier Drive. The previous tenants vacated seven weeks ago and after extensive advertising the property is still vacant. She suggested we drop the rent by $15 a week to $170 a week. I telephoned Alan Jones of XYZ Realty and Mary Collins of ABC Realty who are the other main agents in the area. Both confirmed $170 a week was a realistic market figure. Consequently I approved the rent reduction.

As you can see there may be considerable work and responsibilities involved, and if you don't take them seriously you may have problems.

Joint Powers Of Attorney

If you, as the donor of a power of attorney, are concerned about conflicts of interest or burdening one person with too much responsibility, you may give two people **joint powers of attorney.** This requires **both** to agree to any action on your part. Should you do this, it is wise to specify that the survivor may act alone if the co-attorney dies.

The Practical Solution

There is no doubt that having a power of attorney in place is as basic as having a will, and in practice couples usually give powers of attorney to each other and also to one or more of their children. Another should be given to a person such as your solicitor, accountant or financial adviser who is outside the family. They cost around $100 to draw up and last for a lifetime.

Summing Up

- An enduring power of attorney lasts until revoked by the donor or until the donor dies.
- Make sure it is properly witnessed.
- An enduring power of attorney comes into effect the moment it is signed.
- Acting as an attorney can be an onerous responsibility. Therefore, keep good records.
- It may be wise to have more than one person as your attorney.

35

MAKING A WILL

That was a great game of golf, fellers.

BING CROSBY (last words 1977)

For some strange reason many people have trouble finding the time to make a will, which is why nearly 30% of Australians die intestate. Maybe it's because they don't want to face the reality of death; in fact I have even heard some use the expression "**If** I die". However, you spend the greater part of your life struggling to accumulate assets or finding ways to spend them. Surely, then, it makes sense that you have a say in who receives the proceeds of your estate?

Terms To Know

Let's start off with the basic legal definitions:

Beneficiary: A person who is entitled to receive part of the deceased's estate.

Bequest: A gift of personal property under a will.

Codicil: A document whose purpose is to amend or explain the original will. A codicil is usually drawn up to amend the original will if the testator does not want to execute a new will.

Executor: The person who has the responsibility of putting the provisions of the will into effect.

Intestate: To die without leaving a will. A person dies partially intestate if the will validly disposes of only part of the estate. If this happens, the balance of the estate is dealt with under the laws of intestacy.

Letters of administration: A document issued by the court if a person dies intestate, or without naming an executor, or if the executor named in the will has died. The document gives a person known as the administrator the power to administer the estate and act as executor.

Predecease: Die before (somebody else).

Probate: A certificate granted by the court that effectively certifies the will is valid, and gives authority to the executor to administer the will.

Testator: The person who makes the will.

Making A Will

It is a simple matter to make a will but, as there can be serious legal consequences involved, it is best to spend $120 or so and have it done by a solicitor. Certainly you can pick up a do-it-yourself will kit cheaply at a legal stationery shop and this may suffice if all you are going to leave is the family home and a few hundred dollars in the bank. However, if you follow the advice contained in my books, you will probably leave much more than that so you may as well do the job properly. Remember that leaving a badly drafted will can sometimes be worse than leaving no will at all.

Both your solicitor and your financial adviser should be involved in making the will because, if you are like most of our clients, you won't completely understand all your assets. Your financial adviser will be able to provide a list of managed funds such as unit trusts, insurance bonds and superannuation, and also brief the solicitor on the social security implications. A further benefit, as you will see later, is that a properly drawn will may save you or your loved ones from losing the aged pension.

There are also capital gains tax considerations to think about, and many of these have been covered elsewhere in this book.

Prior to preparing your will, you should list every asset of substance and then ask:

1. Who do I want this to go to?
2. Will there be capital gains tax if it does?
3. If capital gains tax is payable, who will pay it?

You should also think about what you wish to happen if a beneficiary dies before you, or if you and your spouse die together.

To protect the estate from your will being contested, you should specify why a particular person is receiving only a small bequest. For example, if your eldest son has received generous help along the way to the detriment of the other children, your will should state why the others are getting more than he is. It also pays to mention by name, and with reasons, other people who are to be left nothing under the will if there is a chance they could lodge a claim on the estate.

Remember, too, that inflation is still with us. Therefore, if you expect to live for many years it might be better to express some bequests as a percentage of your estate, and not a fixed dollar amount.

Anybody of sound mind over 18, or anybody younger than 18 who is married, has the legal capacity to make a will. The will lasts until it is revoked but, as a revocation is automatically inserted in a new will, we could say it stands until you make a new one.

However, be aware that a will is automatically revoked upon marriage or remarriage unless the will is made in anticipation of marriage. It is a common practice for two people to make wills just before they get married because they usually have more exciting things to do on their honeymoon.

> KEY POINT: A will is automatically revoked upon marriage or remarriage unless made in anticipation of marriage.

To be legal a will must be in writing and signed and dated on each page by the testator and two witnesses who signed **in the presence of each other** and the testator. The witnesses cannot be beneficiaries or spouses of beneficiaries. If you make a mistake and need to alter your will, the alteration should be signed by the testator and both witnesses. It is important that there are no pin holes in the will, or glider clip marks on it. If the will is challenged, such marks may be evidence that the testator added a codicil at a later date.

The will must also include the name of the person or persons you wish to act as executor. They may also be beneficiaries of the will, but there is no need for an executor to know the contents of the will until you die.

Once the will is signed, it should be kept in a safe place such as in safe custody at your solicitor's office, or in your own safe deposit box at the bank. Don't keep it at home in case it gets lost or damaged, but do make sure your family and executor know where to find it.

Choosing An Executor

It is wise to nominate two executors in case one dies; if both are alive when you die they may prefer to share the burden. Look for similar qualities in an executor as you would when choosing somebody to whom you would give a power of attorney, but understand that the person to whom you have given your power of attorney need not be the same person as the executor of your will. Furthermore, your power of attorney automatically ceases on death, so cannot be used afterwards. Your executors should be people who are young enough to outlive you, and who are capable of carrying out the duties involved.

I suggest you should ask their permission before you name them as executors. Even though this is not a legal requirement, it is the courteous thing to do, and may prevent the situation occurring whereby the executor refuses to act. The executors should have some business or administrative experience because they will have the responsibility of handling your affairs when you die. If you are unable to find anybody suitable you can appoint your accountant, solicitor or a trustee company.

Trustee companies specialise in acting as executor of estates, but you would be unlikely to appoint one if your affairs were simple. However, they are probably an appropriate executor if winding up the estate is going to be a long-drawn-out and involved affair as often happens with grazing partnerships, or where a business becomes part of the estate. Their fees are calculated as a percentage of the estate, so you would need to discuss their possible appointment with your solicitor or financial adviser to satisfy yourself you were getting value for money by appointing a trustee company as executor instead of somebody else. The main considerations are the complexity of your affairs and who, if anyone, is available to handle them after you die.

Duties Of An Executor

The duty of the executor is to ensure the instructions of the testator, as expressed in the will, are carried out. However, the executor must also comply with the relevant laws, and if there is a conflict between what the laws require, and what the will states, the executor must comply with the law.

The first job is usually to arrange the funeral and then to get a copy of the death certificate and locate and list the assets. If the deceased has taken the advice I offered elsewhere in this book, there will be a comprehensive list of assets as well as instructions regarding the funeral. However, many people never get around to listing their assets and the executor then has to go through whatever documents and bank statements are available to try to put it all together.

The executor is supposed to advise institutions such as banks, fund managers and the Real Property Office of the death. However, in practice, much of this is done by the family solicitor or the trustee company if one has been appointed.

If the estate is a large one, the executor will probably have to apply for probate, which is a legal term for having the will "proved" in a court of law. This cannot be done until advertisements have been placed advising of the intention to apply for probate. The purpose of this is to protect a person who transfers assets in accordance with the will from claims under a second will that might turn up. Even though the size of the estate of itself does not make this necessary, it is a requirement of most share registries and fund managers that they must sight the Grant of Probate before transferring assets to the beneficiaries. Most estates of a reasonable size contain shares or managed funds, and this is the real reason the executor of a larger estate needs to apply for probate.

Sometimes clients ask what happens if they don't appoint an executor. In reality, the appointment of an executor is a standard clause in all wills, so the situation is unlikely to arise unless they die intestate. What *is* a common occurrence is that the executor is unwilling to act. This may be because they feel they do not have the skills or the time to do the job properly. Quite probably, they have had the experience of being an executor before, and do not want to go through it again. An executor who is unwilling to act can file a notice in the court to this effect and can then nominate a new executor, usually after consultation with the deceased's lawyer, financial adviser and relatives.

What if your executor is dead when you die? Then the executor of your deceased executor's estate can also act as the executor of your estate if probate of the predeceasing executor's estate has been granted.

An executor can be paid a fee for the time spent in administering a will, but only if the will specifies this. If the executor is a solicitor, he or she will usually charge by the hour; if a trustee company is appointed the fees are based on the value of the assets in the estate.

Joint Tenancies

You should understand the difference between assets held as joint tenants, and assets held as tenants in common. Joint tenancies are known in law as "will substitutes", inasmuch as they take the place of a will and even have precedence over the will. If an asset (such as a house) is held in **joint tenancy** the entire asset passes to the survivor on death of the other joint tenant irrespective of what the will states. This happens even if the deceased dies intestate, in which case the balance of the estate is divided in terms of the laws of intestacy. If assets are held as **tenants in common** the part owned by the deceased may be transferred in terms of the will.

If you do not fully understand the importance of this automatic transfer of ownership, and don't ensure your assets are held in the right names, your property may not pass on at your death in the manner you hoped.

EXAMPLE: *Mrs Green was widowed and then remarried late in life. She had two children from the first marriage. Her second husband was well-off and her intentions were that her husband retain their home on her death and that the balance of her assets be divided between the two children. She made her will just after she was married.*

Three years later the couple used a large part of their assets to buy an expensive unit at the Gold Coast to use as a winter retreat. They sought no advice and bought this property as joint tenants. She died a year later and the unit automatically went

*to her husband. This deprived the children of the money she had
invested in this asset and all they can do is hope the husband
will transfer half the property to them. If he refuses, they have
no legal rights.*

KEY POINT: Ownership of an asset held in joint tenancy
passes automatically to the survivor on the death of one of the
owners. This happens irrespective of what is stated in the will.

Intestacy

If a person dies intestate, the estate is divided up under the laws of
intestacy. The way it is required to be done varies from State to
State, but in some States de factos have no automatic rights and
have to claim under family maintenance provisions. The way the
estate is divided depends on whether there is a surviving spouse,
but if there are no kinfolk found the entire estate goes to the
Crown. We have found in practice this seldom happens, because
long-lost relatives come from near and far in the hope of a windfall.

In some States, the spouse or de facto is automatically granted
the family home irrespective of its value. This is why you should
ensure your parents have a valid will. Your retirement plans might
go off the rails if your sole surviving parent started living with a
gold-digger and then died intestate.

A Double Accident

It is important that both parties in a relationship have wills.
Suppose one has a will, and the other doesn't, and they are both
killed in an accident together? If there is doubt as to who died first,
there is a presumption that the younger outlived the older. If as a
result of this presumption, or in circumstances where it can be
proved that the one with the will died first, then all assets held by
the couple jointly will fall into the estate of the one without the will.

In that circumstance the family of the intestate party will inherit
all joint assets. For most couples this will include the family home,
bank accounts, shares and other investments. Only those assets
that were owned solely by the party with the will, will be
distributed in accordance with that will.

If both parties have a well-drawn will, the parties can ensure that
all of their assets, including joint assets, will go to the intended

beneficiaries rather than only to the next-of-kin of one of the parties.

Contesting A Will

Clients often ask what rights family members have when people have a change of heart in their old age, and change their will to leave all their money to a young person they have just met, or to an obscure charity. It happens regularly and, when it does, the family has the right to contest the will.

There are four valid reasons to contest a will:

1. **Under the family maintenance provisions of the relevant state Act** – when a dependant believes he or she has a valid claim.
2. **Undue influence** – if a person receives what other family members feel is an overgenerous bequest because of the influence he or she exercised over the testator.
3. **Suspicious circumstances.**
4. **Lack of capacity** – when there is doubt that the testator was of sound mind when the will was executed.

In cases where an older person leaves most of his estate to a younger person he has not known for long, the grounds to contest it may be that the testator had ceased to be of sound mind, or that the family members had rights under the appropriate family maintenance law. If this happens to you, and you feel you have even a vague claim, discuss it with your solicitor. You may have more rights than you thought you did. However, bear in mind that contesting a will can be a difficult and expensive task with the burden of proof being on those who are contesting it. Take legal advice by all means, but be prepared for a struggle.

In one case a grazier and his son had worked the family property together for years on the understanding that the son would inherit the property. Upon the death of his wife the grazier remarried and changed his will to leave everything to the new wife. When the father died the son made a claim against the estate and was given a share on the basis of his contributions to the father's estate over many years. He had been seriously disadvantaged and had a number of dependants who relied on him for support, and for whom he could not adequately provide for from his own resources.

If you are the one making a will, and feel your family could contest it on the grounds of lack of capacity, you can cover your actions by having a doctor attend the signing of the will and confirm you were of sound mind at the time. This would make it almost impossible to contest on the grounds of your lack of capacity.

> KEY POINT: You may have rights even if you are left out of a will.

Forming A Trust

An efficient method of estate planning can be to form a discretionary family trust as discussed in chapter 12. Once the trust is created, a new will can be made leaving certain assets to the family trust but, to save stamp duty and possible capital gains tax, these assets are not transferred until the death of the testator. This can be highly effective if there is a desire to keep assets separate because there has been a second marriage, or if a couple receiving the aged pension desire that one of them continue to receive it after the other dies.

You should always take advice before using a trust because there are some traps for the unwary. Your own residence is not exempt from capital gains tax if it is owned by a trust or a company. Furthermore, your wishes regarding the disposal of your assets may be disregarded when you die, if a hostile trustee gets power to make important decisions.

EXAMPLE: *Jack had two children by his first marriage, which ended in divorce. He then married Karen who had a child by her first marriage. To safeguard the interests of his own two children, Jack set up a discretionary family trust and included Karen, himself and all three children as beneficiaries. He appointed Karen and himself as trustees. The marriage was happy for the first year but relations turned bitter. When speaking to his solicitor Jack learned to his horror that if he died Karen would become sole trustee with the power to vest all the trust assets in the name of her child only.*

A unit trust instead of a discretionary trust may have been a better vehicle to use in this case, because the assets of each unit holder are kept separate. Alternatively a company could have been appointed as trustee of the discretionary family trust with Jack and his accountant or solicitors as directors.

Some Common Questions

Can a beneficiary refuse a bequest under a will?

Unless an asset is held in joint tenancy, in which case it passes automatically to the survivor, a beneficiary may refuse to take a bequest. If the bequest is refused, the asset goes back into the residue of the estate and is distributed with it. This could be appropriate when the bequest may cause loss of all or part of the aged pension.

> **EXAMPLE:** *A couple had substantial assets but were still way under the limit for the aged pension assets test. This entitled them to all the fringe benefits and some pension. The husband died leaving all his shares, bank accounts and managed investments to his wife. Because the single pension assets test is much lower than the test for a couple, she was in danger of losing all her pension and the fringe benefits as well.*

The solution was to refuse the bequest in which case it went to the children. She kept her pension and had the pleasure of watching the children enjoy the money.

If I am separated and living in a de facto relationship, what rights does my wife have?

If she is named as a beneficiary in your will she retains whatever rights she had under that will. You can execute a new will revoking the previous will and leaving her out, but there is a possibility she still may be able to claim against the estate under the Testator's Family Maintenance provisions.

If I get divorced, what effect does that have on my will?

From the date of the issue of the Decree Absolute signifying the marriage has ended, the former spouse has no rights under the will either as a beneficiary or as an executor.

What rights does a de facto have?

These rights vary from State to State. In some States, if you are separated from your spouse, and die intestate, your de facto inherits your spouse's share of the estate if the relationship has exceeded two years. In other States, a de facto has rights only under the Testator's Family Maintenance provisions.

How can I make sure specific bequests go to the ones I want them to go to?

You can gift them before you die or be very specific in your will. Also, ensure you give your solicitor accurate and full instructions, preferably in the form of a list of assets with the names of the people they are to go to written next to them.

It is well known that family heirlooms often vanish soon after death and it is probably better to give them away before your death. Then you have the pleasure of giving, and also know they are going where you want them too. An alternative method used by some people is to place stickers bearing the name of the intended beneficiary on the underside of items such as antique furniture and silverware, although this is obviously open to abuse.

What happens if a beneficiary named in my will dies before me?

If you leave money to your children or grandchildren, and they predecease you, the bequest may still form part of their estates. This does not apply to your siblings. If they predecease you, their shares go into the general residue of your estate.

Conclusion

You should now understand the importance of having a will and of conferring with your financial advisers and solicitors to ensure it reflects your wishes. Because circumstances change, it is good practice to look at your will at least once a year when you are doing the annual review of your financial position.

The next chapter is of special importance to anybody who is in business for themselves, or who is thinking of going into business. It will show you how to protect your hard-earned wealth from creditors.

Summing Up

- Making a will is an essential part of planning your estate.
- Choose executors who are younger than you and have the ability to see your wishes are carried out.
- A will is revoked upon marriage unless made in anticipation of marriage.
- Carefully consider the capital gains tax consequences of any bequests.
- A family trust may be an appropriate vehicle in some situations, but take expert advice before forming one.
- Joint tenancies take precedence over the will.
- Don't have just one beneficiary in your will in case that person dies before you.
- A beneficiary may refuse a bequest.

36

PROTECTING YOUR ASSETS FROM CREDITORS

Prudent men in their dealings incur risk.

VICE-CHANCELLOR BACON

Wouldn't it be a shame to spend years building up all those assets for your retirement and then lose them, because you got involved in a bad business venture or an inappropriate investment? I have gone into this subject in detail in two chapters in *More Money with Noel Whittaker* and you should read those when you get time. Meanwhile, I'll show you now the principles of safeguarding your assets from creditors.

Let me stress I am not condoning the actions of those rogues who prey on unsuspecting creditors by going broke regularly, and starting up again next day under a different name. Nevertheless, we now live in an age of consumerism, and Australia is following the trend in America where everybody will sue everybody else given half a chance. For example, in the financial advisory industry we have been advised that we can be held negligent if a client has insufficient life assurance, and we do not sell the idea of getting more assurance forcefully enough. A client of mine who is a pharmacist now reluctantly refuses to treat small injuries that need first aid for fear of being sued.

I also believe it is unfair for decent people to lose all their assets because of some quirk in the law, just because they did not know how to put simple safety barriers in place. Furthermore, my limited experience with the law has convinced me that court battles are to be avoided at all costs.

When you are considering protecting your assets, the first step should be to think about your situation, and decide if you are in the risky area. If you work for a boss and have no intention of going into business for yourself, you probably have little to worry about, provided you have your car covered with compulsory third party insurance and have a public liability clause in your house insurance policy. However, if you are involved a business venture, or have given personal guarantees, or work in an area where you may be sued for negligence, you should study this chapter carefully.

Let me start with a warning. In order to protect your assets you must take them out of your name and put them in the name of another person or entity. This involves losing control to a degree, but this is the price you have to pay.

The Principles Of Protecting Your Assets

1. If you are in business use a trust or a company. Do not operate as a sole trader or a partnership.
2. Don't sign personal guarantees for your business, or for any other people, if you can possibly avoid it.
3. Build assets in the names of other people or other entities.
4. Keep debts in your personal names, but the assets in the name of somebody else.
5. Accumulate assets in the superannuation area.
6. If you are sued for a large amount, and the action has a chance of success, act quickly to shift assets.

Let's discuss these in detail.

The right business structure

Trusts and family companies are the best vehicles if you have your own business because they enable you to spread income around to save tax, and because they are separate legal entities. This means they can sue and be sued in their own right, in contrast to a sole trader, or a partnership, where it is the individuals who are sued if something goes wrong.

Worse still, in a partnership all partners are jointly and severally liable for partnership debts. "Jointly and severally" means individually or all together. Think about the following:

> **EXAMPLE:** *You and two friends start up a landscaping business that consists mainly of quoting on jobs, buying materials, hiring labour and making sure the work is done properly. At last you win a big job that involves doing $200 000 worth of work for a builder who is constructing a large building. Your joy is short-lived. The builder goes broke when you have just finished the job. Because you were short of working capital you have bought all the materials on credit. Suddenly you are left with a bad debt of $200 000 owing to you by the builder, while you are faced with invoices of $120 000 that have to be paid to your own suppliers.*
>
> *You have your own home, but your business partners are two nice young people who hardly have a dollar to their names. Because it is a partnership you can be held liable for all the debts. It would have been different if you had been trading using a company or a trust. Then the company or the trust, not the partners, would have been liable for the debts of the business.*

> KEY POINT: In a business partnership all partners are jointly and severally liable for the debts of the partnership.

Avoid guarantees

In all of my books I have stressed the danger of guarantees and you should avoid them if at all possible. However, you often have little choice. In the landscaping example above you all may have been required to sign guarantees if you were trading through a company or a trust, because people who give credit know the devices used to dodge personal liability. Nevertheless, the suppliers may be keen enough to get your business that you can talk your way out of it. As a compromise you may at least have been able to negotiate with the suppliers that the guarantee of each member of the business be limited to a third of the debt.

Build assets in other names

If you are in business, and are vulnerable to being sued or losing money in other ways, you should accumulate assets in the name of your spouse, or in the name of other vehicles such as a family trust. Don't wait to do this when trouble looms, you may be forced to reverse the transaction. It's like taking out insurance –

the time to do it is when everything is fine and there is not a hint of trouble suspected.

This is why, when you are investing money, you should always consult with both your accountant and your financial adviser about the best person or entity to hold any investments you make.

Be aware that putting all your assets in the name of a spouse can cause complications if a marital separation occurs. It can also make the family vulnerable if the spouse goes into business or signs any personal guarantees.

Have debts in personal names

I have written at length[1] about using interest-only financing for investment property in conjunction with a sinking fund. In short, you do it by keeping your investment loan at its original level, but accumulating assets separately that will one day be sufficient to pay off the debt. The theory is that you can earn a higher rate after tax in your sinking fund than you can by using the extra funds to reduce your loan.

Think about two people who are both high-earning professionals near the end of their working lives. We'll call them Jack and Don.

EXAMPLE: *Jack and Don are partners in a firm that has just been sued for negligence. Each has the family home in his wife's name but both have luxury beachfront units that are each worth $500 000. These units were bought in their own names to get the tax benefits of negative gearing. Jack has been paying his loan back quickly because he knows his working life is nearly over. Consequently his debt is down to $60 000. Don's debt is still $400 000 because he has been ploughing all his surplus money into his sinking fund. This consists of insurance bonds in his wife's name that are now worth $340 000.*

Contrast the two positions if their firm loses the negligence action and Jack and Don face bankruptcy. Jack will lose the unit because the creditors will force him to sell it. However, Don has little equity in the unit because his equity has been effectively invested in the insurance bonds in his wife's name. Here it is safe from Don's creditors, and even if the creditors did manage to force a sale of Don's unit, his wife could redeem her bonds and try to buy it back.

---

1. See the chapters on Negative Gearing and Borrowing Smart in *More Money with Noel Whittaker.*

Build money in superannuation

One of the best features of superannuation as an investment is that the money is generally safe in the event of your getting into financial strife. This principle will not be true if the bulk of the money you have in superannuation is from last-minute large sums you deposited into superannuation as the creditors are storming your office. However, the money will not be able to be taken from you in the event of your bankruptcy, provided you made reasonable contributions when you had no reason to believe your financial affairs were heading for trouble.

Remember that money in superannuation is tied up until age 55 at least, and can still be divided with your spouse if you get divorced.

Gift it away

The most effective way of putting assets out of the hands of a liquidator or trustee in bankruptcy is to gift them away. However, once you do this you lose control of them and you may be liable for capital gains tax and stamp duty on the transfer. Obviously it is not something to be done lightly, but let me relate one experience to show you how easily unexpected financial problems can happen.

EXAMPLE: *The Doe Brothers had been running a large and profitable company for years. One day, without warning, a* *supplier of that company served them with a writ for several million dollars. Apparently his claim was that he had been a silent partner of the business and was owed several years profits. The brothers were stunned and quickly denied it. After four years, $300 000 in legal costs, and immense worry they won the case in court. They said, "Even though we knew his case was totally without foundation we were on edge till the last moment."*

You never know when a frivolous writ can hit you and, worst of all, you seldom know what the outcome of a court case will be. In these days of high legal fees you could also be faced with paying the costs of both sides if you lose.

If you are faced with a writ, don't wait for the outcome of the action. Talk seriously to your accountant and legal advisers about transferring assets to other family members or to other entities. A writ is not proof of guilt on your part; it is nothing more than a claim by another party. Provided the gift was not made fraudulently it cannot be set aside after two years have passed from the date of the gift. There are few court cases that can be settled in less than two years.

> KEY POINT: Once two years have passed from the date of gifting money away, it is almost impossible for the Trustee in Bankruptcy to reverse the transaction.

Putting It Together

That completes the six main ways of securing your nest egg. To help you make sure you understand it all let me tell you about Mr and Mrs Smart, who run a highly profitable business and have got their affairs fairly safe from creditors.

The business is run by the company Smart Holdings Pty Ltd as trustee for the Smart Family Trust – a discretionary family trust. Mr and Mrs Smart are both directors of the trustee company and they and their four children, as well as other relations, are beneficiaries of the family trust. If any creditors of the business want directors' guarantees, Mr Smart gives his guarantee but points out that Mrs Smart, being a nervous type of woman, will never sign guarantees. If that is not acceptable, the Smarts take their custom elsewhere.

The business operates from a building owned by the Smart Unit Trust. There is a registered lease in existence and the business pays market rent to the trust. Their family home is in the name of Mrs Smart because they know that it will not be exempt from capital gains tax if owned by the family trust or the family company. All other assets are owned by their self-managed superannuation fund, or by their children or by the Smart Unit Trust.

Their arrangements are perfectly legal and very secure, provided they stay happily married. The only asset of the discretionary family trust is the business, and all the assets of the family, except the family home and superannuation, are owned by the unit trust, which is a separate entity entirely from the discretionary family trust.

Conclusion

You now know the ways of protecting assets that are used by most leading business people. It is information that could be worth hundreds of thousands of dollars to you. At date of writing, Australia was flirting with the American system of contingency law actions where lawyers could initiate an action and be paid a percentage of any monies won as fees. If this develops, some of you who are in business may face court battles regularly, and protecting your assets will become even more important.

We'll now consider ways you can have a simple record-keeping system. It may take a few hours to set up, but the benefits will be worth it.

Summing Up

- To protect your estate from creditors you need to place the assets in the name of another entity such as a spouse, trust or company.
- Never give personal guarantees if you can avoid it.
- Superannuation is a useful place for money you want to protect.
- Divorce can upset the best-laid plans.
- If you receive a large writ, take advice about gifting assets away immediately. Beware of the tax and stamp duty implications of doing this.

37

KEEPING THE RIGHT RECORDS

Next to being prepared for death with respect to Heaven and his soul, a Tradesman should always be in the state of preparation for Death, with respect to his books.

DANIEL DEFOE

In this chapter we'll focus on two types of records, those you are required by law to keep, and those that are prudent to keep. Now I appreciate that keeping records might be a chore, and the temptation is often to toss everything into a drawer and sort it out when you get around to it. However, we live in a time of change and increasing complication, and a good record-keeping system is not just essential for tax purposes – it will also save a lot of time and worry when somebody dies.

Think about the Tax Office first. Taxation now works on the self-assessment system, and the Tax Office staff treat what we put in our tax returns as correct. However, when they select any of us for an audit, we have to be able to produce all the documents that are relevant to the transactions in question.

But, even if it wasn't a Tax Office requirement, it makes sense to keep good records to ensure you are on track with your asset-building program. As the great American broadcaster Earl Nightingale said, "People with goals succeed because they know where they are going." Good records are like a road map, they tell you exactly where you are now, and help you decide the best way to get to the next step.

Tax Office Requirements

In general terms, a business must keep its records for 5 years, and an employee for 42 months. These dates start from when the tax return was lodged. Remember, you may spend most of your time as an employee yet still carry on the business of an investor in rental property, shares or managed funds. If so, the records that are relevant to your "business" must be kept for 5 years, too.

The basic information needed about investments such as property, shares and unit trusts is the date each investment was bought, the sum paid, the buying costs if any, number of shares or units issued where appropriate, and full information about any income or distributions. All reinvested share or managed fund dividends should be treated like the purchase of a new investment. If you carry out any capital expenditure on your rental properties you should record the cost of the work done and the date it was carried out. Naturally you should also keep any documents such as invoices and receipts as evidence of the work done.

Some stationery shops sell special registers that are designed for keeping track of investments, but many of our clients find a loose-leaf ledger with a page for each investment works just as well and is a simple and inexpensive way to start. Other clients have a separate ring binder for each investment and record details on a sheet, which is always kept on top, and file the miscellaneous paperwork behind it.

No matter which method you use, there should be a page headed up with the name of the investment. In separate columns record the date purchased and the amount paid. If shares, unit trusts or insurance bonds are involved, list the number of shares or units issued to you, and then keep a running total that you adjust when you increase or reduce your holding.

THE XYZ IMPUTATION TRUST

Date	Number of units acquired	Cost of units	Details	Progressive balance
01/01/94	10 000	$5 000	Initial investment	10 000
30/06/94	680	$375	Reinvested distn.	10 680
15/08/94	5 000	$3 000	Further purchase	15 680

When a particular type of investment is totally sold, list details of the selling price and the costs of sale, then remove the sheet and file it in the back of the book in a separate section labelled "Sold".

Make sure you keep the distribution or dividend advices, because share dividends may have "franked" and "unfranked" portions and the tax treatment is different in each case. Unit trusts often have most complicated distributions that may include as many as four separate components for tax purposes, but fortunately the fund manager usually sends out an annual summary with it all explained. The easy way to keep track is to have another loose-leaf page headed "Distributions" filed next to the sheet for each investment. Glue or staple the distribution statement to this page and it will be ready for your accountant at tax time.

Each time you receive a distribution statement, check that the total number of units or shares held agrees with your running total. If you want to follow your investments closely you could have a third loose-leaf page for each investment on which you record the daily or weekly values.

If you have taken my advice and joined your adviser's portfolio review service you may be able to skip much of the record-keeping about buying and selling as long as you tell your adviser promptly of any acquisitions or disposals. You should still keep good records of the income distributions for your tax return.

Records relating to assets on which capital gains tax may be payable must be kept from the date the contract to buy was signed until 5 years have passed from date of disposal. That may be 30 years or more. If you have incurred any capital losses the records must be kept from the date of acquisition of the asset until 5 years have passed from the date you lodged the tax return in which you claimed these losses.

Listing Your Assets And Liabilities

In *More Money with Noel Whittaker* I showed you how to prepare a personal balance sheet that listed all your assets and liabilities. This became the basis of your wealth-building plan. It is good practice to make a list of your assets and liabilities every year because it provides feedback on how well you are doing in achieving your financial goals, and stimulates the mind when you are planning for the next year.

An easy way to do this is to design a simple form that incorporates the details needed and then take several photocopies for future use. You can then fill in a new form each year. Another method is to key the data into your computer, or to use one of the many record-keeping computer programs such as my *Wealth Creator on CD-ROM* that are now available. Once you have done the time-consuming job of keying in the initial information, it is a simple matter to update it regularly.

Safe-Deposit Boxes

Your documents should be kept in a safe place yet be readily accessible if you need them quickly. Probably a safe-deposit box at the bank is one of the most effective methods to use, and the annual cost of the bank holding your box or envelope is about $50 a year. This is less than installing a safe at home.

The bank safe custody is secure and bank staff cannot open your box without your being there. However, banks do not insure the contents, nor take any responsibility for loss, so if you keep all your spare cash and jewellery in the box and you lose it in a bank robbery, it is you, and not the bank, who suffers the loss. Accordingly, you should make sure your household insurance covers jewellery and cash stored in safe custody at the bank.

The appropriate items to keep in your safe-deposit box are passports, title deeds, scrip, debenture and managed-fund certificates, rare stamps and coins, insurance polices and your wills. If you have funeral bonds or special instructions for your funeral, it is better to keep these at home where they can be found quickly. Don't forget that banks close on weekends and public holidays.

General Information

It is worthwhile to keep a list of your main assets at home together with other information that may be useful to your spouse if you die or become disabled, or to your next of kin if you live on your own. The following check-list will help you compile your own list, but remember it is no more than a guide. There are almost certain to be other items that apply to you. In the next chapter I have included a specimen list that was drawn up by a friend of mine that contains even more detail.

Watch Nominated Beneficiaries

Be careful to check who you have nominated as beneficiaries of insurance policies such as insurance bonds. We regularly

CHECK LIST

Locations of:

- [ ] Your wills
- [ ] Your powers of attorney, and who has been nominated as your attorney
- [ ] The title deeds for all your properties
- [ ] Documents such as scrip or unit trust certificates that evidence ownership of assets
- [ ] Your safe-deposit box if you have one

Details of:

- [ ] Your bank accounts
- [ ] Any money, valuables or mementos you may have hidden in odd places around the house or in the garden
- [ ] Your insurance policies, when they mature, their approximate value, and the names of the beneficiaries
- [ ] Your superannuation
- [ ] Your rollover/approved deposit fund/pension particulars
- [ ] Your credit cards
- [ ] Any loans you may have
- [ ] Tax file numbers

encounter situations where a spouse has been nominated as a beneficiary prior to a divorce, but the party who owns the policy has forgotten that this clause remains in the policy after divorce. It is a simple matter to change a beneficiary if a divorce happens, provided you remember to do it. A practical way to overcome this problem in advance is to alter the beneficiary clause to read "in terms of my will" when making the original investment.

Conclusion

It will take you a few hours to get the above information together, but the effort will be worth it. You will have the peace of mind of knowing that your affairs are in order, and you will have the fun of keeping track of your progress each year. That, in itself, is one of the best learning experiences there is.

Next we'll discuss arranging and funding a funeral. It's an important job but one that most people keep putting off.

Summing Up

- Good records are essential for tax purposes and also help you stay on track with your wealth-building program.
- Make sure you keep all your dividend and distribution advices.
- Know the different time limits for which records must be kept for tax purposes.
- When you carry out capital expenditure on your rental properties, you should record the amount spent, the date, and details of the actual work done.
- Don't keep your funeral instructions in your safe-deposit box.

38

FUNERALS AND FUNERAL BONDS

A great deal of money is expended on funerals and that, in itself, seems to betray a lack of confidence in the resurrection of the dead.

REV. EDWARD HENDERSON

You seldom read much about funerals in money books, but death is a fact of life, and grief is a process that it is better to go through than to try to ignore. Maybe you still have to suffer the death of one or both of your parents and, in any event, a knowledge of the funeral process is useful when you are doing your own estate planning.

Death comes to all of us, but most people prefer to leave thinking about it till another day. As a result they are usually unprepared for the important decisions that have to be made when loved ones die, and they may suffer a lot of unnecessary stress.

In this chapter we'll discuss the procedure that should be followed when somebody dies, think about the process of the funeral itself, consider ways of paying for the funeral and then list the information it is useful to keep on hand.

When a death occurs

Just as a birth requires a birth certificate, so a death requires a death certificate. This is usually issued by the doctor attending the deceased person, but if the deceased has not been seen by a doctor in the three months prior to death, the coroner must be notified. The word "coroner" means "of the Crown", and the coroner was originally a government official who had the responsibility of investigating any suspicious death. The coroner still has that role but also becomes involved when people die

343

suddenly or in a range of circumstances that include accidents, fires and suicides. Then, before a funeral can take place, the body is taken to the Government Mortuary where an autopsy is performed to determine the cause of death.

If a person dies suddenly at home, and has not been attended by a doctor in the previous three months, the police should be called. They will arrange for the body to be taken to the Government Mortuary and the coroner notified. When the deceased has been under the care of a doctor, but that doctor cannot be contacted, the doctor who comes from the after-hours medical service will issue a temporary certificate that enables the funeral director to remove the body. Next day the deceased's own doctor will view the body and issue the death certificate.

About half of the deaths that occur happen at hospitals, about 25% occur in nursing homes, 20% at home and 5% elsewhere, such as when accidents occur.

In practice, a funeral director will be unlikely to remove the body from the place of death until the death certificate is issued, but once that happens it is usually the funeral director who orchestrates the proceedings from there. Once the death certificate has been issued the next of kin, or the executor of the will, should phone the funeral director, who will ask for some brief information, and then arrange a face-to-face meeting.

The meeting can happen at home, or at the funeral director's office, but most people prefer the last-mentioned option so that they can choose the coffin or the casket[1] at the same time. The important matters that will be decided at this meeting include the time and place of the funeral, the type of coffin or casket, the cost of the funeral and whether burial or cremation is preferred. Once these decisions are made the funeral directors will collect the body and attend to such details as arranging the venue and the celebrant, and placing the appropriate advertisements in the newspapers.

You should be gaining an appreciation now of why it is so important to have discussed these fundamental decisions in advance. It is almost certain to be a stressful time and will be much more stressful if you are in a quandary over whether a loved one wanted an expensive casket or a plain coffin, or to be buried or cremated.

---

1. A casket is dearer than a coffin and is rectangular. A coffin is tapered at each end.

The cost of the funeral

Funeral directors tell me the cost of a normal funeral is between $2300 and $2700 for a cremation and about $3300 to $3700 for a burial. The burial costs more, because there is a plot to buy and digging fees to pay. However, if you choose cremation there could be the additional cost of a niche, which may be $600 or more. You can save this cost if you scatter the ashes, which is another reason to have given some thought to these matters in advance.

The funeral costs include the coffin, all disbursements such as advertising, church fees and burial certificates, as well as the funeral director's charges for doing all the work from transporting and preparing the body to arranging the funeral.

The funeral cost need not be paid before the funeral and in most cases payment is arranged by the executor to come from the estate when it is being administered. However, most banks will issue a bank cheque in favour of the funeral director for the cost of the funeral if there are sufficient funds in the deceased's account.

Viewing the body

About 15% of families choose to view the body and there is usually little extra cost involved in this because the embalming process is carried out by the funeral director whether a viewing is required or not. Obviously, viewing the body is a choice for each family, but the article in the October 1992 edition of *Choice* magazine (pages 22-26) mentioned the positive reactions felt by those who had been through the viewing experience. Funeral directors recommend you have the viewing if you are in any doubt. Then you will not have regrets later when it is too late to do it.

The grief process

It is well known that the best way to handle grief is to express your emotions and get it out of your system. However, we live in a culture where many people, especially males, believe it is wrong to cry in public, and as a result do not gain the benefits of grieving. My mother died suddenly at age 54, when I was 21. As I was the oldest child the job fell to me to look after the rest of the family. Consequently, I never went through the grieving process because I was too busy taking care of the others. In any event I thought it was weak to show how badly I was hurt by her death. The result was that for the next 33 years I started crying whenever I thought about her and it was only when I finally allowed myself to pour out my emotions at a counselling session in 1994 that I became able to handle that death that took place so long ago.

The funeral process is often a time of grief, but it is also an opportunity to hasten the grieving process and so speed the healing process. Feel free to express what you feel. If you don't do it then, you will probably have to do it later.

Paying For The Funeral

It makes sense to make your funeral plans in advance and, if you wish, to set aside money for your funeral by way of funeral bonds or funeral plans. They may sound similar, but there are significant differences between them.

Funeral bonds

One of the best ways to provide for your funeral is to invest some money in a funeral bond. This is a highly effective investment, particularly for pensioners, and helps to ensure you cover an essential element in your estate planning – paying for your funeral. A major benefit is that the fund in which the money is invested is a **tax exempt** fund, which enables your savings in this area to grow in a tax-free environment. Contrast this with insurance and friendly society bonds that pay tax at up to 39%, and superannuation and rollover funds that suffer tax at 15%. The leading funeral bond funds are conservatively run and your money is secure.

For pension eligibility purposes neither the growing value of the asset nor the bonuses that are added each year are taken into account. This enables pensioners to transfer assets to a tax-exempt area where it does not reduce their pension. Furthermore, they gain the peace of mind of knowing their funerals are taken care of.

You can buy funeral bonds through licensed security dealers. The entry fee usually varies between 3% and 4% and there is no exit fee unless you regard death as the ultimate price. The funeral bond brochure will contain a form that enables you to transfer the ownership of the policy to a nominated funeral director. This may be useful if you have entered into an agreement with that funeral director for a fixed-price funeral.

The drawbacks? There is good news here, for the drawbacks are slight. You lose access to the money, which in many cases is a good thing anyway, and there is a limit of $5000 on how much you can invest. There is also a requirement that the money be used for genuine funeral expenses. If not, these bonds would degenerate into another "tax fiddle".

This raises two questions:

1. What are "funeral expenses"?
2. What happens if I put in too much?

Funeral expenses

"Funeral expenses" include:

- the cost of acquiring the site and digging the grave
- the cost of transporting the body to the funeral parlour from anywhere in the world
- the funeral director's fees
- the offering to the celebrant
- cost of the coffin, hearse and cremation
- cost of obtaining statutory documentation
- cost of death notices and floral wreaths.

At the date of writing, the cost of an average funeral was about $3000 but you can expect this to rise with inflation. However, the earnings of a funeral bond should do much better than inflation because they are exempt from tax. Therefore, you should not put too much money into a funeral bond, particularly if you expect to live for a long time, because you might become overfunded. We have found that a once-only investment of $2000 per person is appropriate for most people.

Overfunding

It is important to heed your adviser when investing in funeral bonds because different fund managers have different requirements. For example, some fund managers insist on a copy of the death certificate and an account from the funeral director so they know how much to pay out. If there is an excess of funds the money is forfeited by the estate.

In contrast, other managers are happy to pay excess funds to the estate. These funds interpret the tax laws differently and believe the limit of $5000 imposed on any one investor is sufficient restriction to ensure the tax-free status of the bonds is not abused.

A funeral bond can fund only one funeral but funeral bonds are often taken out in joint names. If the bond is in joint names, and one party dies, the survivor has the option of keeping the bond intact for his or her own funeral, or cashing it in immediately to pay for the first funeral.

Funeral Plans

Funeral plans are somewhat similar to funeral bonds, but most contributions are made by regular instalments of possibly $100 each at a time that is convenient to the member. The maximum contribution is $5000 and neither the asset nor the accruing bonuses are subject to the assets or income tests for aged pension purposes. They are used mainly by people who wish to arrange a prepaid funeral with a funeral director of their choice. The rationale is that you pay for your funeral in today's dollars and then the earnings on the plan ensure that the plan value keeps up with the increase in inflation that will cause the cost of the funeral to rise.

The major difference between funeral plans and funeral bonds is that funeral **bond** funds are tax-exempt but your money is unable to be withdrawn till death. In contrast, funeral **plan** funds pay tax at the **highest marginal tax rate** before the earnings are added to your plan, but you can **withdraw your money at will.** The funeral bond funds will, therefore, pay a much higher rate of return because no tax is deducted from the earnings.

If you do withdraw the money in your funeral plan, the accrued bonuses are treated as taxable income and must be included in your tax return in the year the money was returned to you.

KEY POINT: Funeral bond funds are tax-exempt, but the money in them is inaccessible until the death of the owner. Funeral plan funds pay a high rate of tax, but the money is available at call.

When you join a funeral plan and arrange for a prepaid funeral, you usually nominate a specified funeral director to conduct the funeral and the name of the funeral director is listed on your plan certificate. You also have a meeting with the funeral director to decide what you wish to spend on your funeral, and the type of funeral you want. Some funeral plans incorporate a tiny life insurance policy that ensures there is sufficient money for your funeral if you die before you have paid all your instalments.

If there is a surplus of funds after the funeral has been paid for, it is refunded to the deceased's estate.

Preparing For Your Funeral

I'll now reproduce extracts from a document that a friend of mine drew up for the help of his family, and particularly his wife, in the event of his early death. He is a retired senior banker and it is obvious that he is used to handling the family finances. Our firm has found that in most families one person has responsibility for the administration of the money. That's fine, but it may leave his or her spouse in the lurch in the event of sudden death. If you prepare a document that is similar to what follows it will help greatly. Naturally, you will have to adapt it to suit your own requirements. You will notice that much of the following information duplicates that which I mentioned in the previous chapter.

FUNERAL INFORMATION

For the Death Certificate.

Full name

| Birthplace | Date of birth |

| Years in Australia | Age at marriage |

| Place of marriage | Date of marriage |

Occupation

Full name and birthdate of spouse (including maiden name)

Full names and birthdates of children (living and dead)

Father's full name

Mother's full maiden name

Special wishes.

☐ I wish to be cremated at...

☐ I wish to have my ashes placed in a niche near my family or at...

☐ I wish to have my ashes scattered over the ocean at...

☐ I wish to be buried in the cemetery at...

☐ I have a prepaid plot. Details are kept in...

☐ I have a prepaid funeral plan with (Funeral Directors)...

☐ I have a funeral bond that nominates (Funeral Directors)...

☐ I wish to have the following items placed in my coffin...

☐ The people I especially wish to be notified about my funeral are...

☐ My preferred funeral music is...

☐ I want you to give me a good wake

House security - I suggest you arrange with a security firm or a friend to look after the house when the funeral is being held as the funeral will be advertised and criminals will know it may be vacant then.

HELPFUL INFORMATION

Will.

My Will is located at...

The executors are...

Death Certificate.

Before you can do much regarding our financial affairs you should get a copy of the death certificate from the Registrar of Births and Deaths. If you phone they will send out a form and you can return it with a cheque. Otherwise it takes two trips to the city - one to order it and another to collect it a few days later.

Bank Accounts.

☐ The accounts are in my name
☐ The accounts are in joint names

Go to the bank and ask them to close our joint accounts and open a similar one in your name. The bank will probably do this without a copy of the death certificate.

Cheque Account.

Account number

Name of our Bank   Branch

The following payments come out of this account by direct debit...
(a)

(b)

(c)

(d)

The one for my life insurance should now be cancelled.

Savings Account.

Account number

Name of our Bank   Branch

This account earns interest on daily balances.

Safe Custody Box.

This is kept at...

It contains our Wills, Life Insurance and the following papers...
(a)

(b)

(c)

(d)

HELPFUL INFORMATION

Credit Cards.

Bankcard number

It is usually in my wallet otherwise in one of my hiding places such as...

This will need to be cancelled. As your card is linked with mine, yours would be automatically cancelled also and you would need to ask for a new one for yourself.

Mastercard number

I only have this card for use overseas. They charge interest on all purchases on it from day of purchase whereas with Bankcard interest is only charged if you are late in making payments. As your card is linked with mine yours would be automatically cancelled also and you would need to ask for a new one for yourself.

Visa Card number

American Express Card number

Defence Service Homes.

We have a loan from these people. Interest is only at ......% and the fire insurance is very cheap and comprehensive. You get a notice each year around January.

Our Home.

It is mortgaged to...

The person who handles our affairs there is...

Contact Phone Number

☐ The title deeds are held by them
☐ The deeds are held in safe custody by the Bank

Before you can sell the house it would need to be transferred into your name and once again you would need a copy of the death certificate. I suggest you see our solicitor who would attend to the transfer to your name for you.

Insurance.

Our Insurance Brokers are...

The person who handles our affairs there is...

Contact Phone Number

Apart from the house insurance through Defence Service Homes above, all our other insurance is arranged through our insurance brokers. They will guide you when the renewals fall due.

Telephone.

You would need to change the listing. If you are concerned about being on your own you may omit the house number.

HELPFUL INFORMATION

Accountant.

Our accountants are...

The person who handles our affairs there is...

Contact Phone Number

Solicitor.

Our Solicitors are...

The person who handles our affairs there is...

Contact Phone Number

Financial Advice.

Our financial advisers are...

The person who handles our affairs there is...

Contact Phone Number

If he/she is not available talk to...

We are on their Review Service and they have details of all our investments. The certificates for these investments are in the safe custody box. I have an allocated pension and you will need to make an appointment to vary the pension or take the balance as a lump sum.

Life Insurance.

Our life insurance is with...

The person who handles our affairs there is...

Contact Phone Number

Our policies are as follows...
(a)

(b)

(c)

They are worth approximately $...

The policies are in our safe-custody box.

Superannuation.

Our superannuation is with...

The person who handles our superannuation is...

Contact Phone Number

HELPFUL INFORMATION

Medicare.

Our number is...

Our card is in my wallet. There are no payments to make, but take our card to their nearest office and they will arrange a card in your own name.

Private Health Insurance.

Our Health Insurance is with...

Number   Table

The person who handles our affairs there is...

Contact Phone Number

The book is kept in...

You will need to arrange with them for the insurance to be in your name with a payment frequency that suits you. I think my death entitles you to claim a funeral benefit from them.

Tax.

Our tax file numbers are...

(a)

(b)

Pension.

Our pension numbers are...

(a)

(b)

RSL.

The name of the RSL Branch we are members of is...

There is a funeral benefit there of $...

Motor Vehicles.

I now get them serviced at...

For smash repairs I have always used...

Our car insurance is with...

The registrations are in joint names and would need to be changed to your name. I suggest you leave it until the registration is due. Don't forget that when you sell the second car there may be a refund of insurance and registration available.

Summing Up

- Don't be afraid to discuss your wishes for your funeral with your spouse or next of kin.
- If a person dies without having been attended by a medical practitioner in the preceding three months, the coroner must be advised.
- Funeral bonds are tax-exempt, but the funds are inaccessible until death.
- Funeral plans pay tax at the highest marginal rate, but the money is available at call.
- Make the time to prepare a detailed list of your affairs.

That's a comprehensive list isn't it, and it has probably reminded you of other items that should be mentioned. It should also have made you more aware of the importance of keeping good records.

Conclusion

Coming to terms with one's mortality is sometimes a difficult thing to do, and such actions as making a will, signing a power of attorney or listing your wishes for your funeral may not come easily. Nevertheless, the fact that you have read this far shows you are serious about enjoying a secure retirement. You will find if you take the time to make out a list as described above you will feel far better about your financial affairs as well as being firmly on the path to living well in retirement.

We'll now turn to the aged pension. You may not need it but it's nice to know it's there if you do.

39

PENSIONS AND BENEFITS

Get even – spend the inheritance.

A BUMPER STICKER

We'll now discuss pensions and benefits, but let me start by assuring you that Australia has one of the most generous social security systems in the world. However, it is such a complicated system that most people don't understand it properly, and consequently often fail to make full use of their pension entitlements.

The system offers both **pensions** and **allowances.** A **pension** is the term for government assistance paid to people who are regarded as needing long-term support or having retired permanently. An **allowance** is a generic term used for most other forms of government assistance. That is why we may talk about an aged or disability support pension, but an unemployment allowance.

There is now such a vast range of payments available that it would be impossible to cover them all here. However, if you feel they might apply to you, call in at the local office of the Department of Social Security, which will supply all the details. In this section we shall focus on the aged pension as this will affect the majority of you at some stage, either for yourself or your family. Also remember that successive governments are continuing to fine-tune the system, and changes to the pension and benefit rules are still being announced regularly. The result is that we have reached a stage where most retirees seeking the aged pension need the help of independent financial planners to arrange their affairs to best advantage.

356

Eligibility

To qualify for an aged pension you must have reached pensionable age and have lived in Australia for ten continuous years, or five continuous years combined with five years of broken residence. You may also be eligible if you came from a country with whom Australia has reciprocal arrangements. Pensionable age for men is 65, and it is 60 for women who were aged 60 before 1 July 1995. Since 1910 the pension age for women has been set at five years less than the age for men in recognition of women's lower income, broken employment patterns and reduced capacity to save for their retirement.

However, in recognition of the increasing role being taken by women in the workforce, the pensionable age for women is being progressively raised to 65. The following table gives details:

Age at 1 July 1995	Pensionable age
From 58.5 to less than 60	60.5
From 57.0 to less than 58.5	61
From 55.5 to less than 57	61.5
From 54.0 to less than 55.5	62
From 52.5 to less than 54	62.5
From 51.0 to less than 52.5	63
From 49.5 to less than 51	63.5
From 48.0 to less than 49.5	64
From 46.5 to less than 48	64.5
Less than 46.5	65

If you are a couple, and only one partner is of pensionable age, the one who has reached pensionable age may apply for a pension in their own right. If the pension is granted it will be half that paid to a pensioner couple.

Rates Of Pension

At 30 June 1997 the rates of pension were $353.20 a fortnight for a single pensioner and $585.60 a fortnight (combined) for a couple. If a couple are forced to live apart, perhaps one is confined to a nursing home, they receive a higher pension.

The pension is subject to both an income test and an assets test, which results in the pension dropping as income and assets rise. While these tests appear straightforward, for example the pension drops by one dollar for each two dollars earned, the continual rule changes have made them complicated to administer. To determine eligibility for a pension, applicants are tested under both tests and the one that produces the least pension is the one used. The two tests are discussed in detail in the next chapter.

Fringe Benefits

All pensioners (irrespective of the amount of pension received) qualify for certain fringe benefits, which may include a health card, reduced fares on public transport, and concessions on telephone, electricity, gas, motor vehicle registration, dog licences and rates. Pensioners value the fringe benefits highly as they can be worth as much as $1500 a year. The amount and type of fringe benefits vary from State to State and also between different local authorities. The office of your local alderman and State member will be able to give you more details.

Commonwealth Seniors Health Card

From 1 July 1994 the Commonwealth Seniors Health Card (CSHC) is available to Australian residents of pensionable age whose assessable incomes under the pension income test (not taxable incomes) are below the pension cut-out level. Most people who qualify for this card are not eligible for a pension because of excess assets, or because they have not lived in Australia long enough to qualify under the residency conditions.

The CSHC provides access to pharmaceutical concessions, hearing-aid concessions and dental treatment under the Commonwealth Dental Health Program.

Seniors Cards

Seniors Cards are issued by most State governments free of charge. The eligibility criteria varies from State to State, but in some States both pensioners and non-pensioners can take advantage of the benefits offered. Holders of the card may be entitled to concessions on a range of government services, which may include rail and bus travel, motor vehicle registration fees and the cost of electricity. Seniors Card holders also enjoy discounts from a range of participating businesses who offer such diverse products as clothes, travel, dry cleaning and smash repairs. The State department that administers the Seniors Card distributes a booklet every year listing the services available, and part of the cost of this booklet is paid for by contributions from the businesses listed in it.

Mature Age Allowance

A mature age allowance (MAA) was introduced in March 1994 because the Government recognised:

- it is often harder for older people to find work and may be almost impossible once they reach their late fifties or early sixties.
- the tough income test applied to unemployment benefits reduced the capacity of the older unemployed to look after themselves when they retired.

To qualify you have to be at least 60, but less than pensionable age, at the time you apply. Applicants must have been registered with the Commonwealth Employment Service for nine months prior to their claim and also be in receipt of benefits. However, once MAA starts to be paid, there is no requirement that its recipients actively seek work. It is obvious the Government believes that MAA applicants have become virtually unemployable and it is a waste of time to tie up resources by forcing them to keep applying for jobs that they have no chance of getting.

Since July 1996 new grants of MAA are assessed under the allowance income and assets tests, which are stricter than the aged pension tests. The recipient must have had no recent workforce experience. This allowance is automatically superseded by the Age Pension at Age Pension age. Recipients are entitled to receive the Pensioner Concession Card.

Deferred Retirement Bonus Plan

The May 1997 Budget included a bonus for people who continue to work past pensionable age. Naturally it is available for all, but it is aimed primarily at people who work for themselves in small business with relatively low incomes and who have little to sell when the time comes to retire. Under the plan, a bonus of 9.4% of pension entitlement will be paid as a tax-free lump sum for each full year of "work" beyond pension qualifying age.

The bonus will be payable for up to five years of "work", which is defined as paid employment for at least 25 hours a week. It will be calculated by multiplying their assessed pension entitlement by 9.4%, multiplied by the number of eligible years of "work".

> **EXAMPLE:** *Tom and Sue are both working, but Tom is eligible for age pension from 3 July 1998. Tom works the required 25 hours a week for the next five years and applies for the aged pension on 3 July 2003 when he turns 70. He is granted a pension of $290.10 a fortnight ($7 542 a year). Sue does not reach pensionable age till August 2000 but she chooses to wait to 2003 when Tom starts his pension. She is also granted $290.10 a fortnight.*

The bonuses are calculated as follows:

	Tom	
Starting aged pension	*$7 542*	
"Work adjustment"	*$3 545*	*7 542 x 9.4% x 5*
Bonus	*$17 725*	*3 545 x 5*
	Sue	
Starting aged pension	*$7 542*	
"Work adjustment"	*$2 127*	*7 542 x 9.4% x 3*
Bonus	*$6 831*	*2 127 x 3*

They are entitled to a tax-free bonus of $24 106 between them.

Note that Sue would have been better off to take the $7 542 a year pension as soon as she qualified for it, unless she was also working.

Taxation Of Pensioners

Aged pensions are regarded as taxable income, but pensioners may claim a tax rebate if their total income does not exceed $21 377 (including their pension) for single pensioners, and $16 684 each for a couple. The maximum tax rebates are $1 229 for a single pensioner and $868 each for a couple, and are allowed when total taxable income is not more than $11 545 and $9 740 respectively.

The tax scales are arranged so that if a single pensioner earns no more than the allowed $98 a fortnight in addition to the pension, and a couple earns no more than their allowed $172 a fortnight, there is no income tax payable. A pensioner couple can split the rebate if their incomes are out of balance so as to be in the same position for tax as if their incomes were equal. For every $8 earned over the rebate thresholds of $11 545 and $9 740 the rebate reduces by a dollar. Pensioners pay the same rates of tax as ordinary taxpayers once the rebate is eliminated.

> **EXAMPLE:** *A single pensioner receives a pension of $317.20 a fortnight and earns $170 a fortnight from other investments. Therefore total taxable income is $487.20 a fortnight or $12 667 a year. The rebate is calculated thus:*
>
> | | |
> |---|---:|
> | *Taxable Income* | *$12 667* |
> | *Less rebate threshold* | *$11 545* |
> | *Difference* | *$ 1 122* |
> | *Loss of Rebate* | *$140 ($1 122 divided by 8)* |
> | *Rebate available* | *$ 982 ($1 122 less $140)* |

We have already discussed how investors on lower taxable incomes could reduce their tax bill by investing in company shares or equity trusts that produced "franked dividends". A franked dividend of $1000 should reduce tax by approximately $180 for a taxpayer in the 20% tax bracket, therefore shares or equity trusts paying franked dividends are a tool for pensioners to use to reduce their tax. Reread the section on dividend imputation if that is not clear to you.

You And The Department

I have noticed many pensioners are afraid of department staff and fear they will investigate every dollar spent. In my experience these fears are unfounded. Treat the staff with courtesy and you will find, in most cases, they will be helpful and sympathetic. Remember, the department staff are government employees trying to administer difficult laws – there is no point in abusing them for a situation over which they have no control.

Because the Department of Social Security is a large one, and the rules are so complex, wrong assessments are not uncommon. This is when a relationship with a good financial planner pays off. Most financial planners are happy to help their clients fill in any forms that are required and to liaise with the department when it appears a wrong assessment has been made. It is unfortunately true that many pensioners are "worriers" and they gain peace of mind by letting their financial planner conduct any negotiations with the department that are necessary.

Conclusion

Whether you are retired, or saving for retirement, you should make the best use of every dollar you have. Therefore, if you can qualify for even a dollar a fortnight of pension you should go for it. The fringe benefits that accompany that tiny sum will be worthwhile if you become ill, and even a few extra dollars will help pay your electricity bill. When you read the next two chapters you will notice that the laws are generous and, even if you don't qualify today, it may be possible to put a strategy in place that will start to give you a pension in a year or two.

This chapter has been a light read but I did that deliberately to get you ready for what is to come. You may be staggered by the complications that will be revealed in the next two chapters. The plethora of changes have made pension maximisation a nightmare for pensioners and their advisers. Consequently, pension planning is now too difficult to do on your own.

I therefore suggest you get into the habit of having regular sessions with a competent independent financial adviser and start planning for retirement now. By maximising superannuation, by judicious gifting where appropriate and by the acquisition of a good spread of investments you should make your retirement free of money worries.

Summing Up

- The pensionable age for men is 65 and for women 60. It is gradually being raised for women to age 65.
- You are eligible for the fringe benefits if you receive even a small amount of pension.
- Pensioners may be eligible for a tax rebate.
- Most pensioners will benefit by seeking advice about their affairs.

40

THE ASSETS TEST AND THE INCOME TEST

Perhaps one has to be very old before one learns to be amused rather than shocked.

PEARL S. BUCK

We'll now move on to the assets and the income tests, the two major tests that are used to determine your eligibility for a pension. The Department of Social Security applies both tests and the one that produces the **least** pension is the one used. It's hard to discuss one test without a knowledge of the other, so you may find it easier to read through this chapter briefly before studying it in detail.

The purpose of the tests is to limit eligibility for pensions to those in need. However, you will soon notice the tests are overly generous in some ways, extremely tough in others and are full of anomalies and inconsistencies. To make it worse, the tests are out of kilter. For example, a couple with assets of $176 000, as well as their own home, are entitled to a full pension under the **assets test**, but they would be unlikely to receive a full pension under the **income test**, if the assets were invested in the traditional areas of cash, bonds and shares.

The Assets Test

The assets test is quite generous. Your own home, and up to two hectares area around it, is **not** included, so a person seeking the pension can live in a mansion and still qualify. The test catches

363

almost every other asset such as household contents, vehicles, life assurance policies, caravans, boats and investments. It does not assess your interest in an estate not yet received, medals or decorations for valour, aids for disabled people and money paid in advance for funeral expenses or a funeral plot.

When valuing depreciating assets such as your furniture, motor car and boat, remember the assessable value is present net **market** value, **not** replacement value. A house full of furniture might be worth $30 000 if you had to replace it, but you may be pushed to get $5000 for it if you died suddenly and it was auctioned on your front lawn. Similarly, if you wish to find out the value of your car, drop it into the local branch of Shonky Autos and ask what is their best cash offer for a quick sale.

KEY POINT: Assets such as your furniture and your car are valued at net market value, not replacement value.

There is another class of assets called deemed assets. This term applies to assets you have given away in the last five years but which, for eligibility purposes, are still given a value by the department. We'll cover them in the next chapter.

Everybody is allowed a certain base level of assets and you do not start to lose part of your pension until your assets exceed these base levels. The base levels are higher for those who do not own a home, but there is an anomaly. The income test is the same for home owners and non-home owners. Therefore, non-home owners suffer more under the income test than the assets test. The base levels at 30 June 1997 were:

	Non-home owner	**Home owner**
Single	$212 500	$124 000
Couple	$264 500	$176 000

Once assessable assets exceed these base levels the pension reduces by $3 a fortnight for every $1000 of assets over the limit.

An **abridged version** of the assets test scale is shown on the next page to help you understand how this works. Because the aim of this chapter is to explain the principles, I have limited it to **home owners** as they are the majority, but remember your own home is not included in the assets. The department, or your financial adviser, should be able to give you a copy of the full tables if you ask for one.

Notice in the next table how the pension drops as the assets increase, or to put it another way, how the pension rises as assets

Single pensioner		Couple	
Total assets	Fortnightly pension	Combined assets	Fortnightly pension combined
$124 000	$353.20	$176 000	$585.60
130 000	335.20	190 000	543.60
160 000	245.20	220 000	453.60
190 000	155.20	250 000	363.60
210 000	95.20	295 000	228.60
220 000	65.20	360 000	33.60

decrease. It is important to understand this because a $10 000 drop in assets increases your pension by $30 a fortnight or $780 a year. Therefore, giving away $10 000 to your family has a similar effect as placing that $10 000 in a debenture earning 7.8%. We'll discuss that in depth soon.

The Income Test

Now we'll look at an abridged version of the income test table and find out how this test and the assets test work together:

Single pensioner		Couple	
Fortnightly income	Fortnightly pension	Combined fortnightly income	Fortnightly pension combined
$ 98.00	$353.20	$172.00	$585.60
120.00	342.20	260.00	541.60
180.00	312.20	360.00	491.60
250.00	277.20	500.00	421.60
300.00	252.20	600.00	371.60
400.00	202.20	800.00	271.60
550.00	127.20	1000.00	171.60
750.00	27.20	1300.00	21.60

This has given you a brief over-view of the tests. Now let's move on to the difficult question of what the department defines as income" for income test purposes.

What is income?

Exactly what is "income" for income test purposes has plagued financial planners for years, and the sometimes inconsistent and conflicting rulings from the Departments of Social Security and

Veterans' Affairs have not helped matters. To further complicate matters, the Tax Office takes a different view entirely.

The difficulty of determining what was income started with insurance and friendly society bonds, which did not start to become popular until the early 1980s. The essence of the problem was that the income on these investments is not paid to the holder, but is added to the original capital in the form of bonuses. Even though the increasing value was assessed under the assets test, the Department of Social Security did not take the accruing bonuses into account as income for the income test. They assessed it in full when the bond was cashed in. Pensioners, and their advisers, took advantage of what they saw as a loophole in the income test and money poured into friendly society bonds and insurance bonds. The Department plugged that loophole, but the system remained inconsistent.

In September 1988 radical changes were announced that saw managed funds such as share trusts and market-linked insurance bonds given a notional income rate of 11% per annum. This caused an outcry, as the returns from these types of products fluctuate. It was seen to be most unfair to treat an investment as earning 11% when it may have done much less than that. Finally the system was overhauled, and replaced by a simplified deeming system that came into effect on 1 July 1996. The system is fair, and is not unduly complicated, but you may understand it better if I explain why deeming was introduced in the first place.

The Original Deeming Rules

The deeming rules place a notional interest rate on certain assets for income test purposes. The main target initially was interest-free bank accounts, and this caused a rash of bad publicity when the concept of deeming was introduced on 22 August 1990. Much of the publicity was irrational and was centred around comments like "It's a free country. Why shouldn't I keep my money in an interest-free account if I want to." In fact, the deeming rules didn't prevent pensioners keeping money in interest-free accounts; they treated such monies as earning the deemed rate for income test purposes.

Why would a pensioner want to keep money in interest-free accounts? Because, until the introduction of the deeming rules, pensioners lost most of their valued fringe benefits once they ceased to get the full pension. Thus a loss of even one dollar of pension could cost $1500 of fringe benefits. It was another silly rule and, to get around it, many pensioners kept large amounts of money in interest-free accounts. Naturally this practice was encouraged by the local bank managers who saw it as a great way to boost the branch profits.

The introduction of the deeming rules coincided with a new rule that pensioners would be eligible for all the fringe benefits irrespective of how small a pension they received. From that date there was nothing to be gained, and plenty to be lost, by having money in interest-free accounts.

The Revised Deeming Rules

You now know that deeming is a process whereby the Government deems that some investments are earning a certain sum for income test purposes. The original rules applied only to cash-type investments, but the revised deeming rules apply to assets such as debentures, bank deposits, friendly society bonds, insurance bonds, shares, and managed funds such as equity trusts. However, they do not apply to rental houses, land, allocated pensions and annuities. We'll consider these later.

At date of writing the deeming rates were 4% on the first $30 000 ($50 000 for a couple) and 6% on the balance. These rates can be varied by the Minister for Social Security at any time, but, any changes will be made to coincide with the March and September pension indexation increases.

Pensioners should seek the highest-earning secure investments available because, if their investments earn less than the deeming rates, they will still be assessed as if they were earning 4% or 6%. The good news is that actual earnings higher than the deemed rates will be assessed at the deemed rates not the actual rates. Gifts[1] in excess of $10 000 in a year, and loans made by pensioners, are also subject to the deeming provisions.

EXAMPLE: *Just before they applied for the pension, the Browns gave their daughter an interest-free loan of $60 000 to help her buy a house. If the Browns have other financial investments of $50 000 (which will be deemed at 4%) the department will assess the $60 000 loan as if it is earning 6% and add $3600 to the Browns' income for pension purposes. As*

---

1 Gifts are discussed in detail in the next chapter.

a result their pension will reduce by $1800 a year if they are up to the allowable income level now. It will be also treated as a $60 000 asset for the assets test.

The Tests in Practice

Now that you have a basic knowledge of the way the system works, let's go through a simple example.

A pensioner couple own their own home, and have other assets as follows:

Personal effects	$ 5 000
Car	$ 10 000
Boat	$ 3 000
Debentures	$100 000
Shares	$ 50 000
Bank accounts	$ 20 000
Total assets	$188 000

From the assets test table earlier in this chapter you can see that their assessable assets are just under the $190 000 level in that table. Therefore, under the assets test, they are eligible for a combined pension of a little more than $543.60 a fortnight.

Now we'll find out how they fare under the income test. Irrespective of what the financial assets are actually earning, their deemed income is $9200 a year or $354 a fortnight calculated on their $170 000 on financial assets thus:

4% on the first $50 000	$2000
6% on the balance of $120 000	$7200
Total deemed income	$9200

If you now scan the income test figures you will see they are entitled to a pension of a little less than $491.60 a fortnight. As this is lower than the amount to which they are entitled under the assets test, the income test is the one used. They are entitled to a combined pension of just over $491.60 a fortnight. That's simple isn't it?

Now think about another couple who own their home, who are entitled to a combined pension of $585.60 a fortnight, and who have assessable assets of exactly $176 000. Provided they do not earn more than $172 a fortnight, which is the base level for the income test, they qualify for the full pension.

What would be the position if their elderly aunt died and left them $40 000, which they invested in a range of financial assets? Their assets now increase to $216 000 and the excess of $40 000 over the base limit would reduce their pension by $120 a fortnight to $465.60 a fortnight. Remember every $10 000 of extra assets causes a reduction in pension of $30 a fortnight. Now they need competent financial advice. Their pension has dropped by $120 a fortnight because of excess assets, but they have now become entitled to a reassessment under the income test.

Because their pension has dropped to $465.60 a fortnight they are entitled to earn another $240 a fortnight under the income test, because each dollar of pension lost entitles a pensioner to earn two extra dollars income. The $172 a fortnight limit no longer applies to them. This could be achieved by some casual work, but if that is not possible they could restore some of the lost pension by reducing their assets. This could be done by investing in exempt assets such as funeral bonds, or by gifting money to their children. This is covered later in the book.

Allocated Pensions

Since allocated pensions have become popular, there has been much debate about the proper way to assess them for both tests. Since 1 July 1994 the value of the balance in an allocated pension fund has been treated as an asset for assets test purposes unless the investment was made before 1 July 1992. The amount of the annual allocated pension, less a deductible portion based on the pre 1983, concessional and undeducted components, is included under the income test.

From 1 July 1998 all allocated pensions, and allocated annuities, will be treated equally. The balance of the account will be assessed as an asset for the assets test and the income, less the deductible portion, will be regarded as income for the income test. This is a simpler and more generous treatment, but all pensioners will have to have their portfolios reassessed after 1 July 1998.

EXAMPLE: *Harry is 65, has $150 000 in his allocated pension fund and starts to draw an allocated pension of $14 000 a year after 1 July 1998. His life expectancy is 15 years. For the assets test the value is $150 000. For the income test it will be only $4000 a year calculated as follows:*

Annual pension $14 000
Less Deductible Portion $10 000   ($150 000 divided by 15 – his
                                     life expectancy)
Assessable Income $ 4 000

Annuities after 1 July 1998

From 1 July 1988 the Social Security treatment of income streams will divide them into three categories, short term, medium term and long term. They will be treated as follows:

1. **Term 5 years or less.** The purchase price will be assessed for the assets test and the income will be assessed under the deeming rules.

   EXAMPLE: *Judy has $100 000 of financial assets and invests $50 000 into a three-year annuity with a return in full of capital at the end of the term. The balance of $50 000 will be an asset for the assets test. For the income test she will have a deemed income of $3000 (6% of $50 000).*

2. **Term – between 5 and 15 years.** The account balance will be assessed for the assets test, but unless it has a 100% residual value, which is most unlikely, the balance for assets test purposes will be changed as it reduces. For income test purposes the income will be the pension paid less that portion of it that represents a return of capital.

   EXAMPLE: *Bob invests $70 000 into a 10-year annuity paying $7700 a year with a return of capital of $20 000 at the end of the term. $5000 of capital will be used up every year of the 10-year term, so each year the account balance will drop by $5000 for assets test purposes. For the income test he will be assessed on a deemed income of $2700, being the $7700 less the $5000 which represents a return of his capital.*

3. **Term – 15 years, or the life expectancy of the investor if that is less than 15 years.** These products will enjoy exemption from the assets test. The pensions must be non-commutable, have a nil residual value, and the size of the payment in any year must be fixed. They must have limited reversionary benefits, but indexation will not be required. The income will be the gross pension paid less a deductible amount that will be based on the purchase price divided by life expectancy or the term.

EXAMPLE: *A pensioner couple's assets are so high that they receive minimal age pension. They withdraw $100 000 from debentures where it is earning $7000 a year and invest the money in a 15-year annuity, with a nil residual value, paying an income of $9500 a year. Their assessable assets reduce immediately by $100 000 and their pension increases by $7800 a year. For income test purposes the income is $2824, being $9500 less the deductible portion of $6666 ($100 000 divided by 15). Their total income has increased from $7000 a year to $10 300 a year.*

Note that new rules apply to **all** pensioners from 1 July 1998. Therefore it will be important for anybody who has taken out private pensions before that date to have a review with their adviser.

Beating The Assets Test

The assets test is the harsher of the two tests. Consider a couple who are getting a part pension. If they suddenly received a legacy of $100 000 it would reduce their pension by $7800 a year under the assets test, but by only $3000 a year under the income test. Here are some strategies to reduce the asset test's impact:

1. Reduce assessable assets by spending money on your own home, on living expenses and travelling, or by selling the home you have and buying a more expensive one to live in. These methods will all use up surplus assessable assets but should be done only after a lot of thought. There is no point in doing foolish things just for the sake of the pension.

2. Invest some money in funeral bonds. These are friendly society bonds whose fund enjoys a tax-free status with the only catch being that the proceeds must be used for funeral expenses. We have found pensioners feel comfortable putting $2000 or $3000 in funeral bonds as they know there will be money for a decent funeral. The other advantage is that neither the accruing bonuses nor the value of the bond is assessed under income or assets tests.

3. Gift up to $10 000 a year. Contrary to popular belief, there is no State or federal gift duty in Australia and anybody (including pensioners) may gift away as much as they wish. However, from 1 March 1991, a single pensioner, or a couple, have been allowed to gift away $10 000 a year for assets test purposes. Any excess over $10 000 will be held as an asset for five years from the date of the gift. Full details are in the next chapter.

4. Convert some assets to an income stream by buying an annuity with a duration of at least 15 years, or for your life expectancy if it is less than 15 years. You learned about these in the previous section.

Naturally all the above strategies should be discussed with your financial adviser, but they illustrate how your position can be improved by some careful planning.

Estate Planning

Pensioners should be careful when making out wills as the amount of allowable assets for a single person is less than that for a couple.

> **EXAMPLE:** *Mike and Dot had assessable assets of $200 000 and were getting most of the pension. Mike died suddenly and left all his assets to Dot. This took her over the assets test limit for a single person and she lost the pension entirely. Had he left the bulk of the estate to the children[2] she would have been able to claim the whole pension plus all the fringe benefits.*

If you have nobody to leave your money to, consider a bequest to some of the many worthwhile charities that exist. They are usually run by hard-working volunteers who welcome a little extra money. This is far better than leaving it to people you have never met, or letting it end up in general revenue.

---

2 This is only practicable if the children can be trusted to "do the right thing" if the surviving parent needs financial assistance.

Conclusion

You may now have a better understanding of the way the income and assets tests work, and may appreciate why some pensioners in the past have been vocal in their criticism of the definition of income. However, despite the definition problems, the tests are generous overall and this chapter may have shown you ways you or other family members can benefit from them. In the next chapter we'll look at gifting assets in more detail.

Summing Up

- Your own home is not included in the assets test.
- Assets such as furniture and cars are valued at sale value not replacement value.
- A person applying for a pension is assessed under both the income and the assets test. The test that gives the least pension is the one used.
- There are major changes to the treatment of private pensions after 1 July 1998.

41

GIFTING MONEY AWAY

You pays your money and you takes your chance.

PUNCH 1846.

"What's to stop me giving it all away and getting the full pension?" That's a question we hear continually and the simple answer is "Nothing". Now I don't suggest you do that, but the truth is that the Department of Social Security goes back no further than five years when assessing your eligibility for a pension. Therefore, if five or so years before you reach pensionable age you decide to gift away enough assets to make you eligible for some pension, you may do so.

There is a good reason why this plan may backfire. The Government is almost certain to change the rules in those five years between when you gift away your assets and reach pensionable age, and you may be caught out. It would be a shame to give away the bulk of those assets you strived to accumulate and find yourself reduced to living in poverty.

However, there are many cases when gifting money away makes a lot of sense – this is what we shall explore in this chapter.

The gifting rules work as follows:

1. A person or a family may gift away $10 000 a "pension year"[1] for pension purposes. Thus Miss Smith who lives alone may gift $10 000 a year; Mr and Mrs Jones who are a pensioner couple may gift $10 000 a year between them. They are not allowed to gift $10 000 each.

---

1. Each person has their own "pension year", which begins on the starting date of his or her original pension.

2. Gifts in excess of $10 000 in any one pension year are held as an asset for the assets test for a period of five years from the date of the gift, and a deemed income is attributed to them for the income test.

The following example will show you how the gifting rules work generally.

EXAMPLE: *Mr and Mrs Jones received a legacy of $25 000 late in 1994 but, without seeking advice, gave it away on 1 January 1995 so as to maintain their existing pension. They had made no gifts in the previous 12 months. The first $10 000 will be regarded as a gift and will cease to exist for departmental purposes. The balance of $15 000 will be held as a notional asset until 31 December 1999. During that time it would cause a reduction in their pension of $1170 a year if they are assessed under the assets test and are above the bottom assets limit, or a reduction of $300 a year in pension if they are assessed under the income test.*

The income test treatment is calculated by assessing the gift of $15 000 at 4% (the current deeming rate), which produces a notional income of $600 a year. A pensioner couple may earn $172 a fortnight and still retain the full pension, but once they reach this figure the pension reduces by $1 for each additional $2 earned. Hence, in the example above, the $600 of notional income reduces the pension by $300 a year.

Using The Gifting Rules

The gifting rules are most effective to get around the **assets test** as the **income test** only penalises the pensioner by reducing the pension by $1 for each $2 of income earned, there is little point in gifting away $10 000 that may be producing $700 a year when the result will be to increase the pension by $350 a year. You would be $350 a year worse off.

However, a gift to reduce assets because your pension is assessed under the assets test may be one of the most effective investments you can make.

EXAMPLE: *A pensioner couple had assessable assets of $340 000 but income of only $18 000 a year. Thus they were affected by the assets test and not the income test. If they gifted a total of $10 000 to their children they would receive an* *immediate rise in pension of $780 a year and have, as a bonus, the pleasure of watching the children enjoy it.*

This is an effective yield of 7.8% on the $10 000 gift, which makes it a most effective investment in a climate of low interest rates. Remember, the gifting rules work on pension years not calendar years, so if your pension anniversary is 30 May you may make a $10 000 gift on 28 May and a further $10 000 gift on 1 June.

The Best Strategy

Let's suppose you have a genuine reason for helping your family by giving them money. Here are some pointers:

1. Stay away from interest-free loans. The money lent will still count for the assets test and, worst of all, will be treated as an asset for as long as the loan is in place. If five or six years pass by, and you decide to gift the money, the five-year period will start then. If you are assessed under the income test you will be deemed to be earning the deeming rate with a subsequent reduction in your pension. It's a lose-all-the-way situation.

2. Split the money between a gift and a loan. By doing this you can substantially improve your pension position.

   EXAMPLE: *A pensioner couple wish to gift $100 000 to one of their children but are concerned about the effect on their pension. If they gift the whole $100 000 now the first $10 000 will be treated as a gift and the balance of $90 000 will be held as an asset for the next five years. A better strategy is to lend $40 000 and make the balance of $60 000 a gift.*

   The first $10 000 of the $60 000 gift portion will be allowed as a gift immediately, and the balance of $50 000 will be held for the next five years. The loan of $40 000 may then be reduced each pension year by the simple action of forgiving (making a gift of) $10 000. Compare the situation over five years:

   Irrespective of whether they are assessed under the income test or the assets test the couple are far better off using the combined gift-loan method than by making a straight out gift. As you can see, the gift-loan strategy produces a total deemed asset value of $90 000 in the first year, $80 000 in the second year, $70 000 in the third year and so on. Notice also how much more effective this is under the assets test than the income test – each year they receive $780 a year extra pension under the assets test but only $200 under the income test.

	Gift of $100 000		Gift and loan combined	
	Asset	Deemed income	Asset	Deemed income
Year 1	90 000	5 400	90 000	5 400
Year 2	90 000	5 400	80 000	4 800
Year 3	90 000	5 400	70 000	4 200
Year 4	90 000	5 400	60 000	3 600
Year 5	90 000	5 400	50 000	3 600
Year 6	NIL			NIL

The above example uses 6%, which is the deeming rate for financial assets over $50 000 owned by pensioner couples at the date of writing.

Gift Duty

There is no gift duty in Australia and people are free to gift away a million dollars, or more, a year if they wish. However, there is State stamp duty to pay on transfers of assets such as property and shares and this varies from State to State.

Conclusion

You have now come to the end of the money section of *Living Well in Retirement*. The route has taken you through such diverse areas as the bond and share markets, capital gains tax, dividend imputation, dealing with your adviser, reading a prospectus, superannuation, rollover funds, retirement villages, estate planning and the aged pension. The size of the book and the range of topics shows what a complex and important issue retirement planning has become and you should now be much better equipped to handle it all.

We'll now change course and look at the physiological and psychological areas of the ageing process. It's my favourite subject and one in which medical science is discovering important knowledge every day. I think you may be pleasantly surprised at what the future may hold for you.

Summing Up

- For pension purposes a person or couple can gift no more than $10 000 a year each pension year.
- A gift in excess of $10 000 in any one year is held as an asset for five years for the assets test. Furthermore, a deemed income is given to it for the income test.
- Prefer gifts to interest-free loans where possible.

42

THE AWAKENING

There is no such thing as "on the way out". As long as you are still doing something interesting and good, you're in business because you are still breathing.

LOUIS ARMSTRONG

Sometimes you are lucky enough to stumble across a fundamental truth. Usually it just sneaks up on you quietly and yet, once you have had the experience, your life is changed forever. It happened to me in 1974 when I read *Think and Grow Rich* by Napoleon Hill. I picked up that book as one person, but when I had finished reading it I was a different person. My life was radically different from that day and, as readers of my other books will appreciate, I made a vow then to promulgate Hill's material for the rest of my life.[1]

The major lesson I got from *Think and Grow Rich* was that I did not have to live any longer with my self-imposed limitations – at last I had found a way to tap the potential that was inside me. It was a message I sent out to the world in *Making Money Made Simple* when I told readers that the aim of that book was to show people they could have far more than they thought possible if they made the best use of what they had starting today. Judging by the letters from readers that keep arriving, the book has done just that, but I continue to be amazed by the potential people have and what they can achieve once they know how to unlock it.

Another awakening happened in 1993 when my wife, Geraldine, started studying gerontology as part of her psychology degree. Then the word "gerontology" conjured up to me images of

---

1. The chapter styled "The Torch" in *Making Money Made Simple* tells the story of Hill's quest for knowledge and how this knowledge has been handed down from generation to generation.

helplessness, incontinence, dementia and all the problems we associate with elderly dying people. I just didn't want to know about it. Repeatedly she would try to start a conversation on the subject, but her efforts fell on deaf ears. I was always immersed in writing an article, or studying the latest tax ruling.

Finally she handed me a folder on attitudes to the aged that had been compiled by the Office of Ageing. As she gave it to me she said, "You should leave this in the reception area of your office; it is information many of your clients will find very useful." This suggestion did not go over well with me at all for I was still totally negative about the topic. Although I did not realise it then, I was practising denial; my own fear of losing my independence and becoming a senile, feeble old person was so strong that I would ignore any information about the subject.

Fortunately, although I have a fear of losing my independence, I also have a great thirst for knowledge. One day, curiosity got the better of me and I started to browse through the folder. As I did, my interest quickened and I started to feel the same sense of awakening that happened 19 years before when I read *Think and Grow Rich*. You see, the material wasn't about bed-wetting and helplessness at all. It was about potential – the potential of older people to live happier and healthier lives than most of us younger (I was 53 then) people had even considered.

The excitement was back and now I had a new challenge. I had already managed to pass on the basic principles of prosperity in the other books I had written; now my task was to pass on some of the principles of ageing happily and healthily. What made it more interesting is that it fitted in so well with Napoleon Hill's research – success principles are universal. They contribute to health and happiness as well as prosperity.

In these five chapters I'll try to give you a glimpse into the ageing process and how to stay happy and healthy till a ripe old age. Unfortunately, the size of this book restricts the amount of material but develop the habit of browsing in book-stores and looking for books on the subject. You will probably find it an exciting experience.

We'll take it step by step, but be aware that I have stuck with theories that are generally accepted and have quoted only conventional research. If you browse in any alternative bookshop you will find a huge range of books and magazines offering theories that may meet with the disapproval of many members of the medical profession. I neither approve of, nor condemn, these publications because medical knowledge is growing quickly and what is out of favour today may be "in" tomorrow. After all, it's your life, and you will have to make up your own mind and follow what works for you.

Let's look first at community attitudes to ageing and where the population is heading.

The Ageing Population

There is no doubt that the average age of Australia's population is rising as the proportion of older people grows. For example, in 1881 people over 65 constituted 2.5% of our population; the number had grown to 11.4% by 1991 and was forecast to be over 20% by the year 2030. However, this is not just because people are living longer because of medical advances; it is also because our birth rate is dropping as people choose to restrict the number of children they have.

Life expectancy has shown extraordinary increases. A male born in 1881 had a life expectancy of 46.5 but this had risen to 72.6 by 1986. In just over 100 years we have raised the time we can expect to live by a staggering 56%. Obviously this rate of increase will not continue, but the fact is that many people living now can expect to live well past 85. However, few of us want to live longer if the quality of life is missing. That is the purpose of including this material in this book – to show that those years can be happy and healthy ones.

This raises the question "What is an older person?" The answer is difficult to define. American financier Bernard Baruch said he would never grow old because "to me old age is always 15 years older than I am"[2], but other writers have claimed that number should be 30 years. Office of Ageing research indicates that "people tend to put a 30-year gap between themselves and old age until they are in their mid-forties or older". "Old age" is not defined as the person's own age until they are in their seventies, and in some cases later than this.[3]

Demographers usually define an aged person as somebody who is 65 or over, but the reason for this is obscure. Certainly it corresponds to the eligibility age for pensions in many countries, but it is hard to know which came first – 65 as the eligible age for pensions because that was regarded as time to retire, or retirement age set at 65 as that was when pension eligibility started.

Whatever the number there is no doubt that most people feel young inside no matter what their ages are, and get a shock at school reunions to find themselves surrounded by so many older people who were once in their class. It is also true that there can be a vast difference in biological age even when two people have the same chronological age and, let's face it, what matters is the biological age. When you mix with a group of people you must have noticed the difference in attitude and appearance of people who have lived the same number of years.

Community Attitudes

So most of us will feel young at any age, and can expect to live to 80 or more. Then how does the community in general view the older generation? This is the biggest problem of all and one that I touched on earlier in this chapter. Many people, and that once

---

2. Reported in *Newsweek*, 29 August 1955.
3. *Community Attitudes to Ageing*, 1991 Resource Paper No. 1, Queensland Office of Ageing.

included me, have an **incorrect and dangerously misleading** view of aged people in general. The prevailing attitude is that our aged citizens are people who are sick and handicapped, who live in institutions where they behave like children and who are a drain on society. Butler, Sunderland and Lewis point out, "Medicine and the behavioral sciences have mirrored societal attitudes by presenting old age as a grim litany of physical and emotional ills. Until 1960 most . . . literature on the aged was based on the sick and institutionalised, even though only 5% of older people were confined to institutions. Decline of the individual was the key concept."[4]

It's a pity these views still prevail for they are so wrong. In Australia less than 7% of older people live in institutions and no more than 12% of older people use community services such as Meals on Wheels. Contrary to being a burden on society, the majority live with their spouses and do not require help with their daily activities.[5] Over 70% of those over 85 do not suffer from dementia, and rather than being a "drain on society" older people are more likely to provide financial help (such as a loan) or practical help (such as child-minding) to their families.[6]

According to Office of Ageing research, the group with the worst perception of older people was younger people, who believed older people had "lost the ability to do things". In contrast, skilled tradesmen had the best perception of older people because of their regular contact with them in a business environment. A friend of mine who is a hot-air-balloon pilot has a very positive view of older people because the type who take balloon flights are "active and outgoing".

It is also unfortunate that many employers won't hire people over 50. In 1988 TESCO, the second-largest supermarket chain in the United Kingdom, adopted a "Mature Entrant Program" for staff recruitment and retention and, as part of that program, surveyed 50 managers and 80 older workers. The responses[7] from these 50 managers, when older people were compared with younger workers, were:

4. Butler, Lewis and Sunderland, *Aging and Mental Health,* 4th ed., Macmillan Publishing Company, New York, 1991, p.65.
5. Minichiello, Alexander, Jones, *Gerontology,* Prentice Hall, Sydney, 1992, p.3.
6. *Ageing: Myth and Reality,* Resource Paper No. 6 Queensland Office of Ageing.
7. Kern, Ann, reported in the September 1992 edition of *Ageing Action,* a publication of the Queensland Office of Ageing.

- 80% said the older workers were better with customers and were more reliable.
- 78% said the older workers were more responsible.
- 74% said the older workers were less likely to be absent.
- 56% said the older workers were more efficient.

For their part, the older workers who were surveyed attributed their health and well-being to exercise, companionship, challenge, a feeling of belonging and "lots of laughs". We'll look at these factors in more detail in the next chapter.

How We React

How does society react to this generally negative perception of old people? They react by focusing on the small minority who conform to the stereotype or by denying the ageing process itself. Take a look at any newspaper and see how many articles you can find about healthy, active 70-year-olds. The papers will feature stories about "lonely old people" who are the victims of crime, or of gullible "old people" who have lost thousands of dollars by handing over their "life savings" to fly-by-night crooks who knocked on their door offering to correct non-existent building problems.

Naturally, there will also be features on the harm done to old people as government funding cuts hit nursing homes and hostels, and there is almost certainly the occasional photo of a dignitary visiting an institution where all the residents are confined to wheelchairs.

When I was browsing in the library of the Office of Ageing in Brisbane I was struck by the tenor of the advertisements and articles in some of the publications[8] on file that were intended to be read by the older generation. Many of the advertisements proudly stated how the advertised product might help the reader "recover from the operation" or "feel well again". Is it any wonder the stereotype of the helpless old person continues?

You can see evidence of the denial of the ageing process everywhere. Most of the advertisements in women's magazines feature young models, and the message in most of the

---

8. These were not those produced by the Office of Ageing.

advertisements is about improving your looks either by losing weight, changing your make-up or by smearing Product X on your face to stop the signs of ageing.

Probably, when you think about it, focusing on the minority is normal human behaviour. Most professional people are honest and make the headlines only when one of their number does the wrong thing. The majority of businesses do their best to treat their customers well, but only the few who rip their customers off are newsworthy. Most children grow up to be responsible citizens, but the relatively small number who go astray are the ones we see on the 6 o'clock news. So it is with the attitude to the elderly.

One of the greatest dangers of stereotyping older people is that the belief can create the result. Once we start to regard older people as a nuisance, dependent and in bad health they may tend to act that way. As always, the solution is to raise our collective awareness, and help our older generation to continue to reach their full potential. To ignore this does not just deprive them of fulfillment in their later years. It also denies society in general the talents they have to offer. Best of all, by helping them, we help ourselves. One day we will all be in that group.

Conclusion

We can sum up what we have covered so far by saying that the majority of older people are leading healthy, productive lives and do not conform at all to the stereotype that society has thrust on them. That information alone must give us all hope for a fulfilling time in our retirement years, but there is more to come. It is obvious that some people age well and others don't. Let's explore that next.

Summing Up

- The community has a false and negative image of older people.
- Our population is ageing and life expectancy is increasing.
- Older people are not a drain on society. Most of them give more than they get.
- Most older people live happy, productive lives.
- A common reaction to the problem of growing old is to reinforce the stereotype or to deny the ageing process.

43

THE AGEING PROCESS

Half our life is spent trying to find something to do with the time we have rushed through life trying to save.

WILL ROGERS

The fact that we all age is undeniable – just look at a photo of yourself 10 years ago – but there is also no doubt that some people age better than others. Would you like to be among those who age well? I'm sure you would. When I ask clients the question "How long do you want to live?", most of them will reply, "As long as I am healthy."

Let's accept that the majority of old people are not senile or institutionalised and that the goal of everybody is to live a long and healthy life. How do we achieve it? What can we control and what must we accept? Gerontologists all over the world are studying these and similar questions but, even though there are hundreds of books written about the ageing process, you must understand that it is a relatively new field. There weren't a lot of aged people about 100 years ago. Furthermore, the most useful studies take many years.

For example, cross-sectional studies carried out in the early part of the twentieth century appeared to prove that IQ declined with age. How did they find this out? They measured the IQ of groups of people of different ages and noted that the older people had lower IQs than the younger ones. However, the results were later disproved when they started taking "longitudinal" studies. In contrast to cross-sectional studies, researchers doing longitudinal studies start by testing a group of people and then continuing to give parallel tests to the same people over a long period to observe what changes occur in their responses. Obviously longitudinal studies are the best ones to do, but they are time-consuming and expensive, and the results may suffer a little because invariably some of the members of the group being studied move away, or die, or just get tired of taking part.

Nevertheless, several successful longitudinal studies have been done, and one of the most famous of them was conducted in Brisbane through the University of Queensland. In 1965 Professor Elsie Harwood and her colleague Dr George Naylor sought volunteers over the age of 60 to take part in a longitudinal study to examine the ageing process. It was styled "Operation Retirement".

In a paper delivered at the 13th Annual Conference of the International Association of Gerontology in New York in 1985, Elsie Harwood and another colleague,[1] Lex Irvine, made the following observations:

"Operation Retirement" is now in its twentieth year. The normally ageing subjects first empanelled (1965 to 1967) over the age of sixty, numbered in all 404 volunteers ... The plan was to undertake serial testing of intelligence ... Those over 90 years old who offered to be available for the first 10 years did not achieve this, but nine who have grown old in the study are now in their nineties. The average age is now 84.

The study was concerned with ageing persons living normally in the community (not actually in care). We know that ... some 93% of people over 65 years of age are domiciled independently. Results after 10 years showed that annual decrement was not a matter of serious concern until after the age of 80, when it amounted to an annual average loss of 2%.

A most important finding was that some subjects showed no decrement at all after 15 years, and some have even improved their scores. These tended to be people who had participated in the learning experiments. Eighty panel members participated in each of the learning experiments, some taking part in both. The first was a German translation exercise; the second, recorder-playing, was a first introduction to musical notation for many of the subjects. Fifty-five took an examination in German translation after eight months of weekly lessons and daily "homework". Of these, 37 passed at the Senior Level, seven with A grades.

---

1. Dr George Naylor died in 1980.

Both groups insisted on continuing these activities . . . under their own initiative and management. The oldest successful German student was 89. The oldest recorder player at the last practice was 98. One German student went on to matriculate and take a BA degree at the age of 75.

These experiments demonstrated the mental and social benefits of appropriate stimulation of ageing brains, and highlighted the importance of avoiding, or of overcoming, the effects of disuse.

Moreover, a retrospective study (Harwood and Enticknap 1983) of the relation between formal learning in retirement years and retardation of intellectual decline showed that decrement in the serial intelligence scores of the non-participating panel-members was greater than in either of the two learner-groups (German or recorders).

Finally, it was found that if the independence of the ageing population can be maintained and their mental function appropriately stimulated, the effects of disuse can be minimised and their enjoyment of the "third age" can be enhanced.

My copy of that paper was given to me by Lex Irvine who co-authored it. His comments were, "You can sum it up by saying that the decline of intelligence was only slight although there was a decline in manual dexterity. The critical factor was the motivation of the participants."

As you can see, it's very much proof of the adage "What you don't use you lose", which is a theme you will notice comes through continually in this section on ageing.

A leader in the field of research into ageing is Dr Ellen Langer of Harvard University. Her famous book, *Mindfulness,* starts off with the following intriguing statement: "One day, ten years ago, I conducted an experiment which was to change the whole way I thought about life."[2] She then went on to describe the experiment that is quoted in so many text books on ageing.

For the experiment, Langer and her colleagues gave elderly residents of a nursing home some house plants to care for, and let each resident have a choice as to which plants they received. The residents were told they were responsible for the care of the plants and had to decide where to put them, and when to water and feed them. A separate "control group" of similar residents on another

2. Langer, Ellen, *Mindfulness,* Harvill, London, 1991, p.13.

floor were also given plants "to keep" but were told that their plants would be looked after by the nursing staff.

After just three weeks all but one member of the first group showed a significant improvement in alertness and physical well-being. In contrast only 21% of the control group showed any improvement. Eighteen months later 15% of the first group had died and 30% of the control group, twice as many, had died. The survivors in the first group continued to be "significantly more active, vigorous and sociable"[3] than those in the second group and their health had continued to improve. The simple act of giving these institutionalised people a little responsibility had wrought extraordinary changes.

In another study[4] Dr Langer in 1979 took a group of men aged between 75 and 80 and placed them in an environment of life 20 years past. She re-created an atmosphere of 1959, television programs of that era were played, and the subjects were supplied with magazines such as *Life* and *Saturday Evening Post* from that time. The subjects had to act as if the clock had been wound back 20 years and they were all aged 20 years younger.

Langer claimed that the men as a whole looked younger by about three years after the experiment, there was a uniform tendency for hearing to improve, hand strength increased steadily, there was an increase in sitting height, they showed greater manual dexterity and tests showed there had been improvements in intelligence. That's powerful stuff, isn't it?

It is clear from reading *Mindfulness* that Dr Langer herself is unsure as to what this project actually proved, but she points out "some of the 'irreversible' signs of ageing were altered as a result of psychological intervention". Her somewhat philosophical conclusion is that "The regular and 'irreversible' cycles of ageing we witness in the later stages of human life may be a product of certain assumptions about how one is supposed to grow old. If we didn't feel compelled to carry out these limiting mindsets, we might have a greater chance of replacing years of decline with years of growth and purpose."[5]

There is a common thread in the research of Professor Elsie Harwood and Dr Ellen Langer that is repeated in most of the textbooks on ageing. It is that human beings need to use their

3. Ibid., p.92.
4. Ibid., pp.109-121.
5. Ibid., p.121.

minds and their bodies, and that they are happier and healthier when they are responsible for something. This has lessons for all of us who are trying to age well and we might get some more clues if we find out why women live longer than men.

Why Do Women Live Longer?

The figures show that women live longer than men – the big question is why. According to the renowned gerontologist Robert Butler and his colleagues, "In the United States women outlive men because of the higher male mortality from arteriosclerotic heart disease, lung cancer and emphysema (associated with tobacco intake), industrial accidents and toxicity, motor vehicle and other accidents, suicide, cirrhosis of the liver (associated with alcoholism) and so forth. These account for perhaps three-quarters of the sex differential in mortality – the other one-quarter is unclear. Lifestyle, life stress, hormonal differences, genetic differences in immune resistance, and other possible differences between the sexes must be further studied."[6]

Thinking about the findings of Harwood and Langer it seems to me that another reason for the longer life expectancy of women is that many of the older ones today have spent their whole life being responsible for other people. First it was supporting the husband getting started in his career, then it was raising the children and finally it was looking after the husband when he retired. Furthermore, at no stage were they given a rocking chair and a gold watch, and told they were too old to be of any more use to the employer. It's a bit like Dr Langer and those flowers, isn't it?

Predictors Of Successful Ageing

Robert Butler and his colleagues also mention the impact of the socio-economic group on life expectancy. "Demographic data shows conclusively that an increasing life expectancy follows in the wake of increasing income and status ... Most studies fail to take note of wealth beyond yearly income. Yet such wealth enormously affects the capacity to maintain health (through greater opportunities for rest, good nutrition, recreation, emotional

---

6. Butler, Lewis and Sunderland, *Aging and Mental Health*, 4th ed., Macmillan Publishing Company, New York, 1991, p.11.

security and status) and to treat illness (through greater access to the finest acute and chronic care)."[7]

Professor Jon Nussbaum of the Oklahoma Centre of Ageing, University of Oklahoma, argues that the three main predictors of successful ageing are:

1. sufficient financial resources
2. a history of good health
3. a network of friends.

I have already alluded to the importance of sufficient financial resources, and the benefits of a history of good health are self-evident. After considerable research, Nussbaum concluded, "If an elderly individual . . . feels a high level of closeness towards their family and friends, then these individuals will have higher levels of life satisfaction and in addition, these higher levels of life satisfaction will reinforce the interaction and closeness felt by the elderly."[8]

However, as Nussbaum told us at a seminar in Australia in June 1994, the family can at times be a negative influence by reminding the old person of loved ones who had died or by encouraging dependency. "Nursing staff often report that the worst emotional times for elderly people are the moments prior to and following a family visit."[9]

Butler refers to the Seattle Longitudinal Study (Schaie) that showed wide individual differences in intellectual changes over time, but also that there was a **large number** of elderly persons showing little decline even in their eighties. Schaie concluded that the factors that characterised those with little decline were no cardiovascular disease, at least average income, an active involvement in life and having been flexible in attitudes and behaviour in mid-life.[10]

When you think about these factors, it is clear that the absence of stress is a major factor. A person who is healthy most of the time, who has good relationships with family and friends, who is free from financial worries and who has an attitude that is flexible enough to cope with the normal daily challenges of life should be

7. Ibid., p.13.
8. Nussbaum, J.F., Successful Ageing: A Communication Model, *Communication Quarterly,* Vol. 33, No. 4, 1992, p.263.
9. Nussbaum, J.F., Communication, Language and the Institutionalised Elderly, *Ageing and Society,* Vol. 11, 1991, p.154.
10. Butler, Lewis and Sunderland, op.cit., p.71.

fairly free from stress. Contrast that person with another who has an unyielding attitude, money worries, difficult personal relationships and poor health, and it is easy to see why the less stressed person should live longer. In the case of the stressed person, it is also reasonable to believe that the attitude may have been responsible for their losing a job or missing out on a promotion, which may have contributed to the money worries that in turn caused the stress. It all goes round and round.

Ageing Is Not A Disease

One of the major misconceptions is to treat ageing as if it were a disease or that it inevitably brings disease with it. Certainly there are diseases such as cancer, heart disease and arthritis that occur more often in older people, while alcohol-induced cirrhosis of the liver, or cigarette-induced lung and throat cancer affect older people because the effects may take years to manifest themselves. However, as Dr Robert Gingold says in his splendid book *Successful Ageing,* "Symptoms that develop in later life are due to illness, not age. It is not normal to feel ill in later life. The elderly are in fact survivors who have suffered less disease than their contemporaries who have not lived to old age."[11]

It was not till the late 1950s that researchers started to study healthy old people, and according to Butler[12] the findings of the National Institute of Mental Health (NIMH) were "surprisingly optimistic, and in general reinforced the hypothesis that much of what has been called ageing is really disease. Decreased cerebral (brain) blood flow and oxygen consumption were found to be probable results of arteriosclerosis rather than an inevitable consequence of ageing".

The NIMH studies also showed that healthy elderly had high self-esteem, a sense of ongoing usefulness and tended to be self-starters who were not frightened to make new contacts or become involved in new activities.

In *Ageless Body, Timeless Mind,* Dr Deepak Chopra includes depression, lack of a regular daily routine, job dissatisfaction, financial worries, loneliness, excessive worry and self-criticism as factors that accelerate ageing. In contrast, happy long-term relationships, job satisfaction, financial security, ability to laugh

---

11. Gingold, Robert, *Successful Ageing,* Oxford University Press, 1992 p.5.
12. Butler, Lewis and Sunderland, op.cit., p.75.

easily and taking regular holidays are just some of the positive factors that retard ageing.[13]

The best news comes from Dr James Fries. In *Aging Well* he points out, "There are far more aspects of aging that can be modified than cannot, and the most modifiable features are the ones that most of us think of as the most important."[14]

In the **unalterable** list he includes greying of the hair, loss of skin elasticity, development of cataracts, fibrosis, farsightedness and high-tone hearing loss. In the ones we can modify he mentions physical fitness, heart reserve, mobility, blood pressure, intelligence, memory, general reaction time, heart disease, cancer, arthritis and agility.

Conclusion

I hope by now you are starting to feel some of the excitement I experienced when I began studying the ageing process. All the research shows that if you take care of yourself, have a good network of friends, stay active, keep the right attitude and have financial security you can look forward to a long healthy life.

However, it's also like a finely balanced three-legged stool. If you become lonely you may not eat or exercise, and thus may get sick. If you suffer the loss of a loved one you may become depressed and withdraw from your circle of friends. As always, being aware that this can happen is one of the best ways of preventing it.

By now you should understand the ageing process better, and appreciate that you have a large degree of control over it. We'll now take the next step and consider easy ways to stay in shape.

Summing Up

- The study of healthy elderly did not start till the late 1950s. Until then the focus was on the sick elderly.
- Studies show little decline of intelligence with age.
- Attitude is important.
- There are many steps you can take to ensure you age well.
- Ageing is not a disease and people should not feel unwell just because they are growing old.

---

13. Chopra, Deepak, *Ageless Body, Timeless Mind*, Random House, Sydney, 1993, p.69-70.
14. Fries, James, *Aging Well,* Addison Wesley, Sydney, 1991, p.11.

44

STAYING IN SHAPE

We spend the first 40 years of our life neglecting our bodies to make money – we spend the next 40 years spending money on our bodies to try to repair the damage.

AMANDA GORE

In both *Making Money Made Simple* and *Getting it Together* I pointed out that life involved making choices, and the difference between the financial winners and the financial losers was that the winners kept making better choices. I even gave chapter 16 of *Getting it Together* the title of "It's Up To You" and started with the quote from Vernon Howard "You need only choose . . . and keep choosing as many times as necessary. That is all you need to do. And it is certainly something you can do. Then as you continue to choose everything is yours."

That book is written for young people, and the theme of that chapter was that they should choose to start managing their money properly, and choose to develop skills that would take them to the top of their industry and eventually enable them to start their own business. It's really no different in retirement. You need to choose to manage your money properly, and choose to develop health habits that will keep you in good shape for most of the rest of your life.

Now the stark reality is that you need to do the work to get the results. If you are young that may mean studying while others are working, and not always buying what takes your fancy. If you are older it may mean exercising when you feel like staying in bed, or knocking back the second slice of the chocolate cake. That's the bad news – the good news is that every good choice you make gives you dividends that far outweigh the effort that was involved in carrying it out.

It's also interesting that, just as most young people can't be bothered with such chores as budgeting or developing their skills, many older people can't be bothered making the time to stay in shape. As always it's the minority who make the effort and enjoy the results. Butler and colleagues point out "Demographic data show conclusively that an increasing life expectancy follows in the wake of increasing income and status."[1] The ability to make the right choices affects life in all areas. Fortunately it is an ability that can be learnt, but, in the areas of health and wealth, the earlier you start, the greater the benefits. Remember the magic of compound interest way back in chapter 1.

An interesting experience for me in February 1994 was spending a week at Camp Eden, a health retreat nestled away in Currumbin Valley near the Gold Coast. I went there to discover how I would feel after a week of extremely healthy living, because I had fallen victim to the Christmas syndrome and had gorged myself for more than a month on good food and wine. I was starting to feel like a car that desperately needed a tune-up. The week at Camp Eden involved vegetarian food, a daily massage, strenuous exercise that included yoga and bush walks, and lectures on diet and nutrition. For the first two days my head throbbed mercilessly from caffeine withdrawal, but thankfully that passed and I had no further problems.

The overwhelming feeling after a week was how lithe and supple my body felt, and how much energy I had. The sad truth was that I had forgotten how supple my body used to be and how good I could feel. There is a lesson for all of us in that – our bodies are not meant to get stiff. They stiffen up only because we neglect them.

Let's now consider ways to keep in shape. I'll cover a range of areas briefly and let you choose the ones you want to explore further. However, remember that we often have good intentions of keeping to an exercise and healthy eating program, but find that we lack the motivation to keep at it. The solution for me is to regularly feed myself a range of motivational inputs through books and audio tapes and by mixing with health-conscious people. It's far easier to stay away from too many beers after golf if your playing partners are similarly inclined.

---

1. Butler, Lewis and Sunderland, *Aging and Mental Health,* 4th ed., Macmillan Publishing Company, New York, 1991, p.11.

Remember, too, that it takes 30 days to establish a habit and that it is better to change direction slowly. Too many of us start New Year's Day with a host of resolutions, and see them gone before dusk when some friends arrive with a bottle of wine. It is far better to set realistic expectations and follow them.

Best of all, it's never too late to start, if you do it gradually. Even if you are totally unfit you can walk 100 metres today, and increase it by 50 metres each day. After just 3 months you'll be walking nearly 5 kilometres.

Exercise

The benefits of exercise are obvious, and probably the only reason many people don't do it is that they never get around to it. The way to solve this is to make it part of your routine, preferably when you get up, so you won't be distracted by events that happen later. If you plan to do it when you come home from work, there is always the possibility of a work crisis arising to hold you up or for other temptations at home, such as TV, to distract you.

The previous chapters on the ageing process have mentioned that a strong cardiovascular system helps to keep us healthy and one of the major benefits of aerobic exercise such as brisk walking, jogging, cycling or swimming is that it strengthens the cardiovascular system. Furthermore, walking with your partner is a delightful way to get in touch, and the benefits are mental as well as physical. Physiotherapist Amanda Gore, who writes "Wellness" columns in many Australian newspapers, advocates a daily 4-kilometre walk in 30 minutes, and while this speed took me three weeks to achieve, I am now happily walking 5 kilometres most days in 40 minutes. The dogs love it, too!

If you are into walking, buy the book *Walking*[2] by Casey Meyers. My reaction when I first picked it up was to wonder how anybody could write a 300-page book about walking, but Casey does it splendidly. To him, walking is the ultimate exercise and he puts his case with great enthusiasm. It's motivational, as well as containing all the information you would ever need to know about the subject.

Diet

There have been thousands of books written on diet and I don't intend to spend a lot of space on it here. It is acknowledged that

---

2. The Australian edition of *Walking* is published by Random House, Australia, RRP $22.

both exercise and diet can assist in reducing the incidence of blood pressure and cancer and can also have a large role in improving general well-being. Probably the key is moderation, and to listen to what your body tells you. Whenever I am required to go to a business breakfast, I forsake my normal breakfast of apple juice and muesli for the bacon and eggs, Danish pastries and croissants that are always served up at such functions. Invariably after these big breakfasts I feel dreadful for the entire morning.

Alcohol And Caffeine

These two substances are a part of our Western culture and I confess to enjoying both. Apparently, neither one does you too much harm if consumed in moderation, but too much caffeine can lead to heart palpitations and insomnia, while the effects of alcohol abuse are well known. The doctors I know suggest that three cups of coffee or tea a day is a moderate intake of caffeine, and the National Health and Medical Research Council has recommended that "light" consumption of alcohol is no more than two standard drinks a day for women, and four standard drinks for men. They also recommend you have at least two alcohol-free days a week to give your kidneys a rest, and to break the habit of drinking every day.

In my experience, too much drinking of alcohol is caused by having nothing else to do. By scheduling activities that need concentration or exercise into your leisure time, you can often avoid falling into the trap. We have also found that a glass of freshly squeezed orange juice tends to stop the 6 p.m. craving for a drink.

A leading ear, nose and throat specialist told me that there is a synergistic effect that occurs when large amounts of alcohol and cigarettes are consumed together. Apparently, each aggravates the other and greatly increases the damage that each one does. This is why "alcoholics are increased risks for serious diseases that include cancer of the throat, mouth, breast, stomach, pancreas and liver".[3]

Nicotine

Smoking causes more deaths than road accidents because it kills over 50 Australians every day. It is known to be a major contributor to emphysema, lung cancer and ulcers. Moreover, as

---

3. Pfeiffer, George, *Taking Care of Today and Tomorrow,* The Center for Corporate Health Promotion, Reston, Virginia, 1989, p.82.

Dr James Fries points out, "accelerated development of atherosclerosis is the most important problem resulting from smoking. This results in heart attacks and strokes, heart pains, leg pains and many other problems."[4] Believe me, it's an awful sight to see a person who has lost both legs because of heavy smoking.

Fortunately, there is now a strong public awareness of the dangers of smoking, and most offices and public places are becoming smoke-free zones, which helps to cut down the temptation. According to Dr Robert Gingold, the good news is that most smokers of mature age want to quit, and once they do, the dangers associated with their past smoking drop away fairly quickly.[5] Even after just six months of quitting smoking, the risk of heart disease is greatly reduced.

Staying Flexible

Doing exercises to stay flexible is one of the most important activities you can do if you want to feel good as well as live a long time. In *Walking,* Casey Meyers quotes Mayo Clinic physical therapist Phil Orte who said, "Flexibility is one of the three pillars of fitness along with muscular strength and cardiovascular endurance. Getting older doesn't automatically mean getting stiffer. Careful stretching can help you stay flexible."[6]

There are exercises designed to assist flexibility and it is also highly desirable to have a stretching session after you have done your normal aerobic exercise such as walking. One of the best ways to stay flexible is to take up yoga. I was introduced to it at Camp Eden and enjoyed it so much that I decided to take it up. Devotees of yoga testify to the feeling of peace it gives them as well as the physical benefits but, if you consider yoga, be aware there are different types of it. Make enquiries to find the one that best suits your goals and your temperament.

Massage

Massage is one of the oldest forms of healing and it is accepted that it will relax muscle tension, help keep the body flexible and generally increase vitality. Dr Deepak Chopra claims that a daily

---

4. Fries, James, *Aging Well,* Addison Wesley, Sydney, 1991, p.79.
5. Gingold, Robert, *Successful Ageing,* Oxford University Press, 1992, p.147.
6. Ibid., p.72.

self-massage with sesame oil is good for the immune system[7] and Geraldine and I, who practise his sesame-oil massage, find it beneficial. Certainly, a regular massage is a great stress reducer and there are also claims that the act of touching another gives the masseur benefits as well.[8]

A weekly massage may be outside your budget, but there is nothing to stop couples giving a free massage to each other or at least doing the sesame-oil self-massage. The benefits it offers are too good to ignore.

Alexander and Feldenkrais Techniques

The Alexander Technique is another method for improving almost all aspects of your health by improving the way you use your body. It was developed by F. Matthias Alexander, a Shakespearian actor, in Tasmania in the late nineteenth century when he developed hoarseness of the voice, and found that the doctors he consulted were unable to cure him. After months of observing himself in a three-way mirror he discovered that his posture and the way he moved his spine were causing the problem. He cured himself and spent the rest of his life teaching the Alexander Technique as it became known throughout the world. Devotees included the author George Bernard Shaw and the singer Dame Nellie Melba.

The Feldenkrais method is of a similar genre to the Alexander Technique but concentrates more on gentle manipulation of the limbs and puts more emphasis on the wholeness of mind and body.

If you wish to explore either method further, teachers can be found through the Yellow Pages.

Meditation

Meditation is not some strange religion, nor does it involve sitting cross-legged on a bed of nails dressed in a robe. It is a method of reducing stress by relaxation that is now used successfully by people in all walks of life. Remember, stress is a major shortener of life.

---

7. Chopra, Deepak, *Perfect Health,* Transworld Publishers, Sydney, 1992, p.204.
8. Maxwell-Hudson, Claire, *The Complete Book of Massage,* Simon and Schuster, Sydney 1994, p.8.

I first became aware of the benefits of meditation when I used the techniques involving meditation and visualisation that are taught by Bert Weir in his Centre Within course[9] to give up smoking. My interest in the subject grew when I heard renowned author and speaker Wayne Dyer say repeatedly, "Once I couldn't imagine my life with meditation, now I can't imagine my life without it." Just one of his many references to meditation is: "After meditating I know that I can accomplish anything! Some of my most profound ideas, my very best speeches, and my most personally satisfying writing emerge after meditating. And my appreciation for my loved ones can only be described as a peak experience."[10]

Dr Deepak Chopra claims transcendental meditation (TM) lowers biological age and points out: "The connection between ageing and stress hormones has been strongly demonstrated, but the problem of how to control these hormones remains. However, (meditation) goes directly to the root of the stress response by releasing the remembered stresses that trigger new stress. Levels of cortisol and adrenalin are often found to be lower in long-term meditators, and their coping mechanisms almost always tend to be stronger than average."[11]

After reading Chopra's claims, Geraldine and I took a course in TM in April 1993 and have been enjoying its benefits ever since. Because of my busy schedule I confess I sometimes don't get

9. The Centre Within course is offered by the Relaxation Centre, Brisbane.
10. Dyer, Wayne, *You'll See It When You Believe It*, Schwartz Publishing, Melbourne, 1989, p.17.
11. Chopra, Deepak, *Ageless Body, Timeless Mind*, Random House, Sydney, 1993, pp.162-63.

around to doing it, but then my body gives me a warning sign by producing that stressed-out feeling that feels like a steel band around my forehead. The moment I meditate, and it only takes 20 minutes, I feel like I have had a week's holiday.

I'll let Amanda Gore give us the last word on meditation. Amanda was having a typical (for her) day that involved catching the first plane from Sydney to Brisbane, giving an all-day seminar, making an after-dinner speech and then getting up at 5.30 next morning to drive 100 kilometres to Caloundra to give another all-day seminar. It was a Friday afternoon, and we had grabbed a half-hour between the seminar and the speech to exchange some ideas. I asked her how she managed to keep up the pace. Without hesitation she replied, "I couldn't do it without meditation – I'll even set my alarm clock early tomorrow morning to have time to meditate before I leave."

Conclusion

Notice how it all fits together. The diet and the exercise and the relaxation exercises all combine to keep you healthy and feeling good if you take the trouble to do them. Remember, the aim of this book is not simply to make you live longer, it is to make you live longer and feel great. We'll now look at ways to prevent minor problems becoming major ones.

Summing Up
- Staying in shape is a matter of choice.
- Our body is our most important asset.
- Make changes slowly – don't start off with a burst and then give up.
- In every field the winners are those who make the right choices.
- Flexibility in body and mind is the goal.
- Give your health the priority it deserves.

45

BEFORE IT'S TOO LATE

A little neglect may breed mischief. For want of a nail, the shoe was lost; for want of a shoe, the horse was lost; for want of a horse, the rider was lost.

BENJAMIN FRANKLIN

I hope by now you are convinced that you have a good chance of living to a prosperous, healthy old age if you make the choices that will lead you to that destination. However, it is important to take steps to ensure you continue to move in the right direction, which is why, in the earlier part of this book, I have stressed the importance of having an annual financial check-up. But remember, you have another asset of incalculable value that requires a regular check-up. That is your body.

The importance of this was brought home to me recently when the father of a close friend of mine was admitted to a nursing home at the age of 90. My friend was bitter because his father was now blind because of serious glaucoma, and it seems it may have been much less severe if his doctor had checked for it, and treated it, in earlier years.

This chapter will focus on what you can do to correct minor problems before they become major ones, and, because my area of expertise is tax and finance I am indebted to my good friend Dr Toby Ford who has assisted me with much of the material in this chapter. As well as being a sought-after speaker and commentator on health issues, Dr Ford is a partner in the Wesley Corporate Health Program, Brisbane, which specialises in preventive medicine.

Unfortunately in Australia preventive medicine does not get a high priority from governments and most medical fees for check-ups, as opposed to treating illnesses, do not get a subsidy from either Medicare or the private health funds. They are all happy to pay out thousands of dollars once you get sick, but are reluctant to pay out hundreds of dollars for consultations that may prevent you needing to claim the big money. It's a strange world, isn't it?

Dr Ford and I started off by looking at the results of the August 1993 Suncorp survey of nearly 1300 Australians, which examined how they "live their lives, treat their bodies, and view their health". There was good news and bad news. The survey showed that 66% of Australians take positive steps to keep to a fixed weight, 80% take some form of exercise, but only 50% exercise strenuously at least once a week.

However, 42% feel under a great deal of stress at least once a week, only 52% visit the dentist at least once a year, 50% have never had their cholesterol checked and 70% have never had an examination for skin cancer. This is particularly worrying as only 43% use sunscreen. Worst of all, the Suncorp survey showed that a massive 80% of Australian men have never had a check for either prostate or bowel cancer. The survey also showed that women over 45 were more concerned with having a proper diet and eating properly than men over 45, which may have more than a little to do with the increased life expectancy of women.

These results show clearly that there is still much that Australians can do to prevent the onset of illness. Even following the simple principles outlined in the previous chapter will go a long way to keeping you well, but it is also important to try to detect potential problems while they are in their early stages.

We'll now look at ways to do that, and you should understand that, while medical practitioners do not recommend unnecessary check-ups, there is general agreement[1] that certain routine tests should be carried out on a regular basis. Dr Ford stressed the importance of making your doctor aware of your family history. For example, one of your parents may have died of a stroke at a young age, or a sister may have died of breast cancer. This knowledge will help your doctor decide what tests are important for you.

---

1. A comprehensive list is contained in *Preventive Medicine in General Practice* prepared by the Preventive & Community Medicine Committee of the Royal Australian College of General Practitioners.

In general, the recommended tests for those over 50 are these:

Weight

An annual weight check. That does sound basic, doesn't it, but being overweight contributes to many diseases including heart disease, diabetes and arthritis. The best thing about the problem is that it is reversible. Dr Ford points out that a low-fat diet is usually more effective than a low-calorie diet because, with a low-fat diet, the weight drops off slowly but stays off. Also, most people find it easier to stick to a low-fat diet than a low-calorie diet.

Blood pressure

An annual check. It's a simple test, and control over blood pressure can reduce death from strokes, heart disease and renal failure. People with high blood pressure should have more regular checks as recommended by their doctor. Exercise has been found to be useful in reducing blood pressure.

A single blood-pressure reading can be influenced by alcohol, smoking or stress. Therefore, an abnormal reading should be followed by further checks when you are in a more relaxed state, and when you have abstained from alcohol or tobacco for at least a day.

Cholesterol

An annual check-up, unless the level is so high that more frequent checks are recommended. The National Heart Foundation recommends keeping overall cholesterol levels under 5.5 mmol/l, but you should be aware that there are two types of it – high-density lipoproteins (HDL) and low-density lipoproteins (LDL). HDL is the "good" cholesterol that helps prevent atherosclerosis, while LDL is the "bad" one that causes all the problems. It is the ratio of these two substances, more than the total, that needs to be monitored. Exercise and dietary changes can improve the balance.

Dental check-up

Every six months, to remove plaque and to treat decay while in the early stages. Loss of teeth is not part of ageing, it is tooth decay and gum disease that cause the problems. Dental care is most important because good teeth help older people to chew properly and to retain their facial appearance. Modern dental technology can now help most people retain their natural teeth all their lives.

Glaucoma

Every five years, unless there is a family history of glaucoma. It is a disease that results from increasing pressure inside the eye that can lead to irreparable damage to the optic nerve and the retina. Glaucoma tends to be genetic, so those with a family history of it should be particularly aware of the importance of regular testing.

Prostate examination (men only)

Every two years. A manual prostate examination is quick and painless, and may enable cancer of the prostate to be detected and treated in the early stages. There are also blood tests that can indicate prostate problems, but these are most effective when taken over several years so a trend can be observed.

Pap smear (women only)

Every year unless your doctor believes you are not at risk. The major goal is detection of cancer of the cervix, body of the uterus or rectum. The examination may also lead to detection of cancer of the bladder or colon.

Mammography (women only)

Every two years, unless your doctor decides you are in the high-risk group. It is regarded as an effective screening tool for those over 60 and is capable of detecting breast cancers of less than 2 cm in size that are undetectable by manual examination.

Immunisation

Every 10 years with adult diphtheria and tetanus (ADT) booster, but if more than 10 years have passed it is recommended that the patient should be re-immunised with three injections. Those over 65 should also talk to their doctor about being immunised annually against influenza, and anybody who is travelling in underdeveloped countries or who is at risk because of their lifestyle should be immunised against hepatitis B.

Sigmoidoscopy

Every two years. After lung cancer, colon cancer is the most common fatal cancer. Sigmoidoscopy is an examination of the colon using a special instrument that enables the doctor to view the interior surface. It is regarded as an effective method of detecting colorectal cancer, which occurs mainly in people over 50. People of 50 and over should have an initial examination, and then one every two years or as recommended by their doctor.

Many doctors are now giving a colonoscopy, which is a much more detailed examination of the colon, in lieu of sigmoidoscopy. Your doctor will guide you.

Skin examination

Every year, but more often if recommended by your doctor. Dr Ford told me it is common to see people, especially men over 50, with serious skin malignancies who have been continually putting off having them checked. Usually it is only after pressure from other family members that they show the suspicious spot to their doctor.

Conclusion

As you can see, most of those tests don't cause too much discomfort and they could save your life.

This chapter, and the three before it, have given you an insight into the possibilities of staying happy and healthy for many years after retirement. But remember, this does not come by chance; the sooner you start forming the good habits the sooner will you reap the rewards.

You should now be ready for the final chapter in this long book – living well in retirement.

Summing Up

- Many Australians still neglect their health.
- Regular check-ups may enable many diseases to be cured in the early stages.
- Make your doctor aware of your family medical history.
- You don't wear out – you rust out.
- There are areas in which we can all make improvements.
- If you are in doubt about a symptom, consult your doctor immediately.

46

LIVING WELL IN RETIREMENT

Most people face the future with apprehension – that is because they haven't planned for it.

JAMES ROHN

By now you should know that a long life and a healthy, happy, and prosperous retirement are likely for those who work towards that goal. The theme that is repeated continually in this book is that to do this you should have adequate financial resources, a strong network of emotional support and continue to use all your physical and mental abilities. However, these things don't just pop up of their own accord – you have to plan to make them happen.

In 1986 Dr Robert Williamson and his colleagues interviewed a sample of white-collar workers who had been forced into retirement after being retrenched from Bethlehem Steel. Follow-up interviews were done in 1991 to observe changes in attitude and behaviour. Their conclusion was:

"Satisfaction is markedly greater when one can plan one's retirement. Specifically, the longer one has to plan one's retirement, the higher will be his or her satisfaction and happiness. The main finding from our surveys was the importance of a sense of control. If the individual is allowed a maximum of autonomy in planning his or her retirement, the enjoyment of retirement is much more probable. Not least their experiences underline the truism that if one has adequate income, health and a zest for living or a vital set of interests retirement can hardly fail to be a success."[1]

---

1. Williamson, Rinehart and Blank, *Early Retirement,* Plenum Press, New York, 1992, p.262.

If we accept that as being true, the big question is how do we achieve it. Unfortunately, most people hardly give a thought to retirement until they are at least 40, and probably put it in the "too hard" basket for another 10 years. Then the employer will announce a redundancy scheme, or a friend will take early retirement, and they wake up to find themselves 50 or more, with possibly five years or less to the retirement day. That's when the grim reality sets in, and they go to see a financial adviser to ask the question "Can we afford to retire when we choose?".

To prevent that happening, start developing strategies now to enable you to come to retirement prepared for it. Understand, too, that you will have to work on developing a multi-dimensional awareness if you have not done that already. It is human nature to focus on the immediate and ignore the future, and far too many of us have our lives involved only in our children and our work. There is a price to pay. At some stage we will realise that the children have left home and are busy with their own lives, and we are due to finish work in a few months. The two points of focus and support in our lives are about to vanish.

Now it need not be like that. You should start to think of your life as one that has several dimensions, and work on developing each dimension. They are:

- the health dimension
- the financial dimension
- the relationship dimension
- the activity dimension
- the spiritual dimension.

Let's reflect on each one in the light of what I have written so far, and notice particularly how they all mesh. Provided we do not neglect any one of them, every action we take to strengthen one dimension automatically strengthens the others.

The Health Dimension

Most of us have a large degree of control over our health and the two major principles are "What you don't use, you lose" and "Prevention is better than cure". Furthermore, one of the greatest enemies of our health is stress, which can be caused by overwork, attitude and problems in relationships.

Overwork should not be a problem in retirement, although many of our retired clients say they have never been so busy in their lives. But retirement is a period when we have much more discretionary time available, and putting at least an hour a day towards staying healthy is just good commonsense. However, just as it's easier to keep a car out of a bog than to get it out once it's bogged, it's also easier to stay in shape than to get in shape. Don't wait till you retire to start getting your body in order.

Make manageable changes

Dr Toby Ford says the key is to make manageable changes. He says, "If people come to me and I find they are overweight, drink to excess, and smoke 40 cigarettes a day, I don't advise them to make all the changes in the first week. Even if they try hard they will almost certainly fail, and be worse off than before. It is better to start by trying to get them to cut the cigarettes to 20 a day, and to change to light beer. They can probably do this, and will then establish a success pattern which will put them on the right track so they can continue to make further small changes."

Notice how staying in shape affects the other dimensions. Suppose you and your partner choose to go to a yoga or aerobics class before dinner. The shared activity will not just be good for your health; it will be good for your relationship because you are sharing an activity. Furthermore, you will save money as you probably won't eat as much that night, you will be helping reinforce the habit of not drinking alcohol every day, and you may be making a new network of friends in the class.

Learn to handle stress

Stress causes ageing and illness so it makes sense to learn to handle it at as young an age as possible. A certain amount of stress is good for us, but far too many stresses are self-induced and could be easily prevented. In his audio-cassette album *Real Magic,*[2] Wayne Dyer tells how his life changed when he discovered that "the traffic doesn't care". He was referring to his previous habit of fuming and getting stressed out every time he got caught in traffic. What do you do if a rude person cuts you off in traffic? Do you give yourself a dose of stress or just accept the fact that some car drivers are rude? The incident has happened and nothing you can do is going to change the past. What you can do is choose how you react, and by choosing not to get stressed you are being good to your body.

---

2. *Real Magic* is produced by Nightingale Conant, Chicago.

Another way to cope with stress is to prepare for it. Bangkok in Thailand is noted for its traffic jams, yet an architect there has solved the problem by having an air-conditioned van converted to a mobile office complete with fax, phone, and drawing table. He has hired a driver and can now work in peace, irrespective of the state of the traffic, while other architects are complaining about being hours late for appointments.

Re-framing,[3] which involves changing how you view an event, is another way to handle stress. Epictetus (AD90) said, "Men are disturbed, not by the things that happen, but by their opinion of the things that happen", and Morarji Desai believed "Life at any time can become difficult, life at any time can become easy. It all depends upon how one adjusts oneself to life." For example, if one of your investments turns bad, you can brood over it for years and complain continually about investment advisers, and the dangers of any investments except money in the bank. Alternatively, you can accept the loss, reflect on what you can learn from the experience, find a way to use the tax losses, and console yourself with the fact that you may now get more aged pension because your assets have shrunk.

Don't become the stereotype

Have you ever been to America? If so, you probably found that within a week you were developing an American accent. There is something in our psyche that seems to make us tend to copy those around us. This can be particularly dangerous as you are getting older because there are so many negative stereotypes about.

But there is more to it than just what people say around us. There is self-talk – our daily dialogue with ourself. Once you fall into the trap of considering yourself old, your self-talk will start going along the following pattern "I'm too old for that", "not at my age" and "I'm getting old".

That kind of talk may be literally fatal. As Cavanaugh and Green pointed out, "What one says to oneself largely determines what, and how well, one does . . . it is rare in psychology to stumble across such a pervasive phenomenon as the belief in oneself . . . self-evaluation is one of the most important aspects of memory in older adults."[4] Their study was concerned with memory and how it

3. My book *Getting it Together* has a whole chapter on re-framing.
4. John Cavanaugh and Elizabeth Green, *Aging and Cognition: Mental Processes, Self Awareness and Interventions,* Elsevier Science Publishers B.V. (North Holland), 1990, p.189.

was affected by the subjects' impression of themselves but, as you can see, they believed the concept was relevant to all aspects of life. Think about it – if your self-concept can change your memory, what else must it be able to do?

Another stereotype is that old people are worriers. I used to think that because so many clients have said things like "Mum is a worrier". To my surprise studies do not validate this view, and have shown that younger people worry more than older ones. For example, a study carried out by Powers, Wisocki and Whitbourne compared the worry level of older people (median age 77.6) with college students. The students scored higher (worried more) on the total worry scale, and on the financial and social worries sub-scales. There were no differences on the health worries sub-scale. The conclusion was, "The elderly have been exposed over the years to many instances of frustration, loss and stress and have had many years experience in coping. Perhaps the profit from these experiences serves them well in old age. The young on the other hand have not had much opportunity to learn the lessons taught over a long period of time and thus worry more."[5]

If you have been telling Mum that she is a worrier it may be interesting to start telling her you admire the way she has always coped. It may change her self-talk from "I'm a worrier" to "I'm strong and I can cope", with resultant benefits to her mental and physical health.

The Financial Dimension

There is strong evidence that having sufficient financial resources in retirement is a major contributor to happiness and living healthily to a good age. Why is this? Mainly because people with money are often (not always) free from the stress of money worries, and they can afford nutritional food and good health care.

I have stressed throughout this book that the best way to have financial security is to start building assets when you are young to give compound interest time to work. Furthermore, you should establish a relationship with a financial adviser as soon as possible in your life so you are able to judge his or her ability, and you

---

5. Charles Powers, Patricia Wisocki and Susan Whitbourne, Age Differences and Correlates of Worrying in Young and Elderly Adults, *The Gerontologist* vol. 32, no. 1, 1992, p.82.

should experiment with a range of investments, so you don't arrive at retirement thinking the only investment choices are leaving it in the bank or buying a rental house.

Understand the reality of money

As you approach retirement it is also necessary to put money in context, and appreciate what it can and can't do. Remember I wrote that being free from money worries, eating good food, and having good health care are major factors in living to a healthy old age. Think about them one by one:

1. Freedom from money worries is very much a state of mind. There are thousands of pensioners with scant financial resources who are sublimely happy living on the full pension, because they have learned to be happy living on what that pension will buy.

2. Good food need not be expensive food. Even if it were, you could probably grow most of what you need.

3. The problems relating to finding good health care can be minimised if you ensure that having private health insurance gets priority when you are doing your budget.

Don't forget that many of the best things of life really are the free ones. Geraldine and I find that going for a walk together is one of the day's highlights, and the pleasure we derive every day from the vases full of flowers we have in our house is inestimable. Many of them come from our rose garden, which cost relatively little to establish. The best entertainment is cheap, for there is always at least one radio station playing good music, and the library is full of books.

From my experience I think it fair to say that the amount of money you have is not nearly as important as your perception of it. If you feel it is adequate, and you manage it well, you should not have money worries.

Share the knowledge

If you have a partner make sure you are both aware of the family financial situation. We have found one person becomes responsible for the money in most relationships. When this occurs, the other partner can be left in a mess if the person handling the money dies or becomes disabled.

By sharing the role of financial manager with your partner you are gaining communication skills that will strengthen your relationship, as well as raising your awareness of finance. This helps to reduce conflict about money, which is often caused when the partner who does not handle the money wants to spend more than the budget can bear.

Have regular check-ups

Suppose you were travelling to an important destination and you missed one of the main turn-offs. The longer the time that elapses before you discover your mistake the harder it will be to correct it. This is how it is with the financial world. Markets fluctuate, economic conditions go from boom to bust and back again, fund managers can lose key staff, and the laws relating to tax, superannuation and social security benefits are continually changing. If you have not made provision for an investment monitoring service, and an annual check-up with your financial adviser, you may well not make the best use of your precious resources.

Understand, too, that we live in an age of specialisation. That is why forward-thinking financial advisory firms have developed networks with a range of related professionals such as lawyers, accountants, lending institutions and even medical practitioners who can help clients achieve their goals.

Making money in retirement

Some people are scared about having too much time on their hands in retirement, but you can turn that time into dollars if you have hobbies that either make money or save money. Growing your own vegetables and making your own clothes saves money, while hobbies such as toy-making and orchid growing can bring in money.

Be wary about going into business after you retire if you have no business experience and the venture requires a considerable outlay of capital. The majority of small businesses fail, and you could lose a large sum at a time in your life when it is hard to replace it. If you are thinking of starting a new business, such as buying or setting up a book-store, try to spend some time "learning the ropes" by working for somebody who has a similar business.

However, if the business is one such as multi-level marketing, where the initial outlay is only a few hundred dollars and you have no liabilities for leased premises or equipment, you should investigate it. Just remember your rewards in life are proportional to your efforts, so expect to put in huge efforts if you want huge returns. Don't let that put you off if you find the concept attractive. Many people in good multi-level marketing organisations are happy making $500 a month and enjoying the network activities. The extra money makes life a little easier and they are keeping their mind and body active.

The Relationship Dimension

Statistics show that people who live alone have higher death rates than others and that they suffer more disorders such as accidents, tuberculosis and psychiatric disorders. Until recently it was thought this was because they did not take care of themselves as well as those people did who lived in relationships. However, Alice Day argues there is now evidence that just being in a relationship, or enjoying a network of social relationships, can have direct beneficial results "operating through some quality of interpersonal relationships of meaning to the individuals involved".[6] She continues, "The evidence is compelling that social relationships have generally beneficial effects on health, not solely or even primarily attributable to the role they play in alleviating stress or in helping older people to deal with their anxieties or fears".[7] In other words, just the fact that you have somebody can make the critical difference.

But here's another interesting fact; most of our older citizens are widows who do live on their own, and many of these are healthy, happy, active people who do take care of themselves. What can we deduce from this that will be useful for those of you who live alone now, or who are likely to suffer the loss of a partner eventually? It's not the living on your own that matters – it's the relationships you have that make the difference.

A study by the United States National Institute of Mental Health showed that greater social activity tended to "maintain health by stimulating more physical and mental activity, by providing a social network and by maintaining a sense of self-esteem and social worth".[8] Furthermore, the study found that those who did

---

6. Alice Day, *Remarkable Survivors,* The Urban Institute Press, Washington DC, 1991, p.36.
7. Ibid.
8. *Introduction to the Study of Human Aging,* Rockville, Maryland, National Institute of Mental Health, 1971, p.17.

not survive into their seventies were those who "tended toward withdrawal from social contacts".[9]

Whether you choose Alice Day's interpretation of the research, or stay with the more conventional views, it would appear that it's not living alone **per se** that causes the problems. I suggest it's the habits that many people, especially men, develop when they live on their own. These habits are often symptoms of their loneliness, and include drinking to excess, smoking and not eating properly. If you accept that view it is still not inconsistent with Day's argument, for if people who live alone do have a strong support network of friends they might not be lonely, and if they aren't lonely they are unlikely to develop the symptoms of loneliness.

No matter how you think about it, everybody needs somebody else. Whether this be a spouse, partner or social network is less important than the fact that they are there.

Understand the differences

To have fulfilling relationships with the opposite sex you have to understand that men and women are different. I didn't appreciate this till we had a daughter (who was the third child born after two boys). The American comedy writer Dave Barry put it well: "When we look at actual children, no matter how they are raised, we notice immediately that little girls are in fact smaller versions of actual human beings, whereas little boys are Pod People from the Planet Destructo".[10]

Two books on the subject that you may find enlightening are *You Just Don't Understand* by Deborah Tanner and *Men are from Mars, Women are from Venus* by John Gray.[11] Read them with an open mind and then discuss them with your partner or your friends. Even if you don't agree with the authors, the discussion may help your present relationships, or help you to understand why other relationships have problems.

Successful relationships come from open communication and shared feelings and experiences. The more you can share with your partner and friends the better will be the quality of the relationships and the stronger will be your support network.

---

9. Ibid.
10. Dave Barry, *Dave Barry Turns 40,* Ballantine Books, New York, 1990, p.64.
11. Both books are readily available.

Forming relationships

You may be reluctant to make new friends if you have lost your partner or have moved to a new location. However, it is important for your health and happiness that you make the effort. This is why it makes sense to take up sports or hobbies before you retire, for you have a head start if you can join a golf club, bowls club or bridge club. But don't despair if you haven't taken up a sport prior to retirement; it's never too late to learn, and you will find plenty of others in your situation when you pluck up the courage to go along.

If sports or cards aren't your idea of fun there are always book clubs, theatre groups, church groups or craft groups, and you will find most charitable organisations are always looking for volunteer helpers. This is a most effective way to meet new friends as well as raising your self-esteem.

The Activity Dimension

People thinking about retirement often express some apprehension, which is understandable because it's the beginning of a new period of life, and the two greatest concerns are whether they will have a deficiency of money or a surplus of time. But, as the Early Planning for Retirement Association points out, you have to decide whether retirement means retiring from life, or "retiring to a more satisfying life without the obligations of work".[12] Remember I mentioned before the danger of having only your work and your children as your major interests. This is why you should think about the other activities you will have in retirement, and if possible start them well before retirement.

In *Getting it Together* I advised young people to work towards having their own business. This is to enable them to have greater control over their income, and the hours they worked. The advice holds good at all ages because if you have your own business you can often reduce your hours as you near retirement age and achieve a nice balance of work and leisure. There are others such as medical practitioners, writers, music and speech teachers and sports coaches who can work for almost their whole lives, at a reduced pace if necessary, and they should not face a time problem as they grow older.

---

12. *Life Planning For Leisure in Retirement,* Early Planning for Retirement Association, Melbourne, 1984, p.10.

Get some goals

I have written at length in my other books about the importance of setting goals. Briefly, goals do the following:

- give our life direction
- provide new challenges
- help us achieve at a higher level
- make us more productive.

How many times have you heard somebody say they had a friend who retired at 65, started sleeping in later and later, and was dead by 67? Just be aware that the only reason we do not want to get out of bed in the morning is that we have no reason to get up. Goals provide that reason and they can make our life so rich, busy and fulfilling that we will wonder how we ever had time for work.

The way to set goals is to take a quiet hour with pencil and paper and do a dream list. Put on that list everything you ever wanted to do. Maybe it's to cruise up the Amazon, learn a new sport, develop a new strain of rose, live in Tuscany for a year, break 80 at golf, write a book, learn a musical instrument or a foreign language, get a degree, open a coffee shop, or develop superb fitness. Add all the little jobs you have been putting off, such as fixing up the garden, cleaning out the garage and sorting out the record collection, and you will find you have more than enough to get your mind into top gear.

Then you can start to make plans to achieve your goals. When you are doing this, understand that there are many ways to reach them. For example, if travel is your goal and money is short, you may consider organising a special-interest group to travel to your preferred destination. Often, if there are enough participants, the organiser gets a free ticket.

The Spiritual Dimension

The spiritual dimension is the hardest one to explain because it may have different meanings to different people. To me, a person with a spiritual dimension has a sense of being an integral part of the universe, of being at peace with that, and also knowing their reason for existence. Mother Theresa of Calcutta may spring to mind, but we can all contribute in our own ways. As Henry van Dyke said, "Use what talents you possess, the woods would be very silent if no birds sang except those who sang the best." Dr Wayne Dyer has written a whole book about it, and buying that book[13] may be a good place to start if you wish to explore the concept further.

Even though we tend to focus on work during the middle years of our lives, there are other things that may give us more fulfillment when we become aware of them. For example, the Institute of Social Research (1974) at the University of Michigan found: "While there is interplay between the satisfactions people derive from the different aspects of their lives – work, family, marriage, housing – people reserve their greatest satisfaction from those parts of their lives that are the most intimate and personal."[14]

If that is true, it may be appropriate to write down what activities give you the best feelings. They are the ones you should explore.

There is also an experience that gerontologists believe happens to almost everybody before they die. That is the need to reflect on their life, to put it in order, and find some meaning for their existence. It may be a time to heal old wounds, come to terms with their mortality, reframe some painful incidents or relive some happy moments. The term for this is reminiscence. Butler, Lewis and Sunderland believe the process gives a "sense of serenity, pride in accomplishment and a feeling of having done one's best".[15] I'm not arguing with that, but doesn't it make sense *to do it now?* Don't wait until you turn 90 to make up with the friend you fell out with, to grieve for the event that made you sad, or to start doing something that you will be able to look back on with pride.

Whenever I think about death I am comforted by the views of Socrates. He said, "Let us reflect and we shall see that there is a great reason to hope that death is good." He went on to argue that death had to be either the end of everything, or the start of a new spiritual phase. If it was the end of everything, it was going to be like a long blissful sleep and even a "great king" has had few better nights than one spent in blissful sleep. If it was the start of a new spiritual phase one could look forward to having endless discourses with the most interesting people. "What would a man give if he might converse with Orpheus . . . or Homer?"[16] Perhaps a modern-day philosopher may have added "or converse with God".

13. Wayne Dyer, *You'll See It When You Believe It,* Schwartz Publishing, Melbourne.

14. Richard Prentis, *Passages of Retirement,* Greenwood Press, Westport, Connecticut, 1992, p.5.

15. Butler, Lewis and Sunderland, *Aging and Mental Health,* 4th ed., Macmillan Publishing Company, New York, 1991, p.112.

16. S.E. Frost, *Masterworks of Philosophy,* Doubleday and Company, New York, 1946, p.53.

Conclusion

As we near the end of this book it might be appropriate to think about how you view retirement, for if you retire at 60 and live till 85 you will be spending almost a third of your life retired. Clients have given the following reasons they look forward to, or fear retirement.

POSITIVE ASPECTS	NEGATIVE ASPECTS
Can do what you wish	May be bored
Can function at own pace	Will miss the buzz of work
Chance to travel	May have money worries
Can give up work	Career coming to an end
Enjoy more time with partner	Too much time with partner
More time with family and friends	Loss of purpose
Can play more sport	Loss of work role
Freedom	Fear the ageing process
Can participate in social projects	Getting closer to death

Notice that most of them are in the category of "is the glass half-full or half-empty?" One person fears boredom, another looks forward to having the time to fulfil more of his or her goals. It demonstrates the importance of attitude, and there is no reason not to have a positive one. The information that keeps pouring in about the growing opportunities for people over 70 and 80 is staggering, and it all points towards the "third age" as being one of the most exciting and fulfilling times in your life if you decide it will be.

Summing Up

- Start to plan your retirement now.
- Success leads to success.
- Continue to make manageable changes.
- Don't become the stereotype and conform to what you think others expect of retired people.
- Your perception of whether your financial resources are adequate may be more important to your happiness than the extent of those resources.
- Research studies show that younger people worry more than older people.
- Retirement does not mean retirement from life.

47

EPILOGUE

No Spring nor Summer Beauty hath such grace, As I have seen in one Autumnal face.

JOHN DONNE

We've travelled a long journey together, and I confess the size of the book is much larger than I intended when I started the project. Unfortunately, the problem all along has not been in finding material, but deciding what to leave out. Therefore, you should treat this book as the stepping stone to more knowledge, not as an end in itself.

Remember, too, the secret of a happy, prosperous and healthy retirement is to prepare for it well before it happens and understand that, while retirement is a time of adjustment, it is not a time for fear. It is a time for anticipation, which presupposes you have made a lot of plans so you have something to anticipate.

There is now strong evidence that how you live in retirement will carry on from how you lived before it. If you were adaptable, generous, optimistic, healthy, keen to learn, had a good network of friends and were involved with life before you retired, you will probably stay like that afterwards. On the other hand, if you were fearful, distrustful, unwilling to learn and unwilling to participate in life, you will almost certainly find life in retirement is even worse.

Obviously, the younger you are when you start to make the small manageable changes in your life the more effective the process will be. But we can't change the past, and in any event I'm not sure what "young" means any more. What I do know is that the future is going to be fulfilling for those who make the choices that will keep them moving in the right direction. My wish for you is that you will be one of them.

The Noel Whittaker Wealth Creator

ON CD–ROM

Design your own future

The interactive tool that will enable you to take charge of your own finance and monitor your progress on a regular basis.

The Wealth Creator *includes:*

- A retirement planner so you can work out when you can retire
- A capital gains tax calculator to aid you in buying and selling decisions
- A loan calculator incorporating a gearing calculator
- A budget planner so you can simply prepare and update your budget
- A net worth statement that lets you keep track of where you are
- An insurance list on which you can record all your possessions

It is also a teaching aid. It includes an animated section that teaches the basics of compound interest, negotiating, business structuring and borrowing.

Don't stop now!

Mail or fax this coupon today for a comprehensive brochure and order form.

☑ **YES Noel, I'm serious about becoming financially independent and want to improve my knowledge.**

Please forward me an ORDER FORM containing full details of the material you have available to help me.

Name:_____

Address: _____

_____Postcode: _____

Tel.:_____

MAIL or FAX this coupon to:

Noel Whittaker
Whittaker Macnaught Pty Ltd
Level 5, Santos House
215 Adelaide Street, Brisbane Q 4000

Tel.: (07) 3221 1022 Fax: (07) 3221 9682
E-mail: noelwhit@gil.com.au

SAVE the price of this book!

EVERY ORDER for *the Wealth Creator* on CD-ROM will receive a **FREE** autographed copy of one of my books. To select your gift, all you have to do is tick the appropriate box on the order form.

Index